RUSSIA—LOST IN TRANSITION

THE YELTSIN AND PUTIN LEGACIES

RUSSIA—
LOST IN TRANSITION

THE YELTSIN AND
PUTIN LEGACIES

LILIA SHEVTSOVA

TRANSLATED BY ARCH TAIT

CARNEGIE ENDOWMENT
FOR INTERNATIONAL PEACE
WASHINGTON DC • MOSCOW • BEIJING • BEIRUT • BRUSSELS

Carnegie Endowment for International Peace
1779 Massachusetts Avenue, N.W.
Washington, D.C. 20036
202-483-7600, Fax 202-483-1840
www.CarnegieEndowment.org

The Carnegie Endowment for International Peace normally does not take institutional positions on public policy issues; the views and recommendations presented in this publication do not necessarily represent the views of the Carnegie Endowment, its officers, staff, or trustees.

Typesetting by Oakland Street Publishing
Printed by United Book Press
Photos courtesy of *Kommersant*
Special thanks to Beth Schlenoff for her graphic design assistance.

Library of Congress Cataloging-in-Publication Data
Shevtsova, Lilia Fedorovna.
  Russia lost in transition : the Yeltsin and Putin legacies / Lilia Shevtsova.
    p. cm.
  Includes bibliographical references and index.
  ISBN 978-0-87003-236-3 (pbk.) -- ISBN 978-0-87003-237-0 (cloth)
  1. Russia (Federation)--Politics and government--1991- 2. Russia (Federation)--Foreign relations. I. Title.
  DK510.763.S494 2007
  947.086--dc22   2007034896

12 11 10 09 08 07   12345   1st Printing 2007

CONTENTS

FOREWORD

Russia is at once an ancient land and a new country. This dual reality suggests a profound challenge that Russia faces in defining itself today. The challenge has to do with the seemingly unyielding frictions between the emerging shape of a new Russia—at last free of the imperial entanglements, communist ideology and Soviet dictatorship—and the patterns of its millennium-old culture and proud history. Russians and Russia-watchers alike have learned that the habits of an autocratic superpower die slowly and the ways of a liberal democracy can take time to flourish.

The period in between is commonly called a "transition." For Russia, being "a country in transition" is a scientific-sounding but largely empty phrase. It signifies a journey with a known point of departure but a far less certain destination. It refers to a period when the balance between continuity and change is believed to have tilted decisively toward the latter. Of course, for those who do not subscribe to Whig or Hegelian theories, change is not necessarily progress; it is an *opportunity* for progress.

In the present volume, Lilia Shevtsova examines how Russia has responded to the opportunity for progress during these early years of post-Soviet transition. Shevtsova provides a comprehensive assessment of the new Russia that has been built under the leadership of the nation's first two presidents, Boris Yeltsin and Vladimir Putin. Her work represents a major contribution to our understanding of Russia's quest for a modern national identity, which is one of the most important political dramas of our times.

Shevtsova is clear-eyed about the virtues and flaws of Russia's leaders and its elites. Her insight into "Yeltsin's ability to repudiate and to restore tradition simultaneously" sets the stage for her fascinating inquiry into the complex, often contradictory dynamics of a country "lost in transition." Implicitly comparing the present period with the times of Peter the Great and the Bolshevik Revolution, Shevtsova remarks that "Putin's destiny may be to confirm that Russia cannot be modernized from above." She questions, furthermore, whether Russia can find a "third way" or a "special path" as an alternative to "genuine modernization," which must be guided by trust in the organic development of civil society, not the power and wisdom of the state.

Few countries have endured the degree of turmoil that Russia has experienced in the twenty years since the unraveling of the Soviet Empire was unwittingly set in motion under Mikhail Gorbachev. Russia's territory today is its smallest size since the early 1700s. While its economy has been growing thanks largely to rapid exploitation of non-renewable natural resources, Russia's population of 140 million souls is in decline due to stubbornly low fertility and high morbidity rates. Yet the quantitative aspects of Russia's existence are in many ways less important than its qualitative dimensions. Indeed, for Russia's transition, questions of institutional development, political culture, and philosophical orientation are paramount.

Every empire in human history has had its own logic for coming into being and its own logic for falling apart. Muscovy started as an isolated principality and grew into a mighty empire, ruled first by divine-right czars and later reconstituted by ideologically mandated commissars. Over a few centuries

Russia's geographic reach grew steadily, by exploration and by conquest, seeking to unify the vast Eurasian continent. Along the way, the Russians proved powerful and resilient enough to withstand foreign invasions and other disasters. Russia almost always had a big idea—as heir to Kievan Rus, lamp of Eastern Christendom, Third Rome, bastion of Counter-Revolution after Napoleon, and fortress of world communism. Yet ultimately the Russo-Soviet Empire declined and fell because of the inherent ungovernability of its disparate lands, the chronic misery of its peoples, and the frequent brutality of the state.

What is left in the wake of imperial collapse is in principle an open road, a field of enormous possibilities and great expectations, but also a fragmented national identity fraught with anxieties and questions. It is significant that Russia has managed to avoid the considerable risks of chaos, disintegration, and social strife that could have readily ensnared the country. Yet, if Russia has avoided the worst, neither has it decisively reached for the best.

As Shevtsova observes of the new Russia under Yeltsin and Putin, "no one had ever democratized an imperial superpower." When will nostalgia for past glory and resentment of lost prestige yield to a dynamic vision of national rebirth? What will be the character of a new Russian society? What will be its national purpose? How will Russia's leaders and citizens define the ideals of their land? Russia, *quo vadis?* These vexing questions still hang over Russia's path to building a genuinely prosperous and just society.

The answers to these questions are of profound interest not only to Russians but also to its neighbors and partners in the West. Shevtsova has important things to say about the limited role of the outside world in Russia's development. She makes abundantly clear that transforming Russia is a project that belongs to Russians themselves. If Russia cannot be modernized from above, neither can it be modernized from outside. To say that the external role is limited is not to say that it is entirely absent. Shevtsova is frank about the errors of commission and omission made by Russia's would-be foreign supporters in recent years.

Shevtsova's writing is animated with the spirit of liberal democracy and a sense of historic possibility for Russia. The author is also a realist who knows that Russia's "history and culture do matter." In a sense, her principal objective is to examine the difference between Russia *as it has been* and Russia *as it could be.* Shevtsova understands that Russia cannot be a fully "normal" country until it works through its uniquely abnormal history. Her analysis is nowhere more poignant than in her discussion of the events of the autumn of 1991, which she calls "the decisive moment for postcommunist Russia," a time when the "liberal project" had perhaps its most decisive opening.

The liberal project—establishing limited government, constitutionalism, the rule of law, respect for individual liberty—has not been a dominant theme in Russia's statecraft. Indeed, it has been more akin to a "minority report" in Russian history, with a series of significant episodes: the early years in the reigns of Catherine the Great and her grandson Alexander I, the Decembrist movement of 1825, the reforms of Alexander II in the 1860s and 1870s, the 1905 Revolution, and the February Revolution of 1917. Each of these awakenings contained important seeds of progress yet ended in a greater measure of disappointment for Russia.

That the post-Soviet period still represents Russia's most dramatic and hopeful break with its past and an opportunity for progress; that Russia's ambiguous and contradictory modes of development under Yeltsin and Putin have nevertheless managed to avoid highly plausible national catastrophes; that, notwithstanding the current retrenchment of the state and the ominous shrinking of civil society, material life is once again improving for ordinary Russians—these points are not much in dispute. Yet the legacy of this historic period remains deeply uncertain.

As this book goes to press, its author has remarked that Russia seems to be "waiting for Godot." The reference aptly sums up the near-term uncertainty about the identity of the country's next president. On a deeper level, Russia continues its long wait for a time when the name of its leader matters less than the will of its citizens.

MARK MEDISH
VICE PRESIDENT FOR STUDIES–RUSSIA, CHINA, AND EURASIA
CARNEGIE ENDOWMENT FOR INTERNATIONAL PEACE

PREFACE

Russia retains its capacity to surprise. The world thought it knew where it stood in the 1990s, as Yeltsin's Russia struggled to find a new identity, watching with increasing disappointment Russia's inability to sort out its problems, taking its weakness for granted. Sixteen years after the collapse of the USSR, however, Russia is back in the news, startling the international community with its assertiveness, ambitions, capriciousness, and unpredictable vector.

Russia's twists and turns and uncertainty about its ultimate destination oblige us to revise our ideas and assessments of it constantly. Those who were delighted by its revolutionary transformation into a young democracy after the fall of the USSR today talk of a restoration and the return of authoritarianism. Those who lamented its demise as a nation today predict a return to superpower status. Many who yesterday expected Russia to be integrated into the West today worry about the possibility of a future confrontation. Those who saw it as a success story now see intimations of catastrophe, while those who despaired of Yeltsin's Russia are proud of Putin's Russia.

Russia's trajectory, and the political legacy of Boris Yeltsin and Vladimir Putin, matter.[1] This, after all, is a country that can make a serious difference to how the world responds to such challenges as international terrorism, nuclear proliferation, energy security, the volatility of a vast territory between Europe and Asia, and the problems of Iran, Iraq, and the Middle East. What can we expect from Russia in its next political phase?

1. I have discussed the presidencies of Boris Yeltsin and Vladimir Putin at length in my previous books: *Yeltsin's Russia: Myths and Reality* (Washington, D.C.: Carnegie Endowment for International Peace, 1999) and *Putin's Russia* (Washington, D.C.: Carnegie Endowment for International Peace, 2005).

ACKNOWLEDGMENTS

I owe my deep gratitude to a number of people for their invaluable advice and encouragement. The Carnegie Endowment for International Peace and Carnegie Moscow Center are institutions that have created a perfect atmosphere for my efforts to follow the unfolding of Russia's story. I thank Carnegie President Jessica T. Mathews, and Vice Presidents Paul Balaran, Mark Medish, Thomas Carothers, and George Perkovich for their unflagging support. I also thank James F. Collins, Director of the Russia and Eurasia Program, for his insights.

I am also indebted to Mikhail Gorbachev, former president of the USSR, who read the Russian version of the manuscript and helped me with his critical judgment, rigorous argument, and generosity of spirit. Special thanks also go to Carl Bildt, foreign affairs minister of Sweden, who, amidst his hectic schedule and domestic and international commitments, found time to read the manuscript and give his view on it. Special appreciation also goes to Strobe Talbott, president of the Brookings Institution, whose ideas and observations have been always helpful in my writings and who this time gave me generous comments.

My friends Arnold Horelick, David Kramer, Angela Stent, and Andrew Kuchins read the manuscript with extraordinary care and helped me in every conceivable way with their insights and critical comments. I have also benefited from my other friends and colleagues, first of all Rose Gottemoeller, Thomas Graham, Igor Klyamkin, and Dmitri Trenin, who have shared with me their ideas and helped me to promote the book. I thank Carnegie Vice President for Communications Peter Reid for his advice and enthusiastic promotion of the book.

I am indebted to Arch Tait, the translator, who conveyed my thoughts to the English reading audience. I also thank Sam Greene for his advice on the translation.

Special appreciation goes to Carrie Mullen, Carnegie Endowment director of publications, who coordinated the editorial process and gave the book higher priority; her support was essential at every stage. I am also indebted to Ilonka Oszvald, production manager, who shepherded the manuscript through production and played an invaluable role in the editing. Natalia Bubnova helped me in countless ways. I am grateful to my friends and colleagues in and outside of the Carnegie Endowment and in and outside Moscow for sharing their thoughts with me.

I thank editor Lorraine Alexson for her commitment that made a difference, proofreaders Carlotta Ribar and Beth Richards for their attention to detail, and Tina Wong Coffron for marketing the book. My thanks go to Marina Barnett, the Russia and Eurasia Program manager and Ann Stecker, program assistant of the Russia and Eurasia Program in Washington, and my coordinator Anna Bessonova for creating a most helpful atmosphere for my research in Moscow and Washington. Thanks to Andrei Shelutto, the designer, for finding the graphical form to convey my message on Russia lost in transition.

I am grateful for the generous support of the Carnegie Corporation of New York, the Charles Stewart Mott Foundation, and the Open Society Institute to the Carnegie Moscow Center.

And finally, thanks to my family—my mother, Maria, my husband Igor, and my son Oleg—for their understanding and forbearance that were tested repeatedly.

Chapter 1

BORIS YELTSIN: A REVOLUTIONARY WHO PRESERVED TRADITION

Russian history is first and foremost the history of personalized power—of the concentration of all the levers of power and resources in the hands of a leader standing above society, of a succession of leaders and their regimes. It is true that in the new Russian context, political leadership acquires a contradictory nature. Leading Russia out of communism required a leader who could act as a battering ram to destroy the old order. That person had to be an outstanding and charismatic politician with the courage to break with the past and force the political class and state authorities to leave the past behind. This person needed a strong personality and the ability to lead. However, to introduce a system based on political rivalry and competition requires quite a different kind of leader, one prepared to "abdicate the throne" and transfer at least some executive power to other institutions. The criterion of Boris Yeltsin's success or failure is not only the extent to which he managed to free himself of the communist mentality and his country of communism, but also his ability to prevent the disintegration of Russia, establish friendly relations with the West, and succeed in creating a free market. The crucial question is to what extent he succeeded in overcoming Russia's underlying tradition of personalized power, which, as recent Russian history has proved, could be

1

presented as an anticommunist package with pro-Western stripes based on market rules.

Those who are interested in Russia will puzzle for years to come over Yeltsin's personality and rule, trying to decide whether he was a reformer, a revolutionary, a liberal, or a conservative. Did he aspire to lead Russia into the future, or was he more concerned with putting a brake on society's transformation, fearing a potentially dangerous forward momentum? What is the nature of the link between Yeltsin and his successor, Vladimir Putin, and is Putin's period in office a continuation or a negation of the Yeltsin years? Perhaps it is too early to answer all these questions, and the dust must settle before the key trends of Yeltsin's legacy and its impact on Putin's rule become clearer. I will nonetheless risk making some observations on Boris Yeltsin's role and his legacy, viewing it in the context of events following his departure from the Kremlin.[1]

Yeltsin's rule was paradoxical and rife with contradictions from the outset.[2] Despite the hostility between Yeltsin and Mikhail Gorbachev and their seemingly opposing goals, it was to be Yeltsin who completed what Gorbachev had unintentionally begun—the final destruction of an empire, a superpower, and a one-party state. If Gorbachev had never anticipated that destruction, falling victim to *the law of unintended consequences*, Yeltsin consciously set out to finish the demolition of the USSR. For a time he hoped to create a new, anticommunist, and anti-Soviet union under his leadership, but he was soon forced to abandon that aspiration and concentrate on Russia. Although Gorbachev, the architect of perestroika, intended to breathe new life into the Soviet Union, and Yeltsin, the instigator of the Belovezha Accords, which dissolved the USSR in December 1991, pursued opposite goals, they jointly brought the Soviet project to an end. Neither had any wish to go down in history as the gravedigger of the Soviet Union. As regards Yeltsin, his role in the dissolution of the USSR largely determined the nature of his subsequent leadership and influenced how the post-Soviet Russian system would develop. His period in office shows continuity with Gorbachev's policies, but it also laid the foundation for rejecting the spirit of Gorbachev's perestroika. Russian politics and power have evolved on more than one occasion through this synthesis of incompatible tendencies and steps leading to unintended consequences and ramifications.

During Boris Yeltsin's presidency, the Russian political class was forced to reject, or decided it was in its own interests to reject, basic principles that had governed the perpetuation of power and the state in Russia for centuries. For the first time the regime sought to legitimize itself through elections rather than through ideology, communist totalitarianism, or czarist succession to the throne. Rallying Russia by confronting the West was abandoned. A free market was introduced, weakening the state's control of society. Finally, Russia began learning how to live in an environment of political pluralism. Admittedly, renunciation of some principles was less than final, as Vladimir Putin's presidency was to show.

What remained of the traditional exercise of power at the end of Yeltsin's rule? The elite had preserved some basics of the Russian matrix—the traditional organization both of the regime and of society, with the principle of indivisibility remaining key. Power remained personalized and monolithic. There had been no dispersing of authority among the branches of government. The Russian leader continued to hold the main levers of control. He was elected, but he was not accountable to the electorate. The merging of power and business was just one more manifestation of the principle of indivisibility. State interests retained their primacy over those of the individual and society. The elite and the majority of Russians continued to see Russia's great-power status in world politics as fundamental, which is defined by the Russian term *derzhavnichestvo*: "Russia is a great power or it is nothing"—such was (and continues to be) the overwhelming consensus.

Even when a new society and new institutions began to emerge, the Kremlin played by the old rules. If the fundamental principle of democratic elections is that "the rules are clear, but the result is uncertain," the Russian elite was determined that the rules should be uncertain and a result favorable to itself guaranteed. Rather than make provisions for an alternative regime and rotation, the elite stressed continuity. Samuel Huntington's observation that two election cycles are sufficient for a country to become democratic proved not to apply to Russia, where regular elections, including Yeltsin's two presidential elections, provided a smokescreen for backsliding from Gorbachev's liberalization.

A free market, though rudimentary, came into being under Yeltsin, but as the state was above the law, it took the form of "oligarchic capitalism," premised on a deal between major property owners appointed by the Kremlin and the ruling team. This meant that the institution of private property was never legitimized in the minds of the public, with the result that Yeltsin's successor was able to set about revising the results of privatization.

In foreign policy, Yeltsin continued Gorbachev's withdrawal from confrontation with the West, but where Gorbachev had broken the mold of international relations, compelling the West also to seek new policies and think in new terms, Yeltsin not only failed to find a new global role for Russia, but also failed to understand new international realities. To the last he was torn between cooperating with the West and fulminating against the nature of that cooperation and Russia's inferior position. His aim was to make Russia an ally of the West, but after his departure, the country moved in the opposite direction.

Yeltsin's presidency gave rise to a hybrid system that regulates relations between the regime and society on the basis of conflicting and irreconcilable principles: state authorities are elected, but candidates to elective office are appointed from above, and elections are manipulated; the rule of law is enshrined in the constitution, but surreptitious deals are the order of the day; although society has a federal structure, the center dictates policy to the regions; there is a free market, but officials constantly meddle in the economy. This system was not fully established in the Yeltsin period and remained unconsolidated, leaving space for other forces—from orthodox communists to radical liberals—and for movement in any direction. Chameleon-like, the hybrid could assume different colorations, at one moment appearing more authoritarian, at another more democratic. Its mixed nature and lack of ideology enabled it to survive by means of reincarnation, but it was plainly without strategic direction and wholly focused on self-preservation. At some point after 1993, when Yeltsin dismantled the Soviet parliament and edited his own constitution, establishing a hyperpresidency, Yeltsin's hybrid began to evolve into a neo-patrimonial regime that was based on a leader that holds all power and delegates its functions and authority to an entourage and to competing clans.

To understand the nature of Yeltsin's leadership, it may be useful to compare it with that of his predecessor. Mikhail Gorbachev, the last Soviet leader, tried to the end to develop "socialism with a human face." At the same time, lacking the courage to reject socialist views and leave Communist Party ranks, he was the first leader in Russian history to attempt to reform the traditional Russian state, which was symbolized by an omnipotent leader that stood above society. Gorbachev rejected the notion that power was sacrosanct by nature and also abandoned three other major props of the Russian state: militarism, the claim that Russia was doomed to follow a "special path," and its attempt to have its "zones of influence" in the international arena. Yeltsin completely abandoned the socialist ideal and became an anticommunist. It was he who finally destroyed the old state, which allows us to regard him as a revolutionary. However, he also set about restoring what Gorbachev had tried to undermine: autocracy. He began to concentrate power in his hands, and it was Yeltsin, not Putin, who began the move back toward the restoration of the old model of governance, albeit without the trappings of Soviet communism.

Yeltsin's Russia demonstrated the ability to repudiate and restore tradition simultaneously. The fact that the first Russian president legitimized the authority of the state through elections made it impossible for the regime to resort to the ways of the patriarchal past. It now had to seek popular support using liberal democratic mechanisms hostile to the Russian matrix. Yet the political actors who might have effected and pushed forward the transition to a new form of governance had not yet appeared, new interest groups had yet to take shape, new property relations had not yet taken root, and the leader was not ready or able to move things in that direction. Russia was stranded in a civilizational wasteland, with no wish to return to the past but lacking the resources to embark on a new path of development.

Yeltsin's style of leadership and the regime he created hardly fit any democratic format. It could not be captured by well-known definitions, such as Philippe Schmitter's "democradura," Guillermo O'Donnell's "delegative democracy," Michael McFaul's "electoral democracy," or Fareed Zakaria's "illiberal democracy." These definitions did not convey fully the flavor of Yeltsin's rule and its strange combination of monarchic powers and style with elements of political pluralism and competition. To express this mix of incompatibilities, I use the metaphor of an "electoral monarchy." But, of course, Boris Yeltsin had much more power than another "republican monarch"—Charles de Gaulle, with whom he has often been compared—and much less accountability.

Observers will argue for years to come over whether Yeltsin could have created a genuine democracy in Russia. Let us consider three factors that affected Russia's development in the 1990s: its historical legacy, the institutional obstacles to the transformation process, and the role of the leader and behavior of the elite.

The history of the Russian state, which for many centuries was based on a strict centralization of authority and repression of the individual, could only ever be a hindrance to the liberalization of Russian society.[3] Before Gorbachev, no one in Russia's history had even attempted to assail the principle of autocracy, and tentative efforts to liberalize the country invariably ended in failure. Alexander II's nineteenth-century experiment with "constitutional autocracy" was unsuccessful, and Alexander III, recognizing that trying to mitigate autocracy might destroy it, reverted to tradition. Nikita Khrushchev's thaw in the 1960s had to be reversed, and it appeared to confirm the Soviet elite's suspicion that any tempering of the political climate and attempts to liberalize the regime could undermine the foundations of the state. In the postwar period, Russia was not shaken by revolutions like those that affected Poland, Hungary, and Czechoslovakia, countries that had prewar memories of freedom and political pluralism. Their experiences prompted the appearance in those countries of a viable opposition prepared to work against the system and of pragmatists within the ruling class prepared to countenance political pluralism. At the crucial moment, in the late 1980s, when Gorbachev threw open Russia's windows on the world and the country awoke, Russia had neither a credible anti-systemic opposition ready to dismantle the old system and build a new one, nor pragmatists capable of living and functioning in an atmosphere of political pluralism.

No less influential was the fact that Russia missed out on the period in European history when the spirit of constitutionalism was abroad, bringing with it a recognition of the importance of the rule of law. Before European society was democratized, it registered a major achievement in the nineteenth century by establishing the *Rechtsstaat*, which embodied the principle that the state itself had to be subject to the law. Russia missed what Ralf Dahrendorf has called "the hour of the lawyer," in failing to form the basis of a liberal constitutionalism. Without that basis Russian society could not successfully move to the next stages of transformation: "the hour of the economist" and "the hour of the citizen."[4] That Russia never embraced that principle was reflected in the fact that, after the fall of communism, even the liberals preferred to be guided by political expediency rather than by rules and preferred to rely upon a leader. Neither had

Russia mastered such other fundamentals of liberalism as civil rights, independent institutions, the inalienability of private property, and the full disestablishment of the Church.

In Russia, the interests of the state traditionally took priority over those of the individual and centralization of power was always bolstered by territorial expansionism. Initially, early in Russia's history, the need to protect the population and a weak state from raids by hostile tribes required the creation of a protective buffer of colonial territories. Subsequently, the centralized state, its ideology an amalgam of the Byzantine concept of autocracy (but without any constraints) and of the traditions of the Golden Horde of the Mongols, somewhat updated later by Peter the Great, proved incapable of developing other than extensively, by annexing territories and peoples. This meant constant warfare, with the intervals between wars spent seeking out the next enemy. The centralized state, constantly repressing society in order to survive and perpetuate itself, required a great-power mission and a continual strengthening of its great-power status, compounded by a suspicion of the outside world. Aspirations to great-power status in turn encouraged further centralization, thus creating a vicious cycle. After the fall of communism, Russia's claim to great-power status remains an important means of rallying society and preserving the centralized state. To this day the elite's vision of the Russian state is based on territory, military power, international prestige, and personalized power as the means of attaining them, and, finally, on identifying an enemy to justify that form of governance. Even after the collapse of communism and the dissolution of the USSR, this tradition of a centralized and arbitrarily governed state, quite alien to European principles, holds sway over the political thinking of Russia's ruling class. Thus, its historical legacy does not give much ground for optimism about the country's future.

It would be unfair to overlook the objective difficulties of the process of transformation that Russia faced in the 1990s. Before then no one had democratized an imperial superpower with messianic pretensions. The Russian elite needed simultaneously to create a new political framework, learning in the process how to legitimize it through elections, and to create a new state. The two tasks of attempting to democratize a regime and form a new state are not easy to reconcile, and trying to accomplish them simultaneously can lead to dramatic events, as the fragmentation of Yugoslavia demonstrated. Dankwart Rustow and Robert Dahl, and later Juan Linz and Alfred Stepan, rightly warned that a precondition of successful democratization is a stable state ("No state—no democracy"), and in the early 1990s Russia was in the midst of state collapse. As if that were not enough, Yeltsin and his team were obliged to attempt *four revolutions* at once: creating a free market, democratizing the political regime, liquidating an empire, and seeking a new geopolitical role for a country that had only recently been a nuclear superpower. The industrially developed world had passed through the phases of nation building, developing capitalism, and political democratization in sequence. Russia had to achieve all three in one leap. Moreover, all successful postcommunist transitions began with the establishment of a new political system, whereas in Russia the sequence was different. The Russian transition began with the privatization of property before independent political institutions were introduced.

Russia was out of luck not only in terms of its history and systemic constraints, which seemed to rule out a liberal transformation before it had even begun, but there was also the leadership factor and the role of the political class. Although when Yeltsin came to power Russian society as a whole and the political class in particular accepted that the old system was unsustainable, it was not yet ready to unite in building a new one. The events of 1990–1992 showed that even the most liberal politicians were not really up to introducing a liberal political system. A mixture of naïveté, neuroses, brashness, and social insensitivity were typical of the political class and did little to help Russia find its way to new values. In the 1990s, Russian liberals envisioned democracy as consisting mainly of elections, but only for the purpose of guaranteeing their power. They never conceded the possibility that their rivals might win, which from the beginning created the danger of election manipulation. An elite with such a mind-set was incapable of making the compromises and the pacts that were the basis of a successful transition to democracy. Embarking on the project of constructing a new Russia, the elite had no consensus regarding either the country's past or its future. The fall of communism was not on the whole seen as having discredited the Russian tradition of autocracy, with the result that there was no total repudiation of the former rules of the game and the political stereotypes. Responsibility for the fact that Russia never subjected its history to critical scrutiny lies primarily with Yeltsin and his ruling team. Not only did they not try to establish a new national consensus on democratic reforms, their egocentrism deepened the divisions within society, goading elites into warring among themselves over who was to get their hands on property and power.

In the early 1990s there was no "subject of transformation," that is, there was no political force or group capable of transforming Russia. The intelligentsia had been the driving force behind the thrust to democratization during Gorbachev's perestroika, but with Yeltsin's coming to power, it lost out. It reaped neither political nor economic benefit from the collapse of communism. On the contrary, the prestige of intellectuals declined. They found themselves collectively excluded from politics, both because of the collapse of financing for science, education, and the arts in which they were employed and because the new authorities had no further need for them. Regrettably, those intellectuals who did find a niche in the apparatus of government agreed to play by the bureaucracy's rules. No middle class with a corporate interest in liberal democratic reform emerged in the 1990s. Indeed, quasi-middle class groups serviced the bureaucratic oligarchic stratum. The elite that rose to the top after the collapse of the USSR was split into competing groups, each claiming a monopoly on power. As no alternative elite appeared, worldly-wise Soviet party officials, admitting a little fresh blood to their ranks, succeeded in providing the basis of a new ruling class. They not only restored their power but also gained control over property, which made them more powerful than they had been under the communist regime.

Society was too inexperienced to develop independently into a civil society under Yeltsin. The Kremlin's new occupants had come to power on a wave of democratic enthusiasm, but not only had they no intention of promoting the development of civil rights and liberties, they systematically obstructed the process, turning their backs on the democratic forces that had helped their rise to power, most notably the "Democratic Russia" movement that had helped Yeltsin to power in 1991. Society was compelled to hand power to a single individual on trust. Yeltsin was given the Kremlin's omnipotence on condition that he would not revoke the freedoms that had been granted. This bestowal signified a new social contract between Russia and its leader, although admittedly not formalized in any institutions and hence vulnerable.

Part of the trouble came from the Marxist assumptions of the technocrats who formed the first Yeltsin government. They supposed that introducing a capitalist economy would be enough, and they ignored the need for new institutions and the crucial importance of subordinating the state to the rule of law. As a result, they reconfirmed Adam Przeworski's conclusion, based on the interaction of democracy and capitalism in Latin America, that without stable liberal institutions, a sustainable liberal economy is impossible.[5] Indeed, in the absence of viable independent institutions and rule of law, economic reforms can become a destabilizing factor that pushes the ruling class toward authoritarianism in order to defend its interests and its property.

The second and third waves of democratization in Europe showed that integrating transitional societies into the European community was a crucial factor in ensuring the success of their democratic reforms. Unfortunately this proved impossible in the case of Russia. Europe was having difficulty digesting East

Germany and was not willing to engage in further self-sacrifice. Russia for its part, having begun the building of a new state, could not surrender sovereignty to supranational institutions.

In short, Russia lacked the full complement of prerequisites for a successful transition. Admittedly, a number of successful transitions to democracy have shown that effective leadership and political engineering can compensate for the absence of some prerequisites, provided the elite is ready to break with the past. "We cannot exclude the possibility of transcending those conditioning factors by political leadership and political engineering," wrote Juan Linz.[6] India, Taiwan, and South Korea have proved that democracy can take root both in non-European, non-Christian, and even (in the case of India) economically problematical societies if the leaders and the elite see democracy as best serving national interests. The leadership of Adolfo Suárez in Spain, F. W. de Klerk in South Africa, and Václav Havel in Czechoslovakia eased the democratic transition in their countries, which lacked certain prerequisites for democracy. In Poland, a democratic-minded elite was able to counteract the authoritarian tendencies of its leader, Lech Walesa, and build a pluralistic society. Even a lack of democratically inclined leaders and elites need not exclude a successful transition, as Giuseppe Di Palma and Albert Hirschmann have shown, because democracy can be built by pragmatists who appreciate the ruinous nature, not least for themselves, of an autocratic system. "In any discussion of the importance of a democratic political culture and traditions, it should not be forgotten that many new democracies were not made by democrats but by people who had more or less passively supported nondemocratic regimes. The nondemocrats of yesterday can become democrats, even convinced democrats," wrote Di Palma.[7] It is difficult to say how far a reform-minded leadership and socially responsible elite in Russia might have compensated for the lack of some preconditions of democratic transition. Indeed, the transformation of a communist state, empire, and superpower would differ from transformations in Latin America, Southern Europe,

Central Europe, and Eastern Europe. There is no doubt, however, that had Russia had leaders willing to build independent institutions and who were aware of the importance of the rule of law, they could have eased Russia's transformation into a law-governed state. Alas, Yeltsin was no Russian Suárez, and the Russian liberals and democrats were ill prepared for the role played by their colleagues in Eastern Europe in the 1980s and 1990s. Nor had Russia in the early 1990s pragmatists prepared to think along new lines. As a result, the country was unable to accelerate its maturation as a civilization, which proves that history, culture, and tradition do matter.

This does not, however, mean that Russia had none of the conditions that might have set it on the road to freedom and political pluralism. I firmly believe that the decisive moment for postcommunist Russia was the autumn of 1991. At that moment, after the defeat of the August putsch attempt by Communist Party apparatchiks desperate to prevent the dissolution of the USSR, Boris Yeltsin had a huge mandate for change from the Russian public. About 70 percent of Russians were prepared to see Russia move toward a liberal democracy. Many were unsure what exactly democracy was, but they accepted it as both an ideal and as a way of life. Moreover, in post-Soviet society, people were attracted by individual freedom, Western standards of prosperity, and the Western way of life. Russian society had not been ready in 1917 to insist on its freedom and therefore handed victory to the Bolsheviks. In 1991, however, society was no longer an obstacle to breaking with the old Russian system. This society had given Yeltsin its support: he could have used it to build a new, pluralistic Russia. He could have introduced a constitution with checks and balances to constrain the power of the state and its leader's omnipotence. There could have been new elections for both the presidency and parliament on the basis of a new constitution. In autumn 1991 Russia would unquestionably have supported those reforms and even the Soviet parliament, which remained on the scene, would have voted them into law, just as the Spanish *cortes* and the communist parliaments of East European countries had authorized a transition to a competitive political system. The revolutionary experience of Central and Eastern Europe and the West's very existence could have helped Russia at least to weaken its dependence on its history and traditions.

Yeltsin went in the opposite direction. He set about consolidating his personal power. In the process, he retained elements of the Soviet state, which meant that the old parliament was preserved as the main focus of power. That could only lead to a confrontation between executive and representative authorities, which was the situation from 1991 to 1993. Yeltsin's decision to embark on economic reforms while refusing to introduce independent institutions inevitably reduced reform to a mechanism for delivering privatized state property into the hands of the "old new" ruling class. In Yeltsin's defense, note that at that time not even the liberals and democrats saw a need to repudiate such vestiges of the USSR as the old parliament and constitution and to initiate political reform. Yegor Gaidar's team believed it could simply rely on a strong leader. It never occurred to those who considered themselves liberals and democrats that there was a need to establish a system of checks and balances. Government liberals had to wait only until 1992 to see how misplaced their trust in Yeltsin had been, when he sacked their government and formed a new one under bureaucrat Victor Chernomyrdin. The first team of Russian liberal technocrats overestimated the potential of the first Russian president. The team itself also appeared unready for the challenge. The Gaidar team's concept of liberalism went little further than privatization, which it implemented so that, no doubt without realizing it, it laid the foundation for an authoritarian oligarchic regime. In the absence of independent institutions, and given the regime's disregard for the rule of law, this outcome was inevitable.

In this way Yeltsin, his team, and the Russian political class, which at that time wanted to appear liberal and pro-Western, let slip a chance to lay the basis for a system that would guarantee liberal freedoms and competition. Even given the obstacles that there undoubtedly were, a leader and a team resolved to move beyond the confines of autocracy could have enabled Russia to progress much further along the path to a new way of life.

Could this leader and this elite, given their origins and ignorance of anything other than the Soviet system, have behaved differently? Gorbachev, who belonged body and soul to the Communist Party apparatus, managed to begin dismantling the Russian tradition without external prompting. He did not foresee the consequences of his endeavor, but all reformers start by shaking the foundations of the status quo without knowing where their actions will lead. If they could see into the future, no doubt many would have second thoughts. Yet the still-communist Gorbachev began dismantling a system that could have survived for some time, proving that leadership could become the key factor of the breakthrough. Looking back at Yeltsin's presidency, we can conclude that for a short time in the autumn of 1991, Russia, at least theoretically, had a chance to escape from the burden of its history and traditions and to outflank its national mentality and habitual ways of thinking and behaving. That Yeltsin and his liberals did not even attempt to do so tells us that tradition and history were stronger than the courage and vision of Yeltsin's team, and they made a window of opportunity irrelevant.

The limitations of Yeltsin's leadership resulted from more than his career and mentality as a Soviet functionary. They were also the result of the way in which the USSR was dissolved, which can be described as a coup d'état carried out against Gorbachev in December 1991 by the leaders of Russia, Ukraine, and Belarus, that is, Boris Yeltsin, Leonid Kravchuk, and Stanislav Shushkevich. With the disappearance of the USSR, the vast majority of the Russian population was cut off from the support of a paternalistic state controlling their lives and from their roots and previous identity as well. They were totally disoriented and had no idea what they were to face in the future. Millions of ex-Soviet citizens were never to find a place for themselves in the new circumstances. Many sank to the bottom of the social scale, fell into poverty, and lost all hope of being able to return to a normal life. For millions of Soviet citizens, the sudden collapse of the USSR was a tragedy. As one of those who had destroyed the USSR, Yeltsin could not afford to let an opposition come to power that would hold him responsible for the act. Even today, most Russians look nostalgically to the days of the USSR, which they remember as a time of stability, and forget the experience of living in a totalitarian and, later, an authoritarian state. In a 2006 public opinion survey, 71 percent of respondents regretted the dissolution of the USSR, while 22 percent did not. Twenty-four percent considered that its dissolution had been inevitable, against 65 percent who considered it could have been avoided.[8] Of course, that does not mean that these people are ready to restore it; it demonstrates the extent of their dissatisfaction with a new reality. Nonetheless, their complicity in the destruction of the Soviet Union was a factor that obliged Yeltsin and his team to do everything they could to cling to power. Soon, events occurred that precluded any chance that Yeltsin might create conditions for genuine political competition.

On October 3, 1993, Yeltsin shelled parliament. After the demise of the USSR, parliament became the focus of a national populist opposition. Destroying it by force, however, with the spilling of blood, meant the end of any hope of governance by national consensus and a return to fist-fighting to resolve conflicts. In 2006, 60 percent of those surveyed blamed Yeltsin for his action against parliament and considered his use of force to be unjustified. (At the time, only 30 percent held that view.) From today's perspective there are hardly any doubts that the use of force to dismantle parliament in 1993—despite its having become a reactionary symbol—pushed Russia in an authoritarian direction. At the time, however, many liberals and democrats saw no other exit, demonstrating how difficult it is for the Russian political class to learn the art of finding peaceful solutions to conflict and clashes of interests. In the end,

Boris Yeltsin, together with the political elite—the part that supported parliament as well as the part that supported the president—drove Russia into a trap, forcing society to make a choice between two forms of undemocratic government: returning to a new version of the Soviet system or opting for anticommunist authoritarianism. The destruction of a parliament left over from the Soviet era narrowed, and perhaps even ended, any prospect that Russia might see an expansion of political freedoms and political competitiveness for the time being, not least because a pluralistic democracy can hardly be introduced through force and bloodshed. For only a short time in 1991 Russia had a chance to choose liberal democracy, but by violently putting down the opposition in 1993, Yeltsin signaled that he was no longer prepared to countenance political struggle and free elections.

The superpresidency that ensued after the forced resolution of the conflict between the executive and representative powers was enshrined in a new constitution adopted in December 1993. Yeltsin amended that constitution personally and was instrumental in pointing it toward authoritarianism. The shape of the new regime bore the hallmark of the victory of a particular political force and had the nature of that victory stamped all over it. Individuals who fight to the death are hardly likely, after destroying their opponents, to start fostering political competition. The new constitution proclaimed the power and freedom of the people but set superpresidential power in stone, which undermined both the people's power and their freedoms. Under this constitution the president is not one branch of power but is above all branches. It is he who "determines the basic direction of the state's domestic and foreign policy" and who is "the guarantor of the constitution of the Russian Federation, and of the rights and freedoms of individuals and citizens." In reality, the powers of the Russian president are much the same as the powers of the Russian monarch were in 1906–1917. It was the Yeltsin constitution that established the institutional framework for an authoritarian, neo-patrimonial regime, as even Yeltsin aides freely admit. Yeltsin's assistant for legal issues, Mikhail Krasnov, says, "This constitution prevents any development of democracy.... It liquidated a system of checks and balances, making the president omnipotent; and that is a tragedy."[9]

When analyzing Russia's transformation we would do well to recall Joseph A. Schumpeter's five requirements for democracy, of which he stressed the importance of "the human material of politics—the people who man the party machines—are elected to serve in parliament, rise to cabinet office," emphasizing that they "should be of sufficiently high quality."[10] The quality of the human material of the Russian elite was insufficient for it to strive to expand civil freedoms. This applies also to the liberal technocrats summoned by the regime to implement reforms. All of them, from Yeltsin economic ministers Yegor Gaidar and Anatoly Chubais to Putin's economic ministers, German Gref and Alexei Kudrin, accepted the logic of authoritarianism.

The key responsibility for Russia's trajectory has to be shared by Yeltsin's close entourage and ruling team, which included quite a few people who had been viewed, and even now are viewed, as liberals. Under the banner of fighting communists, they ended up together with other political and business-class factions that were protecting their vested interests, newly acquired property, and self-perpetuation. For Yeltsin's entourage his political regime became an instrument not to achieve noble goals, but an end in itself. That is why they so desperately tried to keep in the Kremlin a man who was barely alive. During the presidential elections in 1996 they miraculously succeeded in having a sick man elected president of Russia. But at what a price! The election accelerated Russia's slide toward a fake democracy that includes the mechanisms of presidential succession and electoral manipulation.

Ironically, the Communist Party proved a much stauncher supporter of political competition and learned more rapidly how to behave as parliamentarians and in the cut-and-thrust of politics than those who professed to be liberals and democrats.

Finally, no new Wittes or Stolypins, who had been the staunch supporters of reform in the Russian political class in czarist days, emerged in postcommunist Russia because the system does not allow modernizers the independence that czarism felt able to live with.

The great responsibility for the missed opportunity to democratize Russia lies fairly and squarely with Boris Yeltsin. A leader's quality is seen in his capacity to rise above pressures from society and the political class and to offer a new vision. Yeltsin showed no such ability, preferring to react to events that he did not always foresee or manage to control. Beginning in 1995, he became increasingly physically incapable of carrying out his functions and even of fully understanding what was happening. The power of the presidency was usurped by the Kremlin "court," a few members of the Yeltsin family, and its favorites. Yeltsin's second presidency not only made a farce of national politics, it managed to discredit those elements of liberal democracy that Yeltsin himself had helped to introduce.

In 1995–1996 Russia faced the dilemma of whether to hold free and fair elections and risk the return to power of the communists, or keep the ruling clique in power by "managing" the elections. The experience of Eastern Europe showed that the genuine election of communist governments by no means consigned those countries back to the past. Communists found themselves obliged to implement liberal reforms. In Moldova the Communist Party included among its goals joining the European Community and respecting the norms of democracy. These, of course, were communist parties that had successfully evolved in the direction of social democracy. How Gennadi Zyuganov's Communist Party in Russia might have evolved had he been given the opportunity of winning the election is difficult to say. It is worth remembering, however, that Yevgeny Primakov's government, which the communists supported in 1999, did not reject free-market principles and democracy and even led Russia out of a deep economic crisis without undermining market rules. The consequences of keeping an ailing

Yeltsin in the Kremlin by reneging on free elections are obvious: it provided a basis for the return of authoritarianism, albeit in an anticommunist incarnation.

In this connection we must also recall the role played by the West at the beginning of the Russian transformation. Was it crucial and important, or insignificant? In the 1990s Russia was dependent on international financial institutions and on the economic assistance of the Western community and beyond— on the West's help in forming a new civilizational agenda. That is, it needed advice on how to build the market, how to introduce the rule of law, and how to form independent institutions. In addition, Yeltsin and his team were seeking integration with the West, which made them particularly responsive to Western advice and Western influence. Most of the Western leaders, however, were not only unprepared for an ambitious program of assisting Russia's transformation, they failed to see how much was at stake as the new Russian state took shape or to appreciate its potential impact on the world whether it succeeded or failed. Watching the Western reaction to Russia at that time, one got the impression that a small part of the West looked on with curiosity as its once-mighty but now pathetic opponent thrashed about in the water, not knowing which way to swim. Would it sink or swim? they wondered. Another part genuinely tried to help Russia adapt to the new realities, but even those who recognized the scale of Russia's challenge were unable to find effective means to support its reforms. U.S. president Bill Clinton was the only Western leader who made Russia's integration into the West and its transition to democracy a foreign-policy priority and saw Russia's reforms as an important guarantee of international stability and America's security. He argued that Russia "must be a first-order concern" because "the world cannot afford the strife of the former Yugoslavia replicated in a nation as big as Russia, spanning eleven time zones with an armed arsenal of nuclear weapons that is still very vast."[11] Clinton called for a "strategic alliance with Russian reform," and his administration adopted the view that the United States should become involved in Russia's development. The chief architect of the administration's Russia policy, Strobe Talbott, outlined the U.S.'s "Strategic Alliance with Russian Reform" in the following way:

> Russia is on the path toward becoming a modern state, at peace with itself and the world, productively and prosperously integrated into the international economy, a source for raw materials and manufactured products, a market for American goods and services, and a partner for American diplomacy. It should be the U.S. policy not just to prevent the worst but also to nurture the best that might happen in the former Soviet Union.[12]

In fact, this was the third Western attempt to push forward democratic transformation in the twentieth century. The first was American assistance for the democratization of defeated Germany and Japan after the Second World War; the second was the transformation of the former communist states in Central and Eastern Europe and the Baltics. Both times, independent U.S. efforts and joint efforts with Europe were successful, proving how much the outcomes of transition depend on the integration of the transition societies with the structures of the West. The third attempt, this time to embrace Russia, had mixed and, in some cases, counterproductive results.[13] In the matter of security, the United States succeeded in helping Russia to sort out the Soviet nuclear legacy, and created a new security framework for the West, filling the niche left by the collapsed USSR. The Russian elite, however, now has other thoughts about this process, blaming Washington for using Russian weakness in its own interest. In the economic area, the Clinton administration helped to forge the Washington Consensus, which focused on macroeconomic stabilization and high-speed privatization, that became the key instruments of Russian reform and that at least partially contributed to the emergence of oligarchic capitalism. Analyzing the U.S. factor in Russia's transformation at that time, Arnold Horelick and Thomas Graham wrote:

The United States squandered the reservoir of goodwill Russia had for it at the time of the Soviet breakup.... Russians came to understand that the U.S. was prepared to deliver much less assistance to Russia ... than they had expected. The close identification with an increasingly feeble Yeltsin; strong support for radical reformers, with their thinning popular support base; public insistence on reform programs most Russians believe led their country to ruin ... have caused increasingly more Russians to question the wisdom, judgment, and benevolence of the United States.[14]

In terms of the U.S. impact on Russia's reforms, both its supporters and its opponents have overestimated American influence on the Russian trajectory, and the Americans themselves underestimated the complexity of the challenge at the time.

In truth, all Western leaders made a double mistake, first, by relying on Yeltsin and believing that he would guarantee a Russian transition, and, second, by emphasizing the economy and neglecting the role of political reform. They would have been more instrumental in helping a democratic- and market-oriented Russia if in 1991 they had advised Boris Yeltsin and his team to organize new elections, adopt a democratic constitution, and build a new state based on the rule of law, and then move gradually to privatization, premissing it on the development of new institutions.

Instead, Western leaders adopted policies that were convenient and politically conducive to great photo-ops. Western advisers of near-celebrity status, like Harvard's Jeffrey Sachs, together with Russian technocrats, promoted what turned out to be disastrous advice about "big bang" privatization in the absence of an adequate legal structure and workable financial institutions. It took years, however, for failure to manifest itself, and in the meantime, the West was happy with Russia's anticommunist thrust and its unproblematic foreign policy. It continued to believe that Russia was moving toward democracy. It was not difficult to see why Western political circles did not insist on the strengthening of political pluralism in Russia and why the West silently accepted Yeltsin's manipulations of presidential elections in 1996. It feared that the communists might return to power, or the nationalists. Those anxieties were vigorously encouraged by Russia's liberal technocrats. No wonder the resultant oligarchic capitalism and *electoral monarchy*, masquerading as democracy, came to be associated in the Russian popular imagination with Western influence and gave rise to a deep-rooted mistrust of both liberal democracy and the West.

In the end the West failed to contribute effectively to the Russian transformation also because it lacked a common strategy, supported by both Europe and America, to induct Russia into its civilization; it failed to understand the complexities of Russian politics and was often naïve in its assessment of Russia's political players and their intentions. Only in the autumn of 1991 was there a real opportunity to include Russia in Western institutions, even if only as an associate member of the North Atlantic Treaty Organization (NATO) and the European Union. Neither the West nor Russia saw this. It was not only the Russian elite, but the Western elites too, that were caught out by the collapse of the USSR and failed to see the historic nature of the choice they could have made. The first NATO enlargement was a sign that the West had made its goal the integration of Eastern and Central Europe, though at the expense of its relationship with Yeltsin's Russia, which meant that the leading Western political circles had reconciled themselves with the idea that Russia could not be embraced. It would have to swim alone.

The lack of success of Russia's reforms did not particularly alarm the West, where many had already written Russia off both as an adversary and as a spoiler. They saw its stagnation either as inevitable or as a temporary step before democratization, and as posing no great threat to the West. The resurgence of a self-possessed Russia under Putin took Western political circles by surprise. There had been no expectation of such a turnaround, let alone the reappearance of a potential adversary. To this day quite a few Western politicians are evidently unaware of the role, even if it has been marginal, they played in Russia's evolution by strengthening its mistrust of them, in particular by bombing Serbia, expanding NATO, initiating the Iraqi war, and in general applying double standards in their policies.

Chapter 2

HOW WILL YELTSIN
GO DOWN IN HISTORY?

The creation of a hyperpresidency did not produce the expected consolidation of Yeltsin's power. Having defeated his rivals and with the Kremlin at his command, Yeltsin was unable to enjoy the fruits of his victory. He was a fighter by nature and came alive when it was time to do battle with his latest foe, but he was completely incapable of working constructively, formulating a vision, and creating social consensus. Having no enemies to fight, he locked himself away in his study or at his dacha and watched without interest as power was siphoned off by favorites fighting among themselves for slices of state property that were suddenly up for grabs.

The survival during Yeltsin's presidency of a number of freedoms, particularly freedom of mass media, is no testimony to the democratic credentials of his regime. It was instead a form of elite pluralism and often reflected the vested interests of oligarchic groups close to the Kremlin. The participation of democratic-minded politicians and journalists in the political struggles of the Yeltsin era created an illusion of freedom and competition, but these players had little influence on the Kremlin's decision making. The decentralization of power was also not an indication of democracy; it merely reflected the fact that feudal clans were emerging in the regions that were even more hostile to democracy than the federal center was.

To counter nationalist and populist left-wing opposition, Yeltsin resorted to liberal and democratic rhetoric. In part this rhetoric evidently reflected his mood as he attempted to free himself from the restrictions of Soviet and communist dogma and stereotypes. He achieved a measure of success, abolishing the dominant role of the Communist Party of the Soviet Union (CPSU), forming a government of young technocrats, and continuing rapprochement with the West. The lack of any culture of democratic thinking, the conservatism of intellectual and political forces, his personal limitations, and a predilection for using power to further his personal goals left Yeltsin and even the most liberal members of his entourage unable to see liberal democracy as a system of government. They plucked from that system elections and press freedom but rejected such other components as the rule of law and the concept of a system of checks and balances. Even those who claimed to be proponents of the liberal ideal decided to back Yeltsin personally rather than the development of a civil society.

The way Russia evolved after Yeltsin tells us that he failed to create either a firm foundation to underpin the freedoms that emerged during his period in office or to ensure that they could not be revoked. After his departure, society looked for an "iron fist," which is in itself an unambiguous assessment by the Russian people of his rule. Let us, however, bear in mind that Yeltsin's authoritarianism no longer harked back to the Russian patriarchal tradition. Ironically, the first Russian president tried to legitimize his personalized power through liberal ideas and principles and a pro-Western foreign policy.

Yeltsin will go down in the history of Russia as a paradoxical leader pulled in opposite directions. After 1993 he possessed immense formal powers yet was incapable of implementing his decisions. By nature someone who wanted to be "the Great Leader," he lost public support and had to cajole oligarchs and regional bosses in the provinces and resort to populist policies.

A leader whose ideal was the president as the only political institution standing above society, with all levers of power in his hands, his destiny was to preside over an era of decentralization. A politician who hated compromises, he was forced constantly to make deals. He proclaimed the building of democracy as his aim but fostered autocracy. A president who won elections, he became a screen for the cliques hiding behind him. A man with an outwardly strong, charismatic personality, he ended up struggling with a lack of self-confidence and strove to conceal his incompetence. Yeltsin was a revolutionary who ultimately stopped transformation in its tracks. He abolished communism, but his regime was able to survive only thanks to the communist threat, clinging to ideological anticommunism as a means of rallying society even after communism had been defeated. Yeltsin's instincts on many occasions were right. He supported free speech, Russia's relations with the West, and the building of a free market, but his performance ruined all his key achievements and brought back authoritarianism with a strong patrimonial and oligarchic flavor.

The manner in which power was handed over to his successor only emphasized the authoritarian complexion of the system Boris Yeltsin had created. Yeltsin's hasty departure from the Kremlin on the eve of the new year of 1999 had little in common with a democratic transfer of power. His departure seemed preferable to the protracted paralysis of his leadership, but the artificial bringing forward of the presidential election and the way it was controlled by the Kremlin proclaimed the arrival of a new Russian tradition: the appointment of a presidential successor and his subsequent endorsement through elections stage-managed by his entourage.

How will Russians remember Yeltsin? The majority of the ordinary people will remember the time of his governance as being the most trying time of their lives. During Boris Yeltsin's presidency 90 percent of the Russian population suffered a sharp reduction in income while 32 percent began to live on incomes below the poverty threshold. In the 1990s about 14 million people—the population of a small country—lost their jobs and homes. Under Yeltsin only 24 percent of those who did have jobs were paid on time, and for almost half (49 percent) the delay was protracted for months and even years. Per capita consumption in Russia fell to the level of Congo and Cameroon, and Russia's gross domestic product decreased by 49 percent. Some decline in the living standards of Russians was inevitable, but social degradation on this scale was largely a result of the Kremlin's indifference to the social cost of the transformation the country was undergoing. Russian society at large could not feel gratitude to Boris Yeltsin. In 2000, according to one of the most reliable polling organizations, the Levada Center, 56 percent of respondents viewed Yeltsin's role and his presidency negatively (18 percent viewed it positively). On January 10, 2000, soon after Yeltsin resigned, only 4 percent of respondents expressed regret. In 2005, 49 percent of Russians wanted Yeltsin to be charged for his failures and "unlawful actions" during his presidency (31 percent said that he should retain immunity, and 20 percent were not sure of their position). In 2006, the number of those who thought that his rule was a disaster reached 70 percent (13 percent continued to view him positively).[1]

As for the Russian political and intellectual class, it viewed Boris Yeltsin along party and ideological lines. Communists and nationalists were unable to forgive Yeltsin's having brought down the superpower and the Communist Party's hegemony. Liberals for quite a long time were unable to make a final assessment of the Yeltsin years. Most of them, while giving Yeltsin credit for his support of freedom of speech and the media, for his economic liberalism, and for his pro-Western foreign policy, could not avoid the pessimistic conclusion that Yeltsin was after all responsible for the trajectory Russia has taken after his departure from the Kremlin. The pro-Kremlin factions more often than not also evaluated Yeltsin's leadership with suspicion or openly blamed him for social and political chaos and disorder. Here are a few examples of how pro-Kremlin observers today think of the first Russian president. Viacheslav Nikonov: "He was a man of extremes, more of a great destroyer than a great creator"; Maxim Dianov: "If Yeltsin faced a choice between democracy and power, he would have chosen power"; Alexander Dugin: "I condemn everything he did.... He destroyed the USSR, a great state. I regard this as a historic crime, and he failed to build democracy."[2]

When we turn to Western assessments of the presidency of Boris Yeltsin, we find that most of them are more positive than are those of the Russians. Peter Reddaway's and Archie Brown's criticism of Yeltsin's term in office contrasts with a generally benevolent attitude toward the first president of Russia. Peter Reddaway and Dmitri Glinsky wrote, "The Yeltsin regime ... had a comprehensive ideology that ... consisted of a peculiar blend of three elements: Social Darwinism, which sees survival of the fittest and neglect of the weak as the iron law of social progress; the 'postmodern' cult of the autarkic self, which scorns civic obligations and community values; and traditional Russian fatalism."[3] Archie Brown was no less tough on Yeltsin, arguing: "Yeltsin's main merit as the president of post-Soviet Russia was that he preserved many of the freedoms introduced by Gorbachev, including some that became attenuated after his departure. His principal demerit was that he helped to discredit the very ideas of democratization and democracy which had evoked real enthusiasm in the last three years of the Soviet Union."[4]

Strobe Talbott's memoir *The Russia Hand* might be an example of an attempt to give balance to the contradictory angles of Yeltsin's leadership as viewed by a person who had been building the first model of a Western partnership with the new Russia. Talbott described Boris Yeltsin as a personality with erratic tendencies but who "knew one big thing"—on the most important issues that had constituted the casus belli of the Cold War: democracy versus dictatorship and cooperation versus competition abroad. Yeltsin, in Talbott's view, "was on the right side."[5] Leon Aron's *Yeltsin: A Revolutionary Life* is another example of a positive view of the key Yeltsin vector and of his contribution to Russia's transformation. Deliberating on the legacy of the first Russian president, Aron wrote: "The political organism that he [Yeltsin] forged is full of severe defects, both genetic and acquired, yet capable of development and of peacefully thwarting Communist restoration without succumbing to authoritarianism."[6] Overall, "Russian Democracy" is how the Yeltsin period was characterized by a majority of Western analysts and political leaders in the 1990s, and that description is prevalent to this day.

The evaluation of Boris Yeltsin's leadership depends on what criteria and standards are applied. If Boris Yeltsin's presidency were judged on the basis of his dismantling the empire, superpower, and communism, then one would see it, of course, as highly positive. If an evaluation were done on the level of sustainability of his liberal and democratic achievements, and on the social and human costs of his policies, its final assessment would be the opposite. This explains the disconnect between the Western and Russian narratives of Yeltsin's role. The West perceived communism and the Soviet empire as the main threat, so anything anticommunist and anti-imperial was endorsed and supported. The risk of the reappearance in Russia of authoritarianism, but with an anticommunist and anti-Western tinge, has not been appreciated or has even been brushed aside by the majority of observers. At that time Western governments and the Western political community also harbored illusions about the power of liberal technocrats, supposing that their market reforms would lead automatically to the democratization and Westernization of Russia. The names of Yegor Gaidar and Anatoly Chubais had a magical effect in the West, and while the technocrats retained their prominent positions, all other actions by the Kremlin were met with indulgence. Finally, the West wanted to avoid nasty surprises for itself and the rest of the world following the dissolution of the USSR. To resolve geopolitical issues, particularly those related to nuclear security, the Western leaders—sometimes consciously and sometimes not—played down the question of the democratic credentials of the Russian authorities, hoping for their gradual democratic and liberal maturing. The time evidently came when they started recognizing Yeltsin's inability to advance democratic reform in Russia further and understood the contradictory nature of his leadership, but those limitations were redeemed by his readiness to cooperate with the West internationally. Stefan Hedlund, pondering the reaction to the Yeltsin period, wrote,

> Why so many observers allowed themselves to be deluded for so long into viewing it [Yeltsin's time] as a success is an intriguing question. Perhaps it had much to do with a laudable and heart-felt desire that Russia really must succeed. Perhaps it was due to the overwhelming salesmanship of the reformers and their foreign consultants. Or perhaps it was driven by the conviction of many economists, that a rules-based market economy represents a societal default position of sorts."[7]

Russian reflections on Boris Yeltsin and his legacy have been defined by a different set of criteria. First of all, how did he solve the social and economic problems of society? How secure did people feel during his tenure? How far did Yeltsin move Russia toward well-being and a fair system of governance? And, finally, how sustainable has his legacy been: which elements of that legacy have survived and which have not? These deliberations have led most Russian observers and ordinary Russians to a negative judgment of Yeltsin's rule, which, by the way, is reflected in the fact that Russian society has supported Vladimir Putin, hoping that he would be an antidote to his predecessor.

In retrospect, if we view transformational leadership as Joseph Schumpeter did, as a "creative destruction," which means not only dismantling an old system but also building a new one, then Yeltsin was pretty good at negation. Still, he failed to create a sustainable foundation for a liberal and democratic state. Moreover, Yeltsin was apparently prepared to tolerate democracy as long as it did not threaten his position, and he was ready either to renounce or ignore the most important principles of democracy (although not without wavering) in defense of his own power and both his own security and that of his family. His appointment of a successor is a convincing example of his convictions and attitude toward democracy. Of course, the constraints that limited Yeltsin's leadership, external and personal, did matter. George Breslauer argues that whether a leader is treated as a tragic figure or as myopic depends on whether the leader had a chance to succeed in a system-building endeavor, taking into account all constraints.[8] It may take some time and historical distance to have a better and dispassionate view of Boris Yeltsin's leadership and of all the obstacles he had to deal with.

To summarize my thoughts on Boris the Second (taking Russian czar Boris Godunov as Czar Boris the First), I would expect the first president of Russia to go down in history as a leader who failed to meet the expectations of the Russian people. During his time in office Russians began to enjoy unprecedented freedoms, although these freedoms resulted from the efforts of Gorbachev, who had removed the shackles from Russian society and created the possibility of emancipation. Under Yeltsin, however, and with his active connivance, Russia began slipping back to the past after failing to cope with its freedom. It was Yeltsin who could not stop infighting among the elite and handed over power to his favorites, enabled cliques to help themselves to state property, and allowed Russia to drift back toward authoritarianism. Some see this authoritarianism as essential if Russia is to modernize. Others see it as guaranteeing stability, while still others see it as both. It is paradoxical that the degeneration of Yeltsin's leadership strengthened demands, not for independent institutions as a means of avoiding a repetition of that leadership, but for more powerful, authoritarian rule.

Boris Yeltsin, the first president of Russia, died of heart failure on April 23, 2007. His death provoked much speculation, some of it heated, about his role and his leadership. It poured in from around the globe. The West continued its previous line in its perception of Yeltsin's rule, which was viewed favorably. Bill Clinton, in a *New York Times* article published after Yeltsin's death, in summarizing his friend Boris's contribution, wrote:

> He made the compromises necessary to get Ukraine, along with Belarus and Kazakhstan, to give up its Soviet-era nuclear weapons. He pulled Russian troops out of the Baltic states. He made Russia part of the diplomatic solution to the crises in Bosnia and Kosovo. And much as he opposed the enlargement of NATO, he accepted the right of Central European states to join the alliance and signed a cooperation agreement between Russia and the alliance.[9]

Ironically, the majority of Russians would criticize and even loathe Boris the Second for the things Clinton and the Western world praised him for, which shows how different the Russian and Western perceptions of Yeltsin are. *Financial Times* columnist Martin Wolf wrote an obituary that reflected popular sentiment in the West's approach to the Yeltsin legacy. "Yeltsin's remarkable story may be seen at best as a partial success and at worst a gross failure. I regard it as being closer to the former assessment than to the latter. The Russia of today is not the one that a European, or indeed a Russian, liberal hoped for. But it is, surely, far better than the Russia of three decades ago. For that, Yeltsin deserves credit," wrote Wolf.[10] The West praised Boris Yeltsin most of all for his role as the terminator of communism and of the evil empire rather than for building a new Russia.

Yeltsin's death forced the Kremlin to change its line on the first Russian president, which had been pretty critical. Putin decided to choose a softer approach to his predecessor, who was raised by the Kremlin's propaganda to the status of "builder of modern Russia." In his annual state-of-the-union message, Putin recognized some of the failures of Yeltsin's past, but only as inevitable mistakes made while implementing the proper course. The Kremlin was rewriting history and changing its view, offering a definition of Yeltsin's presidency that would create an honorable place for his successor. "A man has died thanks to whom a whole new era began. A new democratic Russia was born: a free state open to the world, and a state in which power really does belong to the people," Putin solemnly declared. Giving Yeltsin his due, Putin behaved in a humane way, and it was apparent that he had warm feelings for his political godfather. At the same time, however, Putin had to be practical. He had to think about his own role in Russian history. The rhetoric he chose after Yeltsin's death demonstrated that Putin had decided to emphasize continuity with his predecessor, most of all for the sake of his own image. Having Yeltsin hailed as the founder of a new democratic state gave Putin the opportunity, through the process of succession, of using the democratic elements of Yeltsin's image, to neutralize his own authoritarian blemishes.

After learning of Yeltsin's death, some Russians changed their view of his rule to a softer attitude, which proves that Russians forgive those dead leaders they had blasted during their rule. According to a Moscow survey, after Yeltsin's death in April 2007, 29 percent of the respondents said that Yeltsin's contribution had been "mainly positive," while 40 percent insisted it had been "mainly negative" (and 31 percent had no opinion). A significant part of Russian society still viewed Yeltsin's part in Russian history as a failure.

For Russian liberals, Yeltsin's death provided a new impetus to return to the past, rethink the past fifteen years, and compare it with the present period. Suddenly many of them felt nostalgia for the previous epoch and the man who symbolized it— with all his erratic habits and urges, passions and limitations, failure and mistakes, his thirst for power and his stubborn will, as well as his intellectual and political inadequacies. For many liberals, the old bear was human—a sensitive, compassionate, and suffering person compared with the reticent, consciously unemotional, and cold second Russian president.

Emotions and nostalgia for the previous era make bad companions in the assessment process. One thing about Boris Yeltsin is, however, clear. His was a dramatic leadership, if we take into account the gap between his intentions and the results of his activities, between his initial agenda and the fact that he himself buried it. He was a revolutionary who paved the way for an antidemocratic restoration and the failure of revolutionary dreams.

Vladimir Putin's appearance on the political scene and the way in which the succession issue was resolved in 1999–2000 signaled the end of Russia's hopes for democracy. The first and possibly fatal blow to these hopes was dealt, however, not as many suppose by ex-KGB Lieutenant Colonel Putin. They were destroyed by Yeltsin and his entourage when they abolished free elections.

Chapter 3

THE COMING OF VLADIMIR PUTIN: A NEW REGIME TO PRESERVE AN OLD SYSTEM

The brisk, youthful-looking man who ascended the dais of the Russian parliament with a spring in his step in August 1999, glanced with cold gray eyes at his audience, and promised to "kick the shit out of" Chechen terrorists, instantly won the heart of Russia. To a public fed up with Boris Yeltsin, who could barely speak and from whom there was no telling what to expect, the appearance of Vladimir Putin—brusque, athletic, and with a military demeanor—seemed like the answer to its prayers. With his impassive features, this unknown had neither political experience, a political career behind him, nor, in all probability, any ambitions of power. To everybody's surprise, including, apparently, his own, he was suddenly the ruler of the omnipotent Kremlin and was effortlessly enjoying popular support. If the aim in choosing Putin was to conserve the autocratic tradition, then Yeltsin's successor and the manner in which power was transferred to him were flawless. Yeltsin's retinue had correctly gauged society's mood and the image needed for it to support a new leader. Putin was brought in as a symbol of the stability, order, and strong leadership that Russia, weary of Yeltsin's cavorting and erratic behavior, felt it needed.

Why was it Vladimir Putin, an unknown officer of the intelligence services, who was not even a member of Yeltsin's charmed circle, who was chosen to succeed him? Explaining Putin's qualifications, Yeltsin said, "He is not a maximalist." Anatoly Chubais explained the choice: "He is equidistant from all factions."[1] That is hardly an adequate explanation.

What did the Russian elite and the Russian public need as Yeltsin's rule drew to its close? His team needed to evade responsibility for the failures of the 1990s and to safeguard its personal security, and economic interests. The political class as a whole wanted guarantees that their property was secure and it wanted to see an end to the warring between cliques. The public longed to live in peace and hoped tomorrow would be an improvement over today. But there was more. In August 1999 tragic events occurred that abruptly changed the mood in Russia and opened the way for new policies: the attack by Chechen separatists on Dagestan and the bombing of apartment blocks in Moscow, Volgodonsk, and Buinaksk, which resulted in the deaths of hundreds of ordinary people, created a huge demand in Russia for a protective state authority. All other aspirations were forgotten, and the people's first concern was for their personal safety. Responsibility for the explosions, which terrorized society in such a timely manner and eased the transition to a new reign, was officially laid on Chechen terrorists even before the investigation had begun. The fear that swept the country had a dramatic effect: if people had not supported the Kremlin's first war in Chechnya during Yeltsin's presidency,[2] a significant part of the Russian population now unhesitatingly and unquestioningly gave carte blanche to a new leader who promised to restore order and save them from the terrorists. Russia returned to its familiar sense of being under military threat.

The nature of the new leadership chosen by the Kremlin also became clear. The ruling elite did not want another charismatic leader and revolutionary; it did not want a heavyweight with his own power base; it did not want an ambitious politician. Nor did it want anyone engaged in questionable dealings, as were most Russian politicians of the times. The Kremlin's principal need was for an individual close to the security forces who would be able to rely on their support to defend the regime. It wanted someone who could provide cover for the outgoing team and respect its commitments to it, someone without dictatorial tendencies, someone not a part of the era that was ending and capable of reacting to new challenges, somebody with the ability to rule the country and who knew how the state machinery worked, and, finally, someone who was predictable.

Putin was the right man, in the right place, at the right time. He entirely met the job specifications for the Yeltsin team's successor and, moreover, had a good track record. Putin had proved his capacity for loyalty by rescuing his previous boss, the Petersburg mayor and one of the most influential liberals of the "first wave," Anatoly Sobchak, from facing justice when he was accused of corruption. Putin had already shown his loyalty to Yeltsin when, as the director of the Federal Security Bureau (FSB), he leapt to the president's defense in his confrontation with parliament and the public prosecutor's office when Yeltsin and his family were accused of corruption in 1999.

Time has shown that Vladimir Putin coped brilliantly with the tasks he was entrusted with. He not only ensured the safety of the ruling corporation, but also managed to fulfill the hopes of society. He was, admittedly, unable to satisfy all members of the Yeltsin team or all their expectations. At some point he also disappointed Yeltsin himself. When asked what Yeltsin thought about Putin, Yegor Gaidar said, "He is not happy with the way things are going. He is more critical than I am." Even if Yeltsin was dissatisfied, he avoided criticizing Putin publicly. Only once did Czar Boris lose his nerve and allow himself to make comments that revealed his true concerns about Putin's rule. This happened when Putin decided to return the old Soviet symbols, including the music of the Soviet anthem. "I am categorically against using the Soviet anthem as the Russian anthem. We can't play with these things," Yeltsin allegedly said. But he never did that again and apparently had very strong reasons to abstain from further criticizing his successor.

The Yeltsin family, now far removed from power, may also not be completely satisfied with the man to whom they gave the keys to the Kremlin: they lost the political leverage that they had enjoyed and apparently hoped to retain. Some of the old Yeltsin oligarchs had no reason to be pleased with Putin, especially Yeltsin's *éminence grise*, Boris Berezovsky. They were pushed out of the Kremlin and Berezovsky was even obliged to seek political asylum in London. It was inevitable that some members of the old team would be disappointed. If Putin were to have the appearance of an independent leader, he could hardly remain encircled by puppet-masters who called him by the diminutive form of his name, *Volodya*, tried to blackmail him, and wanted to tell him what to do. He needed to show his power, and in his first open letter to the public in February 2000, Putin suggested that he was not going to be another Yeltsin. "Our first and most pressing problem is a weakening of will, a loss of political will and tenacity in seeing policies through: hesitation, vacillation, putting off difficult decisions," the successor wrote, transparently distancing himself from Yeltsin's impotence. Given the model of power that had developed in Russia, if the new leader were to preserve the system, he had no option but to jettison old ballast, including the individuals who had put him in the Kremlin and who wanted to order him around.

However, as far as the basic interests of the outgoing team and its security were concerned, Yeltsin and his closest entourage had little cause to complain. Although Putin expelled the Yeltsin "family" from the Kremlin, he ensured their safety and safeguarded their property. Neither did the Russian political class and big business (with the exception of the old Yeltsin oligarchs who had strong political ambitions) have cause for complaint. Putin looked after their interests too. He needed, however, to have a legitimacy beyond that conferred on him by Yeltsin, and that necessarily included an element of rejection of Yeltsin's legacy. Accordingly, Putin set about creating his own power base, exploiting his high presidential approval rating (which in 2000 was 73 percent, with 17 percent disapproving and 10 percent having no opinion) to shape his own political regime. The emergence of Putin's regime completed the system of personalized power whose foundation had been laid by Boris Yeltsin. In the process, Yeltsin's successor exploited the public's hostility toward Yeltsin.

"Everything changed, and everything stayed the same," Russian writer Fazil Iskander commented on the life around him. The same was true of Russian politics. Let us examine the continuities and discontinuities of the Yeltsin and Putin regimes. Yeltsin indulged both allies and opponents, decentralized power, accorded big business a privileged role, and exercised a monarchic style of rule. During Yeltsin's presidency there was a constant turnover of personnel and a changing of policy that created the illusion of progress, or at least of change. Putin, in contrast, set about building his "pyramid of power," emphasizing subordination, strengthening the role of the bureaucracy, bringing members of the security services into the government, centralizing control, and eradicating opposition. Yeltsin was constantly provoking a revolutionary ferment and in-fighting between the factions of his court, which enabled him to act as referee. Putin preferred orderliness and constancy, was reluctant to reshuffle personnel, and was intolerant of attempts to influence him. Putin's style, unlike that of his godfather, is not remotely monarchic. He appears to see himself as the "CEO of Russia" and he and his colleagues view Russia as a business corporation. If Yeltsin's main aim, particularly during his second presidency, was simply to hold on to power, Putin, at least initially, saw power not as an end in itself but as a means of modernizing Russia. During his second term, power for him increasingly became a means of maintaining the status quo, which suggests a drift back to the logic of Yeltsin's regime.

If Yeltsin's model can be classified as a moderately *authoritarian oligarchic* regime, then Putin's rule resembles the *bureaucratic–authoritarian* regimes of Latin America in the 1960s and 1970s.[3] This is a system of government under which power is concentrated in the hands of a leader who relies on the bureaucracy, security forces, and big business. The reformist potential of such a regime is, of course, fairly limited and it is sustained by the inclusion of liberal technocrats. The system works only if the leader manages to keep the constituent factions of his regime under control, not allowing interest groups to tear one another's throats out. Workable authoritarianism relies on the leader's charisma, security forces loyal to him, and effective state apparatus. In the absence of any one of these, the leader can soon find his power usurped by the bureaucracy or security forces. The evolution of Putin's regime has shown that the balance between personalized power and the bureaucracy, always dominant in Russia, is crucial to its nature. Both the Yeltsin and Putin regimes have one common feature: having "more power than they could swallow," they had to begin sharing it with their entourage, proving that both leaders evolved toward neopatrimonialism.

No sooner was Vladimir Putin elected a new Russian president in March 2000 than he made clear the direction he intended to take. He began by ridding the political arena of anything resembling opposition. His first act was to subjugate the independent television and press owned by the oligarchs, first attacking the most popular channel, NTV, controlled by Vladimir Gusinsky, who was close to the Yeltsin faction. The Kremlin employed a ruse that was to be exploited regularly against individuals targeted by the new regime. The prosecutor's office and the courts were pressed into service. They could always find something (alleged nonpayment of taxes or whatever) on which to base a lawsuit. Next, it was the turn of the upper chamber of parliament, the Federation Council, which was stripped of its independence, and regional leaders were deprived of their right to represent regional interests there. After the upper chamber, it was the turn of the lower chamber of parliament, the state Duma, where the Kremlin created a propresidential majority that voted as instructed by the presidential administration that continued to be the most powerful institution. The president divided the country into seven districts that, not by coincidence, were the same as the military districts. He appointed his own representatives to the districts, some of whom wore epaulettes, in order to lick into shape the regional elites, which under Yeltsin had been getting unruly. Finally, the president returned control of regional sections of the "security ministries" (the Interior Ministry, Special Services, the prosecutor's office, and the tax service), which had been reporting to the governors, and to Moscow, turning them into the eyes and ears of the sovereign. Having started the bandwagon of recentralization rolling, Putin purged the political arena of even the slightest manifestation of independent political initiative. The elite and the public, transfixed by Putin's popularity rating and triggered by their hope of restored order, helped him to put on their chains and gags and locked themselves in their cages.[4]

Why did Vladimir Putin undertake this recentralization of power? Was it his political outlook? Was it a result of pressure from the political class? I believe the crucial factor that explains how Putin's rule developed is the logic of the system he inherited from Yeltsin. It was under the first president of Russia that a constitution was adopted that placed the leader above society and created the framework for further development. It was under Yeltsin that a privatization took place that bound the regime and business to each other. It was under Yeltsin that the mass disenchantment with liberal democracy began, as it came to be associated in the popular mind with corruption and the exercise of power by shadowy factions. It was under Yeltsin that society started to look for a strong leader who would restore order. Even if, against all the odds, a true democrat had come to power in 2000, he would have been hard pressed to steer the country in a different direction. There was no popular force in Russian society capable of implementing a democratic agenda, and besides, people were tired and had no wish to endure another bout of painful reforms.

No less important was the Russian elite's "quest for certainty," something that entirely coincides with a worldwide

trend evident in the consolidation of American fundamentalism, European traditionalism, and Japanese and Chinese great-
power conservatism. As we see nowadays, countries with very
different political regimes can have very similar aspirations. The
Russian "quest for certainty" took the form of a rejection of
political pluralism with its uncertainty and unpredictability. In
this context, Putin's personal views, his inclination to rely on
administrative resources and on the machinery of government,
his desire to use the state as a tool for modernizing Russia, his
mistrust of freedom, and his suspicious nature further strengthened a preexisting tendency toward the centralization of power
and the creation of a state whose mission was to protect the
new property owners. This tendency grew even more pronounced when the Kremlin returned to legitimizing power
through war (this time the second Chechen war in the North
Caucasus), which gave an added boost to authoritarianism. A
military threat, real or imagined, has always been used in Russia
to justify the removal of independent political players from the
scene and bullying the others. Intimidated and disoriented,
society made no attempt to prevent this. It gave its consent for
the leader to reestablish order by doing away with political competition and political freedom.

Why was Yeltsin unable to create a pyramid of power when
Putin introduced it without meeting any resistance? The new
president's success in accumulating power was primarily a result
of the immense public support he began to enjoy. In that case,
of course, the question becomes, why was this support given to
Putin, when nobody had ever heard of him, and why did they
support a leader who used power like a bludgeon? The main
reason for Putin's popular support was simply that he compared favorably against Yeltsin in every respect. He was up to the
job, capable of coherent speech, and radiated confidence. He
promised what Yeltsin had failed to deliver: an end to chaos
and corruption. People supported Putin because he looked
nothing like Yeltsin. It was a measure of the desperation, indeed
despair, afflicting Russian society under Yeltsin that a complete

unknown appearing on the political stage could so quickly come to embody the public's hopes. However, merely not being Yeltsin would not have been sufficient to ensure that Putin enjoyed lasting support. Vladimir Vladimirovich had a great stroke of luck at this point: the price of oil soared, providing the financial underpinning for the stability Putin had brought. By supporting Putin as the guarantor of order, Russians had endorsed his arm-twisting style as the inevitable means of a movement toward order.

Putin's security background explains why he began to rely on former colleagues in the intelligence and special services, but it would be wrong to overstate the KGB component in his biography and to see it as the root cause of all his subsequent actions. The reality is less straightforward. Vladimir Putin was a failure in the KGB: his career went nowhere and he was forced to retire. He blossomed only in the radically liberal environment of the mayor of St. Petersburg, Anatoly Sobchak, one of the most energetic gravediggers of communism. Sobchak reposed special confidence in Putin and trusted him enough to let him negotiate with foreign investors and deal with major privatization issues. At that time, these issues consisted primarily of seizing property and fighting tooth and nail to hang on to it. The combination in the new leader's thinking of Soviet provincialism, elements of KGB mentality, and his liberal economic views made him a sought-after commodity in a system that maintained a balance of mutually incompatible tendencies. Putin drew security officials into his team not because he wanted to create a regime of *siloviki* (representatives of the "security" ministries) and hand power over to the successors of the KGB. He chose his team, not on the basis of professional allegiances or ideological or political affiliation, but simply because these were the people he knew. Along with former intelligence service colleagues, he included the liberals and bureaucrats he had worked with in St. Petersburg. This produced a motley entourage, but he succeeded in establishing equilibrium within the new regime. Perhaps unconsciously at first, Putin created the preconditions for new factional in-fighting, which meant that he could act as a referee and avoid the risk of becoming the hostage of any one clique.

As Putin began to build his regime, it was evident that, for a time at least, he had a sense of mission. In 2000–2001, he put forward a package of new measures that included land reform, the introduction of a 13 percent income tax, deregulation of the economy, and administrative reform. At the same time his government started to plan the reform of the armed forces, the pension system, "natural monopolies" (Gazprom, the railway, the Unified Energy System of Russia [RAO UES]), and local government. It seemed that the new president was mulling over how best to modernize Russia and to make it a competitive nation enjoying the respect of the rest of the world. To do so, however, he clearly considered it a first priority to restore governability, and that, in his mind, meant control—and more control. He set about gaining control over people and events, understanding control, with the mind-set of an intelligence officer, as subordination. At this point the president found himself in a quandary: having gained control of the country, he began to doubt the wisdom of reforming it. Reform undermines control. An iron law of autocracy began to operate, which typically leads regimes to centralize all resources. This centralization becomes an obsession and is followed shortly afterward by a determination to defend those resources from rival claimants, which means further centralization.

The recentralization of power achieved by the Kremlin in 2000–2001 whetted the ruling team's appetite, and this time it embarked on a new campaign to destroy independent players in the economy. This was bound to occur sooner or later because regimes based on the personalization of power are intolerant of independent actors, even if their independence amounts to no more than the possession of property. It was the turn of big business, which, under Yeltsin, had come to be called an oligarchy. In 2003 an attack was mounted on one of the most successful of the major Russian oil companies, Yukos. Its principal shareholder, Mikhail Khodorkovsky, together with some of his colleagues, was taken into custody and shortly afterward sentenced to nine years in prison. The main part of Yukos and its "jewel," Yuganskneftegaz, was nationalized. The results of the Yukos affair included squeezing the remnants of the oligarchs out of the political decision-making process; an expansion of state control of the economy; the beginning of a redistribution of property in favor of the new ruling team; the neutralization of political activity by big business; and an increase in the Kremlin's interest in the fuel and energy complex, which came to be viewed as an economic base for the regime.

The Yukos saga can be seen as a watershed. Yeltsin's *oligarchic capitalism* began to be transformed into *bureaucratic capitalism*. The foundations for this had also been laid during Yeltsin's presidency, when the bureaucracy created a tier of appointees, dependent on the state, to manage private property. Taking advantage of Yeltsin's failing powers, these appointees started imposing their will on the regime. Under Putin, the bureaucracy, newly strengthened and recognizing where its interests lay, decided it could do without middlemen and started reestablishing direct control over property.

Chapter 4

IMITATION DEMOCRACY

If the first Putin presidency (2000–2004) still gave the impression of ambiguity and contradictory trends, his second term left no doubts regarding the key direction of its evolution and the nature of the bureaucratic–authoritarian regime that had become fully entrenched. Even the limited political competition that had existed during the previous stages of postcommunist Russia's development was done away with as the election of governors and presidents of national republics was abolished; the ruling United Russia party formed by the Kremlin was handed a monopoly of power; the administrative resource, that is, pressure on society by the federal and local bureaucracy, was exploited without inhibition; the mass media and primarily the national television channels were taken under government control; parliament and the courts were totally subordinated to the executive administration; and the creation of political movements was manipulated by the Kremlin. The center managed without too much effort to liquidate the independence of regional elites, to depoliticize big business, to drive the opposition out of legal politics, and, finally, to rally around itself servile social groups that were willing to support every initiative the Kremlin took. A special forum was created for the most loyal: the Public Chamber, whose function was to mimic civil society.

The presidential administration changed electoral legislation beyond recognition, extinguishing even the slightest hope that individuals not sanctioned from above might get into government. Long before the end of Putin's second term, the Kremlin began preparations for the perpetuation of power by seizing total control of the electoral mechanism. The independent liberal deputy Vladimir Ryzhkov, not without bitterness, has proposed that the term "elections" should no longer be used in Russia: "A new term is required; for example, 'recharging' would be more accurate. Recharging the old authorities every four years for a further term and for all terms to come." Previously an individual opposition politician could win a regional constituency seat. All regional constituencies were now abolished, and only candidates on party lists could get into parliament. A new law on parties, however, made it impossible to create parties without the Kremlin's consent. Those democratic parties that still existed would be unable to gain any seats in parliament because the barrier to entry was raised to 7 percent of the vote, which is more than any party would be able to obtain without the support of the Kremlin. Because small democratic parties might be able to get into the Duma by forming a bloc, a law was passed banning blocs. An opposition candidate could be prevented from taking part in elections for the most trivial reason, for example, if he or she had made a spelling mistake when filling out the necessary forms. If by some miracle an oppositionist did manage to stand, he or she was prevented from campaigning because a law was passed allowing any criticism of the regime to be classified as extremism, which would disqualify the candidate. So that the populace should not unexpectedly embarrass the regime, the authorities abolished the right to organize referendums, removed the "None of the above" box from ballot slips (which had enabled malcontents to show what they thought of the authorities), and did away with the minimum turnout required for elections to be valid. The authorities could now get themselves elected even if only one or two people turned out to vote. The Communist Party that had ruled the

USSR would have envied the enterprise and meticulousness with which total control over Russian politics was established after the collapse of communism.

Russia's political trajectory since the disintegration of the Soviet Union in December 1991 has undermined several scholarly beliefs about democratic transitions, causing observers to acknowledge that the "third wave" of democratic transitions fizzled out when it reached Russia. Many who once saw Russia as a "democracy with adjectives" ("electoral democracy" was the most popular cliché), those who believed that "immature" democracies evolve ineluctably into the full-fledged variety, have now been compelled to define Russia as an autocracy. Others perceive Russia to have fallen into a "political gray zone" between democracy and dictatorship, a view that recognizes that the political teleology presumed by the very term "transition" does not accord with an empirical reality that has turned out to be even messier than imagined. Russia's experience has clearly undermined a basic assumption of the transition paradigm: the determinative importance of elections.

Russia's postcommunist evolution can serve as a textbook case of failed democratic transition. The Russian experience has simultaneously confirmed that Francis Fukuyama was right when he said that liberal democracy has no plausible ideological competitors, and that there are "few alternative institutional arrangements that elicit any enthusiasm" aside from liberal democracy.[1] The political regime that has emerged in Russia confirms that democracy is the only "broadly legitimate regime form" and that, as Larry Diamond has put it, post-totalitarian regimes have felt "unprecedented pressure to adopt or at least mimic the democratic form."[2] This is precisely why the Russian elite proclaims its democratic credentials while in fact, with consummate skill, adapting democracy to its purposes. *Imitation democracy*, the retention of the formal institutions of democracy in order to conceal authoritarian, oligarchic, or bureaucratic tendencies, and most often all three at once, is not only to be found in Russia but has become the most popular form of political regime in the post-Soviet territories. This, however, indicates that Fukuyama was wrong in another of his predictions, when he foresaw neo-Bolshevism as the most likely rival of liberal democracy in those lands. The real competitors have proved to be the authoritarian regimes that set up Potemkin villages, creating an illusion of democracy.

Russia is perhaps the world's chief, or at least thus far most successful, example of imitation multiparty democracy today, but it is not alone: Venezuela, Egypt, and Iran are also imitation democracies, as was Ukraine before the Orange Revolution. Imitation democracies are in transition to nowhere. Some suppose that the appearance of "doppelgänger," here referring to parallel institutions, is an unplanned and chance result of the democratic wave that swept Russia. They are wrong. Bulgarian philosopher Ivan Krastev is right when he says, "Russia is not an illiberal democracy by default: it is an illiberal democracy by design."[3] In the Russian case we are dealing not with the "collapse" of democracy, as many think, but with the deliberate use of democratic and liberal institutions in order to conceal traditional power arrangements. During Putin's presidency, the Russian elite calculatingly set about constructing an imitation of the democratic project that defies any strict definition. "Russia is not a democracy, and it is not a dictatorship ..., it is a political system of surface stability but turmoil underneath," writes Stephen Kotkin.[4] Indeed, this is a system that proves how deceptive appearances can be.

When Boris Yeltsin was still the secretary of the provincial committee of the CPSU in Sverdlovsk, he ordered that the fences should be painted green in those streets along which the motorcades of Soviet leaders sped when visiting the city. For this he was nicknamed the Sorcerer of the Emerald City. His successor has taken to painting the entire country a cheerful color. "Imitation" is a key word for deciphering political reality in Russia, and it warns us not to believe the evidence before our eyes.

In the end, imitation brings the end of politics as a complex phenomenon. Politics includes a variety of means, instruments, and institutions that represent a plurality of interests that in Russia has already been replaced by a kind of virtual reality, one created by the special class of Kremlin spin doctors who are simultaneously analysts, politicians, and propagandists. As Andrew Wilson put it, spin doctors "operate in a world of 'clones' and 'doubles,' of 'administrative resources,' 'active measures,' and 'Kompromat' (compromising information), of parties that stand in the elections but have no staff or membership, or office ... of well-paid insiders that stand as the regime's most vociferous opponents, and of scarecrow nationalists and fake coups."[5] As a result, the boundary between real and fake is intentionally vague or even nonexistent. This is the only way such *nonpolitics* can exist.

Pseudo-democracy discredits democratic principles, but unless the regime resorts to violence, it also undermines faith in the omnipotence of the authorities. The game of "Let's Pretend" that so engrosses the Kremlin's occupants will sooner or later come back to haunt them. Imitating a multiparty system, freedom of the press, democratic elections, parliamentarism, and a free market may well lead to an imitation of presidential power that conceals the governance of Kremlin cliques. The return to authoritarianism may prove to be a pretense if the elite is unwilling, or lacks the necessary resources, to turn back the clock completely and stops halfway. An imitation system of government and imitation nationhood that can exist only with the aid of illusions and fake politics can be neither stable nor effective. They are transient and have no long-term future.

Putin had no option but to rein in Yeltsin's hybrid system. Under Yeltsin, mutually exclusive tendencies coexisted: elections with nominations to office, political pluralism with autocracy, a free market with state control. On the surface it might appear that, even after Putin's tidying up, incompatible features are retained in the system. But this is misleading. Everything that runs counter to the political monopoly becomes increasingly virtual. The game of "Let's Pretend" also debases political principles. Putin's terms in office show how principles torn out of context are transformed into their opposites: elections shorn of competition become a means for reinstating personal power in the form of a hyperpresidency; a multiparty system with a monopoly of power guaranteed to a single party makes a fiction of political pluralism; a parliament and legal system turned into an appendage of the executive branch discredit both the legislature and the judiciary. Economic liberalism in the absence of democracy and a republican ideal engenders plutocracy. The Kremlin's attempt to pick and choose among principles of social organization confirms Guillermo O'Donnell's hypothesis that a highly organized society can function effectively only when it is able to combine democracy (the rule of the majority), liberalism (guarantees of human rights and freedoms), and a republican tradition (the ideal of social service).[6] Liberal democracy becomes a parody of itself if particular principles are selectively pulled from what must be an integrated system.

One further key word for decoding the reality of Russia is "nonaccountability." The leader is formally placed on a pedestal as the sole legitimate political player. He is the monosubject on the Russian political scene and the only one who has all the means and instruments and levers of power. At the same time he has to shirk responsibility in order to survive. He would otherwise be answerable for every failure of his bureaucracy from top to bottom. Putin, like Yeltsin, is constantly looking for ways to slough off responsibility for his decisions and their consequences, sometimes onto his prime minister, sometimes onto parliament, and sometimes onto his officials, although it is patently obvious that no weighty decision can be taken in the Russian state without presidential approval. The underlying principle of Yeltsin's presidency—the abdication of responsibility—continues to operate under Putin.

Putin's governance differs from Yeltsin's both in style and in substance, but since the structure and basis of state authority remain the same, a change of personalities and regimes has not brought about any radical change in the substance of the system. The inherent contradiction between the system's monopolistic, authoritarian element and the tendency to democracy is still there, although as time has passed, it has increasingly shifted in favor of authoritarianism.

Today's Russian political landscape resembles a desert in which only one stronghold, the presidency, is still standing. Outwardly it seems imposing, but this is again illusory. In their 2006 report for the Trilateral Commission, Roderic Lyne, Strobe Talbott, and Koji Watanabe wrote of the Russian "pyramid of power": "The presidential dependency is like a porcelain vase— hard and rigid and outwardly splendid, but brittle, fragile, and unable to bear a heavy load. It could last for a long time or break very quickly, depending on the pressures on it."[7] The concentration of power in one man's hands inevitably brings about a situation where it is physically impossible for the leader to cope. He devolves some of his powers to the bureaucracy and gradually becomes dependent on it. Stalin had good reason to purge his entourage, and Mao Zedong to conduct a "cultural revolution." They were neutralizing a bureaucracy that had grown too powerful, even if that meant destroying it physically. Augmenting the role of a bureaucracy by making it a substitute for institutions inevitably leads to its aspiring to power and obliges the leader to be constantly thinking of ways to avoid becoming its pawn. Reshuffling officials is one way of reducing the apparat's leverage on him, but Putin prefers consistency and does not like changing his staff. So far he has managed to retain control, if with difficulty, by making ever-greater concessions to the bureaucracy in return for its loyalty.

Despite all the powers of the presidency, it has no effective means of implementing its sometimes correct decisions. Putin has been unable to push through administrative reform or to combat the bureaucratization and corruption of state power of which he speaks in tones of near desperation in his annual addresses to the nation. He has been forced to postpone military and pension reforms and to abandon the reform of social welfare policy completely. He has ceased even to mention reforming Russia's disastrously neglected housing situation. He has been unable to achieve his goal of doubling gross domestic product and diversifying the economy. Instead of reforming the energy sector, he has agreed to increase fuel prices above the rate of inflation, which will be an unwelcome legacy for the next team in power. Every time a particular presidential initiative falls flat, he chooses to forget about it and does his utmost to ensure that the country does the same. It already seems highly unlikely that Putin will choose during the run-up to the election to recall his "national projects," trumpeted by the Kremlin, to reform education, the health service, home building, and agriculture. Most probably, he will need to work hard to make Russia forget some of his other initiatives, and specifically his attempts to resolve the demographic problem. It is not that Putin does not want to realize his pet projects, but that the interests of the ruling caste force leaders to concentrate only on what is important for its survival. In his last state-of-the-union address in 2007, Putin again talked about diversification of the economy and new technology, in this way indirectly admitting that he had failed to achieve those goals during his term.

A president with a secret service background and an administration staffed by officers of the intelligence services could only strengthen the regime's tendency to resort to an administrative resolution of problems. However, in defense of their own interests, those in civilian professions have resorted to this approach no less enthusiastically than the security officials. We are dealing with a heterogeneous ruling class made up of diverse groups attached to the Kremlin court, all of which are busily doing their best to preserve the system. It is worth singling out the intellectuals serving the regime, who emphasize the political importance of order and stability because they are only too aware of their vulnerability and fear for their future if the regime should weaken. Accordingly, if the state authorities were suddenly to resort to violent repression to defend themselves, the authors of the policy, or its propagandists, would not necessarily be representatives of the military or the intelligence services, but former intellectuals and even dissidents turned into spin doctors who have surrendered themselves to serving the Kremlin (Gleb Pavlovsky, Viacheslav Nikonov, and Sergei Markov are the best known of these).

The ruling bureaucratic corporation has achieved much: it has succeeded in imposing its agenda on all manner of ministries, including the public prosecutor's office, the tax office, and, most importantly, the judicial system. It has succeeded in taming the constitutional court, something Yeltsin never managed. As the bureaucratic corporation grows stronger, however, the independence of the leader inevitably becomes more of a problem. Neither the ruling team nor the political class as a whole has any interest in a fully functioning leader. Let us not be blinded by the fact that officially these are menials carrying out the president's instructions. They have immense power over him through controlling the diary of what he does and whom he meets, what he gets told, and by exploiting his professional mistrust of those outside his immediate circle, let alone people with a different way of thinking. Stalin may have been a dictator, but he was dependent on his secretary, Alexander Poskrebyshev, for contact with the outside world. Where a ruling corporation has eliminated all other political forces, the president is increasingly the property of his team. This was true of Yeltsin and Putin, and this will be true of the next Russian leader, unless the system is radically reformed.

The leader within such a type of political regime survives by provoking and resolving conflicts between the various factions in his entourage that allow him to play the role of the arbitrator. In the case of Russia today, the Kremlin's entourage includes liberal technocrats, *siloviki* (representatives of the security services, the army and Interior Ministry, the prosecutor's office, and other law enforcement offices), and moderate pragmatists, who constantly disband, fight each other, and form short-lived and sometimes weird alliances of seemingly ill-assorted bedfellows. This means that a strong leader is needed to control the entourage, but it has happened not infrequently in the history of bureaucratic–authoritarian regimes that different factions have united to remove a leader who no longer suited them. The leader may, of course, try to break from their stifling blockade by bringing in new faces, but Putin is reluctant or unable to do this. He rarely replaces those around him. The substitution of Dmitri Medvedev for Alexander Voloshin as the head of the presidential administration in place in 2003, of Sergei Sobyanin for Medvedev in 2005, of Mikhail Fradkov for Prime Minister Mikhail Kasianov in 2005, and of Anatoly Serdyukov for defense minister Sergei Ivanov in 2007 were rare exceptions. When he falls out with someone, Putin prefers not to discard them but to find a different role for them, as he did with his enemy Vladimir Yakovlev, the ex-governor of St. Petersburg who was made a minister for regional development, and Public Prosecutor Vladimir Ustinov, who was beginning to get ideas above his station, whom Putin moved to the position of minister of justice.

The evolution of the regime during the concluding phase of Putin's presidency shows that it is capable of inventing new ways to keep control over the Kremlin. Many felt certain that the regime would continue to rely on a single dominant party, United Russia, led by state Duma speaker Boris Gryzlov, one of Putin's loyalists. In 2006, however, Putin blessed the creation of a second party of power, "A Just Russia," led by another loyal ally, Sergei Mironov, the speaker of the Federation Council. Where United Russia has tried to formulate a conservative, strong-state ideology, A Just Russia has positioned itself to the left of center. In this new configuration, the regime began to rely on two rival parties, both of which were created by the leader. This new model allows for the existence of at least two other parties, Vladimir Zhirinovsky's Kremlin-friendly Liberal Democratic Party and the Communist Party. The first became an extremely successful business structure that has been selling its parliamentary support to the Kremlin for good money, and the second formally remains in opposition to the regime, yet poses no serious threat. Putin has allowed for rivalry not just between the parties of power, but also between two energy giants that aspire to the role of "national champions": Gazprom and Rosneft. This growth of pluralism within the elite has led some Russian analysts to talk about the liberalization of the political regime. This view has been supported by Western pundits. Steve Sestanovich reminds us that Gorbachev's introduction of more free elections in the Soviet Union soon brought about its collapse because "once you legitimize the idea of political competition, people would want the real thing, not a phony substitute."[8] Sestanovich concludes that the Putin "invent-your-own-opposition strategy" may have the same unintended result because "keeping up democratic appearances means taking risks that can empower your opponents."

In fact, Robert Dahl also believes that the optimal way to a stable polyarchy would be the rise of political competition among the elite, which would allow the culture of democracy to take root first among the political class and ruling team, which would then diffuse to the larger population, and gradually be incorporated into electoral politics.[9] One may hope that in Russia, sooner or later, the imitation of political pluralism will be replaced by the real thing and that, having learned to compete with one another, the ruling clans will allow political competitiveness to spread within society at large. However, today the clans, disguising "elite pluralism," are discrediting the idea of competitiveness and forcing at least part of society to look eagerly forward to a harsher version of authoritarianism to bring order. Besides, the impression is that the ruling groups consciously aim to create a controlled pluralism that would allow the president to play a more active role as arbitrator—a role he could continue to play after leaving office. The appearance of A Just Russia was obviously also motivated by the ruling team's fear that a single party of the bureaucracy could pose problems for the Kremlin if it became too strong, and Putin found the means to neutralize the activity of his first political baby by introducing a new one.

Once again Russia presents us with a paradox: increasingly active clan rivalries within the elite are being used to strengthen the current ruling group's monopoly on power. The Kremlin, however, should prepare itself for the unexpected. The president's new "horizontal power," which allows open competition within the elite, could eventually undermine the "vertical power," the centralized machine of state that Putin began building as soon as he took office. Many questions remain unanswered. How will the role of arbitrator of elite pluralism be handled when Putin leaves office? Will his successor be strong enough to resolve conflicts between the two parties of power and among other competing elite groups?

The regional parliamentary elections in March and April 2007 served as a dress rehearsal for the state Duma vote in December 2007 as well as the first real test of the new party system. As expected, United Russia triumphed in fourteen of fifteen regions, losing only to A Just Russia in the Stavropol region. A Just Russia, the Communist Party, and the Liberal Democratic Party all did well enough to ensure representation in many regional legislatures, and in a few cases the liberal Union of Right Forces party cleared the barrier for representation. These results suggested that the next state Duma would comprise four parties, most likely including United Russia, A Just Russia, the Communist Party, and the Liberal Democratic Party. Even if the Kremlin decides to allow the Union of Right Forces, or Yabloko, which is even more doubtful, into the state Duma, the balance of forces in the lower house will not change. The relationship between the two parties of power, and the Kremlin's management of those parties, will provide the main drama in the next parliament. The other parties, including Yabloko, Russia's oldest democratic party, have been gradually squeezed out of official politics and now face the choice of going quietly or entering the anti-establishment opposition. Only the tamed and loyal are allowed to stay in politics, as well as those, like the communists, who can play the role of imitation opposition since they present no threat to the established political system.

As Putin's presidency nears its end, there is a stalemate: the ruling bureaucratic corporation is still afraid of the leader and obeys him, but the leader is increasingly dependent on them and cannot replace the support on which he depends without the risk of falling. The leader is tied to his team not only through his past and common corporate interests, but also most importantly through their shared mistakes. It is this bond that makes him most vulnerable and dependent on them. Shielding itself behind the leader, the bureaucracy acts independently but in his name, and this discredits and undermines him. Putin continues to distance himself successfully from his apparatchiks in the eyes of the populace, who acquit the president and condemn the bureaucracy. Yet this split in public opinion over the regime, differentiating the leader from the state, cannot continue indefinitely, and Putin's successor could find himself (or herself) in a more precarious situation.

Meanwhile the bureaucracy has society firmly ensnared in its tentacles. The Soviet bureaucracy under Leonid Brezhnev was made up of some seven hundred thousand officials. In Russia today there are 1.5 million, and the number is continuously increasing. For example, in 2004 there were 116 employees working for the Federal Veterinary Inspection Service. By 2005 that number had increased to 20,469. Selling jobs in the bureaucracy has become commonplace. According to media speculation, an influential position in the state administration might cost anywhere from $150,000 to $1 million. Obtaining a job as a traffic controller will set you back $3,000 to $5,000. This shows that any job in the state apparatus can be a source of personal enrichment and the money spent to get such a job is soon fully compensated.

The burgeoning of officialdom is accompanied by a burgeoning of its corruption. If in the West corruption is a deviation from the norm, in Russia it has become a norm by which society is ordered, and the norm by which the political system is organized. Russian corruption received a boost when the state authorities returned to the mechanism of appointing officials on the basis of their loyalty to the leader rather than their professional competence. The bureaucracy's seizure of control over business increased its uncontrollability. A further source of corruption was the nontransparent manner in which privatization was conducted. According to Deputy Public Prosecutor Alexander Buksman, the total value of bribes in Russia yearly totals $240 billion.[10] Approximately 50 percent of Russians consider corruption to be the greatest obstacle to economic growth, but at the same time 55 percent admit they give bribes. According to the index of Transparency International, Russia ranks 121st of 163 states in its level of corruption. True, Russia is not at the top of the corruption league. As assessed by Transparency International, India and China are even more corrupt. It also appears that representatives of the developed democracies, when they find themselves in a corrupt environment, very often act by the rules of that environment. Corruption in Russia has become a key element, the backbone of the state. The problem here is not that certain representatives of the state apparatus can be bought. The problem is that the state itself is built in such a way that it allows the privatization of state functions and mechanisms by its officials. How does this appear in practice? Here are several examples. If a minister redistributes money for medical equipment, one can be sure that his relatives will be in charge of purchasing the equipment and selling it to hospitals. If a general heads the consular office, his wife will be the owner of the travel agency that deals with issuing passports. If a college dean is in charge of a department, his son will be the owner of the building where the department meets. Under Yeltsin, officials were selling their informal support. Under Putin, bureaucracy has privatized the state.[11]

Putin, of course, recognizes the threat posed by corruption, which disrupts the presidential pyramid of power. In order not to allow it to undermine his power completely, he has tried to undertake purges of some law enforcement bodies, accompanied by noisy media coverage. In 2006, for example, dozens of highly placed officials in the FSB, in the customs department, and the prosecutor's office were dismissed. These cosmetic purges have not radically improved matters, and nearly all the dismissed officers were soon comfortably reappointed to other positions. What makes the situation so desperate is that a real battle against corruption might shake the Russian system to its foundations. This anxiety obliges the president to close his eyes to even the most blatant cases of corruption in the top echelons of power. Moreover, if a president with a skyrocketing popularity rating is afraid to undertake a reshuffling and cleansing of his power structure, for fear of provoking instability or even the collapse of his machinery of government, how would his successor, coming out from his shadow, have the courage to do so?

Another trend that causes concern is the growing centralization of resources that undermines the Russian Federation, which is moving toward becoming a unitary state. This trend is most evident in the redistribution of economic resources between the center and the regions. In 1992–1998, the share of regional tax revenues in the federal budget grew from 44 percent to 56 percent. Beginning in 1999, this share began to decline and fell to 31 to 32 percent in 2005–2006. The share of regional expenditures in the federal budget has decreased as well, from 54 percent to 43 percent. By centralizing financial resources, Moscow leaves the regions with huge responsibilities that they are unable to fulfill. This could be the source of growing social dissatisfaction and even turmoil in the regions in the future.[12]

One cannot get a complete view of the Russian political landscape without looking at one more inevitable consequence of personalized power—favoritism. The elimination of independent institutions by the executive makes the executive itself dependent on random individuals in the service of the presidency, individuals who have a vested interest in trying to weaken it. The formation of a political family, or kitchen cabinet, occurs within a framework of authoritarianism quite apart from the physical condition of the leader. It has to do with the technical impossibility of the leader's fully exercising all his tremendous powers. Favorites were a natural constituent of Yeltsin's presidency. During 1995–1996, a political "family" ruled in Yeltsin's name, which included members of his biological family (mainly his daughter Tatiana Diachenko and her future husband, Valentin Yumashev). Under Putin, a lack of developed institutions has also obliged the president to turn to people he trusts, who help a leader burdened with routine matters to do his job. The more powers vested in the presidency, the more the president is compelled to delegate them to confidants. He hands them out to people he knew at university and during his service career, to family friends, and to neighbors from nearby dachas. In effect, everyone Putin has ever known and become friendly with has been given an important position, and if they have no official position, then they help to run the state as members of his kitchen cabinet. So what? the Western reader may say. Every Western leader has the equivalent of George W. Bush's Karl Rove. It is not the end of the world. The difference is, however, that in developed democracies there are systemic checks, among them freedom of the press, political opposition, and independent institutions that prevent favorites from taking over and dominating the system. When these are lacking, the authority of the state is inevitably privatized by the leader's entourage, sometimes without the leader's even noticing.

The logic of favoritism is simple. Having initially obtained only some of the leader's functions, his cronies gradually extend their powers. Putin's loyalists include Sergei Ivanov, Dmitri Medvedev, Nikolai Patrushev, Igor Sechin, Vladislav Surkov, Victor Ivanov, Vladimir Yakunin, Boris Gryzlov, and Sergei Mironov.[13] These are officially well-known figures. There are quite a few names on the list of Putin's "shadow" confidants who might be even closer to him. This practice is not only the result of the president's informal way of dealing with politics but with the way Russian power is still organized today. Which individuals are on "the list" is less important than what evokes their appearance and what results from their actions. The nontransparency of the decision-taking process creates ideal conditions for courtiers to develop influence. The leader, with no institutions to back him up, inevitably tends to convert functional relations to personal relationships based on trust. Forced to rely only on personal devotion, he at the same time constantly expects that his retinue will betray him (and it often does). The leader hands over parts of his power to his favorites; he brings them into the leadership, but if he were to trust them implicitly, he would lose all his power. Thus it has been throughout Russian history, under the czars and during the Soviet period, and so it continues after communism's collapse. The only difference is that today's favorites do not suffocate their leader with a pillow, and the leader refrains from executing favorites who have fallen from grace.

Russia demonstrates an ancient truth: omnipotence is doomed to become impotence, as Guillermo O'Donnell predicted in writing about delegative democracies.[14] This happens if only because a leader who concentrates the totality of power in his own hands is obliged to concentrate totally on the defensive, which leaves him neither the strength nor the energy to implement ambitious plans. The fate of the leader in a bureaucratic–authoritarian regime is not to be envied. All resources are concentrated in his hands, but he is dependent on his entourage. He aspires to grand projects but must live for the day. Sometimes a leader has to trudge this path to the very end of the road, until he has completely lost his power, before recognizing that omnipotence is a dead end. We will never know whether Yeltsin understood this truth. Nor will we probably ever know, taking into account Putin's profession and style of governance, which he performs as a covert operation, whether he understands that his power is fragile, and he has led his country into a dead valley. Much more serious is the fact that society pays the price for the impotence of the omnipotent.

How authoritarian can the Russian regime truly be if it is being pulled apart by the competing Kremlin clans? A corrupt bureaucracy, the fragmentation of the political class, and the degeneration of the army and other security services are all phenomena that reduce the scope for pure authoritarianism, let alone a dictatorship. This does not, however, mean that the next leader cannot attempt to strengthen authoritarian mechanisms in a political crisis, or as a result of his own crisis of confidence. We cannot exclude the possibility that life under Vladimir Putin's (so far) mild authoritarianism may seem the very epitome of freedom compared with what Russia may face in the very near future if the vector persists.

The regime in Russia is increasingly tending toward acts of intimidation of the population, often simply to conceal its own anxieties. Examples include the excessive terms of imprisonment meted out to members of the officially banned National Bolshevik Party, which organizes protest demonstrations; the passing of a law on extremism that means that anybody criticizing the regime can be jailed; the refusal to register opposition parties; and attacks on the leaders and members of opposition movements, who are assaulted by unidentified individuals who are fairly obviously agents of the security forces or members of the pro-Kremlin movements. The harassment of members of the "Other Russia" opposition movement (formed in 2006 by former prime minister Mikhail Kasianov, former world chess champion Garry Kasparov, and the leader of the National Bolsheviks, writer Eduard Limonov) and the use of brutal force against protest "dissenters' marches" in Moscow, St. Petersburg, Nizhni Novgorod, and other cities in the spring of 2007 ultimately show that the regime is gradually sliding toward more aggressive authoritarianism. In the course of 2005–2006 the impression was that the ruling elite might be tempted to use violence, but that it was also afraid of doing so, no doubt aware that it could not control its ramifications. The elite had to fear that the use of force could cause turmoil in society, or could boomerang and the rulers themselves would fall victim to infighting. Besides, the Kremlin did care about its image, especially in the West. At that time it seemed unlikely that the Russian ruling class would be prepared to employ violence against its opposition, quite apart from the fact that there were no forces in society really threatening it. However, a growing orientation toward the use of force is programmed into the regime both by the complexes and fears of the ruling elite, which make it unable to compromise, and by the evolution of a centralized state. I am quite certain that Putin himself wants no further movement toward strengthening the aggressive reflexes of the authorities in the final phase of his presidency, something that would be tantamount to admitting that he has failed as a leader and an architect of national consensus. Chechnya may have shown him the limits of resorting to violence and that there is a reverse side of the coin. But a trend can generate its own momentum, which can drag a vacillating president, or his successor, in its wake. As of this writing in summer 2007, it has begun to seem that constraints that had held back the ruling class are beginning to break down. The authorities' reaction to the "dissenters' marches" in Spring 2007 demonstrated that authoritarianism has a logic which pushes it to crack down on minor opposition groups in order to prevent broader dissent. The ruling team, once it starts to use force, will be unable to step back, and this may bring about a spiral of violence. Whether these apprehensions are justified or exaggerated, we shall shortly find out.

Chapter 5

CAN YOU SIT AND RUN
AT THE SAME TIME?

Vladimir Putin's presidency has not been without its moments of drama. The second president of Russia has had to restore at least a semblance of order, but he has also had to try to advance the project of reform as he understands it. Characterizing the evolution of state power and leadership in Russia, Russian historian Yuri Pivovarov has noted two invariable, intertwined elements: status quo and reform. That means that in Russian history, leaders often had to embody the Pope and Martin Luther simultaneously. Mikhail Gorbachev and Boris Yeltsin were torn by those conflicting roles and Putin has continued this trend, vacillating between irreconcilable alternatives until one of them gained the upper hand.

For someone who was not a politician, Putin has long coped passably with the contradictory demands on him. Presenting himself as the "president of all Russians" and having the support of influential groups with conflicting interests, Putin stabilized the situation and consolidated the society left by Yeltsin and even embarked on new economic reforms. The first Russian leader of modern times who had not been schooled in the Soviet Party bureaucracy, he evolved a technocratic style of leadership unusual for Russia. Putin talks like a modernizer when he speaks of the systemic problems of the Russian state, notably corruption. He was the first Russian leader to begin deregulation of the economy and to attempt to reform the bureaucracy, both of which go to the foundations of the traditional state. Throughout his first term, he continued to aim for a partnership with the West, even when the elite preferred that he should show assertiveness and indeed defy the West. Even when he did criticize the West and the United States, he avoided anything that might have led to a confrontation. Putin continued downsizing Russian ambitions towards the country's more modest resources, which was reflected in Moscow's moderate stance over the United States' abandonment of the antiballistic missile (ABM) treaty, the second round of NATO expansion, EU expansion, and the war in Iraq. Early in his presidency Putin tried to restrain Russian imperial ambitions in the post-Soviet territories by soft-pedaling Russian foreign policy and emphasizing economic and trade interests. He tried to establish a more predictable foreign policy and developed constructive relations with the members of the G8. This pragmatism, bringing goals into line with the resources for implementing them, was most evident in 2000–2003.

Each time he took a step in the direction of renewal, however, Putin guarded his back by making a move in the opposite direction. This backsliding became more apparent during his second term and became a dominant trend. Putin himself put a landmine under privatization and the institution of private property by renationalizing Yukos. Speaking out against corruption, he increased opportunities for it by further centralizing the state authorities and handing over administrative reform to the bureaucracy. Having embarked on a "revolution against oligarchy," Putin retained and even strengthened the major financial and industrial groups that limit competition; handing control of the economy to the bureaucracy, he set the stage for the appearance of *bureaucrat–oligarchs*.

Putin's partnership with the West in his second term has been accompanied by Russia's growing assertiveness and suspicion toward the West, which undermines that partnership.

Having repudiated claims to hegemony over the post-Soviet territories, the Kremlin intervened crudely in the Ukrainian electoral process in 2004, embarked on a confrontation with Georgia and Belarus in 2006 and with Estonia in 2007, and began trying to dislodge Western influence from the post-Soviet territories without having the forces to fill the vacuum thus created. Making political use of Russia's energy resources created a precedent that may come to threaten international stability, particularly if other exporters of natural resources follow that example. Moscow's behavior in the former Soviet space indicates that the mood of the Russian elite, which until recently conformed to the post-imperial syndrome, may develop, perhaps unconsciously for some of its factions, into neo-imperial ambitions.

On a number of occasions, for example, in his readiness to cooperate with the United States after the tragedy of September 11, Vladimir Putin came close to rejecting Russian stereotypes and to becoming a fully fledged partner of the West. However, he thought better of it and retreated. Putin showed that he could be a politician prepared to make changes in domestic policy, but only in order to buttress familiar principles. He was either unwilling or unable to relinquish the four pillars of the Soviet system: personalized power, domination by the bureaucracy, great-power ambitions, and state control of property. More than that, having decided in favor of a neo-patrimonial regime, the president isolated the liberally inclined section of society that could support innovative policy and gave greater scope to reactionary forces and conformists. If Vladimir Putin in his first years as president believed he had a mission to make Russia into a modern state, he subsequently rejected and destroyed his own potential to be a transformational leader. By his second term, it was too late for Putin to return to reform. The logic of the system forced him to concentrate on maintaining the status quo, and higher oil prices allowed him to relax and avoid taking risks. He was able just to carry on swimming with the tide. Putin worried less and less about his image as a politician representing all political interests, and moved even further back toward Russian traditionalism.

When Putin came to power he had three options: he could embark on the creation of a liberal democracy with a separation of powers; he could move to market-oriented authoritarianism, restricting the role of the bureaucracy; or he could choose bureaucratic capitalism, relying on officialdom. Putin chose the third option. Was the first option of moving in the direction of a liberal democracy feasible? For Vladimir Putin to try to break free of the shackles of electoral autocracy, there needed to be liberal democrats able to provide him with effective support; an active desire for democracy on the part of the public; and a recognition of the need for the reform of state power by the political class and its readiness and ability to "think outside the box." These prerequisites were not in place when Putin found himself in the Kremlin. Even the Russian liberals were continuing to hope that the strong hand of an authoritarian leader might complete the transition to a free market economy.

It might have been suicidal for Putin to start introducing checks and balances when he first came to power, but after he obtained solid public backing, he could have embarked on dismantling the old state and ridding it of its archaic features. In late 2000 and early 2001, the president had an opportunity to try to alter the logic of Russia's evolution. Public opinion indicated that 60 to 70 percent of Russians would have supported the creation of a system that guaranteed order under the rule of law, but Putin decided against taking risks. He chose the easy option of governability and began strengthening the administrative and security institutions of the state structure. He chose order through control and top-down governance. Was he afraid he might break his neck? Possibly, although the more likely reason for his choice was not a lack of courage but a lack of faith. The president of Russia evidently did not, and still does not, believe that Russia is ready for modernization without authoritarian control. In fact, however, his presidency has shown the impossibility of a genuine transformation in Russia while top-down governance remains in place.

At first Putin just about managed to combine his dual role of stabilizer and leader with modernizing potential, but as he approached the end of his rule it became obvious that the model of governance he had created ruled out the successful implementation of the reforms that had been instituted at the beginning. A genuine struggle against corruption required a return of press freedom, an independent judiciary, and an independent legislature. In other words, the pyramid of power that Putin had so energetically created would need to be demolished. The president was not prepared to countenance this and accordingly had to reconcile himself to corruption. Indeed, he was obliged to retreat whenever rooting out corruption might have undermined the position of the ruling class.

In the evolution of every leader there are times when he is tested, and those times decisively influence the way he thinks and force him to make choices that affect him forever after and constrain his room to maneuver. These tests establish or strengthen a particular vector in everything the governing authorities undertake. For Yeltsin, the moment of truth came when his conflict with parliament was resolved by force, with civilian casualties. The taboo on bloodshed in Moscow, introduced under Gorbachev, had been broken. Having once resorted to violence, Yeltsin no longer hesitated to use it in the North Caucasus, starting the first Chechen war, in which tens of thousands of people died. Violence had again become part of the arsenal of Russian government, further debasing Yeltsin's presidency. Putin's first moment of truth came in August 2000 with the loss of the nuclear submarine *Kursk*, the pride of the Russian navy. His inaction during the tragedy elicited a storm of criticism from the then independent Russian media. The conclusion Putin evidently drew from this was that he needed to get rid of the independent mass media so that no one should again dare to impugn his leadership or suggest he was weak and unable to respond to challenges. If he had learned a different lesson from the *Kursk* tragedy, Russia just might have chosen a different path.

The president's mettle was next tested in 2003 by the terrorist hostage taking at the Dubrovka theater complex in Moscow. The Kremlin decided not to negotiate with the terrorists and secretly used a lethal gas in the course of the operation. Hundreds of hostages died from gas poisoning, and no provision was made for trying to save them. Doctors were not even told how to counteract the poisoning. The authorities had, however, shown firmness. The leaders of the operation received government awards, if in secret. Society shrugged off this barbaric method of fighting terrorism and, since the presidential approval rating was not dented by the tragedy, Putin assumed that Russia approved of his actions. In the next, even more appalling, terrorist act in the school in Beslan in September 2004, in which twelve hundred children and their parents were trapped, the Kremlin did not hesitate to mount an armed assault. Hundreds of children died as a result of this "antiterrorist operation." The Beslan ordeal confirmed that the prestige of the state mattered more to the regime than human life, which meant that Russia had come full circle, back to the point at which its transformation had begun under Gorbachev.

There have been other landmarks in Putin's presidency that have only strengthened his chosen trajectory. Among these were the Yukos affair in 2003, which consolidated the move toward bureaucratic capitalism; the Ukrainian Orange Revolution in 2004, which put the regime on the defensive; the gas conflict with Ukraine in 2005, which accelerated Russia's transformation into a country that more and more resembled a petrostate with great-power pretensions; and finally, the "dissenters' marches" in 2007, which demonstrated the shift from soft authoritarianism to its harsher version.

Putin's leadership has reconfirmed that in postcommunist Russia, as in the Soviet era, the office of the leader remains of paramount political importance. How may we define and categorize postcommunist leadership in this country? In this context, the distinction drawn by James Burns between *transactional* and *transforming* leaders is useful: transactional leaders introduce incremental changes by means of expedient political brokerage and trade-offs; transforming leaders provide inspiring leadership that makes bold moves to bring about qualitative policy changes.[1] To this categorization of "foxes" and "lions," it would be helpful to add George Breslauer's and Archie Brown's definitions of *transformational* leadership. George Breslauer points out that a transformational leader must: "1) create and legitimize an autonomous public arena; 2) disperse social, economic, political, and informational resources into those arenas; 3) construct new institutions for coordination of decentralized social exchange and integration of the new social order; and 4) plant the seeds of a new political–economic culture that is consonant with the new social order."[2] In Archie Brown's view, transformational leaders are those who preside over systemic changes and guarantee their success.[3] Yeltsin definitely had transformational potential, though of an intuitive variety, especially at the beginning of his leadership. Gradually, however, the transactional side increased, taking the upper hand by the end of his rule. Putin, as Alex Pravda rightly points out, initially struck most observers as a "transactional fox." He writes, "Putin seemed intent on stabilizing the status quo by carefully balancing interests and seeking consensus through give-and-take negotiations, all hallmarks of a transactional leader. With his practical and even technocratic approach to fixing problems, Putin appeared to be less of a political leader than a prudent manager."[4]

True, the second Russian president not only developed an independent style of leadership but made an attempt to introduce innovative politics, restarting economic reforms and moving toward the West during his first presidency. Yet he proved that partial reforms—and even certain transforming elements in the leadership—do not change the logic of the old system. Moreover, those elements only consolidate it and prolong its existence. Bureaucratic–authoritarian consolidation became

Putin's key achievement. There are, of course, different kinds of consolidation. President Putin moves beyond the typical Soviet formula of stabilization, of the Brezhnev and Andropov variety—stabilization that had been aimed to keep afloat a hermetically sealed system. Though Putin's statist thrust clearly resembles Andropov's style, Putin has faced a much more ambitious and difficult task. He has had to consolidate and stabilize a system that includes conflicting trends and principles, one that is impossible to seal completely. He has had to ride two horses simultaneously and in opposite directions, and he has—so far—succeeded in accomplishing this trick. He has ended the convulsive period of Russian development, he has seemingly restored normalcy and built a stronger state, and he has presided over economic growth. Still, "normalcy" conceals insoluble social conflicts. The state is predatory and its strength is a disguise for its weaknesses. Economic growth is produced by an outdated economic model. We do not have to wait long to see how stable and efficient this system is. Political history tells us that consolidation for consolidation's sake, with the major task of strengthening state power, in the end undermines it. This brings us to the conclusion that the second president of Russia, Vladimir Vladimirovich, is leaving the political scene as a *transactional leader* who did everything to prevent systemic change by making many situational changes and shifts that sometimes seemed radical and sustainable.

Chapter 6

PRAGMATISTS VERSUS IDEALISTS

L et us pause for a moment and discuss how Russian analysts view the direction of Russian transformation. The majority of them—let us call them *pragmatists*—say that Russia has the state it deserves, that you cannot leap straight from totalitarianism to liberal democracy, and that you have to move forward a step at a time. There will be time enough to think about liberal democracy, they say, when a middle class has formed and the national standard of living has risen.[1] "All democracies have matured slowly," reiterates a leading Russian analyst, Andranik Migranian, who is followed by all Kremlin pundits (Viacheslav Nikonov, Sergei Markov, Gleb Pavlovsky, and others).[2]

Pragmatists consider Russia to be a perfectly normal country, its level of democracy proportionate to its economic development. Some pragmatists believe that Russia has discovered an enlightened form of authoritarian modernization that will lead to democracy. Yet all pragmatists agree that reforming the economy and capitalism come first, and only after that can you expect liberal democracy and freedom. In fact, they tacitly agree with the Marxist view of history, whereby the political superstructure is strictly determined by the economic base. In the modern period, the guru of the liberals, Friedrich Hayek, argued that we "should trust the economy, and it will bring freedom."

He was probably unaware of his Marxist overtones. There are other doctrines that explain why Russia should be patient: we need first to wait for the Russian people to grow up before taking off the reins and allowing society to decide for itself where it wants to go; under no circumstances should we be in too much of a hurry to create independent institutions; Yeltsin tried to give Russia freedom and almost brought about the country's disintegration. Of late, the busier pragmatists among the Kremlin's propagandists have been arguing that "sovereign democracy" has come to Russia. The term was coined by chief Kremlin ideologist Vladislav Surkov, the deputy head of the presidential administration.[3] The label is supposed to convey that Russia has a right to its own approach to democratic principles and (no less to the point) a right not to be subjected to outside interference. The right to define democracy in its own way is presented as integral to Russia's sovereignty.

Within Russia the pragmatists are in the majority in the scholarly community and the political class. They include a few Russian liberals who blame the West, especially the United States, for all the misfortunes of Russian democracy and suggest that if NATO had not crept up to the borders of Russia, and if the West itself had not fallen short of democratic standards, Russia would by now be one of the developed democracies.

The pragmatists look for support in the views of Fareed Zakaria and those Western pundits who champion the evolution of Southeast Asia, where economic modernization preceded democracy. The ideal for many Russian pragmatists is the regime of Lee Kwan Yew, the architect of the Singaporean economic miracle. They see his ideas as supporting an authoritarian approach to modernizing Russia. Some pragmatists point also to the experience of China, which in their view confirms the modernist potential of authoritarianism. What unites them all, optimists and skeptics alike, is a fatalistic view of Russia, a blindness to contradictory trends within the country, a lack of faith that it can be democratized, and a determination to shoehorn the country into their favored stereotypes.

Their opponents are the *idealists*, who believe that in Russia politics is more important than economics, and that political will can compensate if some of the preconditions for democratization are lacking. Among the idealists are economists Yevgeni Yasin, Andrei Illarionov, and Alexander Auzan, historian Yuri Afanasiev, political scientists Igor Klyamkin and Mark Urnov, international relations analysts Andrei Piontkovsky, Yuri Fiodorov, and Andrei Zagorsky, and sociologist Georgi Satarov. They do not see any insurmountable barriers to a move toward liberal democracy in Russian society. They are convinced that a balance between freedom and order on the basis of the rule of law is possible in Russia, and that economic modernization has no future in Russia while power remains personalized. Within Russia the idealists are marginalized, pragmatists having monopolized the right to speak about and on behalf of Russia.[4]

At first sight reality appears to be on the side of the pragmatists. The Russian populace supports Vladimir Putin and his regime, it does not complain about the state of affairs, and it gives the president an approval rating his G8 colleagues can only envy. Any opposition hopes that the system is about to collapse and that the Russian people will come out onto the streets to demand freedom are wide of the mark. It is sometimes difficult to avoid the impression that the Western world, aware of the limits of its influence, clearly prefers a stable if undemocratic Russia. Western leaders like ex-chancellor Gerhard Schröder of Germany and ex-prime minister Silvio Berlusconi of Italy speak out on the Kremlin's behalf, pleading that Russia is not yet ripe for democracy. In his memoirs Schröder sounds like a veritable Kremlin public relations consultant as he describes the achievements of his friend Putin:

> In his role as the country's president, Putin set about resuscitating state institutions, and it is he who has introduced a semblance of sound legality for citizens, enterprises, and investors.... It would be wholly mistaken to make unrealistic demands of Russia in respect of the pace of domestic

political reform and democratic development, or to judge Russia solely on the basis of the conflict in Chechnya.[5]

Mr. Schröder apparently forgot about the Yukos affair or he has an odd definition of "sound legality," and it is no less odd to hear a Western politician urging the curtailment of demands for democratic reform in Russia.

The failures of America's strategy of "promoting democracy," of which the stalemate in Iraq is the latest, only make more convincing the arguments of the Kremlin's defenders when they urge that there should be no rush for democratic breakthroughs. They see the crises of the "color revolutions" in Ukraine and Kyrgyzstan as further proof that a society "has to be ready for democracy."

Russian idealists concede that a majority of Russians support the existing regime, but only because they see it as a lesser evil or have hopes of gradual reform. Many who voted for Putin in 2004 believed he would deliver the optimal combination of freedom and order. The idealists argue that the people are quiescent because they are able to survive on a personal level, but that their silence can hardly be taken as approval of government policy if only 33 percent of respondents declare themselves satisfied with the current situation. The people are quiescent also because they see no alternative political forces deserving of their trust, but the present absence of unrest is hardly stable if 61 percent of those surveyed in 2007 say they do not trust the government.[6] The idealists claim that, for the first time in Russian history, the people of Russia are ready to live in a free society, and the real problem is that the elite is not.

Let us play the devil's advocate and suppose the pragmatists are right. Let us assume that Russian society really does have to be led toward freedom slowly and cautiously. This does not explain why its ruling class, instead of opening up the system, is busily tightening the screws. If it is impossible to modernize Russia under a democratic system, why is its economic growth declining as the power of the state becomes more centralized?

Can evolution into a petrostate really be described as modernization?

Not long ago the pragmatists were assuring everyone that just as soon as a strong regime was established reform could begin. Russia becomes a superpresidency, but somehow the Kremlin has no time to get around to making the reforms. The pragmatists like to stress how far Russia has yet to travel, comparing it with England in the seventeenth century and America in the nineteenth. Yet somehow the selfsame people manage to claim that Russia is ready to be a fully fledged member of the G8. Russian society may not yet be ready for freedom, but the Russian elite has no doubt that it is ready to sit at the same table as the leaders of Western democracies.

When Western pragmatists (and there are quite a few of them) discuss the situation in Russia, they are often heard to remark soothingly, "It could have been worse." This seems to betray a cynical and supercilious attitude toward a people deemed unready and not mature enough to understand Western values. Poles, Hungarians, Bulgarians, Romanians, and Ukrainians, it seems, are capable of living under democratic norms, but not Russians. Western commentators who deny Russia the right even to aspire to more sophisticated forms of social organization play into the hands of a Russian elite that never ceases to assure its citizens they are much better off without Western ideas.

The logic of some of the pragmatists' arguments, especially those of Kremlin propagandists, is downright perplexing. If Russia is an "energy superpower," as many of them argue, why is its sovereignty so much under threat? If selling hydrocarbons can confer superpower status, has not Saudi Arabia, which sells a lot more, a stronger claim?

The idealists, I admit, have failed to explain why a society that would like to live in freedom allows its elite to curtail its freedoms. Why have the liberals failed so signally to win the electorate's trust? And why are they widely regarded by Russians as quite alien to Russia's culture?

There really is no evidence to suggest that China's and Southeast Asia's authoritarian modernization is applicable to Russia. First, we have to recognize that China's successes have been exaggerated and that economic growth is no guarantee that an economy is competitive or that a country is moving toward democracy.[7] This has been proved by Indonesia, which after a period of sustained economic growth found itself in a state of profound crisis. Second, while Southeast Asia was able to industrialize under authoritarian regimes, as South Korea demonstrated, social and political liberalization was needed before it could move on to a post-industrial economy. Indeed, Russia itself industrialized successfully back in the Stalin era. Third, Singapore showed that in societies with a tradition of Confucianism, authoritarianism can structure a society on the basis of the rule of law. In Russia, however, it merely exacerbates a state of lawlessness. Many countries, from Belarus to Egypt, provide evidence that a bureaucratic–authoritarian state hinders economic reform. The world's experience of democratization has confirmed that Dankwart Rustow was right to claim back in 1970 that a transition to democracy is possible without full economic liberalization. Guillermo O'Donnell and Philippe Schmitter have also proved to be correct in asserting that the transition is possible in societies with only a rudimentary middle class, and that political will can compensate for a lack of favorable socioeconomic conditions. This has been seen in economically underdeveloped countries from Portugal to Poland.

The pragmatists, shaking their heads over Russia's lack of readiness for liberal democracy, in this way justify its backsliding and close off further discussion of how it might develop. If everything is preordained, one should take it easy, go with the flow, and hope that everything will come out right in the end. Pragmatism endorses the neo-patrimonial regime and justifies political inaction and conformism. The idealists, however, also need to think carefully about why an attempt to introduce democracy in Russia failed and how far responsibility for that lies with those who proclaim themselves to be liberal democrats.

While the discussion in the scholarly community in Russia and the West continues regarding Russia's transformation, Vladimir Putin has done his job and soon he will await the verdict of history. He has recreated a state whose mission is to defend the interests of the ruling minority. It remains to be seen whether Russia's elite and its new leader are capable of reconstructing the system before the price of oil falls and a discontented populace takes to the streets, or whether Russia will, as it always does, follow the rule of failure, that is, whether it will break its head against a brick wall and only then, when the situation is intolerable, begin to seek a way out of the mess in which it finds itself, thanks partly to Vladimir Putin.

Chapter 7

SHOULD I STAY OR SHOULD I GO?

According to the new Russian constitution, the president must leave the Kremlin after completing a second term. Thus, for the first time in Russian history, a barrier has been placed in the way of a ruler's remaining in power for an unlimited period, until either he dies naturally or is removed by a coup. Yeltsin was the first Russian leader to relinquish power voluntarily even before the end of his term, but only because he could not physically continue to govern. A successor appointed by Yeltsin was his attempt to preserve the influence of his political group and the continuity of his course. This in itself was a novel approach to attempting to cling to power and Russian tradition.

The Russian political class, however, still cannot bring itself to accept the uncertainty that political competition and free elections entail. The elite has failed to learn to think in terms of alternatives and a change of regime, which is why it tries so desperately to retain control over the transfer of power. As the end of the current regime approaches, the Kremlin team can think of nothing better to do than prepare to hand power over to a loyal person hoping to remain as an influential force behind the throne. It needs to predict who is going to gain control and align itself in good time with the new leader. The country is left to its own devices, and no one knows where it is headed; all problems are put off to another day, and no one is truly governing Russia.

The state becomes paralyzed and cannot function properly until it knows who is to personify it next. Society is expected to be compliant, patient, and passive. Anyone who utters a squeak gets a good kicking from the authorities for preventing them from getting on with their succession project. What really matters is to ensure the continuity of power. So it was under Yeltsin, so it is under Putin, and so it will be under the new leader and for as long as the bureaucratic–authoritarian regime continues in Russia. Accordingly, the second term—no matter who the president is and for as long as the current system persists, with all its problems of continuity—is lost time. The fact that for several years before the elections, the entire country forgets everything other than trying to guess the name of the next ruler or persuade the incumbent to stay on is clear enough testimony to the failings of a system so completely dependent on who occupies the Kremlin, a person who can simply overturn the chessboard and say, "Now we are going to play by different rules."

Given this model of power, Russia is guaranteed continual uncertainty as to whether the leader will remain for a third term and, if not, who will succeed him and what course he will pursue, and who from the old entourage will remain in the Kremlin. For a while the Russian elite was sure that Putin would stay on. All the president's statements that he had no intention of violating the constitution were treated as mere words to camouflage his determination to prolong his grip on the Kremlin wheel. The parachuting into the government of two members of Putin's entourage, Dmitri Medvedev and Sergei Ivanov, his old pals from St. Petersburg, in November 2005, gave the elite to understand that Vladimir Putin was thinking seriously about the best way of transferring power to a successor who would get some government experience. Many in Russia and in the West, however, still have their eyes on the president and cannot bring themselves to believe it is really possible for him to leave the Kremlin, voluntarily walking away from so much power. There are many who repeat, "Putin is going to stay!" like a mantra. Regional authorities, outdoing one another in their displays of loyalty to Putin, are appealing to him not to go. Their pleas reflect not merely the servility of the Russian elite, but also its growing anxiety. With Putin's departure, the current and so energetically massaged patron–client arrangements will lapse. They will have to construct new relationships, and there is no telling whether they will manage to jump onto the running board of the new train. There is a growing fear that with his departure Putin's pyramid will begin to crumble, since it was created for a particular individual. When it goes, they may find themselves beneath the rubble. Not only the elite, but a significant part of society also feels anxious about the forthcoming changing of the guard in the Kremlin and what it may bring.

Developed democracies also face the problem of how to transfer power. Thought has to be given as to how to resolve this issue. In some democracies, for example, in Japan and Great Britain, the departing leader may even recommend his successor, as Prime Minister Junichiro Koizumi did Shinzo Abe and as Tony Blair did Gordon Brown. In developed democracies, however, a change of leader is less fraught because it does not signal any change in the principles by which society and the state are ordered. Democratic leaders not infrequently use their time as lame ducks to ensure themselves a place in the history books. Thus Koizumi, as he came toward the end of his premiership, initiated reforms that would change the character of Japanese capitalism. One could argue that George W. Bush has also been giving thought to the future, not only his own. He has, perhaps somewhat unconvincingly, proclaimed the strategy of promoting democracy. French president Jacques Chirac has similarly, and also unsuccessfully, tried to stake his claim by seeking approval of a new European Union constitution. The important point is that Western leaders, as they approach the end of their time in office, try to rise above the routine vanities of power.

Vladimir Putin, as he prepares to depart, might also have tried to revive the modernization he was thinking about at the beginning of his presidency. He had a chance to step back from Kremlin politicking and begin thinking in terms of the broad sweep of history. Theoretically he had the possibility of moving economic reforms forward and of trying to free the country from its dependence on oil and gas. This, however, could be the play of my imagination, and musings of this kind are unlikely to have occurred to Putin. They are alien to his understanding of governance. The president's priority is to ensure the survival of a regime obsessed with its own interests. To be fair, this is no simple matter. Vladimir Putin is obliged on the one hand to repeat that he intends to step down, thereby announcing that he will abide by the law. At the same time, he needs to give the appearance of intending to stay in politics to retain his influence. Putin's successor will do the same, seeking to maintain the status quo and create the illusion of a mere change of scenery on the stage. The Russian elite will try to persuade him to remain in power because changing a leader who substitutes himself for an entire political system is perceived as a threat to the very foundations of the state.

The moment is inexorably approaching when uncertainty will drive the elite to distraction, and it will desperately want to stop the ordeal. The elite is becoming impatient, wanting the Kremlin to make it clear who will be ruling Russia after 2008. Meantime, Putin has to postpone the moment when he says, "This is whom I recommend." He is likely to continue to deliberate when would be a good time to recommend a successor, and whether he should until he can no longer stay silent. The premature endorsement of a successor could be fatal for him— politically, of course. As soon as the elite is persuaded that Putin really is stepping down, he will find himself abandoned as the Kremlin cockroaches scuttle off in search of a new center of attraction. Worse, a scuffle might break out between the rival claimants to power. As long as the future remains undecided, the president has the ability to control the elite and the transfer of power. This is a departing leader's trump card. Such is the logic of the culmination of a political cycle that will be repeated for as long as the bureaucratic–authoritarian regime continues. But at some point, uncertainty could become unbearable for the elite and vicious fighting might erupt, forcing the leader to carefully balance certainty and uncertainty to prevent events from getting out of control.

Under a system of personalized power, the leader can change his choice of candidates to succeed him, as Yeltsin did more than once, while keeping the main pretender under wraps until the last moment. We can be sure, however, that neither the outgoing president nor the ruling elite wants a strong leader as the successor for fear of dictatorial ambitions. This is why Putin fired Public Prosecutor Vladimir Ustinov, known for his bullish character, in May 2006 and moved him to a less influential job but did not dispatch him totally. It is always better to have dangerous people close by and under watch. Ustinov had been seen as the *siloviki* faction's candidate for the throne and was staking his claim to succession rather too energetically. There can, however, be no guarantee that a more authoritarian candidate will not break through into the Kremlin at the last moment if (and when) Putin relaxes his grip on the reins. There is, of course, a paradox here in that the ruling team, and particularly the departing leader, wants a weak, manageable successor. On the other hand, they have to recognize that such a successor would be incapable of defending their interests effectively, and a weak president could undermine the top-down structure of the government.

Until the successor's identity is finally made public, large queues of potential heirs are forming around the incumbent in the hope that chance will bring them to the surface, just as happened to Putin. If the outgoing president takes too long to perform his last and most important act—announcing who is to be the next occupant of the Kremlin—the candidates might begin to resolve the issue themselves. This is how the Russian electoral monarchy works.

The various factions within the Kremlin will always hope to install their own candidate on the throne and be able to manipulate him. Many would-be puppet masters have harbored similar illusions. The Spanish Falangists supported their young colleague Adolfo Suárez, only to have him put an end to the Franco regime. The Chilean oligarchs invited General Augusto Pinochet to be a symbolic president in the hope of having him at their beck and call, but they too lived to rue their mistake. The army generals in France supported Charles de Gaulle in the belief that he would continue the war in Algeria and return France to her imperial past, but they too were wrong. What a mistake Boris Berezovsky, Yeltsin's *éminence grise*, made in supposing that Putin might be a puppet. That is a misjudgment worthy of the textbooks. Authoritarian power has its own dynamic, which compels a successor to forget his (or her) obligations to his (or her) patrons.

As the political cycle approaches its end, the political elite also energetically sets about redistributing property. That was seen at the end of Yeltsin's period in office, and the same thing is happening as Putin's presidency draws to a close. The seizure of firms and enterprises using the law-enforcement agencies, known in Russia as raiding, has assumed epidemic proportions. Property changes ownership at lightning speed in many different sectors: the car industry, nonferrous metal production, metallurgy, finance, food distribution, and the construction industry. The new owners are people from St. Petersburg who happened to find themselves in the front carriages of trains driven by former St. Petersburg boy Vladimir Putin. The transfer of capital and ownership that has been taking place in the final years of Putin's reign is reminiscent of the shake-up of the Russian economy in the 1990s. The new owners will defend their acquisitions ferociously, and for that they need their own man in the Kremlin.

While the political class has been guessing who will succeed Vladimir Vladimirovich, the incumbent has demonstrated that he is a politician with imagination. He did not want to follow

Yeltsin by automatically appointing a single successor. He decided to have two candidates for the post (Medvedev and Ivanov) and to let them compete with each other, which has complicated the race but at the same time has increased the field for the president's maneuvering. Having two competing loyalists and leaving the public guessing how many more cards he has up his sleeve and who may end up being the joker, Putin can always say that he has guaranteed Russia a fair contest by introducing some pluralism at the top (under his strict control, of course). Will he ever give a sign to the elite and society about whom he would prefer as his successor? This has been the question that so many people in Russia have been mulling over for months. More important than the name of the candidate is the way the incumbent will set out the rules of the game. The logic of the Russian system gives scope for two possibilities. Should the incumbent have problems obtaining a consensus on the candidate for succession or other difficulties in securing the smooth self-perpetuation of the regime, he will have to convey his preferences. Should he wish to have a weak successor with limited legitimacy and only the vague support of the political class, the incumbent would have to maintain an ambiguous attitude and avoid any open endorsement. His choice of tactics will depend on the extent of his control over developments and his future political plans.

In the end, the decisive factor will be what kind of leadership the country is looking for. Yeltsin entered the Kremlin as an anticommunist leader prepared to draw a line through the past. Putin was attractive as a stabilizer of the chaotic uncertainty created by Yeltsin. During Putin's rule, the demand spontaneously being formulated by the Russian public is for a purifier, someone who will campaign against corruption. The regime, in trying to push society in a less dangerous direction, has attempted to offer people a populist formula of stability and divert its attention to consumer aspirations. It is within this context that the "national projects" appeared, which Medvedev tried to implement. Whether this policy will be a political graveyard for

Putin's successor or a springboard to power remains to be seen. Trying to experiment with leadership formulas, the Kremlin has allowed Medvedev to lean more toward a soft version of liberalism and a moderate pro-Western orientation. At the same time Putin himself has understood that it is too dangerous to concentrate on only one scenario of self-perpetuation. Sergei Ivanov was appointed to represent a slightly different model of leadership, one that is much more conservative and statist. Those two options, however, are really modifications of the same model of leadership. The Kremlin recognizes that the stability formula alone is not enough and has started to move more actively, offering a further carrot: Russia as a superpower once again. A rapidly changing situation is obliging the authorities to run in different directions as they try to predict which brand of leadership will most closely answer the popular mood and in which direction they should be trying to steer it. Meantime, an eager crowd of Putin loyalists has been watching events nervously, hoping for a chance and dreaming of repeating Putin's ascendancy to the Kremlin from nowhere. All these people have been brought by the president to the upper echelon of Russian power. Speakers Boris Gryzlov and Sergei Mironov, premier Mikhail Fradkov, head of the railroads Vladimir Yakunin, St. Petersburg governor Valentina Matvienko, head of Rosoboronexport Sergei Chemezov, and a number of lesser known and totally unknown figures have been waiting while the country has been paralyzed.

By mid-2007 there were signs that the authorities had begun trying out [ethnic] nationalism and great-power rhetoric as easy options for mobilizing society—no need to solve social problems or worry about a national consensus. An added bonus is that they can exploit nationalism and "enemy" seeking, not only to solve the problem of the 2008 elections, but also to justify the existence of an economy based on the export of natural resources while continuing the redistribution of property. Wealth can be taken away from both internal and external "enemies" of Russia. Nationalism is a convenient way of retaining control of the revenue from natural resources, which has been privatized by the ruling class. The elite has been quick to understand the trend, starting to demand protection of the "national economy" from foreigners. To succeed with the mobilization formula, the Kremlin has only to initiate a nationalistic television campaign and "cleanse" major cities of criminal non-Slav gangs, and to continue its anti-Western rhetoric to enjoy the support of masses of confused people instantly. If in addition they toy with the idea, for instance, of annexing Abkhazia and South Ossetia, Russia will appear to be avenging the recent years of defeat and humiliation, which would assuage the smarting self-image of the Russian nation. That is an option that seems too far-fetched for now. However, at least part of the political class has been experimenting with this idea for some time. The Kremlin's foreign-policy assertiveness in 2007, demonstrated by Putin's Munich Security Conference speech, his state-of-the-union address, tough rhetoric directed at certain neighbors, and finally, by Moscow's anti-Americanism—all unexpected and shocking for many observers—is a sign that the Russian elite has been turning to the mobilizational pattern of leadership. In this context, both Medvedev and the even more aggressive Ivanov might appear too weak and even too pro-Western for this pattern of leadership.

Playing the nationalist and great-power card would certainly compensate for a lack of other unifying ideas, but there is no guarantee that, having started a campaign of anti-Western and anti-American mobilization and retribution, the ruling elite will be able to stop it. If a new leader is propelled into the Kremlin on a wave of nationalism and statism, it could prompt a move toward a more aggressive version of authoritarian rule or at least toward more active authoritarian patterns. Having let the genie of ethnic hatred and anti-Western emotions out of the bottle, the elite with its new leader will only be able to stay in power by resorting to repression. If that happens, then, needless to say, the faction within Putin's team that has championed friendship with the West and Western leaders will promptly be purged from the Kremlin. While the moderates in the Kremlin are try-ing to control the genie, it is unclear whether they will succeed.

There is a further question: what kind of political regime will be established after Putin? A number of scenarios are theoreti-cally possible between the extremes of rule by a strong individ-ual and rule by a strong bureaucracy. Putin represents a regime built on compromise and mutual restraint between the presi-dent and the bureaucracy. If there are no major shifts in how society and the elite behave, there are grounds for continuing this kind of regime after Putin's departure. Some unexpected complication, however, especially an intensification of the power struggle within the Kremlin or, even more so, a crisis in society, could cause a more authoritarian leader to emerge. The "left turn," with a Russian Perón or Chávez coming to power, is less likely. The Russian ruling class would undoubtedly prefer to see its interests protected by a leader with right-wing leanings, fearing a resurgence of socialist ideas. Of one thing we can be sure: even if an unexpected and nearly impossible scenario comes true and a relatively strong leader comes to power, he will ultimately depend on an apparatus that has long-established skills for bridling the most blatant of dictators.

The state apparatus may be forced to push toward a more aggressive regime while trying to keep the leader under its control. If the leader risks appealing to the people over the heads of the political class, it is also foreseeable that a real, rather than amor-phous, authoritarianism will be reborn in Russia, but this time with a leadership less dependent on the bureaucracy. Both its program and its prospects in the longer term will depend on exactly how the leader appeals to the people. For the time being, none of Putin's would-be successors appears to have the courage or desire to take that step and no one looks as if he can move in this direction, but the evolution of state power in Russia is full of surprises. Given that we already have a situation that is unusual for Russia, one where members of the special services have come to the Kremlin, become part of the ruling team, and seized prop-erty, a new Russian authoritarianism could take a much stronger, militarist form. It is hard to imagine, however, that any type of militarist rule could be sustained in Russia. In any case, the level and forms of authoritarianism of the post-Putin regime could vary, depending on the balance of forces within the Kremlin and on how sure of themselves the ruling elite and its leader feel. Still, one can be certain that key parameters of the system built by Yeltsin and Putin—state control over the economy, neopatrimonialism, social paternalism, and suspicion of the West in the state's foreign policy in the near or even in the medium-term future—will be preserved simply because the system has consolidated and acquired its own logic and because continuity has thus far a broad basis of popular support.

Putin and his closest associates are evidently hoping that he can remain in the role of a Russian Deng Xiaoping. They would like a gentle, weak-willed successor to be a stand-in, expected to give up his seat at any moment if the Russian Deng decided to return to power. The systemic logic does not, however, always conform to the expectations of those who hold it. An additional problem is that the Russian public is unlikely to take to the idea of two centers of power, one in the form of a "technical" president and the other in the form of an unofficial holder of power standing behind him or acting as the premier, the chairman of the constitutional court, or performing any other role. Both the people and the elite would rapidly begin to defer to the elected head of state, who might well acquire a taste for ruling and decide not to be a cipher in the hands of puppet masters but instead a real president. Putin, after all, kicked out his own sponsors just as soon as he had gotten a grip on power. In any case, if Putin wants to stay in power beyond 2008, he may have a chance to do so by putting in charge a "technical president," and staging a return a year or year and a half later (the constitution would allow this). If, however, he takes too long, the successor will succeed in building up his own regime and will dislodge his predecessor from the Kremlin's orbit.

Let us stop here and ask ourselves what ordinary Russians think about Putin's staying in power beyond 2008. When this idea was first mentioned in 2006, the majority of the Russian population reacted very negatively. Since then, however, Kremlin propaganda has succeeded in changing many views, and in March 2007, according to Levada Center polls, 66 percent of Russians were ready to support a change in the constitution that would allow Putin to be elected for a third term. Only 21 percent were against such a change (and 12 percent had no opinion).[1] There were two reasons behind this evolution. First, for many people, even a stagnant status quo would be a lesser evil than unpredictability. Second, one can detect a growing conviction among the people that they have no impact on the political process, that change at the top means nothing, and that if Putin's successor continues his course, why all the hassle and why change the leader at all?!

What fate may await Putin if he leaves the Kremlin voluntarily? If he were the age of Yeltsin when he left the Kremlin, Putin could retire to his dacha and cultivate his garden, but he is still a young man in political terms and full of energy. Russian politics has no opening for someone who has just stepped down from the most important position in the country, which by comparison makes all other positions of no consequence. Putin as chair of the ruling party? Putin as head of the government? Putin as the chair of Gazprom? Putin as adviser to the new president or chair of the constitutional court? The list could be extended, but why would someone recently a demiurge choose to be the menial of his former menial?

Personalized power makes it almost impossible for a former leader to continue ordinary political activity inside Russia, as the fate of past Soviet and Russian leaders confirms. There is no place for them in politics if politics is subsumed in a single political institution. The problem is exacerbated because the new leader of Russia invariably constructs his legitimacy on the bones of the preceding regime. While this tradition continues, there can be no guarantee that Putin will continue to be an influential figure, let alone the center of power after, say, 2009, when the new team takes control of the Kremlin. He may have a different mission, that of cementing a new tradition by peacefully departing from the Kremlin into everyday life, a tradition begun by Gorbachev and continued by Yeltsin but not yet regarded as normal in Russia. Besides, so far no one ever left the Kremlin at the height of his popularity with mass support. If Putin did, despite the odds, succeed in creating a new pattern by continuing to engage in politics after he left his post, subsequent occupants of the Kremlin would not cling so desperately to the Kremlin battlements when it comes time for them to go. There would be a new and even more important tradition. For this tradition to take root in Russia, however, the "monosubject system" would have to be renounced and independent institutions established where former presidents could continue to engage in politics.

The self-perpetuation of power cannot be reduced to a single scenario. Let us look at other ways in which it might develop. If these alternatives are not used as Putin's rule ends, they may be seen at the next changeover of power. The option most favored by the Russian elite is for the president to remain for a third term. Even if Vladimir Putin agrees to leave the Kremlin in accordance with the constitution, his successor may be tempted to stay on. If he does, the repudiation of electorally legitimized authority will make his power less secure. The leader will be dependent on his entourage, and the more vulnerable he feels, the more likely he will be to consider the use of force. There is, however, no longer any mobilizing ideal like communism that might persuade society to reconcile itself to the dictatorship. The Kremlin's old guard has long been preoccupied with more immediate domestic problems and would hardly be likely to rush to its ruler's defense. A constitutional coup of this kind would make it impossible for such a leader in the Kremlin to have normal diplomatic relations with the Western world. Forming a regime along the lines of Lukashenko's regime in Belarus would leave Russia isolated.

It is also doubtful whether such a development would be supported by the Russian public, which has become used to a certain level of freedom. It would hardly be accepted by a significant portion of the elite that would like closer personal integration with the West. A leader who decided to extend his stay would need to consider his exit strategy for getting out of the Kremlin alive, or staying alive in the Kremlin in the long term. Russian precedent offers little comfort. Putin, no doubt, will have pondered these matters. To imagine that he would stay voluntarily underestimates his understanding of the situation and its ramifications. Still, analyzing how authoritarianism might be reproduced obliges us to consider options that make little sense for the leader himself.

As zero hour, the March 2007 election, approached, rumors were spread assiduously about a "third-term party" within the regime that was said to be trying to force Putin to stay in power, partly by discrediting him in the eyes of the West. Those closest to Putin's allies, like the speaker of the Federation Council, Sergei Mironov, in March–April 2007 continued to call for a change in the constitution to allow the president to stay in power for a third term, which only underscored the growing tensions in the Kremlin's clans and their attempts to preserve the status quo. Such proposals, or rather, such trial balloons, each time rejected by Putin himself, could have been anticipated. The self-perpetuation process needs to keep people in suspense until the very end in order to prevent the incumbent from turning into a lame duck, which would result in the immediate collapse of the presidential "pyramid" built around him. In summer 2007, a few stubborn observers still insisted that Putin would remain in the Kremlin beyond his legitimate term, while a majority of others believed that he will return to the Kremlin in 2012. Under this scenario, his successor would keep the seat warm until the end of his term or would leave even before the end of his term. Vladimir Putin seemed to take delight in feeding speculation about his succession project. Meeting with reporters before the G8 summit in Germany, when asked whether he would run in 2012, he said, " Theoretically it's possible. The constitution does not forbid it. But it's very far away. I have not thought about it."[2] Putin mentioned another idea as well—extending the term of the presidency from four to five or even seven years. That comment was enough to trigger a new round of fevered speculation among the establishment, this time about the "technical" president who would be the loyal placeholder. Putin's intention behind toying with the succession scenarios was anticipated—he was forced to keep the political class constantly busy discussing the options and feeding their hope that he would remain in power to prevent fights from erupting. He still has a rocky time ahead of him and he has to control the Kremlin and the country until the moment he must leave his post. An increasingly anxious mood toward the end of Putin's rule fits the logic of an elected monarchy, which ratchets up the uncertainty as the end of a political cycle approaches.

Theoretically, personalized power in Russia could perpetuate itself through a couple of rather risky scenarios: (1) the president loses control of the political process and a struggle for the throne leads to a fragmentation of the elite; (2) the entourage of the president, dissatisfied both with him and his choice of a successor, decides to go it alone, expels him from the Kremlin, and itself seizes power, legitimizing it in any of a number of ways. Putin's ascent to power was, after all, legitimized by restarting the Chechen war, but it was the need to dominate during a complicated time of political crisis and division of the political class that required a state of emergency to keep the fragmented scene together. A consolidated state machine at the end of Putin's cycle does not need to revert to such drastic ways of guaranteeing its survival. Besides, looking at Putin's entourage, one is hard pressed to identify any likely conspirators or people ready to address the emergency mechanisms needed to secure power. Electoral monarchy, however, with its delegating of administrative and political means to favorites, obliges them to defend their own interests, if need be by overthrowing their patron and abandoning even mock elections. In short, given the current system, we cannot rule out the possibility of

palace revolutions. We may tax our the imagination and continue examining other possible approaches to reproducing
power in the Kremlin, which, if not needed in 2008, might be
taken up during a later changeover in 2016 or 2024. The self-
perpetuation of Kremlin power could give us a chance to
observe the ingenuity of the Kremlin spin doctors and the nov-
elties they devise. But I do not think it is worth our time to
dwell on it. So far Vladimir Putin is in control of the situation
and remains the key Russian political actor, which leads us to
conclude that if current trends continue to March 2008, he will
be able to realize his succession project the way he plans to. In
retrospect, the transfer of power may not prove to have been the
most risky event. The real moment of truth will come when the
new leader and his team start deciding how to respond to the
challenges left by his predecessor.

As of this writing, we do not know the future disposition of
political forces immediately before the presidential elections,
and the outcome of Kremlin infighting is not yet clear.

Putin's September 12, 2007 dismissal of Prime Minister
Mikhail Fradkov and nomination of Viktor Zubkov, a little
known former financial watchdog who worked with Putin in
the 1990s, clearly demonstrates that Putin wants to prove he is
still in charge. His surprising move raises doubts about the man-
ageability of the situation within the Kremlin. The reshuffle suggests that Putin has been struggling to orchestrate a succession
that would guarantee his own influence after the transfer of
power. Turning the reins over to someone else is proving difficult and Zubkov's appointment proves that the Russian system
is able to survive by perpetuating uncertainty and suspense.
Surely this is not Putin's last surprise and Russians will continue to guess about his next move.

The country must carry on holding its breath. That is how the
Russian system works. It will be paralyzed every time a
changeover of power is imminent, until Russia reforms the system of power that generates all this upheaval.

Chapter 8

THE *SILOVIKI* IN POWER

For the first time in Russian history, in the person of Vladimir Putin, an officer from a security ministry, a professional representing the KGB's corporate interests and mentality, has come to formally head the regime. His predecessor in the 1980s, Yuri Andropov, although chair of the KGB, had been appointed by the Communist Party to that position to control the state's lethal political weapon, yet he brought none of the mentality of a secret police officer to the tasks of heading the Communist Party and Supreme Soviet. Until now the civil authorities in Russia, both czarist and Soviet, had kept the army and the security forces well away from the center of decision making and under strict control. Stalin, apprehensive that these forces might become too powerful, subjected them to bloody purges and also monitored their officers through the Communist Party. Under the Soviet system, the security forces were the regime's chained attack dog, called upon to protect it from enemies and used in the settling of their private scores, but no more than that. This policy inevitably developed in the security officers an aggressively conservative mentality and a predilection for repressive methods and undercover manipulation. It also resulted in an acceptance of a subordinate role and knowing their place. It is difficult to imagine members of the security forces readily throwing off the inertia of a defensive mind-set and abandoning repressive habits, voluntarily reprogramming their mental computers to eliminate this attitude. In one respect, however, a number of them have managed to change. Moving out of its subordinate role, Putin's team has shown it can learn to give orders.

The conservatism that has prevailed in Russian politics under Putin, which has shown itself in the centralization of power and its reliance on subordination, is related to the fact that the president is a member of the security community and that the nerve center of his regime is staffed by former colleagues. It would be a mistake, however, to suppose that he and his associates, dubbed the *siloviki*, initiated this trend. The evolution of Russian state power in this direction was not begun by the security forces. Rather, the new role of their representatives is a result of that evolution. The invitation to the *siloviki* to take power was to be expected of an oligarchic–authoritarian regime that was losing confidence in itself and had no other means to guarantee its survival. It would never have occurred to Stalin, Khrushchev, or Brezhnev to groom an army general or a representative of the KGB as his successor. When Yuri Andropov, the former head of the KGB, became the leader of the Communist Party, he made no attempt to bring his subordinates into power with him. A one-party state had no need for such insurance. It never entered Gorbachev's mind either. In fact, he reduced the role of the KGB. Yeltsin was in a more vulnerable position and had to devise new ways of defending his power. Under its first president, the post-Soviet regime three times tottered on the brink of a seizure of power by an alliance of the bureaucracy and *siloviki*. A seizure of power would have happened if Vice President General Alexander Rutskoi and parliamentary speaker Ruslan Khasbulatov (both of whom went from being among Yeltsin's closest allies to his worst enemies) had been victorious in 1993 in the confrontation between the president and the parliament; if Yeltsin's bodyguard, General Alexander Korzhakov, in cahoots with Deputy Prime Minister Oleg Soskovets, had been successful in 1996; or if maverick general

Alexander Lebed, who was third in the first round of the 1996 presidential race, had won or if Yeltsin gave him the resources Lebed had been demanding. Three times Yeltsin averted a leap to power by the military and security officials, but himself handed power to the security forces upon his retirement. It was Yeltsin who, in an attempt to guarantee a peaceful old age for himself and security for his family, handed power to members of a caste he had never trusted and against whose aspirations for power he had defended Russia. Putin's team was called in by Yeltsin's team to safeguard its interests, and it did so, consolidating the undemocratic reflexes of the state authorities but also beginning to realize its own group interest.

We can see from this example that personalized power, even if it starts out on the path of reform, is forced to turn for help to those who are professionally there to protect the regime once the regime becomes vulnerable and tries to guarantee its position and perpetuation (here not dominance). In the process it sacrifices its reform potential. A moment comes when not only the security forces but also the civilians working for such a regime become defensive. Liberal German Gref (Putin's chief economic minister), pragmatist Mikhail Fradkov (Putin's premier), and technocrat Alexei Kudrin (Putin's finance minister) work no less actively to ensure the survival of bureaucratic capitalism.

To what extent might society accept the idea of rule by the security forces? In the 1990s Russia had already flirted with a general. This was the above-mentioned General Alexander Lebed (the commander of the Fourteenth Russian army in Transnistria) at the peak of his popularity in the mid-1990s. He traded his chances in the struggle for power for cooperation with Yeltsin and never again soared in the political firmament. Lebed ended his career as the governor of the Krasnoyarsk region, where he committed many blunders before dying absurdly in a helicopter crash. In Russia a number of other, rather less charismatic, generals tried to become politicians, among them such luminaries of the Chechen war as Vladimir

Shamanov, Gennady Troshev, and Konstantin Pulikovsky. The experiment revealed the generals' inability to govern and cured Russian citizens of any further desire to see army personnel in positions of political power.

Under Putin, Russia conducted a further experiment with itself, this time with members of the special services. Once in power, they extended the scope of the security ministries—the prosecutor's office, the Interior Ministry, the FSB (Federal Security Service), the Tax Department, and other law-enforcement agencies, which moved beyond public or political accountability and close to power. The colleagues Putin brought in, particularly Sergei Ivanov, Igor Sechin, Victor Ivanov, Nikolay Patrushev, Georgi Poltavchenko, Sergei Chemezov, and Victor Cherkesov, rose to highly influential state positions. Security officers close to the president now run the presidential administration, which is a shadow government in Russia. They turn up on the board of directors of the largest state companies. They take initiatives that alter the destiny of Russia. It was the *siloviki* who initiated the attack on and nationalization of Yukos and nudged Russia in the direction of bureaucratic capitalism. It is only natural that they should lobby for increased state expenditure for law enforcement and national security. In 2000–2006 such expenditures rose from nearly $4 billion to $20 billion, and in 2007 the allocation was $25 billion. (Expenditure on the FSB is classified information, but according to the Russian media in 2005 it was increased by 25 percent and continues to increase.) Accordingly, and not without prompting from the security forces, Russia is again becoming a country whose first priority is to defend itself against its enemies, the number of whom, to judge by the Kremlin's actions, is ever increasing.

The invasion of government by the *siloviki* has brought into politics the principles by which they operate, in particular an inclination to resolve matters behind the scenes by applying "tough measures" without moral constraint. Russia's political life has become an arena for trickery and blackmail. However, this situation occurred primarily because such are the tools the

Russian political class needed to defend its interests, for which it has been prepared to adopt the expertise of the security forces. Members of the law enforcement organs have not, perhaps surprisingly, monopolized the process of decision making. There are several reasons for this. The imagination of security officers has proved to be extremely limited, as one can see from the fact that their priorities have been mainly personal enrichment and preservation of the status quo. Fragmentation and rivalry between factions within the *siloviki* camp have played a role. Their ability to govern proved deficient. There was no public enthusiasm for the idea of a military regime. The civil bureaucracy resisted subordination to security officers. Finally, there was the pragmatism of the president, who, despite his security background, had no wish to abdicate power in favor of his colleagues, skillfully balancing them with representatives of other factions.

Gradually a differentiation occurred between those security officers who had been successful in gaining control of property and those who had nothing. The insatiability of the officers in the Kremlin can hardly be to the taste of those intelligence and security officers who failed in the privatization process or who were trying to maintain professional principles. The "Manifesto for the Cheka," issued by one of Putin's colleagues, Victor Cherkesov, director of the federal drug control agency, calling upon members of the FSB to work for the good of the people, can be taken as confirmation that there are some among the *siloviki* who do not take kindly to the vibrant activity of their colleagues who occasionally participate directly in criminal activities. The KGB Savonarolas are unlikely to raise a revolt against the KGB capitalists, but it is significant that capitalism has split the security forces, which in the past were fairly united. In the struggle for property, some law enforcement agencies are openly fighting others: the Interior Ministry (MVD) has been pitched against the FSB, the FSB against the Tax Department, the latter against the prosecutor's office, and so on. Federal and regional security officers confront each other in the battle for the ownership of enterprises, the right to exact tribute from entrepreneurs, and for control of the banks. This battle, particularly in the regions, is conducted openly and is violent.

Corruption and criminal activity by representatives of the Interior Ministry, the FSB, the Tax Department, and the prosecutor's office beggar belief. Security officers smuggle goods worth millions of dollars into Russia, provide cover for criminal gangs, carry out contract killings, and pay for the services of the top bureaucrats and prosecutors to cover up their misdeeds. Here is a typical business enterprise of law enforcement agencies: in 2006 Russian customs officers confiscated $200 million worth of mobile telephones from Motorola, claiming they were counterfeit. A short time later the same telephones were found for sale in the marketplace. Entrepreneurs have been obliged to pay the militia and the FSB money for immunity from such practices, which has consolidated the systemic nature of this corruption and further drawn law enforcement agencies into illegal business dealings.

Eventually the criminally corrupt behavior of the representatives of the *siloviki* has become so out of hand that the president himself has become concerned. Putin felt obliged to call in people loyal to him in St. Petersburg to investigate the most scandalous affairs in Moscow, prominent among which was the case of the Three Whales (Tri Kita) company. This firm was smuggling furniture into Russia under the protection of the security ministries, including the prosecutor's office. The results of the investigation were never made public, which means that the authorities had no desire to get to the bottom of this affair. The authorities are rarely able to pursue investigations into the activities of the security structures to their conclusion for the simple reason that revealing the truth about the criminal activities of the representatives of law enforcement agencies could undermine the mainstay of the regime.

The merging of bureaucratic capitalism with the law enforcement agencies has inevitably led to the degeneration of both. Today's Russian security officers are much better at appropriating property and engaging in business than they are in fighting terrorism or enforcing law and order. The most negative consequence of the rise to power and entry into economic activity of security officers is the strengthening of a lawless state operating on the basis of shadowy rules (*po poniatiyam,* as this manner of governance has been dubbed by Russians). When brought into politics, the security service mentality leads to the acceptance of gangland methods in political and public thinking and behavior, a disregard for the law, a penchant for crushing dissent, morbid suspicion, brutality toward the weak, and servility toward the more powerful.

Representatives of the security officers have revived the almost forgotten method of dealing with problems, which, in the Stalin period, was pithily summarized as, "Get rid of the man and you get rid of the problem." The murder in London of Alexander Litvinenko, a former FSB lieutenant colonel granted asylum and citizenship by the United Kingdom, using radioactive polonium-210, a case in which former Russian FSB officers are accused of complicity by the British Crown prosecutor, plainly demonstrates their new sense of impunity. It would be unwise to underestimate the danger that representatives of the security forces, no longer politically or publicly accountable, will move beyond the redistribution of property and be tempted to resort to terror to achieve their objectives. The *siloviki,* now incorporated in the regime, are perfectly capable of seeking a monopoly of power. The root problem, however, is not the overweening ambition of particular officers, but the mentality of the Russian elite that has brought them to power, uses their methods to protect its interests, and has adopted their ethos. With the direct involvement of security officials, the elite has created a state machine that may prove well adapted to the purposes of a new, and now openly authoritarian, regime acknowledging no limitations.

Chapter 9

OLIGARCHY AS MYTH
AND REALITY

By the end of Boris Yeltsin's first term, a select group of wealthy people close to the Kremlin had appeared. They enjoyed access to the regime and used it for their personal enrichment. The aging patriarch had frittered away his popular support and, if he was to have any prospect of winning the 1996 presidential election, he had no option but to strike a deal with newly emerging Russian big business. Afterward, when he had to repay big business for its support, the moment came when the individuals appointed to manage private property became oligarchs.[1] Among that first group were Boris Berezovsky, Vladimir Gusinsky, Alexander Smolensky, Vladimir Potanin, Mikhail Fridman, Mikhail Khodorkovsky, Vladimir Vinogradov, and Pyotr Aven, who succeeded in establishing close contacts with the Kremlin. The oligarchs were initially created by the state bureaucracy to privatize state property. They were the middlemen employed by high officials to serve their purposes but, being intelligent and skillful, they became rich themselves. The president's failings and weaknesses, and his need for support, made the oligarchs extraordinarily powerful and enabled them to dictate their will to officialdom and the president, becoming a force to be reckoned with. The privatization process of the 1990s had left Russia with an extraordinarily concentrated structure of ownership (one that grew even more concentrated during Putin's presidency). By the end of 2001, it was estimated that 85 percent of the value of sixty-four of the largest privately owned Russian companies, with aggregate sales of $109 billion in 2000, was controlled by just eight shareholder groups. This control implies a level of ownership concentration in excess of those found in Western Europe, the United States, or even South Korea, with its chaebols. The individuals who controlled those groups were dubbed oligarchs.[2]

It was not the oligarchs themselves who felt a sudden urge to govern the country. They were brought together by the technocrats and personally by Russian privatization "czar" Anatoly Chubais, as he created Russian big business by distributing state property to a narrow circle of individuals. The oligarchs would never have become a ruling group if they had not also had links with Yeltsin's biological family (the most famous Russian oligarch, now living in London, Roman Abramovich, even earned the nickname "moneybox" from Yeltsin's relatives). Yeltsin's younger daughter, Tatiana Diachenko, was a gift for the oligarchs: she served as a channel through which they could influence the president or his entourage. In this way, she helped to hasten, perhaps unwittingly, the merging of business with the state authorities at the top, and this blending of power and business spread further to other levels of the system. Russian oligarchic capitalism came into being through the joint efforts of the technocrats, Yeltsin's family, and big business.

The Russian oligarchy became a political reality when a representative of big business, Vladimir Potanin, was appointed first deputy prime minister and Boris Berezovsky was made deputy secretary of the Security Council. These appointments legitimized interference by big business in the affairs of state. Having ensured Yeltsin's victory in the election, the oligarchs made the bureaucrats their servants. For the first time in Russian history, the all-powerful bureaucracy went down in defeat; the oligarchs were, however, unable to stabilize the system or to ensure their own continuity as a ruling class. In 1996–1997 they fell out with one another and began fighting among themselves for economic resources, dragging the discredited representatives of the state into their conflict.

Some of the oligarchs had introduced successful innovations. For example, Khodorkovsky created the most efficient oil company in Russia, and Gusinsky formed a modern and, for Russia, wholly original television service. In the process they also used their leverage with the Kremlin and state money or tax-evasion schemes. The other oligarchs, however, Berezovsky, Smolensky, and Abramovich, spent most of their time thinking of ways to extract money from the state and the populace at large.

The meteoric rise of the oligarchs to political influence was possible only because Yeltsin's leadership was in a state of paralysis and he was no longer able to rally the elite or rely on society as a whole. With the arrival of a new and popular leader who was capable of governing, the ruling team did not need the support of the oligarchs. The demise of Berezovsky and Gusinsky, who had hoped to continue to exert their considerable influence on Yeltsin's successor, was inevitable. Khodorkovsky was fated to follow them, not only because he was excessively independent as a businessman and the owner of the juiciest chunk of property, not only because he had succeeded in using parliament and other state organs to pursue his interests, but also because he could not conceal his political ambitions.

The epoch of relations between the new president and the oligarchs was determined less by Putin's personal sympathies or antipathies than by the emergence of a personalized regime backed both by the population and the state apparatus. Not even the classic oligarchies of 1960s Latin America managed to become completely self-sufficient and omnipotent, and they invariably lost their influence when a leader allied himself with the bureaucracy and army or appealed to the population. In Chile the oligarchs even organized a coup to place their appointee in the presidency, but Pinochet promptly shook off their guardianship, demonstrating that dictatorship is incompatible with an oligarchic state. Oligarchs have never succeeded in establishing viable regimes because they have never managed to see beyond their vested interests.

Big business in modern Russia never developed a corporate interest that it could defend collectively. The Russian Union of Industrialists and Entrepreneurs (RUIE), the so-called trade union of big business, failed to become a channel through which the oligarchs could influence state authorities, and they continue to pursue their aims through individual lobbying and separate deals with the state. What befell the oligarchs under Putin shows that oligarchs in Russia cannot aspire to become a ruling class. The regime may exploit big business, and may at times share power with the oligarchs, but its dependency is purely temporary. Once it has reestablished itself and gained the support of other forces, the master of the Kremlin can shake off their influence.

During the past sixteen years, relations between the regime and big business in Russia have been based on a variety of models. In the early years of Yeltsin's presidency, big business, which was just beginning to find its feet, was used by the regime to crush the "red" directors of enterprises. During Yeltsin's second presidency, it was big business that dominated politics. When Putin came to power, he began a cautious policy of keeping business and the authority of the state "equidistant," that is, easing big business out of the Kremlin. For a time it seemed the authorities would stop at a model of corporatism, allowing the institutions representing big business (RUIE and the Chamber of Commerce and Industry, headed by former premier Yevgeny Primakov) to grow stronger and then to enter into dialogue with them. Soon, however, it became clear that the Kremlin had chosen a different model: unconditional surrender of capital to the state.

The removal of Yeltsin's oligarchs did not leave a vacuum. In parallel with the persecution of Khodorkovsky and the state's subjugation of the rest of big business came the formation of the bureaucrat–oligarchs. The director of Gazprom, Alexei

Miller, members of the ruling team already mentioned (Dmitri Medvedev, Sergei Ivanov, Vladislav Surkov, and the rest) as well as the rest of the high officials who sit on the boards of the largest companies, represent a new version of the Russian oligarchy. Let me demonstrate with a few examples of how power and business merge in Russia: Dmitri Medvedev, a first deputy premier, is chair of the board of directors of Gazprom; Sergei Ivanov, a first deputy premier, is chair of the board of directors of the United Aviation Building Corporation; Sergei Naryshkin, a deputy premier, is chair of the board of directors of First Channel TV; Victor Christenko, the minister of industry and energy, is chair of the board of directors of Transneft; Alexei Gordeev, the minister of agriculture, is chair of the board of directors of Rosagroleasing; Anatoly Serdyukov, the defense minister, is chair of the board of directors of Chimprom; German Gref, the minister of economic development and trade, is chair of the board of Russia Venture Company; Igor Levitin, the transport minister, is chair of the board of directors of Sheremetievo International Airport; Sergei Sobyanin, the head of the presidential administration, is chair of the board of directors of TVAL; Igor Sechin, the deputy head of the presidential administration, is the chair of the board of directors of Rosneft; Victor Ivanov, assistant to the president, is chair of the board of directors of Almaz-Antei and Aeroflot; Alexander Zhukov, a deputy premier, is chair of the board of directors of the Russian railroad; and Sergei Prichodko, assistant to the president, is chair of the board of directors of the Tactical Missile Weapons company. This is the team that rules Russia, and this is how it rules Russian property. If we take into account only the capitalization of Gazprom (which is worth $235.5 billion), Rosneft (worth $94 billion), and the Russian railroads (worth $50 billion), we may have some estimate of the wealth these people control.[3] The old Yeltsin oligarchy looks like a group of dilettantes in comparison to the new cohort of bureaucrat–oligarchs.

Officialdom has been seeking less risky and more effective ways of exercising control over property by directly combining the running of the country and the managing of corporations. The leaders of the mammoth monopolies, like Sergei Chemezov, the director of Rosoboronexport, which has monopolized the sale of arms, are likewise bureaucrat–oligarchs who manage their enterprises in the interests of the ruling team. Superficially the arrangement seems similar to the creation of the South Korean chaebols, which are also an example of the intertwined interests of the state and business. The purpose of the chaebols, however, was to focus resources and state support in order to create an economic upsurge. In Russia, the fusion of the state and business under Putin reflects rather the Kremlin's desire to retain direct control over property. There is no evidence that its control has been particularly stimulating for the economy. On the contrary, Russian officials have been learning from the example of Berezovsky, who grew rich not from privatization but from installing his own people in state enterprises and controlling financial flows.

Where does this leave Potanin, Fridman, Aven, Deripaska, and the other oligarchs of the Yeltsin era? They found themselves in a tricky situation. On the one hand, as William Thompson has rightly pointed out, "The oligarchs, after all, had an interest in Putin's state-building project. Having acquired vast fortunes under Yeltsin largely as a result of their success in exploiting the state's weakness, they had much to gain from Putin's drive to rebuild the state."[4] For the oligarchs, rebuilding the state meant more security and guarantees for business. On the other hand, a captain of big business who is not embedded in the Kremlin's unofficial networks is a foreign body. For all his intrigues and protestations of loyalty, he is inimical to the system because he has economic clout and, not being beholden to the president for his company's wealth, may at any moment become an independent player. He may ignore the laws and decisions of the president or officialdom. He may try to subordinate the Duma, like Khodorkovsky did. He may corrupt authorities in his own interests rather than those of the Kremlin. He is a potential threat for the personalized regime, and given the present Russian system, doomed. The last surviving oligarchs of the Yeltsin era have embedded themselves in the structures of bureaucratic capitalism through individual deals. One can only guess what services they now render to the authorities for the privilege of being left in peace. For all that, they can be crushed at any time and they definitely understand this. In other words, property in Russia at the beginning of the twenty-first century remains a gift of the state, symbolized by the leader and his team, just as it has been throughout Russian history. Still, it is a gift that is given under very strict conditions, one of which is unconditional loyalty to the regime and its leader. That loyalty has nothing to do with economic laws. Thus, Russian big business, old and new, is eager to have behind it the support of the state and its guarantee of property rights, but at the same time it has to understand that the state operates on the basis of informal rules and will never give big business a guarantee of unconditional security.

In an attempt to stay afloat, the old oligarchs have sought shelter behind major international companies. Thus TNK created a joint oil holding company with BP, and Lukoil struck a deal with ConocoPhillips. Alternatively, they exploit the political resources of Yeltsin's family, like Oleg Deripaska, representative of the younger generation of oligarchs. The political regime, however, demands the total subjugation of business. This does not necessarily mean that Fridman or Deripaska will suffer the same fate as Khodorkovsky. The Yukos affair showed the Kremlin how negative the consequences can be of mounting a frontal assault on a major corporation, especially one with an insurance policy in the West. At the same time, the Yukos affair demonstrated that, if it sees fit to destroy an oligarch, the Kremlin will stop at nothing. Those remaining big businessmen who remember the license of the Yeltsin years are an endangered species. They must dream at night of selling everything and getting out of Russia. There is little doubt that they long to follow the example of Roman Abramovich, now based in London, who sold Sibneft to the state at a profit and received guarantees of immunity. Even living in London, however, Abramovich is obliged to run errands for the Kremlin. There is ultimately no escape from its clutches. Only the president can decide who may retire from the post of oligarch and when. One must expect that the moment will come when the eyes of the bureaucrats will fall on Potanin's Norilsk Nickel or on Deripaska's aluminum factories, and they will exclaim, "What an outrage that so much wealth should belong to someone other than us!"

The crucial question is whether the new generation of bureaucrat–oligarchs will manage business more effectively than did its previous owners. Hardly. The majority of the new manager–proprietors tend only to extract profit for themselves, with no consideration of the needs of the business. The nonaccountability of the regime engenders nonaccountability in business, which is now linked to it. The new bureaucrat–oligarchs will be less effective than their predecessors, but not because they are prey to avarice. The old ones were no angels in that respect. The instability of property relations, the unpredictability of the centralized state, and, finally, the provenance and inexperience of bureaucrat–oligarchs do not bode well for their entrepreneurial endeavors.

Will relations between the president and the bureaucrat–oligarchs be cloudless? Again, the answer has to be no. The bureaucracy always tries to stifle the leader in its embraces, and a bureaucracy bolstered by control over property will be doubly threatening. The leader will be able to respond to this in one of two ways: either by eradicating the most corrupt and influential oligarchic officials when they become too powerful or by making them accountable to the public and to independent institutions. Putin has been in no position to choose either of those options. Even if he sees the threat from the immensely wealthy bureaucratic corporation that he himself has created, it is now too late for him to reform it. That said, he is in danger of being thrown off the train whenever the bureaucratic caste decides it no longer has a use for him.

The next question is, what will Putin's successor do with these property-controlling bureaucrats who have privatized the state and have squeezed out the old oligarchs? He cannot but understand the danger this powerful group poses for him. Inaction is not an option. If he does nothing, the bureaucratic corporation—which controls the power of the state, the flow of information, and property—will either domesticate him or devour him.

Chapter 10

LIBERAL TECHNOCRATS AS AN ADORNMENT OF THE STATE

The liberal technocrats in Russia deserve separate consideration. These are free marketers who consent to work within a less-than-democratic, or even blatantly undemocratic, system under the direct patronage of the leader. They are to be found in many countries, from Saudi Arabia to China, and from Singapore to Argentina. In most cases they serve a useful purpose, obstructing both the expansion of the bureaucracy and populist policies. In a transitional society they play a crucial role as the only group capable, if supported by the leader, of carrying out painful reforms without having to worry about their popularity or political future. Their role is constructive, however, only if there are other political forces with a developed liberal democratic sensibility to mitigate the technocrats' social insensitivity and excessive managerial zeal. Technocrats can make for a social breakthrough, but they can also be destructive. The success of the reforms of Leszek Balcerowicz in Poland and Václav Klaus in the Czech Republic was due to the fact that the local technocrats were operating in societies with powerful democratic movements. Technocrats without redeeming democratic support operate equally well in the interests of authoritarianism or oligarchy. In Chile, the Chicago Boys were a mere tool of the oligarchy. They played a crucial role in the coup that brought

Pinochet to power, only then to work efficiently under his orders and against the oligarchy.

In post-Soviet Russia the technocrats (the most prominent being Yegor Gaidar and Anatoly Chubais), faced with the weakness of the democratic movement, became politicians. They not only created a free market system, but also, as Democratic Party Yabloko's leader Grigory Yavlinsky rightly notes, facilitated the development of oligarchic capitalism.[1] In 1996–1997 the technocrats, under the leadership of Anatoly Chubais, who, with Yeltsin ailing, was the unofficial ruler of Russia for a time, could have played a different historical role. The popular governor of Nizhni Novgorod, Boris Nemtsov, had been invited by Yeltsin to join the government and, with a popularity rating in 1997 of nearly 40 percent, could have eased the transformation of the technocrats into a liberal democratic force capable of changing the rules imposed by the bureaucracy. The technocrats failed to reform either the regime or themselves. The role of the technocrats under Yeltsin has yet to be thoroughly researched. One question to be answered is how far they facilitated reform and how far they assisted in the consolidation of personalized power under the guise of liberalism. So far, the Russian experience shows strong evidence that the first generation of Russian technocrats has been much more effective in undermining, albeit often unconsciously or unwittingly, liberal democracy than in building it.

During Putin's presidency the technocrats' scope and potential have been limited by the regime's priority of maintaining the status quo. Gref, Kudrin, Zhukov, Mikhail Dmitriev, Arkady Dvorkovich, and other technocrats in the Putin government have found it far more difficult to promote reforms, understanding that reforms might undermine the stability of the system and regime they have been working for. Their room for maneuver has certainly been less than that enjoyed by the Gaidar team in the first years of Yeltsin's presidency, or of Anatoly Chubais and Boris Nemtsov in its final stages, if only because the current Russian system has evolved in a way that rules out reforms that might introduce any element of competitiveness. The new echelon of technocrats must be aware of that. One occasionally has the impression that they are perfectly content to be the liberal adornment of an illiberal, undemocratic regime. The sole achievement of the government liberals has been their success in maintaining financial discipline, but, in the run-up to the elections in 2007–2008, even that achievement might become a victim of the regime's populism.

Today there are two groups of interlinked technocrats: those within the government and those within the party framework of the Union of Right Forces. I have already expressed my doubts about the reform potential of the government technocrats. As regards those in the Union of Right Forces, they are evidently technocrats seeking a political niche that will enable them to survive without being wholly in the president's pocket. The origins of the Union of Right Forces as a free-market party favoring cooperation with the regime make it doubtful whether it has any longer-term, independent prospects. After a purging of the political scene that has removed not only opposition movements but also those that showed signs of vacillation, the Union of Right Forces has found itself obliged to swear allegiance to the Kremlin in order to continue in legal politics. If it strays from the rules laid down by the Kremlin, the Union risks expulsion from official politics. That is something the liberal technocrats are keen to avoid.

At the earlier stages of Putin's presidency, the Union of Right Forces could no longer afford to criticize the regime, although for some time its leaders and ideologists had allowed themselves mutterings of discontent, which had been the only way to retain credibility. The increasing rigor of the regime forced them to seek a compromise and, one cannot help but wonder whether heading into the parliamentary elections of December 2007, their leaders (official leader Nikita Belych and unofficial leader Anatoly Chubais) signed up on the side of the Kremlin. The evolution of that party from mild and hesitant grudges and disagreements with the Kremlin policy to support of the regime merely confirms that it cannot emerge from the Kremlin's shadow. Another reason is that the unofficial leader of the Union of Right Forces, Anatoly Chubais, is the chair of the monopolist RAO UES (which manages the Russian electricity grid). He is not only the godfather of the Russian oligarchy, but also a pillar of the ruling bureaucratic corporation, which includes, in various capacities, all the other technocrats who continue to serve the regime. The fact that, during the run-up to the regional and parliamentary elections in 2006–2007, leaders of the Union of Right Forces were constantly seen on television, where news output is agreed upon with the Kremlin, made it abundantly clear that the Union of Right Forces had surrendered to the regime and in return was being allowed to participate in public politics. In fact, its leaders could not behave differently because its membership base and supporters are mostly loyal to the authorities. In any case, technocrats have agreed, some knowingly and some perhaps not, to act as a smokescreen for the current system as they try to remain in politics. Liberals like Boris Nemtsov who, for some reason remains in the leadership of the Union of Right Forces and continues to oppose the Kremlin, are in the minority, and sooner or later they will be forced into submission or will have to leave the Union of Right Forces.

With the crackdown on dissent, the technocrats have given up sitting on the fence and will most likely end up either loyal to the Kremlin lapdog party or as one of the semi-opposition factions within the chameleon-like governing party. When this occurs it will no longer be possible to doubt that the presence of technocrats with their liberal phraseology on the Russian political scene—both in the government and outside it, serving an illiberal regime—is one of the reasons there is no real liberal movement in Russia, and why bringing together liberalism and democracy has proved so difficult.

A revival of liberalism as an ideology, and of liberal democracy as a political movement, is impossible without a proper understanding of the part played by the technocrats' "liberalism." It may well be that in the future some of the technocrats will join a new democratic movement, but only if they leave the Union of Right Forces, which historically has proved to be one of several "parties of power" despite the fact that it includes a faction of opposition to the regime. Collaboration between the opposition-minded members of the Union of Right Forces and Yabloko in the Moscow Duma elections in 2005, showed that a united front of liberals and democrats is theoretically possible. But the chances of forming a viable liberal–democratic movement in Russia that includes the technocrats, will be nil if the process is again presided over by the Kremlin. Liberalism will have no prospects if those who claim to be its adherents once more try to argue that democracy is a hindrance, or that it will be the next stage after capitalism is established. Despite the complexity of the link between liberals and democrats, neglecting democracy, as the 1990s showed, causes liberalism to degenerate.

Chapter 11

THE TRIUMPH OF BUREAUCRATIC CAPITALISM

The economy Putin is leaving to Russia looks impressive and might be the envy of previous Russian and Soviet leaders. The gross domestic product has risen during his presidency from $200 billion in 1999 to $920 billion in 2006 (in current dollars); gold and currency reserves have risen from $12.7 billion in 1999 to $303.86 billion in February 2007. The reserves of the stabilization fund, into which oil revenues are deposited, have reached $70 billion. In 2006 the trade proficit was more than $120 billion, and the budget proficit is 7.5 percent of the gross domestic product. The Russian economy is now the twelfth largest in the world.[1] In macroeconomic terms, as Anders Aslund argues, Russia "is very strong": no G7 country can compete with Russia in fiscal responsibility.[2] Although economic growth has been slowing since 2005 (from 10 percent in 2000 to 6.8 percent in 2006), it still looks fairly impressive (economic growth in the first half of 2007 amounted to 7.8 percent).[3] A boom is continuing, not only in the extractive sectors of the economy but also in construction, trade, and the service and banking sectors. Russian business has shown that it is able to organize large-scale production, successfully competing against international corporations. Russia, which in the 1990s had to beg humbly for loans, repaid its debt to the Paris Club ahead of schedule. The number of major businessmen in Russia is increasing more than twice as fast as in the United States. In 2005 the number of dollar millionaires in Russia grew by 17.4 percent compared to a 6 percent increase in the United States.

However, as with everything else in Russia, the economy has a false bottom. The causes of the economy's success give no grounds for optimism, mainly because the success is due to high oil prices and has been achieved partially by sectors protected from foreign competition. A collapse of the oil price could plunge the Russian economy into a recession, and people remember what a fall in the oil price means. Gaidar has emphasized that the sixfold decrease in the oil price in 1986 led to the collapse of the USSR, and the twofold fall in 1998 caused a financial crisis that almost finished off a barely breathing Russian economy.[4] The government technocrats try to reassure the public that the economy would survive even if the oil price fell to $25 a barrel, but then they also claimed that the Russian economy was stable in 1998, immediately before its collapse.

Independent Russian economists, like Andrei Illarionov, Putin's former economic adviser, constantly warn that current growth is not based on solid foundations. Many predict an inevitable devaluation of the ruble, which may result in another crisis. They warn that wages and incomes in Russia have been growing systematically faster than productivity. As a result, the share of consumption in GDP has increased at the expense of investment (gross investment amounts to no more than 20 percent of GDP).[5]

There are other causes for concern. The government cannot bring inflation down below 10 percent, and the banking system is not fulfilling its role as mediator: financial flows in the raw materials sector are not being transmitted to other sectors. The banks siphon money off into the shadows, and they service rentiers living off their dividends and sometimes even criminal gangs. The government has no idea what to do about the negative impact of the flood of petrodollars, evident primarily in a strengthening of the ruble that stimulates imports and hits Russian industry.[6] Russia has managed to pay off its national debt (in 2006 it amounted to $48.1 billion), but the corporate debt of Russian companies has risen from $30 billion in 1998 to $159.5 billion in 2006 (that amounts to 16.2 percent of GDP) and the corporate debt of Russian banks in 2006 has increased twofold, amounting to $100 billion. Russia's foreign trade accounts for 45 percent of GDP (in China this indicator is closer to 70 percent), which warns us that the Russian economy is cut off from the rest of the world and that its goods are not competitive.

Russian investors prefer to invest abroad. The number and the scale of deals in which Russian companies acquire assets abroad are quite amazing. This trend is now called "the export of capital." In 2006 investments in the Russian economy amounted to $150 billion and Russian "export of capital" reached $140 billion (according to unofficial sources, more than $60 billion has been transferred from Russia to Britain in the past six years). The names of the people responsible for Russian "export of capital" can be found on the Forbes "rich list." In 2006 foreign direct investments (FDI) into the Russian economy amounted to $31 billion (two and a half times more than in 2005). Still, this constituted only 3 percent of GDP, whereas a good proportion should be 5 to 6 percent, which would give the economy a boost. In 2005 up to 90 percent of FDI was directed into the energy-related areas and in 2006, 60 to 70 percent. (However, the plunging of investments in the commodity areas was a result not of diversification of the economy but of growing risks). Capital inflow in the first half of 2007 amounted to a record-breaking $67 billion (capital inflow for the first half of 2006 was a respectable $42 billion), but most of it was made up of loans and speculative operations.

The World Economic Forum confirmed that in 2006 Russia had fallen from 62nd to 72nd place in its rating for the level of use of information technology. Analyzing the difference between China and India on the one hand, and Russia and Brazil on the other, the observers pointed to the fact that "the former are competing with the West for 'intellectual capital' by seeking to build up top-notch universities, investing in high value-added and technologically intensive industries. Russia and Brazil are benefiting from high commodity prices but are not attempting to invest their windfall in long-term economic development." At the beginning of 2007 Yegor Gaidar maintained that Russia has to deal with two parallel trends: the gradual depletion of the state's revenue sources and increasing social obligations, which may bring a crisis as early as 2015.[7]

That proves that the Kremlin team has no ground for complacency. Indeed, unresolved issues are accumulating for which no one in the Kremlin has a solution. How can Russian business be stimulated? What strategy should be adopted for economic development? How should Russia insure itself against a fall in the price of oil?

There is no more argument about what economic model—dirigiste, liberal, or populist—is developing in Russia. Putin's team has chosen dirigisme, and during his presidency a bureaucratic capitalism has been established that serves the interests of the bureaucratic corporation. The share of the private sector in Russia's gross domestic product shrank from 70 percent in 2004 to 65 percent in 2005 and continues to fall.[8] In 2004–2006 the state's share of the capitalization of the securities market increased by one and a half times to 30 percent of the total, amounting to $190 billion. The state, in the form of the bureaucracy, has not only become an aggressive player in the economy but is also the regulator deciding the rules, which it naturally sets in its own favor. This undermines market principles. The predominance in the Russian economy of "sharks"—state- or partially state-controlled financial and industrial corporations—dents the prospects of small and medium businesses. There are only six small businesses per one thousand of the population, against no fewer than thirty in the European Union. Some 15 million people, about 20 percent of the workforce, are employed in this sector of the economy. That is between three and three and a half times less than the European level. Small- and medium-sized businesses account for only 13 percent of Russia's GDP, which reflects the business atmosphere in the country. Monopolization by sharks rules out diversification of the economy, which requires an abundance of small- and medium-sized fish.

It is surprising that these problems appear not to disturb in the slightest the majority of economic analysts—Russian or Western—who have been in a state of euphoria over the success of the Russian economy for several years now. They have some serious arguments to support their optimism. Dividends are increasing, economic growth continues, initial public offerings (IPOs) are bringing billions of dollars to Russian companies. The total is expected to be $30 billion in 2007, twice as much as in 2006. It might seem that in Russia the economy and politics are quite separate areas, functioning independently of one another, and indeed, for the time being, the negative processes in politics are not preventing people from making money. The moment is approaching, however, when inefficient government will inevitably take its toll in a highly destructive manner—not least on the reputation of optimistic economic analysts.

There is, of course, a logic in the fact that a monopoly of political power in Russia is accompanied by state monopolism in the economy. The tradition of the regime's swallowing property has again prevailed, which testifies to the fact that a personalized regime never tolerates competition in any sphere and seeks absolute control over its environment, even if it damages economic efficiency. I am not by any means saying that all state expansion is a bad thing. We are looking here at intervention in the economy by a particular kind of state, one that does not respect the rule of law and operates on the basis of slippery, unofficial rules. Even these rules the state does not observe consistently. The expansion of a state not based on the rule of law makes corruption inevitable and clear principles inoperable, driving business into a gray area. In fact, in the case of Russia, we are dealing with a bureaucratic corporation that privatized the state structure and through it controls the economy. Ironically, the collapse of communism has allowed the bureaucratic apparatus to use state power in its interests more effectively. Privatization of the state, which is the key economic regulator, does not leave any room for observing property rights or economic laws. No amount of economic reform can stimulate business activity while the state is the servant of the bureaucratic corporation and refuses to operate in a competitive environment.

One of the reasons given by the ruling elite for expanding the state's role in the economy is that Russia needs to create mega-companies capable of competing successfully in world markets, or "national champion companies," as they are called. The elite also considers it a matter of prestige to create gigantic companies in order to confirm Russia's claim to a global role. The creation of national champion companies is proceeding apace, with Gazprom and Rosneft swallowing smaller companies, Aeroflot buying up regional airlines, and companies that design and construct aircraft (Sukhoy, Mig, Irkut, Tupolev, and Ilyushin) merging. Rosoboronexport is monopolizing the arms trade, Transneft is preparing to merge with Transnefteprodukt in the oil industry, and so on. This trend toward creating mega-companies is to be observed also in China, India, and Brazil. There is clearly a pattern here that suggests that countries trying to make a breakthrough create gigantic companies of this kind that can attract capital and technology. Gazprom plays almost the same role in the Russian economy as Tata Group does in India, where its profits amount to almost 2.6 percent of GDP. Experience has shown, however, that gigantic companies supported by the state limit competition and lead to stagnation of the economy. India is managing to prevent this, but in Russia the giant companies controlled by the bureaucracy are holding back economic growth.

The centralization of the economy also partially results from a simplistic understanding of how innovation arises. It is widely believed in Russia that only large companies can make break-throughs in innovation. In reality, as research by the World Bank has found, innovation comes to a significant extent from small businesses operating in a competitive environment. By delegating economic powers to provincial authorities, China has achieved a dramatic improvement in its business climate and in innovation. The centralization of power in Russia, however, and the regime's support for its megacompanies, is leading to stagnation and a preoccupation on the part of economic players with rent-seeking behavior.

While the state is busy reestablishing itself in the economy, no one thinks about reform. This lack of reform effort confirms that a centralized regime is incapable of creating a dynamic and diversified post-industrial economy. Its primary concern is to safeguard its own interests through a pact between the authorities and a section of big business loyal to the regime. Anything threatening that—competition, the inalienability of private property, open court hearings, the transparency of decision making, business ethics, or freedom of the press—must be restricted. Such restriction shuts off the air supply that would enable a normal market to develop. Personalized power, as it ponders ways of surviving beyond 2008, is most certainly not willing to introduce reforms that might cause instability in the run-up to the elections. The price of oil is also at work, enabling the regime to relax and forget reform. Reforms are introduced only in response to a crisis, not when petrodollars are raining down from the skies and you can live, as in the Soviet era, with subsidized consumption.

The functioning of the economy under direct or indirect state control is entirely predictable. "Our state is currently inefficient, and consequently so are the overwhelming majority of state companies," the minister of economic development, German Gref, once admitted.[9] The inefficiency of Russian bureaucratic capitalism is widely acknowledged. "The economy is now at the limit for developing under the existing model," admitted Alexander Shokhin, the president of the Russian Union of

Industrialists and Entrepreneurs. Despite the optimism of the regime as it delightedly counts its petrodollars, an investment famine is increasingly evident. In 2006 the share of Russian banks in investment finance was 5.6 percent. Instead of expanding and investing, private companies are putting their shares on the market because they fear nationalization or a hostile takeover by the financial and industrial groups close to the regime. From 1999 to 2005 both external and internal factors favored economic growth, but it gradually became evident that the resources for extensive growth were nearly exhausted and that the capacity inherited from the Soviet period could not allow the economy to advance further.[10] Business activity is beginning to falter. "We are waiting to see how the saga of the 2008 elections ends and what will happen after the changeover of power," people in Russian business say. Modernization of the entire economic system is needed, something that the bureaucratic state has been unable to deliver, and private business is in no hurry to invest in modernization owing to uncertainty about the future.

Forecasts are being downgraded. The technocrats within the government admit they are unlikely to get inflation down to 2 to 4 percent before 2010, which would allow interest rates to fall to a level where enterprises could borrow to invest. In practice this means that Russians are unlikely to see investment-driven growth and that the economy will continue to function on the basis of consumer demand. Inflation, however, is already reining in this consumer demand, which indicates that the economy is gradually losing its engines of growth and has nothing to replace them with.

These obvious signs of stagnation fail to cool the optimism of the supporters of dirigisme. In search of sustaining arguments, they like to refer to the success of state capitalism in East Asia and China. Perhaps they do not realize that they are calling for Russia to continue along the path that the Asian Tigers abandoned after their model led to crisis. Russia's supporters of a dirigiste economy also prefer to ignore the fact that China's

11 percent economic growth rate is due not to the state sector but primarily to the private sector and low labor costs. China's economic success also results from a low level of social development and the fact that the state does not concern itself with social welfare. If it tries to imitate the Chinese scenario, Russia will risk not only sliding back to the level of a pre-industrial society, but also of failing to insure against upheavals. By giving the bureaucracy a free rein in the economy, the Kremlin has reverted to a point the world has left behind, with the exception of underdeveloped countries, most of which are dependent on the export of raw materials.

It is perfectly true that when Charles de Gaulle, whom some Russian supporters of state capitalism like to mention, came to power, he increased state intervention in the economy. The president of France had his representatives in every ministry and in every province, but they were there to promote reform, not to maintain the status quo, and quite certainly none of them was engaged in a personal "redistribution of economic resources." No less relevant is the fact that French dirigisme was being implemented in the context of an industrial economy.

The Russian bureaucracy, while regaining control of oil, which is the main source of its revenues, does not overlook other natural resources and sectors of the economy in its efforts to get its hands on successful private companies. The regime instills in the minds of people the notion that Yeltsin's privatization was unfair, which indeed it was, but it does so not in order to encourage respect for the concept of hard-earned private property. The ruling elite is preparing public opinion for renationalization, probably selective and with a further redistribution of property. We cannot, however, rule out the possibility that, after the changeover of power in the Kremlin, at least some of today's bureaucrat–oligarchs might be forced out of their positions as managers and heads of the boards of companies, to be replaced by the members of the new ruling team. The old guard is aware of the looming threat and will most likely attempt to convert its current positions into property. A number of bureaucrat–oligarchs might privatize their mega-companies where they sit on boards, trying to get their hands on real money. Lots of it. Accordingly, a new kind of privatization could be expected, one that will create a new generation of billionaires. The new beneficiaries of privatization are unlikely to develop their own businesses since theirs is the psychology of a parasitic class. There is no certainty that the new round of privatization will be seen as fair, and it is unlikely to be the last as property in Russia continues to change hands. Yet, controlling the capital flows of the state companies through affiliated private structures will remain the preferred means of survival for the Russian elite, which means that bureaucratic capitalism will remain the key economic model, unless the system is restructured.

The expansion of the Russian state's role in the economy raises a number of questions. Society loses out from the transition to bureaucratic capitalism, not least because this expansion of the state's activities is funded by ordinary taxpayers. In order to buy out Yuganskneftegaz and Sibneft, the government had to dip not only into the exchequer, but also to borrow money abroad. These debts will be repaid by Russia's citizens. Society loses out also because state companies pay less tax to the treasury and are less efficient managers of property than private companies. It is clear enough who is losing, but it seems reasonable to ask who is gaining. After Ukrainian metallurgy giant Krivorozhstal was privatized by India's Mittal Steel group, the Ukrainian budget received a bonus of $4.8 billion. Russia, in contrast, paid out $13 billion for Sibneft, and it is unclear to whom the money was paid. This raises further questions, this time about the legitimacy of Russian nationalization (and privatization as well) and whose interests it serves. There is more. Incapable of handling its growing obligations, the state hands over its resources to be managed by middlemen, who turn out to be exactly the same bureaucrats or people from their entourage or members of their families. As a result, the ownership of property becomes entirely nontransparent. In formal terms it is owned by the state, but the revenues and control over cash flows are in private hands.

Let us not, however, unduly dismay the Western investor with this description of bureaucratic capitalism. He has a place in the Russian market, and still would even if the entire economy were suddenly to be taken under state control. Russia needs the West, not only because bureaucratic capitalism needs financing and modern technology. The Kremlin needs the West to enhance the status of the ruling team and to ensure international acceptance of Russia's merging of the regime and property. Western investors should, however, keep their appetites within bounds. The Kremlin is already grumbling about such participation of Western capital in the Russian economy as the marriage of Lukoil and ConocoPhillips, which until recently was regarded as more or less acceptable. The authorities will try to further reduce opportunities for Western capital to influence the management of state companies. The main problem for Western investors, however, is less the reduction of opportunities than the question of how far the Russian state will follow its own rules. At this point we have some bad news for Western business people: Russia develops in cycles, and the end of each cycle brings a change of the rules, although they can, of course, be changed several times, even within a cycle.

The Kremlin has changed its mind more than once about which strategically important companies Western investors are barred from investing in. Decisions have been changed and postponed many times regarding the privatization of the Svyazinvest telecommunications monopoly. When operating within the framework of bureaucratic capitalism, the regime prefers to keep the rules vague so that they will be open to a variety of interpretations. Legislation itself always provides the scope for revising agreements with a Western partner, so there is never any certainty that a particular company will not repeat the fate of Sibir Energy, seized by Sibneft, which has in turn been absorbed by the state-owned Rosneft, or the history of Shell, Mitsui, and Mitsubishi, whom the Kremlin forced to sell their shares in the lucrative Sakhalin-2 project, or the experience of BP-TNK, which under pressure from the Kremlin had to sell its stake in Kovykta gas field to Gazprom.

In the 1990s the state and Russian big business had an interest in attracting foreign investment, both because of a lack of resources of their own and in order to establish the free market nature of the Russian economy. Now, however, the Russian elite faces a dilemma. The operations of foreign companies may reduce the dividends produced by Russian business, and the bureaucrat–oligarchs find it more difficult to help themselves to dividends under the watchful eyes of foreign investors. It is also the case that they no longer need Western investment as desperately as they did in the 1990s. But at the same time, the Russian elite and Russian business continue to need the West not only for investment purposes, but also to become integrated into the global economy, which, they feel, is the only way to prosper.

The number of Western politicians and influential personalities in the top echelons of Russian companies continues to grow. Among these is Lord George Robertson, a former Labour cabinet minister and Secretary-General of NATO, who is deputy chairman of the board of directors of TNK. Brian Gilbertson, the former boss of BHP Billiton and Vedanta Resources, took up the reins at Siberia-Urals Aluminum (SUAL).[11] The Russian elite continues its search for highly influential Westerners to become the managers and advisers of Russian firms, attempting to create its own lobby in the West, and this is to be expected. One hopes that the increased participation of Western CEOs in the activity of Russian business will help it to become more transparent. Yet we have to admit that a number of Western entrepreneurs, lawyers, and politicians have evidently demonstrated flexibility in their partnership with the Russian state, since it is hardly likely that the Russian elite would otherwise have been able to use the West as an enormous washing machine for laundering its capital and siphoning off wealth to offshore zones. In some cases, participation of Western business in shady deals in Russia not only appears to legitimize its bureaucratic capitalism but also to spread the virus of corruption to Western economies. The fact that certain Western businessmen ignore business ethics boosts the self-confidence of the Russian elite and strengthens its belief that the West will put up with its rent-seeking tricks.

Russia has been actively expanding in Western markets. The commodity-sector champions are most active in expanding outside Russia (in 2001–2006, the total amount of their investments abroad increased fivefold). Russian business is buying not only into the West's gas and oil distribution networks, but showing growing interest in joining other Western business projects. The first attempt by Russian business to gain control of one of the world's leading companies was the skirmish in which the owner of Russia's Severstal, Alexey Mordashov, tried to take over Arcelor. The attempt failed because Western shareholders were wary and suspicious of doing business with the Russians, who do not have the best of reputations in Europe. This foray, however, showed that Russia has developed an appetite for aggressively playing in the top league. The new Russian expansionist projects "are rolling in." Roman Abramovich, one of the few old oligarchs still close to the Kremlin, has begun— evidently on instructions from Putin's team—creating Evraz Group, a giant metallurgy company, which is aiming to take over American companies. One of the leading Russian banks, Vneshtorgbank, bought 5 percent of the shares of the Franco-German aerospace company EADS and tried to expand its holdings, throwing European shareholders into disarray. French newspapers wrote in a panic, "The Russian cannibal wants to snack on our national property." In response, Putin, while in Paris in the fall of 2006, could not refrain from commenting irritably on the West's anxieties, "People are afraid of us because we are rich and very large." In Munich he soon continued a charm offensive to persuade Western investors that there was no need to be worried about Russia: "The Russians are coming, not with tanks and Kalashnikovs, but with hard cash, and they want to buy rights." The Russian president has said on more than one occasion, in injured tones, that the West would prefer only to buy natural resources from Russia and prevent it from developing and expanding. In Moscow the West's anxiety is seen as a fear of increasing Russian competition, and even liberals share this view.

The expansion of Russian business sometimes triggers conflicts and misunderstandings and very often provokes anxiety in the Western community about the Russian corporate mentality and the fusion between Russian economic and political interests. The Russian ruling class does not understand that what the West is afraid of is that Russia will continue to behave like a bull in a china shop, which Russia often does.

Meanwhile, integration of Russian business into global networks is the most effective way for it to learn the new rules of the game. Both sides, Russia and the West, have to find ways to sort out mutual concerns; Russia's membership in the World Trade Organization (WTO) and further integration of Russia into the global economy could help transform the mentality and behavior of Russian companies.

In this context, a rather peculiar characteristic of the Russian economic model should be mentioned. The Russian state tries to limit the presence of foreign capital in the so-called strategic branches (not only in the military-industrial complex, but in the commodity sector as well), whereas in the food industry and services, FDI constitutes half of the total investment. Russian business in these areas is reluctant to invest heavily. Thus, Russia defends its natural resources, tries to export capital, and at the same time leaves (so far) its consumption market to foreign capital. Possible consequences of this type of development, including social and political implications, have to date been underestimated.[12]

Chapter 12

SOMETHING NEW: A NUCLEAR PETRO-POWER

The bureaucratic component is not the whole story of Russian capitalism. The economic model that has evolved in Russia is beginning to resemble a petrostate, of which the classic examples are Nigeria and Venezuela. A petrostate's economy is typified primarily by its orientation toward natural resources. The Russian oil and gas sector's share of the federal budget in 2006 was 49 percent. Oil and gas accounted for 63.3 percent of exports.[1] A petrostate has certain unmistakable characteristics: the merger between power and business; the emergence of a rentier class living on dividends from the sale of natural resources; systemic corruption; the domination of large monopolies controlled by the bureaucracy; susceptibility of the economy to external shocks; the risk of the "Dutch disease," whereby a large increase in revenues from natural resources deindustrializes a nation's economy; state intervention in the economy; and a gulf between rich and poor.[2] The petrostate has no interest in modernization but in preserving the natural resource economy. All these characteristics are increasingly typical of Russia.

Until quite recently the dependence of Russia's economy on natural resources was seen as a shortcoming (in the USSR the establishment was embarrassed to talk about it). In 2005, however, the Kremlin openly embarked on a policy of funding the restoration of state grandeur through oil and gas sales. The political class found a new drug and tried to galvanize society with the myth that Russia was becoming an "energy super-power." Optimists ecstatically count the income from oil and dream that by 2011 Russia's GDP will have doubled and that the income of citizens will have risen to $2,270 a month. "Russia is again becoming a mighty nation," they affirm, closing their ears to warnings of what Russia would face should the price of oil fall. It is not surprising that they dismiss such warnings: how can you just walk away from an economic model that allows you to sit by a gas or oil tap and do nothing but accumulate petrodollars in the bank? An easy life seems assured for the next few years, and that is as far ahead as the ruling class thinks.

Not all states blessed with natural resources become pet-rostates. The United States, Canada, Great Britain, Australia, and Norway have managed to avoid this fate, but the blandishments of oil, gas, and other natural resources have been resisted only by nations with a developed civil society and responsible gov-ernments. The Norwegians, for example, chose to diversify their economy by harmonizing the aspirations of the oil industry with those of other sectors and interest groups: the fishing industry, high technology, and ecological movements. They took the unprecedented step of restricting investment in the national Statoil company in order to prevent commodities from dominating the economy.[3]

The Russian regime has chosen no less deliberately to rely on natural resources as its means of reviving the economy and strengthening political stability, yet there is no counterbalance of independent institutions and a civil society that might have restrained the self-interest of the natural resources lobby. A sim-ilar folly has been perpetrated by all petrostates, from Venezuela and Nigeria to Indonesia and Algeria, owing to the absence of long-term public accountability of their regimes. Their fates are miserable. One Western economist has compared the impact of oil money on the state and society to Hurricane Katrina.

That natural resources are not the only key to economic success is shown by Japan, where an absence of resources has obliged the Japanese to develop new technologies. States rich in natural resources must feel no less envious of India, a nation poor in natural resources but with a 9 percent growth rate in its economy, with the impact of Bangalore, a major region of new technology, felt worldwide. Forty-one percent of those employed in advanced branches of industry in the United States are Indian. The rise of China too is occurring in a country with only modest natural commodities.

It is difficult to escape the feeling that the Russian elite knows perfectly well what it is doing. They definitely recognize that 75 percent of all known oil and gas fields in Russia are already in production, and that the oil reserves could be exhausted within ten years. It seems unlikely that the Russian elite does not know that 89 percent of oil equipment and 60 percent of the industrial plants of Gazprom are obsolete, that half its pipelines are more than twenty-five years old, and that Gazprom's fields are more than 60 percent exhausted. The natural resource sectors, overburdened by taxation, are being developed more and more slowly. The growth rate of oil extraction is decreasing, despite oil prices being at their current high levels. The extraction of gas is falling by 20 million cubic meters a year. In 2007 a deficit of 4.2 billion cubic meters of gas is expected on Russia's energy balance sheet. By 2015 this deficit is projected to rise to 46.6 billion cubic meters. Moreover, around 70 billion cubic meters of gas is wasted annually, in part because gas is being burnt off.

The Russian economy is exceptionally energy intensive: Russia uses more gas than France, Germany, Great Britain, Japan, and Italy together, which means that the more rapid its economic growth, the more energy it will consume, and the less it will have available for export. This means there can be no certainty that Russia will cope with its increasing international obligations. Moreover, as Russian economist Vladimir Milov has calculated, if a country exports only 2 to 3 tons of hydrocarbons annually per capita, as Russia does, the income will be insufficient to provide for even the most basic needs of the population. This hardly suggests the makings of an "energy superpower."

"We are using the superrevenues from the natural resource sectors for innovational progress," the Russian bureaucrats reassure society, but the promises remain no more than that. The proportion of goods and services in Russia's exports is a mere 1.7 percent, while high-technology exports contribute 0.3 percent. One could feel that the mantra the elite chants so indefatigably about Russia's energy-based international forum is no more than bluff, on par with its claims that Russia is leaping forward into the era of new technologies, and that the purpose of both claims is to distract the public's attention from its plundering of Russia's hydrocarbon wealth.

The notion of Russia as an "energy superpower" with which the elite is so taken is tantamount to an admission of the failure of attempts to diversify the Russian economy. It is a failure that, until recently, threatened to have catastrophic consequences before the unexpected lucky rise in oil prices. The hysteria about energy security that has gripped the world gave the Kremlin a fortuitous opportunity to present its failures as virtues. Gas and oil were transformed into a crucial instrument of Russian domestic and foreign policy, a prop for the Russian state. Visits to the West by President Putin suggest he is engaged exclusively in "natural resource diplomacy" and primarily in "gas diplomacy." True, Russian politicians have recently understood that the idea of an "energy superpower" sounds controversial. They have begun to avoid the term, even accusing foreign observers, as Minister of Foreign Affairs Sergei Lavrov did, of trying "to force this term on us in order to push Russia into the natural resources slot in the system of international economic relations."[4] In reality, Russia continues to behave like an energy superpower.

In early 2006 the Russian authorities defined a novel approach to coordinating supply and demand for energy. It was a "grand bargain" offered by Vladimir Putin to the G8, which the Kremlin hoped the Western leaders would approve at their forthcoming summit in St. Petersburg in July 2006 under Russia's chairship. The details of the proposal were soon provided along the following lines: "We will guarantee you deliveries of energy resources, and you will promise stable long-term purchases at stable prices, specified in long-term contracts. We will allow you to participate in our extraction companies, and you will allow us to participate in your distribution networks." The intention was for the G8 summit to herald the arrival of a new global energy security deal.

It is not difficult to see why the Kremlin is keen to conclude long-term contracts. There is growing concern among the ruling team that Russia might today get into debt, spending billions of dollars developing fields in Siberia and in the Arctic shelf and constructing pipelines to deliver hydrocarbons to customers. If the need for them decreased or the price fell, Russia would go bankrupt. One can also see why Gazprom should wish to obtain direct access to end users of gas "downstream": European consumers ensure the prosperity of Gazprom because the cost of gas in Western Europe is five times higher than in Russia. Putin's offer was not, however, only about safeguarding the solvency of an energy provider and ensuring that Gazprom continued to prosper. The Kremlin's "grand bargain" was intended to return Russia to the club of great powers, and even to dictate Russia's own terms to it.

Not only the G8 but also other consumer countries were less than enthusiastic about the Kremlin's initiative. They are well aware that allowing Gazprom monopoly control of the pipelines and satisfying its ambition to obtain a share in their energy distribution networks would leave them excessively dependent on Russia. Besides, the Kremlin's deal, with its proposal to plan the long-term production and consumption of energy, is altogether too reminiscent of Soviet planning and had little in common with the principles of a free market. Russian state companies are in any case regarded as far from ideal business partners, and the West is concerned that expanding their role might undermine the rules of corporate behavior that in Western economies have taken decades to develop. Russian companies are, to make matters worse, an extension of the state, and the Kremlin can use them as political tools, as it demonstrated in its gas wars against Ukraine and Belarus. Finally, Western investors have learned from the bitter experience of almost all the oil majors in Russia, and have doubts about the reliability of deals with Russian partners. The Russian state has already reneged too often on its undertakings. Those considerations explain why the Western powers were less than enthusiastic about Putin's initiative before the G8 summit in St. Petersburg in July 2006.

Gazprom, Russia's largest corporation and the moving force behind its energy strategy, viewed by the West as a "very shadowy empire," provokes the most serious and quite understandable concerns. Nobody knows how those running Gazprom arrive at their tariffs and dividends or how much is paid to their middlemen. Gazprom, which is attempting to expand internationally, has $25 billion in debt. It is unclear how it regulates its financial flows. The only thing known for sure about the company is that it does not like people to ask too many questions. In short, the West in 2006 had serious reservations about "a grand bargain" that could allow Gazprom to monopolize the European energy market. German analyst Frank Umbach commented:

If Russia is given the opportunity of selling gas directly to consumers in Europe without allowing Western companies into its gas and oilfields, this will increase its monopoly over the energy market even further. For Europe this would be disastrous because competition would be reduced, efficiency would fall as a result, and prices would rise. Even for Russia it would do more harm than good, because there too efficiency would fall and corruption would increase even more.[5]

For the sake of evenhandedness, I should note that Western observers, focusing on one aspect, fail to foresee the possibility of change: the greater the extent to which Russian companies are integrated into Western systems, the more secure Western businesses in Russia will be. For the time being, however, it is the negative consequences of a Russian energy monopoly that are more obvious, for Russia as well as for Europe. The positive side of Russia's global economic integration has been underestimated.

Failing to persuade the West to agree to his "reciprocity" energy deal, Putin started to look for other solutions. In September 2006, at a meeting with Angela Merkel and Jacques Chirac in Paris, he offered a new deal—to redirect future gas flows from the Shtokman gas field to Europe in return for gas-trading concessions. He went back on promises to deliver the Shtokman gas to the United States: relations with Washington were already at a low level. The Kremlin was attempting to play on tensions between the Atlantic allies, something neither Yeltsin, nor Putin had tried before so blatantly. Not receiving a reply, Putin stubbornly returned to the idea at a meeting with Merkel in October 2006, offering this time to make Germany the hub for supplying Russian gas to Western Europe. This must have been a considerable temptation for Berlin. Moscow was offering a Russo-German energy pact that would continue the special relationship established during the Schröder era, which had resulted in agreement to build a North European gas pipeline that would deliver gas from Russia to Europe (this project was dubbed "Nord Stream"). Merkel and Chirac replied jointly to Moscow (apparently, not without hesitation) that their intention was to create an energy alliance within the European Community. This was a polite rejection of Putin's offer. Berlin and Paris preferred not to quarrel with their Atlantic allies. It would have been naïve to suppose that the chancellor of Germany, who in 2007 had to assume the presidency of the G8 and of the European Union, would suddenly agree to a deal undermining the unity of the European Community and the Western world. There were also in the Moscow initiative unwelcome overtones of the Molotov–Ribbentrop Pact and a past that Germany very much wanted to forget.

At this point, Gazprom, having just promised Norwegian and French companies that it would include them in the development of the Shtokman gas field, retaliated, deciding to play hardball with Europe by announcing that it had no need of Western partners and would develop the new field on its own (later the Kremlin would partially reconsider its position). Simultaneously Russian authorities threatened that Moscow would reorient itself toward other energy markets, primarily China and Southeast Asia. Not content with this, Putin announced that Russia would not support the Energy Charter and its Transit Protocol that regulates energy relations in Europe, which he considered not to be in Russia's national interest. He did hint, however, that he might show flexibility if Europe agreed to Russian initiatives.

Early in 2007 Merkel, alarmed by Moscow's unexpected assertiveness and Gazprom's cowboy tactics with Western businesses in Russia, abandoned her usual restraint and gave Moscow a warning, apparently also on behalf of other European states. In January 2007 she said, "I think it is perfectly legitimate for Russia to seek greater access to West European markets. Having said that, we must have reciprocity. If obstacles are being erected to protect Russian companies from European investors, nobody should resent it if the Europeans take reciprocal action." Not long afterward, during the energy conflict between Russia and Belarus, which—as had been the case during the Russo-Ukrainian gas war—caused interruptions in the gas supply to Europe, the German chancellor, now no longer mincing her words, again reprimanded Moscow. "That repeatedly destroys confidence, and you can't build cooperation based on true mutual trust in this way," she warned. It seemed that Germany was on the verge of abandoning its earlier leniency toward Moscow.

In any event, Russian pressure did the Europeans a considerable favor by shocking them into beginning to work out a common energy policy. At the same time, Europe, to avoid being dictated to by Russia, set about seeking alternative energy sources, in particular by looking once more toward atomic energy and returning to the exploitation of local resources, including gas.

Meanwhile, other states are also pondering how they can avoid becoming hostages to Russia, both as sources of energy resources and as transit states owning the pipelines. Until quite recently Moscow confidently held sway over the transit routes of Caspian oil. The Baku–Ceyhan pipeline freed the countries of the Caspian basin of their dependence on the Russian pipeline. Now both Azerbaijan and Kazakhstan are successfully competing with Russia to deliver energy to Europe and Asia, organizing their own transit routes. Competitors have emerged that can try to frustrate the Kremlin's aspirations to make the world dependent on the will of Gazprom or Rosneft. For the next twenty to twenty-five years, to be sure, Moscow has nothing to fear. Europe will be dependent on Gazprom and its pipelines, and the world as a whole, faced with a turbulent Middle East, will have need of Russian crude. Still, there is no doubt that the West and Europe will try desperately to weaken their dependence on Russian hydrocarbons and it is Putin and his team that have forced Europeans to think about alternatives, once again demonstrating how the law of unintended consequences works.

How does Moscow react to resistance to its strategy? Representatives of the Russian government are not disheartened and do not believe they have lost. They evidently suppose that sooner or later the Europeans will accept Russia's terms and that Germany in particular has no other option. Gazprom, meanwhile, continues its onslaught on other hydrocarbon supplies. In October 2006 it obliged Shell, together with its partners, Mitsui and Mitsubishi, to sell it a controlling share in the Sakhalin-2 project.[6] Gazprom increased the pressure on other Western investors: the Franco-Belgian firm Total and Norwegian Hydro, which have licenses to develop the Kharyaga oil field. In June 2007 Moscow forced BP–TNK, which controlled development of the Kovykta oil field, to sell its 62.9 percent stake to Gazprom for just $900,000, a paltry sum for a stake in a project worth about $20 billion when it is completed. Not for the first time, ExxonMobil ran into serious problems in operating the Sakhalin-3 project. It is clear that the state will be revising the terms of the "production sharing agreement" (PSA) concluded with Western investors in the 1990s and that they will be compelled to agree to new operating conditions. These actions raise not only ethical issues but also questions regarding economic efficiency. It is not impossible that Gazprom in the end will be left sitting on vast natural resources with no means or technology to exploit them.[7]

A further development is that Gazprom is changing, from being solely a natural-resource empire that provides 10 percent of budgetary revenues, to being an independent player that subjugates the state. The Russian state is increasingly subordinated to the interests of the gas "monster" that works on its own agenda. The Russian economy, as journalists have aptly remarked, is turning into a "Gazpronomy," serving as an appendage to the gas empire. This may prove enormously damaging in terms of Russia's economic development. Russia has become a subject for experiments performed by the "energy–siloviki" elite, a group that includes representatives of the security structures and the gas and oil lobby. Gazprom itself, bothered by the fact that extracting natural resources involves a lot of hard work, has started transforming itself from a gas company into a manager of the distribution of energy resources, one that aspires to live on the dividends from gas extraction, losing interest in expanding gas production.

After some deliberation at the beginning of 2007 Russia took a step that caused new consternation in the world. Moscow agreed to take part in the creation of a gas OPEC, an organization that might include, besides Russia, Venezuela, Algeria, Qatar, and perhaps Iran, with Russia demonstrating an ambition to become its coordinator. So far observers have been skeptical that a gas OPEC would be technically and politically feasible, thinking it an unlikely project. Yet coordination of their efforts by the gas suppliers is quite possible, and it does appear that European and even American policy makers have good cause to worry. Five potential cartel members control between 3.840 trillion to 4.541 trillion cubic feet of gas reserves and account for nearly 65 percent of the world total. Should the new organization be created, with the potential to coordinate its own policy, it could become a challenge and even a threat for major consumers, most of which are Western countries, making the whole prospect rather disturbing for the West. It is no wonder that the U.S. government in April 2007 expressed its concern over the possibility of a gas OPEC being established, despite doubts that such unification might happen in the immediate future.

Neither the growing assertiveness of the Kremlin toward the West nor the hardening of its policy toward foreign investors has scared off international oil companies, which continue trying to become established in Russia and are prepared to spend money to overcome political risks. There is also always the fear of missing out on something. Western big business is not put off by the lack of consistency in Russian tax legislation, by corruption, or by the ever-present need to obtain the Kremlin's blessing, and it is ready to move into Russia despite all the worries. Investors remain willing to invest, and there is nothing surprising about that. Business has always been cynical and ready to play by local rules—all the more so if there are huge profits to be made. An example of this was the participation of Western investors in the IPO of Rosneft, which swallowed Khodorkovsky's key company, Yuganskneftegaz, at great cost to Western minority shareholders.

By the end of Putin's term foreign investors, despite the Kremlin's rather tough treatment of Western business, demonstrated that they feel more optimistic about Russia than ever before. This was proved by the eleventh annual St. Petersburg International Economic Forum on June 12, 2007, which ended with a record volume of agreements concluded during the event ($13.5 billion worth, as compared to $1 billion in 2006). Meeting with the Russian president at the forum, the CEOs of world business went far in hailing Russia's prospects and praising Putin personally. Royal Dutch/Shell chief executive Jeroen van der Veer, whose company was forced to cede control of one of the world's biggest oil fields to the Russian state at a knock-down price, thanked Putin for helping the company reach a good agreement with the Russian state (!). Anders Igel, CEO of Nordic TeliaSonera, detected in Russia "a strong will to open up and create a more democratic society."[8]

Some Western businesses are ready to accept the informal rules of the game in Russia. The latest example of how they are adapting to Russian conditions can be seen in the charges brought by the German courts against Siemens employees, who have spent around 10 million euros annually in Russia and the newly independent states on bribes.[9]

The Russian state will continue to attract Western partners to implement its projects, but the latter should be under no illusions: foreign companies are regarded in Russia purely as junior shareholders. British Petroleum's joint venture with Russian capital (BP–TNK) was not destined to set a precedent and will remain a monument to the personal rapport between Putin and Tony Blair, which ended in mutual animosity. What can foreign businesses expect from the Russian regime in the future? We already know the answer. The experience of ExxonMobil, stripped of its investments in Sakhalin and forced to tender an offer once again for an oil deposit it thought it owned, and the experience already mentioned of BP and Shell, is sufficient evidence that the Kremlin will continue to play by its own rules. It will set the rules and, when it feels like it, break them. If the ruling class wants to take control of a Western investor's property, it will do so. If the political situation within Russia requires that a Western investor be made into a public enemy, that too will happen, and no amount of friendship between national leaders will alter the situation. The Kremlin will try, within reason, not to let matters get totally out of hand, as that might scare the Western business community away completely, but they should not expect an easy ride, especially if the regime continues to exploit anti-Westernism as a means of rallying the Russian public. The Russian ruling team is convinced that the Western oil majors and other Western companies will be eager to come to the Russian market, whatever the rules are, and so far they find a lot of evidence to prove that they are right.

The arrival in Russia of world-class oil players has controversial consequences for Russia. On the one hand, their presence is economically beneficial for Russia and helps Russian business to develop a new business culture. On the other hand, the activity of the Western companies in an economy that is not diversified and is regulated by informal rules in the end only pushes the country further toward the petrostate. The situation is paradoxical: Western monopolies legitimize the Russian natural resource state by their very presence and exploit it in their own interests, just as they legitimized and exploited other petrostates in the 1960s and 1970s. The Russian state may, however, at any moment renege on its obligations to Western companies. The only question is, who will manage to make more dividends out of this unstable partnership: Western business or the Russian bureaucratic corporation?

Meanwhile, even though Putin's "grand bargain" for exchanging assets with foreign partners was not accepted by Western establishments as the basic model for their energy security, the idea is quietly being implemented in bilateral deals between Russia and a number of European countries that are allowing Gazprom to enter their economies. First were the Germans who, when Schröder was chancellor, let Gazprom buy into the Wingaz distribution company and its subsidiary, Wintershall, in return for allowing the giant BASF to participate in exploiting the South Russia gas field. Russian gas provides almost 25 percent of the needs of the German economy, so Berlin cannot resist pressure from Moscow (although the German E.ON energy company has refused to let Gazprom into its distribution networks). Even as the Western press was discussing the threats associated with Russia's expansion into Western markets, in 2006 the Italian company Eni signed a partnership agreement with Gazprom under which the Italians will join in buying up Russian oil assets, while Gazprom will deliver gas directly to the Italian market and obtain a share of Eni's African projects. Gaz de France has begun negotiations with Gazprom about the possibility of allowing it access to Gazprom's assets. In other states the Kremlin has been even more successful. In March 2007 Putin signed a treaty with Bulgaria and Greece on building a new pipeline—Burgas–Alaxandroupolis—involving these states in implementing Russia's expansionist energy agenda.

Moscow wasted no time in creating a safety net, trying to diversify its transit routes to avoid dependence on Ukraine and Belarus as transit states. On May 13, 2007, Vladimir Putin achieved an astounding victory in a growing rivalry with the West over the energy resources of Central Asia by striking a deal with Turkmenistan and Kazakhstan to build a pipeline from Turkmenistan into Russia's network of pipelines to Europe. This pipeline may carry 20 billion cubic meters of gas annually by 2012. This was a blow to U.S. and European efforts to construct oil and gas pipelines from Central Asia that would cross under the Caspian Sea, avoiding Russia. Vladimir Putin, energetically building his "energy legacy," has outplayed very serious and experienced actors, evidently offering the Kazakh and Turkmen leaders a deal they could not refuse. On June 23, 2007, representatives of the Russian and Italian governments signed a memorandum to cooperate on a 900-kilometer (or 558-mile) pipeline called "South Stream" that will be built by Gazprom and Italy's Eni SpA from Russia through the Black Sea into Europe and will carry as much as 30 billion cubic meters of gas annually.

One might get the impression that Gazprom and the European Community are in a furious race against each other. Gazprom is trying to get established in the European energy market before the EU and individual European governments have come together to nail down a common energy strategy, reform their energy monopolies, and liberalize the energy market. Gazprom finds it much easier to come to terms on exchanging assets with European energy monopolies through separate deals. Not infrequently the Russian side barges in, bullying its partners and paying no attention to the cost to its image. It is in a hurry, and it needs results before the consumer countries have a coordinated approach toward the suppliers. For their part, the Europeans have started to work on a unitary energy policy, and Gazprom's actions are compelling the EU to speed this work up. While hinting at their displeasure at Moscow's bullying approach to energy agreements, and even occasionally venturing to criticize it openly, Western governments tread warily.

Gazprom's hectic expansion, the way it is done, and the goals it pursues demonstrate how deep is the merger of power and business in Russia, proving that its economic goals and especially energy policy have strong political underpinnings. Just a few examples: The North-European pipeline project, mentioned earlier, was considered economically unfeasible in the 1980s, but now the same project, under the new name "North Stream," is presented as one of the most promising routes to link Russia and the EU. Observers cannot conceal their bewilderment, failing to understand how a pipeline costing $7.5 billion suddenly becomes more attractive than a second branch of the Yamal-Europe pipeline costing $2.5 billion that can also link Russia and European countries. True, Russian bureaucracy likes expensive projects that present a lot of possibilities for siphoning off money. But there is a strong political motivation—to bypass Poland and other transit countries.[10]

Another example of politicization of the energy policy is the Kremlin's sudden decision to allow the French company Total to help develop Russia's Shtokman field. The deal was sealed by a call between the French and Russian presidents on July 12, 2007. (Total is to receive 25 percent of a joint company that will develop the project and Gazprom will retain at least 51 percent of the company). It is not difficult to see Russia's motivation behind the deal: the Kremlin, by choosing this particular partner out of several countries standing at the door accomplished two tasks at once. Firstly, Putin was sending a signal to Sarkozy about his readiness to build bridges, which is important for Russia given that its relations with the West have deteriorated.[11] Secondly, by wooing Paris Putin was apparently offering an "advance" for France's opposition to the new EU energy directives and Brussels' attempt to build a joint strategy. This was a brilliant tactical move!

One almost has the impression that the EU bureaucracy provokes the Kremlin–Gazprom team by its lack of vision and stubbornness in pursuing outdated or no-longer relevant norms. This is the case with the Energy Charter treaty and its Transit Protocol, which the EU continually demands that Russia ratify, and which Russia continually refuses to do. Meanwhile, at this stage the Energy Charter, signed in 1994, could hardly serve as the legal framework for energy cooperation in Europe, simply because it no longer matches a now-changed reality. Moreover, Moscow has some ground (in the opinion of Russian independent experts) to consider that Transit Protocol represents a double-standard approach. Both sides—the EU and Russia—need to negotiate a new international legal agreement that would address the issues of energy supply and demand on a long-term basis and would attempt to respond to the concerns of both sides. The EU should expend more effort convincing Russia that energy relations based on multinational principles rather than on separate bilateral agreements benefit both sides, including Russia, which to date Brussels has failed to do. As Vladimir Milov rightly points out, "Europe should concentrate on explaining to the Russian authorities the meaning of the European energy policy and the advantages it has for Russia."[12]

Finally, Russia's petro-power has some peculiarities: the more pronounced the natural-resource, and primarily energy, orientation of the Russian economy becomes, the more energetically the elite tries to compensate for the inferiority complex which generates its great-power aspirations. It does not want to see

Russia turn into a natural-resource appendage of consumer countries. On the contrary, it wants to dictate its terms to them. In this, the Russian energy petro-power differs from its fellow petrostates. A nuclear power with a natural-resource-based economy is something new on the world stage, and the logic of this phenomenon and its implications for world development are not clear. One good thing, at least, has come of Russia's natural-resource bias. Its political class is no longer fixated on nuclear might and does not see its nuclear weapons as constituting the main instrument of its foreign policy. "Hydrocarbon politics," although it can be something of a bludgeon, has less deadly consequences than nuclear weapons.

On the other hand, Russia's heavy-handed use of its gas weapon has shown that energy resources can be used to great political effect, and consumer countries have yet to find a satisfactory antidote. This creates new challenges, not only in terms of energy security, but also for world stability as a whole. We may be sure that, for as long as the world has need of hydrocarbons, Russia will exploit them for political purposes. However, after learning the lessons of the gas conflict with Ukraine in 2005 and with Belarus in 2006, Moscow may proceed more circumspectly. The West and China are not by any means unable to defend themselves, and they are already adept at playing politics in this area, as we can see from the dramatic intrigues being woven around the natural-resource-rich states of the Caspian Sea and Central Asia.

Much more disturbing, at least for Russians, is the question of how Russia will behave when it becomes clear that hydrocarbons are an extremely treacherous weapon that can explode in the faces of their owners. How will it react domestically and internationally when the oil price falls and Gazprom is unable to fulfill its international obligations?

Chapter 13

THE STATE SHAKES OFF
ITS SOCIAL RESPONSIBILITIES

Under Vladimir Putin the majority of Russians are living better. Economic growth has made it possible to mitigate the profound social crisis Russia experienced in the 1990s. The government began paying salaries and pensions regularly; per capita income began to rise. The national average reached $350 a month in 2006, compared with $80 in 2000. Real wages in 2006 grew by 13.4 percent and in the first half of 2007 by 17.9 percent. The number of people living below the poverty line fell from 37 percent in 1999 to 25 percent in 2006 (according to other estimates—from 29 percent in 2000 to 17 percent in 2006); the level of unemployment fell to 19 percent—from 7 million to 5.7 million people.[1] Despite all this, no radical change has taken place in the state's social policy. Upon arriving in the Kremlin, the president set himself two tasks: to consolidate his grip on power and to bring about macroeconomic stability. During his first presidency, he had neither the time nor the courage to tackle the social area. Social reform would have necessitated finally abandoning the state paternalism left over from the Soviet period and dismantling long-familiar pattern of social life, which would have risked destabilization.

Finally, after his reelection in the summer of 2004, Vladimir Putin embarked on something that neither Gorbachev nor

Yeltsin had dared to do before him. He took the risk of beginning to restructure the Soviet model of social policy in line with market requirements. The Kremlin proposed a package of laws to redefine the state's social responsibilities. There were intelligent aspects in this, but most unfortunately the government moved straight into the most sensitive area: the monetarization of welfare benefits in kind. This affected the rights of pensioners, poorer families, and the disabled. It involved a sharp reduction and, in a number of cases, the complete withdrawal of state benefits without adequate compensation for the defenseless segment of the population. The regime abandoned millions of its most vulnerable citizens to their fates. It was obvious that the Kremlin expected that they would accept their lot without complaint, after which it would be possible to begin more complex social reforms. There was a level of cynical calculation in this: the Kremlin anticipated that the reaction of the disabled and the aged would reveal how malleable society was. The regime was sitting on a treasure chest full of petrodollars, yet it abdicated its responsibilities toward the weakest and most vulnerable part of society, even as it continued to raise the remuneration of officialdom and expenditures on national security. The formula behind the Kremlin's new social policy was simple: support the bureaucracy and practice social Darwinism with respect to the poorest in society. Implementing the monetization of benefits, which started in January 2005, drove the groups most loyal to Putin out into the streets in protest, foremost among them the pensioners. For the first time during Putin's presidency, rallies and demonstrations took place that numbered in the hundreds of thousands, including mainly the disabled and the aged. The Kremlin took fright, slammed into reverse gear, and abandoned all further thought of social reform, leaving social welfare and social policy in the same mess as it was before.

One should recognize some improvement in the social situation during the past several years of Vladimir Putin's presidency, brought about by economic growth and increased stability. These improvements, however, are marginal and they are not supported by serious changes in state policy and the strategic agenda. Moreover, after the failure of benefits monetization reform the state has simply refused to perform its elementary functions in the area of social policy. Government's sporadic efforts to plug holes using the old mechanisms of redistribution cannot alter a general picture of the deterioration of society's key pillars.

It appears that economic growth has had no substantial impact on major demographic and health trends. The total population of Russia continued to fall, accompanied by a decline in the level of qualified labor, the aging of the population, and a degradation of its health and intellectual potential—in short, a sharp deterioration of the quality of the nation's human resources. A few facts indicate the scale of the dramatic social problems Russia faces. The population fell from 149 million in 1991 to 142.8 million in 2006; between 1992 and 2005 the natural decrease, the extent to which the number of deaths exceeded the number of births, was 11 million. In 2006, for every 10.3 babies born, 16.3 people died. The average number of children for each woman in the population today is 1.34 to 1.35. To compensate for the natural loss of population, the summary birth coefficient (the number of births for each woman during her reproductive life), should be 2.15, whereas in Moscow the coefficient is 1.29; nationwide it hovers around 1.32. Life expectancy in Russia is extremely low, lagging behind the developed countries by 15 to 19 years for men and 7 to 12 years for women. The mortality of people of working age is exceptionally high. Throughout the world the main cause of death is cardiovascular disease, followed by cancer. External causes of death (murders, accidents, poisoning, traffic accidents, and the like) come between fifth and ninth on the list. In Russia, external causes are the second most common cause of death, which tells us a lot about the quality of life in Russia.[2]

If present trends continue and there is no compensating immigration, the population of Russia in 2025 will be 123 million. Optimistic forecasts suggest that by 2050 the population of Russia will have declined to 102 million, while pessimistic assessments put the figure at 77 million. This does raise the question of how capable Russia will be of maintaining control of its geographical territory beyond the Urals in fifty years' time.

The condition of Russia's human resources is tied to the situation in the health services, which is thoroughly alarming. Only one Russian in three considers himself to be in good health, 40 percent are frequently ill, and 30 percent are suffering from a chronic illness. According to official figures, 60 percent of Russian children are suffering from a chronic illness, which holds out the prospect of the reproduction of an unhealthy population. Some 11.5 million disabled people are excluded from taking an active part in life, and this number increases annually by half a million. In Russia a mere 15 percent of people with disabilities are employed. By comparison, in the United States, 35 percent of the 54 million disabled are in employment, and in Britain, out of 5 million disabled, 40 percent are employed. In China the figure is 80 percent out of 60 million. Diseases that had been eliminated in the USSR are again spreading, among them tuberculosis and plague (according to Murray Feshbach, the total number of cases of tuberculosis in the United States in 2005 was 662, whereas the Russian figure was about 32,000 officially reported, or forty to fifty times higher for a population less than half that of the United States).[3] Russia is on the brink of an AIDS pandemic. In 1999 several thousand people were HIV-positive, while in 2006 the figure was between 800,000 and 1.1 million. The World Health Organization rates Russia 127th among its 192 member states in terms of the general health of its population.

There are about 3 million orphans in Russia. Hundreds of thousands of homeless children wander the streets and live in railway stations. Millions of disabled children are housed in institutions and, receiving no vocational training, have no prospect of being able to fend for themselves as adults. They swell the ranks of the unemployed and homeless. Of 30 million children of school age, 2 million are not attending school.

The list of problems goes on. The collapse of the professional training system means that Russia will soon cease to have a qualified workforce, which will undermine the efficiency of the economy. A further problem is that of displaced persons, of whom, according to official statistics, there are 5 million; in reality there are many more for whom the government is unable to find permanent employment. There is an immigration problem involving tens of millions of people whose status is not regularized and who most often find themselves totally without rights. Housing continues to be critical. On average, each Russian has 20.5 square meters of living space, compared to 40 in Sweden and 60 in the United States. There are 4.2 million families with low living standards and no chance to buy apartments in the housing queue.[4]

One of the most painful social issues in Russia is the situation of its pensioners. Currently in Russia there are 38 million pensioners in a population of 142 million. That means that pensioners constitute about 27 percent of the total population. Over the next ten years this ratio could reach 1:1. How to guarantee civilized levels of life for the older generation is becoming a challenge for the country. Today Russian pensions constitute only one-quarter of salaries, whereas in Europe pensions constitute 60 to 70 percent of a salary, which means that pensioners in Russia are one of the poorest social groups.[5]

Price hikes hit the poorest part of the population. Prices are rising faster than the basic inflation rate: housing prices rose by 35 percent in 2006, kindergarten fees by 29 percent, housing and communal services rates by 18 percent, electricity rates by 17 percent, and gasoline prices by 16 percent. These price rises push the poorer segments of society down the social scale, leaving them without any hope for a better life, and hurt the middle class as well.

A particular cause for concern is the growing gap between the incomes of the richest and poorest in the population: the richest 10 percent now make 25 times more than the poorest 10 percent. (Independent research indicates that financial differentiation may be up to 40-fold.)[6] The differential between the most prosperous and the least favored regions has increased to 281:1 (in 2000 it was 64:1). On the other hand, according to Forbes' lists, there are fifty-three billionaires in Russia with wealth totaling $172 billion. In 2006 alone, twenty new billionaires emerged in Russia. Having one of the highest rates of increase in the number of wealthy people, Russia thus also has one of the highest differentials in the world between the income of the richest and the poorest.

A significant portion of well-off people in Russia include bureaucrats. The salaries of federal officials in 2005–2007 rose by 44.1 percent. That is twice the increase in the average wage. Before the increase in 2005 in Moscow, the average monthly salary of the middle level of executive-branch employees was about $980—plus the supplementary income sources that in some cases are higher than the salaries. The salary, however, and the supplements are not the main source of the bureaucracy's well being—the bureaucracy is benefiting from the fusion between the state they have privatized and business. According to information obtained by the Russian media, higher-level federal officials often make several million dollars a year, and a significant portion of their income comes from private companies, which means that they openly break the law that forbids state officials from having supplementary incomes from commercial activities. (This practice is replicated on all levels of the state administration.)[7]

Russian ministers annually publish information on their incomes and the data shows that they are not poor. A few examples: in 2006 the income of Minister of Natural Resources Yuri Trutnev amounted to $5.2 million; the income of Minister of Information Technology and Communications Leonid Reiman was $4.3 million; the income of Minister of Transport Igor Levitin was $500,000.[8] The members of the government explain that their high incomes are the result of their business activities before they joined the government. There is a general consensus that high incomes prevent commercial activity by high officials while they are in the government. In practice, however, there is no evidence to suggest that this is true.

In the United Nations Human Development Report, Russia is placed 62nd out of 177 states. It is hardly surprising that the Russian population continues to suffer from a sense of uncertainty and constant disillusionment, despite some improvement in morale during Putin's rule. In autumn 2006, only 27 percent of those surveyed considered that things would turn out all right, while 50 percent anticipated no improvement. Thirty-four percent of Russians felt confident about the future; 63 percent did not (3 percent of respondents had no opinion). In the spring of 2007, despite continuing economic growth, Russians were still unsure about their futures and felt frustrated with government policy. According to Levada Center polls, 49 percent of Russians thought that the government could not control rising prices, 47 percent said that the authorities had neglected social issues, and 22 percent complained about corruption.[9] According to a VTsIOM survey in the spring of 2007, only 39 percent of respondents showed a positive attitude toward the situation in education versus 53 percent negative; in the area of medical care, the percentages were 29 and 67, respectively; regarding housing, 15 and 78 percent, respectively.[10]

The social structure of Russian society can hardly guarantee stability. Very wealthy individuals constitute only 1–2 percent of the population; 15 to 20 percent are middle class and can save and have the resources to contribute to the education of their children; 60 to 65 percent constitute the intermediate group sandwiched between the middle class and the poor; 15 to 20 percent are very poor, fighting for survival; and finally, 5 to 7 percent are those who have fallen to the lowest depth of the social scale. We are dealing with an extremely unstable pyramidal structure of a society prone to periods of social turmoil.

In the minds of the Russian political class, social welfare obligations are a burden that it tries to avoid or ignore. The regime has failed, or rather, simply not bothered, to apply the billions of oil dollars that fell out of the sky to easing the lot of the poorest part of the population. To be sure, in 2004–2006 total expenditure on social welfare increased by 31 percent, and in 2007 the budget expenditure on education rose by 60 percent and on health by 30 percent. Yet these amounts are still insufficient to repair the collapsed social infrastructure, and there is a suspicion that the money, allocated in the run-up to elections, will be spent on ineffective programs. At all events, the authorities are far more concerned about defense and national security. In the 2006–2007 budgets, the expenditure on security is 27 percent higher than the total expenditure on education, health, science, social welfare, culture, sports, new housing, and ecology. Taken together, these made up a meager 18.5 percent of the total budgetary expenditure. Moreover, while the 2006 budget proficit was a record 7.5 percent, in 2007 it is expected to be 7 percent and falling. Expenditure on social needs will consequently also fall.

The authorities are so busy "redistributing" wealth and keeping themselves in office that they have no time to think about changing the social psychology of the populace, encouraging those who can to resolve their own welfare problems, and providing for the welfare of those who are unable to do so. Determined to keep society politically passive and dependent on the state, the regime reinforces consumerist instincts and encourages the belief that only the state can help society. When sociologists from the Levada Center asked, "What is the best way to fight poverty," the most popular reply, chosen by 60 percent of those surveyed, was a demand for an increase in salaries and social welfare payments. A further 14.5 percent thought business should take responsibility for the social welfare of the population; 11.4 percent contended that income should be taken from the rich and shared. Only 8.2 percent of Russians expressed a readiness to take responsibility for their own welfare.[11] Accordingly, not without the influence of the regime's policies, the old attitudes that were once typical in the Soviet period remain. At the same time, although the authorities deliberately encourage society to feel dependent on the state, it neither can nor wishes to maintain the level of social security that the Soviet state provided. It makes no attempt to reinforce the social infrastructure by spending its petrodollars, or to create the economic conditions that would ensure a rise in the population's standard of living and create incentives for people to help themselves.

In the run-up to the presidential election, the Kremlin has put forward the idea of "national projects" to resolve problems in health, education, the building of private housing, and agriculture that *were* to be implemented by presidential hopeful Dmitri Medvedev. Alas, there are no mechanisms in those projects for lifting the population out of poverty or for improving the quality of Russia's human potential. The architects of the "national projects" promised handouts to the population purely in order to minimize social discontent before the election. As expected, the national projects have not changed people's perception of developments in social areas. Levada Center polls at the beginning of 2007 have demonstrated skepticism regarding their implementation and their contribution to the well-being of the people. Sixty percent of respondents in March 2007 said that the national projects will not have a positive impact on their lives; 26 percent believed that they will (14 percent had no opinion). Fifty-one percent said that the money will be spent "ineffectively"; 27 percent thought that the money would be stolen. Only 13 percent said that the money would be effectively spent (9 percent had no opinion).[12]

In 2007 the government undertook one more initiative. It decided to use oil money to create the Foundation for Future Generations, following the example of Norway. By 2009 the budget of the foundation should reach $24.4 billion, or $173 a person, compared to the Norwegian state foundation Global, which controls about $290 billion, or $62,000 for each Norwegian. The money that the Russian government puts aside for future generations is hardly enough to guarantee adequate living standards. Moreover, a crisis of the Russian pension fund is coming and has to be dealt with. Its deficit is expected to grow from $4.3 billion in 2005 to $24.3 billion in 2012, which will mean serious problems for the survival of the aging population.

In creating the impression that it is addressing problems, the Kremlin encourages the involvement of business in social welfare, trying to hand over its responsibility for resolving such matters as promoting education, helping the needy, and developing sports and physical culture. An oddly circular situation arises. The population vests its hopes in the state, which supports those hopes but has no intention of satisfying them. Instead, the state attempts to buy society's support with handouts and targeted injections of petrodollars, but this approach can be effective only in the short term.

If society's problems are to be solved, it is essential that social responsibilities be shared by the state and local governments. The latter must be given the authority to provide the basic services needed by individuals and their families: schooling, medical care, public services, and cultural activities. For this to be possible the Kremlin will need to abandon its efforts to embed local government in the state structure; it must develop local self-government and allow local authorities to raise their own revenues. (At present this appears to be out of the question for a Kremlin that has made it its aim to centralize budgetary revenues within the state.) The state also needs to think about providing free access to education and health care for those segments of the population that cannot afford to pay for them and who are currently virtually unprovided for. To make a start in the fight against poverty, small- and medium-sized businesses must be encouraged to create new jobs, especially in the provinces. This initiative requires removing the barriers of bureaucracy and corruption, and this again is impossible without reforming the state and the system.

Finally, to reform Russia's shattered social infrastructure, political will that does not exist in the present regime is needed.

If a state system that panders to a parasitic rentier class while simultaneously nurturing a culture of populist dependency continues to exist with no view to providing social protections, the degradation of social structure in Russia may become irreversible.

Chapter 14

WHAT IS BEHIND RUSSIA'S NEW ASSERTIVENESS?

"Russia is reverting to its imperial great-power paradigm," say some observers of the Kremlin's conduct. "No, it is experiencing the same post-imperial syndrome that all former empires pass through, and sooner or later Russia will start implementing measured policies," others counter. "Russia is behaving in accordance with its own interests and potential," yet others aver. So what is the logic of Russia's foreign policy, what goals is it pursuing, and what is its domestic background?

In the 1990s, despite apocalyptic forecasts, Russia began in a fairly calm manner to downsize its ambitions to align them more closely to its reduced circumstances. The elite seemed to have reconciled itself with remarkable speed to the loss of an empire and of Russia's role as a civilizational alternative to the West. In 1991 and early 1992, Yeltsin and his team even began considering incorporating Russia into such Western structures as NATO and the European Union. Yeltsin demanded that George H. W. Bush and Bill Clinton treat Russia as a favored ally. During this period, the political class still believed that Russia would occupy the niche left by the former USSR, that it would become an equal partner of the United States, but as a democratic nation. Russian politicians did not realize that the West had relegated Russia to a lower division in the hierarchy of states. Having ceased to view it as a key adversary, the West was in no hurry to welcome it as an ally.

The recognition of new realities and of the necessity to abandon overblown ambitions was a painful process. Ultimately, however, the Kremlin in the 1990s accepted the terms of an informal deal offered by Washington, which Arnold Horelick and Thomas Graham dubbed "trading symbolism for substance." The essence of the deal was that the West, and first of all the United States, encouraged Moscow by making such gestures as including Russia in the G7 and creating a Russia–NATO Council, assuaging the wounded pride of its ruling class in return for Russia's more substantive concessions to the West, such as withdrawing troops from the Baltic region, acquiescing to a Western settlement of the Yugoslav issue, and NATO expansion. Having no opportunity and, more importantly, no wish to continue the Soviet foreign policy model, Yeltsin, despite loud protestations of dissatisfaction among the Russian elite, was obliged to accept the demotion of Russia to the position of junior partner of the United States. In the 1990s some Western politicians were unable to conceal their embarrassment at Moscow's readiness to satisfy Washington demands. Richard Nixon even advised the Kremlin to abandon attempts to tie Russia to America and think more about its national interests. But did Russia have any choice? Was it feasible to try to maintain its superpower status or to settle for regional power status after the fall of the USSR? The former was impossible and the latter difficult enough, given Russia's domestic political crisis and the collapse of the former state machinery. Should it seek to dissolve into the West? Neither Russia nor the West was ready for that, and both had their own, differing, views on Russian integration. Ideally, Russia should have found a new formula for advancing its national interests within the framework of a partnership with the West, but a continuing internal power struggle and a failure to understand the need for change in its foreign policy orientation, as well as consternation over the nature of the change, ruled that out.

The "trading symbolism for substance" deal between Moscow and the West worked for a full decade. Cooperation between Russia and the West made it possible to fill the security vacuum that resulted from the collapse of the USSR and to ride out its potentially unpleasant consequences. First and foremost, the number of nuclear states on the territory of the former USSR was limited. To Yeltsin's credit, despite his frequently voiced anger at the West, he did not attempt to play on anti-Western feeling to bolster his political position at home.

Beneath Moscow's outward acquiescence, however, a mute dissatisfaction was seething within the elite, which continued to pine for the lost prestige of a great power, blaming Yeltsin for having surrendered Russia's interests. For a long time this was evident only in verbal eruptions from members of the left and patriotic opposition groups. The Kremlin rebelled just once. It tried to remind the world of its former might when, during the Yugoslav conflict, Russian paratroopers carried out their "March on Pristina" in Kosovo in 1999, seized the airport, and almost found themselves in conflict with the NATO forces. This was the Kremlin's way of trying to force the West to hear its voice during the settlement of the Kosovo problem (a settlement that was not at all ideal); and the role the West played in the Yugoslavia drama raised a lot of questions.[1] However, Moscow's way of proving itself a force to be reckoned with could have had disastrous consequences. Not even this incident stopped the dialogue between Russia and Western capitals, although those sensitive to the mood of the Russian political class could see that its wariness, primarily toward Washington, would yet make itself felt. In any case, a partnership based on asymmetrical resources and continuing differences in values, accompanied by the frustration of one side over its new role and the nature of the partnership, was not sustainable in the long term. This became evident when the early period of Yeltsin's romantic partnership with the West was replaced by the era of Yevgeni Primakov's (Yeltsin's foreign affairs minister) promotion of "multipolarity," which indicated that Moscow had already in Yeltsin's tenure bade farewell to its hopes of seeing Russia included in the West. It began to turn and face the opposite direction.

After his appointment as Yeltsin's successor, Vladimir Putin took time to reflect on the foreign policy priorities of his future presidency. Even for his entourage, his conclusion was remarkable and unexpected. In February 2000, before his election, the new Russian president phoned Lord Robertson, the secretary-general of NATO, invited him to Moscow, and proposed a rapprochement between Russia and NATO that was completely at odds with the anti-Western mood that had become dominant at that time in the Russian establishment. The new Russian leader was soon pleasantly surprising Western leaders with his businesslike approach, conscientiousness, and predictability. No less impressive was that, like Yeltsin before him, Putin intimated that Moscow was prepared to consider integration into the structure of NATO, plainly keen to go down in history as the pioneer of a breakthrough in relations with the West. As the second round of NATO expansion was to show, Putin, unlike his predecessor, did not attempt to blackmail the West with tantrums and demands for a quid pro quo from Western capitals for putting up with the new expansion of the Atlantic Alliance. He did not smash crockery but tried to accelerate Russia's adaptation to the new situation, triggering the consternation of his own team—behavior that further amazed the West.

After the tragedy of 9/11 it seemed that a new formula might be found for Russian partnership with the West. Vladimir Putin provoked high expectations for his new model of foreign policy among Russian moderates and liberals, and his enthusiastic supporters anticipated that "for the first time in Russian history," he would link national interest not "to sheer power and territorial control, but rather to domestic reform, prosperity, and efficiency of governance," and that he "needs the West for Russia to succeed in a globalizing world."[2] Western observers and politicians were equally optimistic. Confirmation of the near euphoria about President Vladimir Putin and his course in Western circles was reflected in the willingness of President Bush to offer Russia the chair of the G8, which was a reversal of Washington's previous position, shared by other G7 members, that Russia should not take the chair until the country achieved democratic and market standards. The heads of the Western democracies issued a statement at the G8 gathering in Kananaskis in July 2002 that emphasized "the remarkable economic and democratic transformation that has occurred in Russia in recent years and in particular under the leadership of President Putin." That was either a reflection of politeness of the Western leaders or a failure to understand the trajectory of the country and the nature of the leadership they were dealing with. The second explanation seems more plausible.

A great deal of water has flowed under the bridge since then, and neither Russia nor the West is talking nowadays about how or when Russia may be integrated into the Western community. The Kremlin has once again caught the world unprepared, with a new drive to regain its role as an independent and aggressive player. Putin is now entirely willing to refuse compromise with the West, is seeking ways to drive the West out of areas that Moscow considers its backyard, and is trying to restore Russia's superpower role elsewhere in the world. Russia's global ambitions are back. "We've started to recover our positions on all fronts, and our offensive has met with unanimous resistance," wrote Russian pundit Sergei Karaganov.[3] Still, not all observers have been impressed by the new cockiness in Moscow. "Behind the rhetoric, Russia's foreign policy is essentially a rearguard action, a matter of using such instruments and influence as Russia currently possesses to prevent further erosion of the country's influence," asserted Sir Roderic Lyne, former British ambassador to Russia.[4]

The West has stopped thinking about its relationship with Russia as a "partnership," to use the term first introduced by Gorbachev, and is looking for more adequate definitions for its downgraded relations, moving from "cooperation" to "selective cooperation," and from there to "engagement," and finally to "selective engagement," fueling Moscow's resentment and leading it to accuse Western governments of failing to deal fairly with Russia and of intending to weaken it. In 2006, the authors of the Trilateral Commission Report, Roderic Lyne, Strobe Talbott, and Koji Watanabe, explained the need to redefine the nature of the new relations and suggested a new formula: "Unlike partnership which suggests that the partners should bend over backward to appear to be agreeing and cooperating even when they are at odds—engagement suggests a high degree of candor and realism when interests and perceptions diverge."[5] Unfortunately, Russia watchers have observed more than once that the sudden reality of the relationship at some junctures makes even the term "engagement" over-optimistic.

What is behind Russia's new and unexpected self-confidence? Largely, of course, it is high oil prices and the world's addiction to hydrocarbons that prompted the Russian elite to conclude that these fortunate circumstances could be exploited. The stabilization of Russia's internal situation under Putin and the resultant social support he gained were also pertinent. Other external factors are relevant: the profound sense of disorientation in Western nations as to how to build a new world order; U.S. setbacks in Iraq and growing global hostility to American hegemony; and the crisis of the "color revolutions," which so alarmed the Russian elite in 2004–2005. All these factors have raised Russia's opinion of its own worth and have revived its interest in world politics. There is, in fact, no telling whether the ruling team genuinely believes in Russia's importance in international politics or whether it is bluffing and consciously exaggerating its capabilities. Domestic policy built on imitation can lead to a foreign policy that also favors creating Potemkin villages, in whose reality the creators themselves may not believe.

Moscow's new self-assurance immediately increased mutual suspicion between Russia and the West. Was that inevitable? There are many reasons why Russia and the West find it difficult to trust each other. The most basic is a difference in fundamentals—in the values and standards both sides are using to structure their systems, organize their states, and consolidate their societies. Russia's way of legitimizing itself and re-energizing itself through great-power aspirations and seeking global influence inevitably provokes the mistrust of the West. In the past century these aspirations led to confrontation between the USSR and the liberal democracies on more than one occasion. Nevertheless, as seen by the Russian elite, great-power ambitions remain a factor of the country's sense of identity and national survival. Even Russia's liberals believe that its geographical situation and security needs mean that it cannot be an "ordinary" or "normal" country, leaving it no option but to seek international influence. Putin and other Russian politicians are, therefore, entirely correct when they claim that relations between Russia and the West have worsened because Russia has grown stronger. The whole point, however, is that this strengthening stems from Russia's return to old patterns of behavior that the West finds inimical and threatening.

Several political reasons, stemming from this organic incompatibility, go some way to explain the estrangement of Russia and the West. First, the Russian political class finds U.S. hegemony unacceptable in a way that America's Atlantic allies do not. Second, the regime in Moscow is consolidating itself domestically by exploiting essentially antiliberal, anti-Western principles. Third, the logic of the Russian system demands resort to force, pressure, intimidation (currently by exploiting energy resources), or a show of force in international politics, without which the regime cannot retain power inside Russia. A weak leader failing to demonstrate a tough hand on the international stage will forfeit the confidence of the elite and have no chance of controlling domestic events. Fourth, the Russian political class now sees its rapprochement with the West as a surrendering of its position and a betrayal of sovereignty and constantly demands reciprocity and trade-offs.

Some commentators on Russia's international behavior try to explain it by the old Russian triad: expansionism, exceptionalism, and messianism, which, according to them, continue to define Putin's foreign policy. Others, on the contrary, believe that Russia has freed itself of its historical legacy and has shaped its foreign policy on the basis of pure economic interests. True, the legacy of the past and old myths and stereotypes are only too apparent in the foreign-policy thinking of the Russian ruling class and cannot be abandoned too quickly, especially when, domestically, Russia has returned to its authoritarian ways. At the same time, the Russian elite has brushed aside its old messianism by reverting to pragmatism. It has rejected territorial expansionism, trying to restore its influence by turning to "soft power"—energy resources—often using it in a rather "hard" way. Soon, however, the Russian elite will be forced to understand the limits of its energy game and how it can backfire. As for the belief in Russia's uniqueness, Putin himself has undermined it by arguing that Russia does not differ much from any other democracy. "We are like you," he says continually, in this way erasing an old Russian myth about a "unique Eurasian destiny" or Russia's "superiority to decadent Western culture," myths always popular among the Russian establishment when seeking to explain why Russia could not change.

Drawing conclusions about the commercialization of Russian foreign policy and, as a result, about a radical change in its nature, would be premature. The blending of power and property in Russia means that there is no division between politics and the economy, which explains why the Russian state so aggressively pursues economic interests, considering them political tools. In this context Russian economic cooperation with its partners will always have a strong political flavor and represent an attempt to serve its geopolitical interests. Conversely, all political steps will have an economic motivation. However, such economic instruments, and in particular energy resources, are not like nuclear weapons and the arms race. They are not lethal. Old drivers of foreign policy are simply fading away and being replaced by new drivers.

The West bears partial responsibility for the ending of Russia's movement toward it, and indeed for its distancing itself from the West. Unfortunately neither the United States nor the West as a whole has found a satisfactory response to the Russian challenge. There are a number of reasons for this. Robert Legvold explains:

> The problem is that neither the U.S. leadership nor for that matter European leaders have ever seriously wrestled with the underlying conceptual challenge: that is, how to integrate Russia with the West when it cannot be integrated into the West, that is, into the institutions that are at the core of Europe (the EU) and the Euro-Atlantic alliance (NATO).[6]

We are dealing here with a systemic trap that the West, together with Russia, of course, failed to find a way out of in the 1990s. So far there is no example of the successful transformation of an authoritarian state outside the orbit of the Western community. Russia could not transform itself without being in some way included in Western structures. That was impossible not only because of its internal problems, but also because Western leaders failed to come up with extraordinary methods for integrating it when such a chance, though negligible, did exist. There can be no certainty, of course, that Russia would have accepted such an offer, but in any case, it was never made.

Could the real enough obstacles have been overcome to enable Russia to continue moving closer to the West? If so, would integration into Western organizations have led to Russia's transformation into a liberal democracy? Who can say? Drawing Russia into the West might merely have legitimized the Russian hybrid or subverted the West from within. Theoretically, a quite different scenario was possible. In the early 1990s the West had the means to influence Moscow more actively and have a broader impact on Russia's reforms than it does now. Alas, the opportunity was missed, and no prospect of repeating the experiment in Russia now or in the foreseeable future seems to be in sight, unless Russia changes its standards.

Under Mikhail Gorbachev, abandoning confrontation with the West, renouncing attempts to view it as the enemy, and his ideas of a "common European home," "new political thinking," and switching to dialogue with the West played a crucial role in the liberalization of the Soviet system. Boris Yeltsin's attempts to make Russia an ally of the West also facilitated Russia's *apertura* (opening) to Western civilization. Putin has reversed that policy, both in terms of again viewing the West as an enemy and of exploiting foreign policy to backtrack and consolidate bureaucratic authoritarianism at home.

Russian foreign policy has returned to its traditional role of serving the needs of domestic order and become the instrument of restoration. Today it increasingly conforms to Lenin's axiom that "foreign policy is a continuation of internal policy." There is nothing peculiar or unique about that. The foreign policies of developed democracies also reflect their domestic imperatives. Turning foreign policy into a domestic policy tool in Russia is a sign that bureaucratic authoritarianism needs extra resources to survive and foreign policy becomes a systemic factor of perpetuation. We see the regime's internal needs behind all Russia's actions on the world stage, whether they take the form of grumbling about American hegemony; selling arms to Syria, Venezuela, and Iran; pandering to Iran; or bullying Ukraine and Georgia. Moscow's opposition to U.S. hegemony derives less from the logic of international developments, which should be driving Russia to work more closely with the United States on counterbalancing, for example, China or fighting international terrorism. It arises from the need to have a mighty opponent whose existence justifies retention of a centralized state. Military aid to Syria and Venezuela has both an economic subtext and a geopolitical basis rooted in Russia's self-image as a state with global interests. Moscow's soft line on Iran is mostly based on anti-Americanism in its domestic consolidation policy and the economic interests of particular groups, ignoring a potential threat emerging on Russia's borders of a regional superpower hostile to Russia.

The most obvious example of foreign policy as a continuation of internal policy is the Kremlin's attitude toward Ukraine and Georgia. Kiev and Tbilisi are being treated like naughty children who are not doing as they are told and need to be punished. The great-power hegemony here is not an end in itself but the means of self-preservation of a centralized state that needs vassals to order around.

Western observers shrug their shoulders and wonder why Moscow is constantly behaving so crassly, managing only to damage its international reputation. In fact, Moscow's actions have their own logic, both when it turns off the gas to Ukraine, when it expels Georgians from its territory, and when it gets engaged in a conflict with Great Britain over the extradition of the suspect in the poisoning of British citizen Alexander Litvinenko, a former Russian national and ex-KGB officer, with polonium-210. The rationale is that of a centralized bureaucratic regime whose interests do not necessarily coincide with Russia's national interests. The subordination of foreign policy to domestic policy aims is also reflected in the weakness of the Ministry of Foreign Affairs, which functions as a translator of decisions made by the president's staff. Those honing the rhetoric of Russia's foreign policy are the same spin doctors who sculpt internal policy myths.

The seesawing relations between Russia and the West are partly due to the West's failure to decide where Russia fits into its system of relationships. The West does not see Russia as an adversary, and Russia, for the time being at least, does not give the West substantial grounds to do so. The West has, however, ceased to trust Russia as a reliable partner. Russia has turned out to be complicated, and having good relations with it needs unconventional approaches, for which those in Western capitals have no time, or for which they are unprepared to make time.

Chapter 15

IS RUSSIA READY TO SET SAIL UNDER ITS OWN STEAM?

Russia's foreign policy has undergone a substantial evolution during Putin's presidency. He began his first term by attempting to establish a partnership with the liberal democracies. At the end of Putin's first presidency (by 2003–2004), as the Kremlin became more confident of its power and increasingly disillusioned with its foreign partners, it began experimenting with a multivector policy, which was effectively a policy of opportunistic vacillation in response to day-to-day requirements.

This policy had a number of advantages for Russia: it began to restore its lost relations with the Asia-Pacific Basin, China, India, the Middle East, and Latin America. Putin's Moscow not only extended the geographical reach of its foreign policy but also moved it to a new dimension. Recognizing that the lever of military force was no longer effective, Russia began concentrating on commercial relations. Bobo Lo was right, of course, when he remarked, "Economization, far from being incompatible with geopolitics, gives it teeth."[1]

A new phase in Putin's foreign policy was seen in 2005. The Kremlin team decided to move beyond its multivector policy and initiate bolder foreign policy initiatives. Efforts to influence the results of the presidential election in Ukraine reflected new ambitions in the Kremlin. In 2006, the minister of foreign affairs, Sergei Lavrov, began talking of a role for Russia as mediator in world crises (he offered Moscow's assistance as a go-between in relations between the West and Iran and between the West and Hamas). He further declared, "Russia ... cannot take anybody's side in the conflict between civilizations. Russia is prepared to be a bridge."[2] Pro-Kremlin analyst Vladimir Frolov pushed it further in order not to leave any doubts regarding a new Kremlin posture:

A consensus has formed in Russia, a national consensus and a consensus among the authorities, to the effect that Russia cannot be integrated into Western structures. And there is no opening for us to be integrated into the East. This means that Russia is destined to remain an independent center of power, whether it wants it or not. It will have to rely on its own code of civilization, doing its best to establish equally distant or equally close relations with other centers of power.[3]

For the first time in fifteen years the Kremlin expressed its unwillingness to integrate into the Western community and conveyed its desire to walk alone, rejecting any strategic choice and attempting to play on several chessboards at the same time, which indicated a strategic rethink.

In late 2006, Russia's foreign-policy doctrine was further developed as Sergei Lavrov put forward two new ideas that clearly reflected Vladimir Putin's thoughts, since only the Russian president has the right to formulate the country's foreign-policy posture. The first was to call for a "geopolitical triangle" comprising Russia, the European Union, and the United States, which would provide "support for collective leadership in managing world developments." The second proposed a transition to "network diplomacy." Lavrov emphasized that what the times called for were "not cumbersome unions with fixed obligations, but temporary, variable-geometry alliances based on present interests and in pursuit of specific goals." Network diplomacy was to provide for "flexible bilateral relations" between states.[4]

Moscow was effectively inviting the world to renounce bilateral and multilateral treaty obligations between states and to base international relations on temporary alliances. This kind of network diplomacy is well suited to Russia's state of chronic indecision about where it belongs. But how compatible would it be with the geopolitical triangle, which was evidently intended to be rather more stable? Both ideas suggested by Lavrov conflict with yet another Kremlin proposal, propounded by the former minister of defense, deputy premier, and presidential hopeful Sergei Ivanov, which appeared to be an invitation to dialogue, but was in reality a proposal to demarcate the spheres of influence between NATO and the Collective Security Treaty Organization (CSTO) under the leadership of Russia, which includes Armenia, Belarus, Kazakhstan, Kyrgyzstan, Tajikistan, and Uzbekistan. This would have returned the world to the age of a division of spheres of influence between NATO and the Warsaw Pact.

The Kremlin's very terminology—*mediator, bridge, network diplomacy, geopolitical triangle,* and finally, *energy superpower*—characterizes the new mood of the Russian elite, one that would like to guarantee for itself the freedom to move in a variety of directions while avoiding obligations of any sort. On the one hand there is an attempt to find a basis for Russia to play a role on its own terms between the West and the rest of the world. On the other, Moscow would like to enjoy a place in a U.S.- European–Russian triumvirate while remaining footloose and fancy-free. This is a dramatic change not only from the spirit of Yeltsin's 1990s, but from the goals of Putin's first presidency.

On March 27, 2007, Russia's Ministry of Foreign Affairs published the long-anticipated "Review of the Russian Federation's Foreign Policy," a lengthy document (one hundred pages). It reconfirms the key features of Russian foreign policy developed in 2004–2006 and seems to be a mix of old and slightly refreshed ideas that justify Russia's reorientation. Moscow has endorsed a return to the old Primakov idea of multipolarity and voiced its increased and hardly veiled criticism of the United States and its model of a unipolar world. At the same time, the Kremlin reconfirmed its interest in "collective leadership," that is, a group of leading international players with "unique responsibility for the state of world affairs," an idea that had been expressed by Sergei Lavrov. This time Moscow decided to expand collective leadership by including the United States, Russia, the United Kingdom, France, Germany, China, and Japan. The Russian ruling team apparently hopes that the idea itself might appeal to Europeans as well as to China and Japan, tired as they may be of U.S. hegemony.

The document demonstrates both the continuing ambivalence of Russian foreign policy and an attempt to play a more activist role in the creation of a new world order. Yet even for supporters of Russia's great role in international relations, the new foreign-policy posture is disappointing because it does not offer specific recommendations on how to build this new role, how to deal with key world crises (in particular, Iran, Iraq, and North Korea), nor does it offer a constructive Russian response to major world challenges, including global warming, poverty, endemic diseases, HIV, migration, radical Islam, and international terrorism.

In practice, Moscow is returning to power politics, but now it is energy based. "The weak get beaten," Putin tells us, evidently referring to what he sees as U.S. efforts to impose its will on Russia. "National security is Russia's first priority," Sergei Ivanov, first deputy premier, agrees. He unambiguously indicates the source of threats to Russia's national security: "The greatest of these is meddling in Russia's internal affairs by foreign states," again a reference to the United States. In search of a banner around which to rally Russians, Ivanov proposed a trinity of national values: "sovereign democracy—a strong economy— military might."[5] This harks back to the playing of a geopolitical game in the tradition of the nineteenth century and in the manner of such geopoliticians as Halford Mackinder, whom the West has more or less forgotten. It is, however, a new kind of geopolitics. It is energy geopolitics.

Under Yeltsin the idea of subscribing to Western values was generally acceptable to the political class. Now, however, any kind of borrowing from the West is regarded by Russian politicians as "an ideological basis for defeatism" and as a "rejection of Russia's own identity and sovereignty." The ever-helpful Kremlin propagandists are busily explaining that the West, primarily the United States, only pretends to fight for democracy and human rights in Russia, while actually being intent on depriving Russia of the "unique role it plays in world energy markets." Accordingly, Russians must defend themselves with all their might from Western influence and oppose the Western, primarily American, understanding of democracy. This is the basis on which Moscow questions its participation in the Organization for Security and Co-operation in Europe (OSCE), asserting that the OSCE is too engaged in promoting human rights and is attempting to impose a Western model of democracy on Russia and its allies.

The Russian elite is again coming to see the surrounding world as hostile. It no longer doubts that the West is aggressive and wishes Russia ill. This conviction gelled after the Ukrainian Orange Revolution in late 2004, when Moscow's unsuccessful attempts to affect the outcome of the Ukrainian presidential election caused the first major conflict between Russia and the West in the post-Soviet territories. The root of the conflict was normative differences, with geopolitics playing a secondary role. Moscow genuinely believes that Ukrainian society took to Maidan Square because it had been inspired and paid to do so by the West. These events at least confirmed that Russia was not prepared for a confrontation with the West. In Ukraine, Moscow was forced to retreat. But this geopolitical retreat at that time was followed by backtracking in Russian domestic politics as well.

Having suffered an embarrassing reversal in Ukraine, the Russian political class did not abandon its belief that Russia has a right to participate in setting the rules of international relations. Indeed, it resolved to step up its efforts. Are the Kremlin's ambitions solidly grounded, and does it have the resources to back them up? This is by no means clear. Moscow's attempts to mediate when tensions rose between the West and North Korea and Iraq were unsuccessful, and it has scored no victories in its efforts to resolve the conflicts in Transnistria, Abkhazia, and South Ossetia. In early 2006, the Kremlin's approach to offering its mediation in the Israeli–Palestinian crisis by talking to Hamas had the appearance of an ostentatious impromptu initiative with little prospect of success.

To be fair, the Kremlin has managed a number of tactical successes. Russia has strengthened its presence in the former Soviet territories, especially in Central Asia, and is obliging the West to take more account of it in its approach to international problems. The Western capitals do their best not to irritate the Kremlin needlessly, recognizing that without Moscow it will be impossible to resolve a number of important issues, from energy security to nuclear nonproliferation. Some Western, primarily European, leaders are buttering up the Kremlin, attempting to negotiate bilateral agreements and thereby giving Russia more room to maneuver in its game with the West. Anyway, today's Russian state gains freedom to maneuver by avoiding the defining of its final trajectory and by stunning the West with spontaneous initiatives which Moscow is not always ready to implement.

Since 2005, relations between Russia and the West have begun to assume the form of "both-friend-and-foe," with collaboration in some areas and mutual containment (or an attempt at it) in others.[6] At first sight this foreign policy hybrid makes no sense at all, but in practice the definition conveys a sense of the Kremlin's efforts to project the incompatibility of the principles underlying its domestic policy into the realm of foreign policy. Authoritarianism combines just as logically with elections as marching in step with the West while believing in a unique and different path, being simultaneously for the West

Boris Yeltsin at a treaty-signing ceremony in Kazakhstan, July 6, 1998.

The rivals: President of the Soviet Union Mikhail Gorbachev and the Chairman of the Supreme Soviet of Russia Boris Yeltsin at the May Day celebration, May 1, 1991.

Inauguration of Russia's first president, Boris Yeltsin, June 1991.

РОССИЯ - США

Boris Yeltsin and Bill Clinton at a press conference in Moscow, April 1994.

Yegor Gaidar and Anatoly Chubais at a session of the State Duma, May 1994.

Chechen woman looks for relatives among corpses, Chechnya, March 1995.

Hostages of Chechen terrorists leave the hospital where they have been held, Budenovsk, June 1995.

Yeltsin's oligarchs (clockwise from upper left): Vladimir Potanin, president of Interros; Mikhail Khodorkovsky, head of Yukos; Boris Berezovsky, an oligarch who wears many hats; Mikhail Fridman, head of the Alfa Group; Vladimir Gusinsky, founder of Media-Most; and Roman Abramovich, governor of Chukotka.

They ruled Russia: Yeltsin's daughter, Tatiana Diachenko, with her husband and former Yeltsin advisor, Valentin Yumashev, at a tennis match, September 22, 2002.

Yeltsin with his wife Naina at the award ceremony for the National Academy of Movie Arts, April 2003.

St. Petersburg governor, Anatoly Sobchak, and his then assistant, Vladimir Putin, at a session of the city legislature, fall 1993.

President Yeltsin and then Premier Putin during the signing of a treaty with Belarus, December 18, 1999.

Premier Vladimir Putin speaks before the State Duma, November 24, 1999.

President Bush and President Putin at a meeting with media after their summit in Moscow, May 24, 2002.

Mikhail Khodorkovsky is taken to prison after his court hearing, May 25, 2004.

A man carries a wounded girl after a terrorist act in Beslan, September 3, 2004.

A Moscow rally of the youth movement *Nashi* (Ours) organized by the Kremlin, May 15, 2005.

Grigory Yavlinsky, leader of Yabloko, Nikita Belych, leader of the Union of Right Forces, and Alexei Yablokov, head of Green Russia party, November 1, 2005.

G8 summit hosted by Vladimir Putin in St. Petersburg, July 26, 2006.

Police attack the dissenters' march in St. Petersburg, April 15, 2007.

Vladimir Putin meets with members of the youth movement *Nashi* (Ours) at his residence, Bocharov Ruchei, May 18, 2006.

Leaders of oppositional movement Other Russia during the dissenters' march in Moscow, December 16, 2006. From left to right: Mikhail Kasianov, Eduard Limonov, leader of the National Bolshevik party, and former world chess champion, Garry Kasparov.

President Putin at a mass in Preobrazhenski Cathedral, January 2006.

Anna Politkovskaya, *Novaya Gazeta* journalist, killed on October 7, 2006.

Russian premiers during the Yeltsin and Putin presidencies (Putin was Russian premier from the summer of 1999 until March 2000). Clockwise from upper left: Viktor Chernomyrdin, Sergei Kiriyenko, Yevgeny Primakov, Sergei Stepashin, Mikhail Kasianov, and Mikhail Fradkov.

Putin's team in 2007 (clockwise from upper left): Sergei Ivanov, deputy premier, Dmitri Medvedev, deputy premier, Igor Sechin, deputy head of the presidential administration, Vladislav Surkov, deputy head of the presidential administration, Boris Gryzlov, speaker of the State Duma and leader of the United Russia Party, and Sergei Mironov, speaker of the Federation Council and leader of the Just Russia party.

President Vladimir Putin, still in power but approaching the end of his term.

and against it. Given such a contradictory model of behavior, the question of which strategy Russia ought to choose, which so many analysts have racked their brains over, proves to be without substance. What choice are we talking about for a state that sees its mission as avoiding a clear trajectory?

In the aftermath of September 11, 2001, the Kremlin unambiguously sided with the United States, which tells us that at existential moments Russia is likely to side with the West, but in times of peace, for as long as the present Russian system is retained, bolstered by great-power aspirations, the country will inevitably return to vacillation. The question is, rather, how long can Moscow continue with a combination of realpolitik, economic pragmatism, aspirations to belong to the same club as Western democracies, and great-power status (*derzhavnichestvo*)? How will it eventually resolve the conflict between such diverse constituents? The hybrid nature of Russian foreign policy is reflected in its style of forcefulness coupled with retreat when obstacles are encountered; arrogance and hesitancy; aspirations to participate in international organizations and a refusal to honor obligations; and bursts of activity and a lack of strategic goals. Such a policy makes it difficult for the West to formulate a consistent policy toward Russia and sometimes obliges it to follow Russia's zigzags.

The Kremlin's urge to be simultaneously the friend and foe of the West, its partner and opponent, occasionally leads to absurdity. Thus, on the one hand, Russia signs a Partnership and Cooperation Agreement with the European Union, becomes a member of the Contact Group during the wars in Bosnia and Kosovo, and cooperates with Europe in the Council of Europe and Parliamentary Assembly and with NATO on the NATO–Russia Council. On the other hand, Russia views the West as an opponent. On the one hand, we have Moscow developing "road maps" for rapprochement with Europe, while on the other it regards Ukraine's move into Europe as a hostile act. On the one hand, Russia had the presidency of the G8 in 2006, but on the other it continues to accuse the West of attempts to undermine its territorial integrity. On the one hand, Moscow views the United States as a partner in the antiterrorist coalition, but on the other demands that Americans should get out of Central Asia, which is rapidly becoming a center for the spread of terrorism. On the one hand, Putin seeks to attract Western investment in Russia, but this approach is accompanied by a barrage of anti-Western propaganda and attempts to force Western investors to sell their assets to the Russian state.

By distancing itself from the West, Russia does not always enhance its sovereignty. At least in some areas Moscow finds itself furthering Chinese interests, in particular through its membership in the Shanghai Cooperation Organization (SCO), which the Chinese are using to expand into Central Asia and to oppose the United States. The Russo–Chinese joint military maneuvers in 2005 were a triumph of Chinese diplomacy, just as Chinese relations were simultaneously worsening with Japan, South Korea, and the United States. It was a time when the United States had even lifted its embargo on deliveries of nuclear technology to India in order to draw it into a containment of China. In the summer of 2005, U.S. Defense Secretary Donald Rumsfeld announced that the Pentagon considered China a potential threat and began demanding that all countries cease arms deliveries to China. This was the moment that Russia chose to hold out a hand to Beijing, which enabled China to raise the stakes in its ongoing dialogue with the United States, which was anxious both to contain China and to cooperate with it. What Russia got out of all this, other than deepening the suspicions of the White House, is not obvious. By aspiring to become a center of power independent of the West, Russia is being lured into the sphere of influence of China. Zbigniew Brzezinski once said of Russia, "Rivalry with America was senseless, and an alliance with China would have meant subordination."[7] Moscow does not seem to notice how Beijing exploits this partnership in its own interests, graciously allowing Moscow to delude itself that it is a leading partner.

Russia's attitude toward China is a tangle of contradictions, which demonstrates that Russia lacks a strategic vector in its foreign policy and in the end is losing the initiative. Russia has an interest in cooperating with its great neighbor.[8] On the surface, Russo–Chinese relations seem a successful partnership, especially in the economic area. Russo–Chinese trade in 2006 amounted to $34 billion, a 40 percent increase, compared with 2005 (in 2007 the volume of trade is expected to have increased by 34.8 percent). More that 90 percent of Russian exports to China are natural resources. China today is fourth on the list of Russia's trade partners (Russia is China's tenth-largest trade partner). Hu Jintao, China's president, who visited Russia in March 2007, and Putin declared their ambition to double bilateral trade to $80 billion by 2010.[9]

Nevertheless, Russia is worried about the growing power of China and its possible expansion into Siberia and East Asia. These fears have increased as a result of the continuing process of depopulation of the Far East and Siberia. About 7 million people now live in the far eastern region of Russia, whereas the population in the northern provinces of China amounts to 110 million people. (Today, however, Chinese migration to Russia does not exceed five hundred thousand people.) Russian analyst Vladislav Inozemtsev warns:

> One day Russia will find itself squeezed out from Central Asia and Russians will leave the Far East themselves. In a confrontation with China, Russia has no chances: its economy is five times less than China's, its population ten times less than China's, its industrial production is thirty times less than China's.[10]

In the Russian provinces bordering China, the population is spontaneously mobilized by a wave of anti-Chinese feeling. Moscow, however, although anxious about China, is selling it the latest weaponry, which emphasizes the gulf between Russia's day-to-day policies and its longer-term strategic interests.

Beijing is boosting its presence in Central Asia, effectively using the SCO for that purpose. Astana and Bishkek obtain arms from China. The total amount of joint Chinese–Kazakh investment in Kazakhstan is some $5 billion. China has allocated loans totaling $600 million to Tajikistan for joint projects. Turkmenistan has received a preferential loan of $300 million. China has decided to extend credits amounting to $920 million to Kyrgyzstan, Kazakhstan, and Tajikistan in 2007 to enable them to finance imports from China. Uzbekistan is receiving a loan of $350 million. This indicates not merely that China is expanding its economic influence in the region, but that it is becoming the main patron and the leading force in Central Asia, proving that Brzezinski's warnings are coming true.

It seems that the Russian political class is choosing to exaggerate the threat posed to Russia by the West without really believing it itself. It seems increasingly worried about the threat from China, but unwilling to admit as much openly, and seems to be facilitating the rise of this neighboring power. Thus, in reality, in Russo–Chinese relations there are a lot of underwater rocks. The relationship is inherently unstable. It is not unimaginable that the growing asymmetry of the relationship as China develops may push Russia into the arms of the West, forcing the Russian elite to terminate its indecision and vacillations, and to seek guarantees from the West to contain China's rise or expansionism. Whether these would be forthcoming remains to be seen.

Immediately after the G8 summit in St. Petersburg, in the summer of 2006, Putin organized his own "G3" summit with Russia, India, and China. The summit was intended to proclaim Moscow's intention of becoming the center of a new coalition. Beijing and New Delhi duly played along. One suspects that these three very different countries had their own reasons for taking part in this collective imitation of friendship, particularly with respect to their relations with the West. Not to put too fine a point on it, creating a semblance of an alternative club to those of the West is covert blackmail of the Western democracies. Coit D. Blacker once saw Yevgeni Primakov's anti-American strategy of pursuing multipolarity by courting U.S. rivals as a bluff. In his words it was a "strategy of driving west while feigning east."[11] The Kremlin continues to use this strategy, while Beijing and New Delhi support the game. It is hardly credible that any of those participating in this strange trinity, which really exists only on paper, believe it has much of a future. All that remains to be seen is which of them will prove to be the most successful blackmailer.

On June 10, 2007, the Russian president again decided to assail the dominance of the few developed democracies by calling on them to recognize a "new balance of power" in the world. "The new architecture of economic relations requires a completely new approach," Vladimir Putin said at the St. Petersburg International Economic Forum, a forum that Moscow intends to turn into the "Russian Davos." Putin bitterly complained that international institutions such as the WTO, which Russia has been trying to join for more than a decade, have turned "archaic, undemocratic, and inflexible," and called on those attending to create a new global economic framework with Russia at its center. Such a system, according to the Russian president, would reflect the new rising powers, like Russia, China, India, and Brazil. It was an open message that Russia wants to change the balance of power. Putin's ideas, as expected, received a cold response from the Western officials in the audience. "Globalization does not respect spheres of influence," Peter Mandelson, the European Union trade commissioner, retorted.[12]

How serious are Russia's demands? Is the Russian elite prepared to embark on a confrontation with the West? Definitely not. The overwhelming majority of the Russian elite has no desire to return to isolation, let alone return to fraught relations with the West. The elite is spending billions of dollars to improve its image in the West. It is trying to attract Western investment in Russia. It wants to expand its presence in the West. It keeps its families and bank accounts in Western countries. How does membership of the G8, or all the energy Putin devoted to making the St. Petersburg G8 summit in July 2006 a success, fit the scenario of Russia's distancing itself from the West? The hard-liners, and especially the *siloviki* who control Rosneft, went to great lengths to organize its IPO (initial public offering) on the stock exchange and to attract Western managers—that means that they too need good relations with the West. Moscow has retained Ketchum, an expensive American public relations firm, and pays for advertisements in the *Washington Post*, the *Daily Telegraph*, and a Chinese daily on a monthly basis in order to improve Russia's image. As if that were not enough, the Russian political class knows full well that, with a military budget of $25 billion, Russia cannot afford a serious deterioration in its relations with the West, where the Pentagon alone spends $419 billion a year on defense.

That is all very well, the skeptic may say, but then how do you explain why Moscow puts a spoke in the West's wheel whenever it gets a chance? Russia obstructs the West in the post-Soviet territories; sells arms to pariah regimes; hinders the implementation of sanctions against Iran and sells it weapons; receives Hamas and Chávez in Moscow; and plays up to China. The answer would be: Russia's behavior does not fit into any tidy scheme. The ruling elite is indeed eager to become integrated into the West on a personal level, and to do a deal on the best possible terms it can obtain. At the same time, it publicly rejects the West and makes it an enemy in order to rally Russian society.

Roman Abramovich, the Russian oligarch who has been the governor of Chukotka since 2000 and lives in Great Britain, is an example of a member of the Russian elite integrating into the West on a personal level. Numerous representatives of the ruling class live in the West and manage their Russian assets from Western capitals even while endorsing an aggressively anti-Western foreign policy by the Kremlin and being demonstratively nationalistic when they are in Russia. This is perfectly understandable. They feel cocky, and they admire their cockiness when they oppose the West. They can remain elite only in a society that is hostile to the West. The overwhelming majority of them, however, would be very reluctant to see relations deteriorate significantly or to be parted from their conveniently schizophrenic mind-set. This is nothing new. It is a new phase of an old policy. Back in the late 1940s, Sir Isaiah Berlin commented on the dual-track policy of the Russian ruling class, "Russia is ready to take part in international relations, but she prefers other countries to abstain from taking an interest in her affairs; that is to say, to insulate herself from the rest of the world without remaining isolated from it."[13]

Russia retreats every time a conflict occurs between its interests and those of the West, beginning with Bosnia and ending with Ukraine. It retreats for want of an ideology that might justify a confrontation with the West; because of the hybrid nature of the regime that, in the interests of self-preservation, refuses to risk conflict; and because of a lack of resources to support conflict with the West. How would a strengthening of authoritarianism reflect on foreign policy? There are some among the elite who have been unable or have chosen not to buy into the West on a personal level, and who are not dismayed by the prospect of conflict with the Western democracies, seeing it as a factor they can use in the struggle for power. At present these hardliners would probably not go so far as to see Russia isolated from the outside world, like an enormous Cuba. How they might behave in the future, however, especially in a crisis, is anyone's guess, so we need to be prepared for surprises in Russia's foreign policy, which will be a reflection of Russia's internal struggle.

The hope for a partnership between Russia and the West on the basis of common interests has not so far produced the expected coming together over moral values that had been the dream of many on both sides. Indeed, an increasing number of conflicts are occurring over the interpretation of their supposedly common interests, and this suggests that for the time being Russia and the West can hardly behave as consistent partners. Their cooperation is ever more situational. Even a common threat is not guaranteed to overcome their mutual suspicion. Vladimir Putin apparently believed for a time that he would be able to maintain close relations with his Western colleagues based on trust, in part through personal diplomacy, even as he closed Russia off from Western influence. He failed, and now to preserve the traditional Russian state he is obliged to put his relations with the liberal democracies at risk. Analyzing Vladimir Putin's foreign policy during his first presidency, Russian observer Andrei Grachev wrote:

> President Putin has shown great dexterity in handling Russia's external relations in a very difficult period. Russia's weakness and the crisis of transition constrained Moscow from having much more than a reactive foreign policy. Using a chess analogy, one could give the president credit for the skill and effectiveness with which he has played his version of "Putin's defense" ... If he fails to resist the temptation to return to the reflexes of superpower behavior ... or succumbs to the pressure of the nationalistic forces, he will be held responsible for the reversal of Russia's journey away from the past.[14]

This concern has materialized during Putin's second presidency.

The resultant relationship between Russia and the Western democracies gives grounds for both optimism and concern. The grounds for optimism stem from the fact that Russia and the developed democracies have existential interests in common, albeit not always understood identically. These interests nonetheless keep them from drifting too far apart, and in moments of a real threat, both sides can be expected to brush aside their different interpretations of common interests. The cause for concern is that the impulsiveness of the Russian elite and its lack of solid principles may eventually prevent the Kremlin from being able to neutralize the consequences of its new aggressiveness. The West, for its part, may make matters worse by failing to understand the processes unfolding in Russia and its neighboring states, and as a result either failing to react or reacting inappropriately.

Be that as it may, the relationship between Russia and the West at the end of Putin's presidency continues to deteriorate. Russia and the West again find themselves divided by mutual suspicion and resentment. It is difficult to see where they will start rebuilding their partnership, whether it will be a real one rather than an imitation, and whether it will be a geopolitical impetus or Russian domestic developments that impel them to do so. The jury is out on those issues.

So far, the nature of the Russian state and the logic of personalized power are the crucial drivers that have been shaping Russia's foreign policy, mentality, and actions. In some cases it has been the West that has given the Kremlin the pretext or motivation to demonstrate a new assertiveness. Yet new variables will inevitably emerge that will push Russia toward a new foreign-policy model, and it is here that several driving forces may be decisive. Globalization, consolidation of the West and its adoption of a more coherent Russian strategy, and new moods and new political leadership in Russia can make a difference. There is, however, a question that provokes anxiety among Russian liberals and democrats: their growing doubts and frustration as to the true intentions of the leading Western powers toward Russia. They fear that powerful forces in the West prefer a stable and stagnant Russia to a Russia that will start a new round of democratization that could lead to the emergence of a competitive state, and transform a stagnant Russia into a more dynamic and prosperous nation. The West has to deal with these concerns.

In the end, the "partner-opponent" model of Russia's relations with the West, being a direct reflection of the Russian domestic hybrid system, cannot radically change unless the Russian system is reformed. This model might be effective in reaching short-term goals and adapting to a changing environment, but it lacks deeper substance and rejects strategic commitments. This is a foreign-policy model for a country that is not ready to choose its final trajectory but at the same time is unready and unable to return to its past. Such a model by a country that remains a regional and global power is a serious challenge for the world.

What about Russian society? How does it view the West? Despite the anti-Western rhetoric of the national Russian television channels and the majority of Russian politicians, Russians still view the West as Russia's partner. In 2007, 46 percent of Russian respondents thought that Russia should orient itself on the European countries (Germany, France, and Great Britain); 45 percent thought that Russia should strengthen its relations with Ukraine, Belarus, and Kazakhstan; 27 percent opted for India and China; 19 percent chose Japan; 15 percent chose the United States; and only 12 percent named old Soviet allies Cuba, North Korea, and the Arab world. This means that Russian society at large is ready for an active partnership with the West, which is the most powerful ground for optimism.

Chapter 16

HOW CAN WE LEARN
TO BE NEIGHBORS?

The former Soviet space continues to diversify. The Soviet republics have been replaced by a variety of political regimes, from unconsolidated democracies to quasi-sultanates. In their foreign policy orientation the new states are being attracted to different centers of gravity. The Commonwealth of Independent States (CIS), which arose from the ruins of the USSR and which Putin called a product of divorce, has become a forum, or club, where leaders who would not otherwise be talking to one another meet.

The newly independent states in the European part of the former USSR are increasingly gravitating into the orbit of NATO and the European Union. Russia and the West are battling it out for influence over Armenia, Azerbaijan, and Georgia, with Iran and Turkey trying to join in. In Central Asia a game is being played by China, Russia, and the West and is being observed by India, Iran, Pakistan, and Turkey. Russia and China are currently trying to counter pressure from the West in Central Asia, but the time may come when Russia has to choose to be either a junior partner of China or an ally of the West in order to contain China. In the post-Soviet territories, a number of integrationist megaprojects are jockeying for position. The Russian-sponsored projects include the Eurasian Economic Community (EEC), which comprises Belarus, Kazakhstan, Kyrgyzstan, Russia, and Tajikistan; the Collective Security Treaty Organization (CSTO), which comprises Armenia, Belarus, Kazakhstan, Kyrgyzstan, and Russia; and the Common Economic Space (CES), which comprises Belarus, Kazakhstan, Russia, and Ukraine. Russo–Chinese projects include the Shanghai Cooperation Organization (SCO), which includes China, Kazakhstan, Kyrgyzstan, Tajikistan, and Uzbekistan. There are pro-Western associations, such as the Organization for Democracy and Economic Development (GUAM), which comprises Georgia, Ukraine, Azerbaijan, and Moldova; and the Democratic Axis, comprising the Baltic states, Georgia, Poland, and Ukraine.

Even within the core of the CIS—Belarus, Kazakhstan, and Russia—conflicts arise. Russia's integrationist initiatives are largely a response to the EU's and NATO's coming within reach of its borders. The members of pro-Russian associations are not expected to allow foreign bases on their territories or to join any other alliances. The members of Russia-led associations do not appreciate these restrictions and are unlikely to develop a strong anti-Western bias as they try to play on several chessboards simultaneously.

Moscow's jealous attitude toward the former Soviet territories indicates that the political class continues to view the newly independent states (with the exception of the Baltic states) as states with limited sovereignty. For the Russian elite they remain an area subject to Russian internal policy. Even the liberals are unable to break free of the snares of traditional thinking, as was evident from Chubais's call to turn Russia into a "liberal empire." This shows how difficult it is for a former empire to reconcile itself to being truncated. One can, of course, seek solace in the fact that all empires have found it difficult to sever links with their former territories and that barely disguised imperialist utterances could occasionally be heard emanating from the French and English political classes as recently as twenty years ago. States like Russia, and indeed Great Britain, as Geoffrey Hosking remarks, find it all the more difficult to part with their former dependencies because they have always had messianic notions regarding their relationship with other lands. In the Russian case, it is even more difficult due to the fact that Russia was a territorially integrated empire.

The interest Russia continues to take in its neighbors is not solely due to a leftover sense of empire. It derives also from Russia's needs for its future development, in particular its wish to ensure stability in the post-Soviet space and to support political regimes that are on good terms with Moscow. Russia wishes to develop economic relations with the newly independent states and to resolve problems that disturb both them and Moscow. The kinds of issues involved are: regulating migration, resolving customs matters, and combating terrorism, the drug trade, and smuggling. The newly independent states are a market for Russian goods and provide labor, transport corridors, and a buffer zone that shields Russia from other potentially unfriendly states. Russia and the newly independent states still have affinities, not only through their Soviet past but also through the interpenetration of their cultures and the continuing role of the Russian language and culture. Although Russia does, then, have solidly based interests in the post-Soviet territories, we have to ask whether those interests facilitate or hinder the modernization of Russia and the newly independent states. Do Russia's integrationist initiatives contribute to greater stability in the region, or do they hinder it?

In the 1990s Russia paid for loyalty by subsidizing the economies of the newly independent states with cheap energy supplies. This did not by any means ease their transformation into fully independent states. Cheap gas also proved no guarantee that those countries would toe the line of Russia's policies. In the summer of 2005, Russian Foreign Minister Sergei Lavrov stated that it was time for the countries of the CIS to start building their relations on the basis of "international practice." An anonymous representative of the Kremlin elaborated that Moscow was dissatisfied with a situation of subsidizing the economies of neighboring states by providing them with cheap energy while "those governing them receive their salaries from the Americans." It became clear that Moscow was preparing to demand a measure of reciprocity: "If we are paying your rent, keep your eyes away from other partners." The intention was to use the commercialization of Russia's foreign policy to obtain political concessions from its neighbors and to exploit energy supplies to create a new, integrated zone around Russia. A new doctrine of "Russia Plus" had been formulated to enable Russia to assert itself using the trump card of its oil and gas reserves.

After the 2005 CIS summit in Kazan, the Kremlin categorized its neighbors as either loyal or disloyal. Any movement by a post-Soviet state in the direction of the West was regarded as hostile behavior. Georgia and Moldova were found to be disloyal and had the price of their gas doubled. The price of Ukraine's gas was first increased threefold and then fourfold. Loyal Armenia and Belarus received assurances that their gas would cost the same as before, in return for economic and political concessions. The Kremlin made it clear even to its allies that it no longer intended to pamper them. In return for cheaper gas Moscow demanded that the new states transfer certain assets into Russian ownership, in particular pipelines and energy grids. Moscow simultaneously imposed sanctions on disloyal states, cutting off the energy supply to Georgia and Moldova and banning imports from those countries, with the intention of forcing Tbilisi and Chisinau back into line.

The 2005–2006 gas war with Ukraine was the first example of Moscow's new policy toward its former "younger brothers." The conflict was sparked very simply when Gazprom raised the price of gas, something for which Ukraine was unprepared. The Ukrainian leadership had evidently underestimated Gazprom's seriousness. It imagined it could come to terms with Moscow and have the price rise postponed to some future date. Moscow showed no readiness to compromise and, in order to force the Ukrainians into accepting its conditions, Gazprom cut off the gas supply. This produced interruptions not only in Ukraine but also in a number of European countries that receive gas from the main energy artery linking Russia and Europe that passes through Ukrainian territory. It became dramatically evident that any energy conflict between Russia and its transit countries would affect Europe, which had not previously considered the possibility of anything so untoward. The Russo–Ukrainian gas conflict undermined Russia's reputation as a reliable energy supplier, but Moscow had no intention of relenting. By 2007, Russia introduced gas "market pricing" for all its neighbors, even those it considered allies. Ukraine has been buying gas at $130 per thousand cubic meters, Moldova at $160, the Baltic states at $160 to $200, Armenia and Azerbaijan at $110, Belarus at $100, and Georgia at $230. The very fact of these price differentials demonstrates a political approach to price formation: recalcitrant countries have to pay more. Not even loyal countries received serious concessions, and in exchange for somewhat lower energy prices, they were compelled to sell prime national assets to Russia. Not all countries were agreeable to the new policy. In December 2006, a further confrontation occurred, this time between Russia and its closest ally, Belarus. This confrontation turned into another energy war, which led to Russia's cutting off the supply of oil to Belarus and by extension to European countries, demonstrating how serious the implications of Russia's commodity-driven policy could be and how controversial its rationale was.

In theory, Russia was right to raise energy prices and introduce market principles into its relations with the post-Soviet states. It changed the relationship from one of imperial–vassal dependency to one based on the principle of sovereignty. It was inevitable that the transition would be painful, both for the states that had become used to receiving subsidies from Russia in cheap natural resources and energy, and for Russia. In the transition to market prices, the newly independent states faced a dilemma. Either they would have to restructure their economies so as to remove their dependence on Russia (which in some cases would be exceptionally difficult in the short term) or they would have to agree to a new form of dependency by handing over control of some of their national assets.

For Russia, it is not only a matter of commercializing its foreign policy in principle because of the fusion between property and state power. The need to have spheres of influence is important as well. There is also the nature of the governing team, which draws heavily on *siloviki* and members of the natural-resource lobby, whose mental stereotypes and readiness for aggressive actions affect policy. (A change of team in the Kremlin may reduce this.) The present ruling team is incapable of separating the economy from political expediency, even though some of its members might wish to. The subordination of the state and all its institutions, from the presidency to the Ministry of Foreign Affairs to the corporate interests of the energy and security elites means that economic decisions will inevitably be biased in favor of corporate and political interests.

Paradoxically, the notion of energy hegemony developed out of the concept of a "liberal empire," that is, an expansion of influence using economic leverage. In practice, however, for Russia the expansion of a liberal empire inevitably turns into Kalashnikov diplomacy. If it is to retain its traditional state, Moscow cannot refrain from exerting political pressure on its partners and allies when pursuing its commercial deals. The belief that Russia has given up its neo-imperial ambitions and entered an era of post-imperial development is clearly premature. Under Yeltsin, it really did embark on a post-imperial phase, with no option but to scale back its influence on the former Soviet territories. Under Putin, the elite revived neo-imperialism backed by the use of energy supplies to bolster political influence.

Conflicts between Russia and Russia's neighbors are an inevitable consequence of the politicization of economic relations (today, energy supplies, but tomorrow, who knows?—perhaps nickel or copper). Demands for economic and political concessions undermine the sovereignty of the newly independent states and weaken their state authorities, which is not something all national elites are willing to put up with. In any case, a number of the states the Kremlin is trying to make dependent on Russia have more attractive alternatives. Only authoritarian regimes, though not all of them, are being drawn in. Prominent among them are those that, like Belarus, find themselves without other options, having failed to find a common language with the West.

This brings us to the Russo–Belarusian gas and oil conflict of late 2006 and early 2007, which was another inevitable consequence of Russia's new energy policy and confirmed certain patterns. It tells us, first, that Russia's gas war with Ukraine was not a one-time affair. The conflict began with an ultimatum, delivered by Gazprom to Belarus in December 2006, either to pay the "market price" for Russian gas or concede joint ownership of the Beltransgaz pipeline, which Minsk regards as one of its national assets. In addition, Moscow delivered another blow to Minsk in demanding its share from the export customs duty on oil products from Russian oil. The ultimatum made it clear to President Lukashenko that Moscow was no longer prepared to subsidize his regime. It is possible that the Kremlin, having driven him into a corner, was hoping to accelerate the long-anticipated integration of Belarus into Russia, on Moscow's terms. In 2007 Minsk had to pay Russia 1 percent of its GDP, or 2.6 percent of the budget revenue, for gas, and around 8 to 9 percent of GDP as its share of the export customs on oil products, which is a heavy burden for any economy. No wonder Lukashenko lost his nerve and rebelled, demanding that Moscow pay for its alliance with Belarus, where there are Russian military facilities, and for the use of Belarus as a transit state. Not content with that, he began siphoning oil from the pipeline that passes through Belarusian territory. Moscow reacted promptly, cutting off the supply to the pipeline, which serves not only Belarus but also Europe, without giving any warning to its customers. As a result of the conflict, the oil supply to several European countries was disrupted. This turned the conflict into another European energy crisis and dealt a further blow to Russia's already tarnished reputation as an energy supplier.

We can draw a number of conclusions from the energy war between Russia and Belarus. In the first place, it resulted from a long, drawn-out failure to create a union state between them. Moscow wanted to incorporate Belarus into the Russian Federation, while Lukashenko, who had no intention of giving up Belarus's independence, fancied the idea of living parasitically off Russia. Yeltsin saw union with Belarus as a way of making amends for having destroyed the USSR, but Putin had no use for harking back to the Soviet myth since he had his new "energy superpower" myth. As a result, an absurd situation arose where regularizing relations between Russia and Belarus was impossible, yet both had the illusion of a union state hanging over them, which in any case did not fit with Russia's concept of the "energy superpower." Belarus faced a dilemma. On the one hand, if Moscow refused to continue the barter deal, its economy faced ruin; on the other, by throwing itself on the mercy of Russia, Belarus would lose its sovereignty—something that neither the people of Belarus nor the Belarusian elite were prepared to countenance.

The second conclusion is that the worsening relations between these states indicated that analogous regimes had evolved in Russia and Belarus, with a tendency to project their internal contradictions into an international conflict. When Ukraine found itself confronting Russia over gas prices, it was forced to restructure its economy more vigorously, expand private initiative, and broaden its economic ties with Europe, but the "last dictator of Europe," Lukashenko, had no such room for maneuver. Left with no alternative, in early 2007, Lukashenko was forced to agree to a deal on Russia's conditions. Moscow did not in fact want to cause his regime to collapse and softened its demands, but even so, the agreement between Moscow and Minsk could only be a stopgap. If Lukashenko could no longer ensure Russia's provision of cheap gas, he would cease to be a guarantor of Belarusian stability. His options for the future were to introduce a full dictatorship or to give Belarus its freedom and lose his power. In either case, Moscow had unintentionally speeded up the political processes of its neighbor, which might equally well push Belarus in the opposite direction of Russia.

In the meantime, any concessions granted to Minsk would merely prolong the myths surrounding relations between Russia and Belarus, at some financial cost to the Kremlin. Further, it would be a disservice to the people of Belarus to remain dependent on Russia because it would delay modernization of the economy and the political maturing of their state. Moscow was merely prolonging its indulgence of Lukashenko (who would continue to try Russia's patience), jeopardizing its great-power status in the process. "Can't you even sort matters out with your transit state?" Moscow's European customers would wonder.

Official Minsk, desperately searching for ways to survive, started to put all the blame on Russia, making it a virtual enemy. Belarusian television worked actively on a new enemy image, blaming Gazprom, Russian oligarchs, the Russian government, and the Kremlin. Lukashenko found himself in a quandary: if he burned his bridges to Russia, he would hardly succeed in getting the support of the West—even if he used the anti-Russia card—unless he was ready to liberalize his political regime. Lukashenko, however, understood that the second option would mean his downfall, and he was not ready for political suicide.

In the end, even Western observers had to admit that in principle, the Kremlin's interest in charging its neighbors more for gas is reasonable. The problem is in Russia's bullying and capricious methods, which can have a destabilizing effect on its neighbors' economies, plus its volatile relationship with energy transit countries and carelessness over the impact on European consumers. Besides, despite the political dimension of Moscow's new approach to supplying energy, not being subsidized by Russia will be to the advantage of the new states because it will force them to reform their economies, save energy, and seek new energy sources. In short, the market will weaken the newly independent states' dependence on Moscow.

Georgia, to escape Russia's pressure, has refurbished its hydroelectric stations, and since 2006 has entirely ceased to import electricity from Russia. The need to economize on energy has prompted Georgia to reform its economy and deepen economic relations with Azerbaijan, Iran, and Turkey.

As Russia ceases to subsidize its allies, it finds it increasingly difficult to demand their subordination. That is all to the good since it obliges Russia to ponder the efficiency of a state system that can only survive on hegemony and by pressuring its neighbors. Meantime, the Kremlin, regarding its oil and gas resources as both a market asset and a political lever, despite the conflicts with Ukraine and Belarus and the damage to its reputation, is pressing ahead with attempts to create a new dependency system in the post-Soviet territories, reinforcing the demands of Gazprom with state pressure. This may lead to more oil-and-gas and transit wars in the former Soviet space. The search for new relationships between Russia, its energy customers, and its transit countries will continue. More surprises may be in store.

Today Russia's neighbors, which depend on it for energy, are compelled either to seek new sources of energy or to embark on political deals with Moscow. Thus, in October 2006 the government of Viktor Yanukovich in Kiev found itself facing the dilemma of whether to make political concessions to Moscow (not to press ahead with NATO membership and not to create difficulties over the Sevastopol base of the Russian fleet), or to face a sharp increase in the price of gas. Kiev decided in favor of concessions and restarted negotiations for Ukraine to join the Common Economic Space (CES) under the leadership of Russia. In future, however, we may expect the newly independent states to seek alternative sources of energy, so the integration of allies around Russia based purely on the need for energy is likely to prove short lived.

The expansion of its presence in the post-Soviet territories is something the Kremlin sees as proof of a resurgence of the Russian state. This is not, however, a matter of primitive retribution, an attempt by Moscow to bring back the USSR. Today's

Russian elite thinks in more flexible and softer categories of dependency. Even so, Moscow believes that the West has no business developing relations with the newly independent states behind Russia's back. The Russian political class feels it is in a "besieged fortress" when it observes a Western presence in the former Soviet Union: American bases, Western investment, the building of oil pipelines that avoid Russia, and attempts by the European Union to mediate the "frozen conflicts" left over from the Soviet era that Moscow controls. It would be an over-simplification to see pressure as the only trend in Russian foreign policy. Healthier attitudes are to be found among the elite, including an acceptance of the need to end nostalgia for a past that cannot be brought back. For the present, however, they are outweighed by a great-power mentality.

Russia's relationship with Georgia continues to be the thorniest. The underlying source of this constant tension is the Stalinist nation-state construct, which, although it collapsed after the demise of the USSR, continues to affect relationships between the nations that fell into its trap. The emergence, with support from Moscow, of separatist republics in Abkhazia and South Ossetia is the most intractable issue in bilateral relations between Moscow and Tbilisi. A factor further hindering a solution of the problem of Georgia's territorial integrity has been the inability of the Abkhazian, Georgian, and Ossetian politicians to compromise. In addition, Moscow does everything it can to retain its influence in the separatist republics, including maintaining tension in those regions where Russia is an official peacekeeper.

In the fall of 2006, relations between Moscow and Tbilisi worsened once again. Retaliating for the detention in Georgia of Russian officers accused of spying by the Georgian authorities, the Kremlin set up a blockade, cutting off all forms of communication and expelling Georgian citizens from Russian territory. Essentially, Moscow's reaction resulted from its inability to accept that the Georgians have no wish to return to the Russian fold. They prefer to shield themselves behind the broad back of the United States, specifically by joining NATO. (In March 2007, the Georgian parliament endorsed the idea of Georgia's membership of NATO, and the U.S. Congress has supported the idea of membership for Georgia and Ukraine.) The prospect of the Atlantic Alliance turning up in a territory Moscow considers its backyard invariably drives the Kremlin to distraction. Moreover, taking into account the old hostility toward NATO in the people's mentality, the prospect is also a pretext for Russian hardliners to rattle their sabres even more loudly. Russian annoyance is caused not so much by what the Georgians do as by a conviction that the Americans are behind everything. Unable to restrain himself, Putin remarked darkly that the Georgian authorities were "acting with the support of foreign sponsors." Moscow's apparent show of force against Georgia was in reality a show of force directed at the United States. Not surprisingly, the more Moscow seeks to keep Georgia in its camp, in part through pressure and threats, the more inclined Georgia is to seek refuge in Western institutions.

All the hot spots in the region are seen as a test by Moscow. Russia claims to act as a peacemaker in the conflicts in Abkhazia, South Ossetia, and Transnistria, but in reality supports separatist forces. For almost sixteen years Russia managed to keep those conflicts frozen. In 2006, however, the conflicts began, as was inevitable, to thaw. One of many factors that inflamed the situation was the discussion of independence for Kosovo. The Kremlin hastened to play the Kosovo card, proclaiming the universal applicability of the Kosovo principle. If Kosovo, which is part of Serbia, can be granted independence, then why have Abkhazia, South Ossetia, and Transnistria, in their struggles for independence from Georgia and Moldova, not been granted independence? Referendums were held in 2006 in South Ossetia and Transnistria in which the inhabitants almost unanimously declared themselves to be in favor of independence. Moreover, many of the voters looked to Russia, expecting it to decide to incorporate the separatist republics into its federation immediately. Dormant passions were awakened.

It is impossible simply to integrate the unrecognized republics into Georgia and Moldova against the wishes of populations that remember bloody conflicts with Tbilisi and Chisinau. Other ways of restoring the territorial integrity of those states need to be sought by guaranteeing broad autonomy to the unrecognized republics within a federal or confederal framework in Moldova and Georgia. So far, however, neither the Georgian nor Moldovan leaders have been able to persuade the separatists or the populations in the breakaway republics that they could live satisfactorily within the framework of Georgia and Moldova. Moreover, corrupt regimes in the separatist republics that find this unrecognized status highly convenient have become ensconced. Any change would threaten their power.

For as long as the breakaway republics exist there will be tensions that could spill out beyond the borders of Georgia and Moldova. Of course it is difficult to resolve the problem of Abkhazia, South Ossetia, and Transnistria while those who took part in the bloody clashes with Chisinau and Tbilisi survive, but neither is it a simple matter to refreeze the conflicts. It is impossible to resolve the conflicts without the help of the international community, and first of all the West, but Russia is generally opposed to international mediation. The international community seems in no hurry to become actively involved.

Russia's relations with Belarus, Georgia, and Ukraine demonstrate that Russia, having consolidated the state and regained a feeling of strength, is looking for a new role in the regional context that may trigger new conflicts in the former Soviet space. In the cases mentioned above, tensions have economic and security dimensions. A crisis in Russia's relationship with Estonia in the spring of 2007 appears to have an existential and historic background that could make it even more difficult to resolve or smooth over its implications. On April 26, 2007, Estonian authorities fenced off a memorial to Soviet soldiers in the center of Tallinn with the intention of reburying their remains in the military cemetery. This not only triggered protests by ethnic Russians in Estonia that turned violent but also ended with Russia's threatening a full diplomatic rupture in relations with Estonia. The Estonian authorities did not find the most tactful way of dealing with the symbols of the Soviet past, especially just before the annual celebration of the victory over Nazi Germany in Russia on May 9, one of the most respected and cherished in the Russian calendar. Even Russian democrats thought that Tallinn had been guilty of an unnecessary affront to Russia's national honor. Nonetheless, it was the Kremlin that intentionally used the event to escalate anti-Estonian hysteria in its "search for enemies."

Even without this unhappy incident, the past will sooner or later begin to haunt Russia as well as other states in the Baltics and Central and Eastern Europe, where Soviet liberation from fascism is viewed as a strategem for installation (as in the Baltic states) or for the introduction of satellite pro-Soviet regimes. The Russian political class has failed to deal critically with its Soviet past, and especially with the period of the Second World War. Conversely, returning to Soviet symbols and trying to use them to reinvigorate the traditional state will only provoke more tension with Russia's former "younger brothers."

The Russian–Estonian conflict over the memorial has raised a number of other issues. If Russia consolidates itself by returning to its Soviet past, could its commercial interests and the interests of the Russian business community play a positive role, neutralizing the consequences of neo-Sovietism? In the Estonian case, these interests have helped to prevent a deepening of the conflict. For Russian politicians, the newly independent states, and especially new European Union and NATO members like Estonia, may continue to be easy targets for proving their nationalist and statist credentials. One may nonetheless expect that Moscow's need to have constructive economic relations with Europe may at least partially temper its desire to harass neighboring countries. There is another factor—the existence in some states, like Estonia, of an alienated segment of the Russian-speaking population can always be used as a pretext for Moscow's bullying, unless the Russian elite changes its key political principles and stops viewing great-power influence and Soviet-era symbols as prerequisites for the state's sustainability. Again, the Estonian experience proves that newly independent states must solve the urgent problem of integrating their Russian-speaking minorities in a way that will prevent hardliners in Moscow from using the alienation of the minorities as an excuse to meddle in the domestic affairs of those states.

Even the states that have declared their loyalty to Moscow are eager to counterbalance Russia's influence. Azerbaijan, to avoid dependency on Moscow, exports its oil through the Baku–Tbilisi–Ceyhan pipeline (built on Bill Clinton's initiative) and is negotiating American involvement in guaranteeing the security of the Caspian. Baku is helping Georgia with energy supplies, despite being charged as much as $235 per thousand cubic meters for gas by Moscow to show its displeasure. Kazakhstan, unhappy with Gazprom's monopoly, is seeking ways of exporting its energy resources to China and Turkey, and through Turkey to Europe, to avoid Russian pipelines. Bishkek has agreed to allow the U.S. military base to remain on Kyrgyz territory, although it has raised the rent.

Energy interests can overrule political preferences. The authoritarian regime of Ilkham Aliev in Azerbaijan might seem a natural partner for the Russian regime, given their similarities, and indeed the local elite understands and prefers Russia to the West. Nevertheless, economic self-interest is pushing Azerbaijan toward the West. (Sixty percent of Azerbaijan's trade is with Europe, while that with Russia is less than 15 percent.) For his part, during the Russo–Belarusian conflict, Ukrainian leader Viktor Yushchenko expressed his intention of meeting with Lukashenko. It is pressure from Moscow that forces these two countries with very different political regimes to find ways of coordinating their actions.

Clearly, energy supplies can substantially alter geopolitical realities. Responsibility for politicizing energy resources in Eurasia lies squarely with Russia, which is now unable to control the implications of the process. Moreover, Russia will soon have to deal with mounting economic problems in its relations with its traditional allies, like Armenia, sandwiched between Turkey and Azerbaijan and totally dependent on Russia. Thus, Russia was compensated for the Armenian energy debt by gaining control over its enterprises but has not been in a hurry to restart production and has continued to raise gas prices for Armenians, obliging them to look for other political solutions.

Conversely, several newly independent states are running to Russia for protection. The Uzbek leader, Islam Karimov, fell passionately in love with Moscow after his regime suffered reverses. Regimes whose leaders are afraid of losing power are coming back to Russia. With the advent of Gorbachev, Russia ceased to play the role of gendarme, but external and internal drivers are pushing it toward resuming that role. Two totalitarian leaders who need Moscow's protection are Lukashenko and Karimov. Although the Kremlin cannot stand Lukashenko and has grave doubts about Karimov, it supports them because Moscow does not want Belarus to fall prey to the West and wants to keep Uzbekistan as an ally.

Needless to say, the more Russia tries to meddle in other states' domestic affairs, the more unpopular it becomes in the very countries it wants to embrace. Thus, in 2004, 78 percent of the citizens of Moldova viewed Russia as a friend; in 2006, 52 percent of Moldovans considered Russia a threat. In 2006, 94.4 percent of the citizens of Tbilisi, who were previously very friendly toward Russia, viewed the Russian state as hostile. Besides, in most of the CIS countries, a change of elites is imminent. Today, the newly independent states with dictatorial regimes are headed by former Soviet officials who actively seek Russian support, but the new ruling class and the new leaders will surely look in new directions, seeking partnerships with China, India, Pakistan, South Korea, Iran, and (who knows?) perhaps even with the West. In this situation the Kremlin's support for the old leaders seems shortsighted.

Russia and its competitors for influence in the former Soviet territories will have to recognize something else. The new states have learned the art of sitting on the fence, conducting what they themselves call a partnership at arm's length, allowing the major international players to court them and seeking to obtain favors from all of them. Sooner or later Russia, China, and the United States will also have to face the fact that the states of Central Asia, the South Caucasus, and the European part of the former Soviet Union are beginning to conclude agreements with one another and are becoming an independent force. Indeed, a number of states like Kazakhstan, Ukraine, and Uzbekistan are already trying to become regional hegemons, with whom even the major world players will have to reckon.

Regarding the newly independent states that are looking to the West, their desire is to join European and Atlantic organizations. The crisis in the EU, amid concerns that it has over-stretched itself in its expansion, has slowed down further European integration. Yet there is no doubt that Ukraine, Moldova, and, eventually, Belarus will be drawn into European structures. Even Armenia, considered loyal to Russia, sees joining the European Union as preferable to belonging to the CIS and is developing closer relations with NATO. The only question is when, in what order, and how the newly independent states will be drawn into the West's sphere of influence. It matters to Russia whether that involvement occurs through membership in NATO or the EU. Moscow would find the former more difficult to swallow, even though Russia, ironically, has better relations with NATO than with the EU.

The GUAM states—Georgia, Ukraine, Moldova, and lately Azerbaijan—are seeking to follow a course independent of Moscow. In addition, Ukraine and Georgia have set up a Community of Democratic Choice in Kiev. Neither organization is particularly effective, but they were created from a desire to jointly resist pressure from Russia. The more the Kremlin twists its neighbors' arms, the more it forces them to look to the west for support—or, like the members of GUAM, to try to organize themselves and together resist Moscow's pressure.

It would be a mistake, however, to conclude that the new states no longer need Moscow. All these states, even those like the Baltic states that have sought shelter in NATO and the EU, have a vested interest in continuing economic cooperation with Russia, and not solely in terms of energy supplies. For most of them, breaking off their links would plunge their economies into crisis. Ukraine, for example, in 2005 exported ferrous metallurgy products to the EU worth $2.6 billion, but its exports to Russia were also worth $2.1 billion. Europe bought Ukrainian machine tool products to the tune of $760 million, while Russia's imports were worth a full $2.2 billion. Ukraine's export of chemical products to Russia grew by 30 percent, while exports to the European Union fell by 2 percent. In 2006 Russia's trade with Central Asia rose to $17 billion, against $13.5 billion in 2005. Russian companies invested $4.1 billion in the region's economy. Belarus, Kazakhstan, and Ukraine have a particular interest in establishing a free trade area with Russia. Other countries, like Armenia, need Russian investments and energy supplies. Azerbaijan, Belarus, Georgia, Moldova, Tajikistan, and Ukraine see Russia as a market for their labor force and as a means of supplementing their budgets. They receive a regular cash flow from Russia, earned by millions of their citizens. For other states, notably Kazakhstan and Kyrgyzstan, cooperation with Russia enhances their sense of security, given their proximity to China. In other words, the newly independent states need to cooperate with Russia, but at the same time they have no wish to become totally dependent on it.

The elites in the new states, even in those that are finding their way to the West, are beginning to recognize that they need positive relations with Russia if they are to develop satisfactorily. After his election in 2006, Ukrainian Prime Minister Viktor Yanukovich went to Moscow to patch up relations. Even the most pro-Western politicians, like the former Ukrainian minister of foreign affairs, Boris Tarasyuk, a supporter of Ukraine's

NATO membership, stated that Ukraine needs to join the Common Economic Space formed by Russia, even as it moved toward NATO. The Moldovan president, Vladimir Voronin, tried for months to be invited to the Kremlin to have Russia remove its trade blockade. He obtained some softening of Moscow's position in return for political concessions (though Moldovan exports to Russia have yet to resume). Russia has yet to find a healthier attitude to its neighbors' aspirations to exist simultaneously in different dimensions, both with Russia and with the West. It has yet to view the newly independent states not merely as a *cordon sanitaire* but as a bridge between it and the West. Admittedly, Moscow has started to learn from the failures of its hardball politics and has embarked on a more cautious policy toward Ukraine. During the political crisis in Kiev in the spring and summer of 2007, the Kremlin chose wait-and-see tactics, avoiding new attempts to interfere directly in the Ukrainian political struggle.

There is logic to Russia's continuing presence in the post-Soviet territories. The demise of the USSR caused a security vacuum in Central Asia and the Caucasus. Instability in Afghanistan and Iraq makes consolidating the stability of Central Asia even more urgent. It is unlikely, however, that Russia will be able to adequately fulfill the role of a stabilizing force alone. It needs to cooperate with the West in the Transcaucasus and with the West and China in Central Asia. There is also a need for Europe's more active involvement to reduce the danger of renewing the tug-of-war between Russia, China, and the United States in those regions.

One might question how far Russia, in its present condition, can contribute to the modernization of Eurasia. If Russia can transform itself, it could be a powerful force for progress and an attractive example for its neighbors. If it remains stuck in a transitional phase, the transformation of the post-Soviet territories will be more difficult. In either case, Russia will remain a decisive factor influencing for all the newly independent states. How they develop will depend greatly on what happens in Russia.

Chapter 17

RUSSIA AND EUROPE: CONDEMNED TO LIVE TOGETHER

There are two dimensions to the relations between Russia and Europe, one international and the other civilizational. Dmitri Trenin was right when he saw the collapse of the world socialist system as an opportunity for Russia to change its geopolitical direction and to change its systemic principles by "joining Europe." He wrote: "By ceasing to be a great power in Europe, Russia has gained the opportunity of becoming a European country," elaborating that this meant "more Europe in Russia," that is, a restructuring of Russia on the basis of European norms and standards.[1] The Europeanization of Russia proved more difficult, however, than many both in Russia and in Europe supposed. Shared economic and geopolitical interests did not automatically bring about a sharing of standards. Even while pursuing common interests, Russia and Europe have ended up mutually disappointed.

The beginning of Putin's courting of Europe was promising. After Yeltsin's disdain of Europe, his constant looking to Washington, and his belief that Europeans were mere executors of the will of the United States, Putin took a lively interest in developing a close relationship with the European states and the EU. He started with Germany, and in October 2001 gave a speech to the Bundestag that was received with enthusiasm by the German establishment. Putin spoke in faultless German, but more important, what he said was guaranteed to win the approval of Europeans. He called for an end to what remained of the Cold War, for the building of mutual trust, and for a uniting of Europe's and Russia's resources. The Bundestag gave him a standing ovation. The Russian leader continued his friendly onslaught, trying to reach a breakthrough in relations between Russia and the European Union. He offered to create a free trade area between Russia and the EU, and to include Russia in NATO projects.

Thanks to the hard work of Putin, Russia and the EU reached agreement on many matters: implementation of a most-favored-nation clause in trade relations between the European Union and Russia; getting the European Union to recognize Russia as a market economy; obtaining Brussels' support for Russia to join the World Trade Organization; reaching a partial resolution of the Kaliningrad issue (the Russian city of Kaliningrad is surrounded by countries that are EU members); and initiating Russia's gradual incorporation of EU trade rules in its trade legislation.

In 2002, Putin took part in the first NATO summit with Russian participation, sitting between the leaders of Portugal and Spain. In May 2003, Russia joined France and Germany in a "coalition of the unwilling," opposing U.S. plans to invade Iraq. Finally, Russia and the European Union adopted four "road maps" to "common spaces": specific action plans for developing cooperation in the spheres of the economy, internal security, freedom and civil rights, external security, research, and cultural and scientific cooperation.

Gradually, however, the rapprochement between Russia and Europe encountered unanticipated obstacles. Quite unexpectedly, NATO proved a more amenable partner for Moscow than Brussels. The first problem to surface was surprisingly technical, involving radically different approaches to decision making by Moscow and Brussels. Russian diplomacy had no tradition of operating by consensus, could not understand how the cumbersome European machinery worked, and experienced difficulties in adapting to the need for all decisions to involve negotiation between all members of the EU. Contacts between the hierarchically organized Russian bureaucracy and the pluralistically oriented bureaucracy of Brussels inevitably led to misunderstandings, breakdowns, and mutual disappointment. Russia demanded the right to participate in the EU's decision making without being an EU member and also wanted special status within the organization. Moscow simply could not see how such a major power as Russia could have no greater rights than Poland or Spain. "Russia is demanding the impossible," European observers complained, refusing to make an exception for it. Although keen to influence the EU's decision making, Russia was not prepared to accept its fundamental principles. For its part, the EU was preoccupied with the implementation and practicalities of expansion and had neither the time nor the energy to devise a workable strategy for Russia, nor for lengthy negotiations with Moscow and explaining to the Kremlin the nature of the EU and its agenda.

By late 2003, it was clear that, despite the creation of a standing mechanism for meetings and consultations, the partnership remained merely formal. Now, increasing points of disagreement were not only over the technicalities of decision making, but also over substance. Moscow and Brussels failed to resolve a number of specific issues, among them the introduction of visa-free travel; a free trade area; full resolution of the problem of Kaliningrad with respect to energy supplies, freight, and fisheries; and extending cooperation in external security. In 2004, Moscow delivered a fourteen-point ultimatum to the European Union suggesting revision of the partnership agreement, trade concessions, and an easing of visa arrangements. Putin made some sharp remarks about the Brussels bureaucracy. In turn, Brussels gradually began to see Russia as a possible source of soft security threats and prepared a response to Moscow's obduracy by laying down "red lines" that none of the European states could cross in talks with Russia. The Common Strategy on Russia, approved by the European Community in 1999, which had aimed at integrating a democratic Russia into Europe, had failed. Deliberating on the current status of EU–Russia relations, Angela Stent concluded, "EU–Russian relations remain beset by contradictions, disappointed expectations and mutual suspicions."[2] Confirming this conclusion from the Russian side, Sergei Karaganov admitted a "dead situation" in the relationship: "Brussels lacks a long-term policy on Russia. Moscow does not know what it wants from the EU."[3]

The cooling of relations between Russia and the European Union was caused not only by unrealistic hopes on both sides, but by Russia's desire for exclusive status in its partnership with the EU, enabling it to flout EU rules. The failure of the relationship had structural reasons as well. Russia and a united Europe represent two diametrically opposed models of development. Europe is aiming to blur the boundaries between nation states, to remove territorial barriers, and to form a new community with policies based on compromise, taking account of the views of minorities and of individual members. Russia, however, continues to emphasize such geopolitical attributes as a strong state, clearly demarcated territory, and national sovereignty, which makes impossible its movement toward integration with Europe.[4]

This fundamental difference in the civilizational dimension and political approaches has led to a succession of disagreements on political matters, primarily on democracy and human rights. Criticism by the European Union of Russia's war in Chechnya and its restriction of civil rights and freedom added to the Kremlin's irritation. Soon Russia's participation in European institutions, notably the Council of Europe and its Parliamentary Assembly, was reduced to little more than countering criticism, exchanging mutual grudges, and increasingly hopeless attempts to improve its reputation.

Despite their differences in values and a plethora of unresolved issues, Russia and Europe are bound together by geographical proximity, cultural similarities, and numerous economic and commercial interests. More than 48 percent of

Russia's trade is with Europe, while a third of Europe's gas needs are met by Gazprom. Eight European countries account for 74 percent of foreign investment in Russia. Trade volume between Russia and the EU in January–April 2007 reached about $78 billion. The presence of European companies in such sectors of the Russian economy as retail consumption, banking services, and commerce is increasing. Nestlé, Danone, Baltic Beverage, Ikea, Auchan, Société Général, and Dresdner Bank are all familiar names in Russia. There is an inevitable tension between the incompatibility of Russian and European values and their shared economic, commercial, and security interests. How relations evolve will depend on which proves stronger— values or shared interests. For now, disagreements between Moscow and Brussels are mitigated by favorable bilateral relations between Moscow and individual European capitals, particularly Berlin, Paris, and Rome, and also by the fact that the European Union needs to trade with Russia. How long, however, can this continue to be the case? The systemic contradictions between Russia and the European Union, especially its parliamentary bodies, cannot simply be ignored. Meanwhile, new sources of conflict between Russia and the EU emerge in the newly independent states that compose a "neighborhood" for both sides. EU–Russia relations have been already tested by growing tensions between Russia and EU members Estonia and Lithuania.

In the 1990s, Europe tried a policy toward Russia of "transformation through integration," supposing that a partnership between the EU and Russia would facilitate Russian reforms. When this approach proved disappointing, Europe began shifting to "integration through transformation," meaning that rapprochement between Russia with the European Union would depend on the extent to which Russia reformed itself and proved willing to adopt European principles.

Russia and Europe now agree to differ, while not ruling out the possibility of close partnership in the future. Admittedly, today their collaborative effort looks like an "imitation partnership," with both sides aware of its limits. A sign of flexibility was the adoption of "road maps for cooperation" in "the four common spaces." This complicated configuration testifies that, while neither side is prepared to advance toward a higher level of relations, neither do they wish to see them cool, even though Moscow and Brussels find it difficult to hide their mutual incomprehension and sometimes hostility. Moscow has, however, learned to get around Brussels by conducting its relations with Europe on a bilateral basis, primarily with Germany, France, and Italy. This does, of course, undermine the unitary approach toward Russia that Brussels is trying to create. "Russia has come to master using EU complexity for its purposes, playing various levels of the organization off against each other—which has not enhanced EU coherence," as Dov Lynch observes.[5]

By late 2006, relations between Russia and Europe had become more strained, primarily because of Russia's energy policy. President Putin, recognizing the alarm signals at a time when relations with Washington also left much to be desired, published an article on November 21, 2006, in the *Financial Times*, where he argued that "Europe has nothing to fear from Russia." He wrote, "Our current goal is to join forces so that Russia and the EU can build a common future as partners and allies. Russia is prepared to work for this and I hope a constructive approach will also prevail in the EU." The Kremlin's wooing of Europe came too late.

At the summits between Russia and the European Union in October and November 2006, the Kremlin failed to persuade European leaders to adopt its vision of an "energy partnership." Russia's unwillingness to ratify the Energy Charter Treaty and its Transit Protocol, intended to demonopolize energy transit, only strengthened the misgivings of Moscow's European partners. President Putin in turn criticized the EU for not fulfilling its own obligations under the Energy Charter, citing failure to open the nuclear materials market and give Russia direct access to this market. Russia and the European Union have been unable to prepare a new Partnership and Cooperation Agreement to replace the one due to expire in 2007. The major reason was Poland's decision to block the procedure until Russia lifts its embargo on Polish meat and agricultural produce. (The embargo, ostensibly imposed because of health concerns over Polish meat, was really part of Moscow's policy to punish Warsaw for being difficult.) Even without the Polish factor, however, Russia and the EU would have had problems finding a satisfactory basis for their future relationship.

What was the European response to Russia? A majority of European leaders, and particularly those in the pro-Russian camp that includes France, Germany, and Italy, have, until recently at least, preferred acquiescence to Moscow. Those Europeans who wished to complain about problems between Russia and its neighbors, Russian corruption, or the deficiencies of Russian democracy received no support from the senior members of the club, while Moscow rebuffed them vigorously. It was obvious that the major capitals of Europe, most notably Paris and Berlin, wanted to avoid tension in their relations with Moscow, fearing it would only make Russia's behavior more unpredictable and cause their economic interests to suffer. The growing rift between "old Europe" and new EU members over Russia, the largely defensive European policy toward Moscow, and the fear in both Brussels and major European capitals of making Russia angry demonstrate Europe's failure not only to adopt a cohesive common strategy toward Russia but also to create a productive and functioning platform for relations with Russia that could withstand tension and include mechanisms for damage control.[6] When Finnish Prime Minister Matti Vanhanen, as EU president, admitted that he was "not sure that Russia [was] heading in the right direction," he confirmed that Europe had failed in its efforts to embrace Russia and did not have a response to Russia's challenge. Today the European Union is at a loss as to how to deal with Russia, which has become its major energy supplier. As one Brussels official said in an interview for the *Economist*, "We don't know what to do about Russia.... In the EU we negotiate on the rules, whereas Russia wants to do deals."[7] The Russian side has been dissatisfied with the EU as well. After the EU–Russia summit on May 18, 2007, and a chain of unsuccessful EU–Russia summits that became heroic attempts by old EU members (principally France and Germany) to mitigate disagreements with Moscow as well as internal tensions between old Europe and its new members regarding Russia, Putin had to admit, "Strengthening the legal basis of the Russia–EU partnership is a difficult issue."[8]

European leniency and politeness are seen by Russia as signs of weakness and irresolution, which makes it tempting simply to ignore Europe or attempt to coerce it. The Russian elite increasingly looks down on Europe, evidently believing it can force it to accept its rules and its agenda, or ignore it. This attitude received a considerable boost when Gerhard Schröder consented to become a Russian bureaucrat, which was seen as confirming that the Western elite could be brought to heel and made to work in the Kremlin's interests. "Every man has his price" appears to be the Russian establishment's conclusion after Gazprom got its clutches on the former chancellor of Germany. This self-conceit put egg on Russia's face shortly afterward when Angela Merkel rejected the Kremlin's offer to make Germany its main energy partner. In general, however, Russia's short-term policy toward the EU has seemingly been successful. Its trademark has been to pick and choose among its European partners, striking bilateral deals with them, mainly with its traditional and loyal partners, like Germany, and with carefully selected smaller countries like Bulgaria and Hungary ready to accept Russia's policy even at the price of breaking the EU common strategy. The Russian daily *Vedomosti* explained the divide-and-rule Moscow policy: "The Kremlin strategy is based on European disunity and selfishness."[9] Moscow could hardly be blamed for exploiting the weakness of its trading partners or for maximizing the economic and political benefits of its riches, its geography, or its current luck. This policy, however, has its limits and will inevitably push Europeans to unite in order to prevent Russia from dividing them. To date that moment does not seem close.

Germany remains the key European partner for Russia. For Putin, the departure of his personal friend Chancellor Schröder from office was a considerable blow. His successor, Angela Merkel, is more restrained in her attitude toward Russia and pointedly refers to "strategic cooperation" rather than to a "strategic partnership." While showing no desire to build a personal relationship with Putin like that of her predecessor, Merkel has demonstrated a willingness to continue a special relationship with Russia that reflects the interweaving of German and Russian economic interests and pressure from German business. There are influential circles within the German elite that support the idea of a new Ostpolitik toward Russia, reminiscent of the policy of Willy Brandt and Egon Bahr of seeking "change through rapprochement." The belief is that a partnership with Russia should be strengthened despite what is happening there, in the hope that it will encourage an evolution toward democracy. The increasingly critical tone toward Russia as well as Angela Merkel's comments in early 2007 indicated German concern that Russia was not playing by European rules. Even more evident was Berlin's intention to proceed with caution and not to allow its dissatisfaction to cross a line that threatened worsening relations with Moscow. In any case, the German government apparently believes that it understands Russia's grievances better than other Western powers and can help to address them, hence Berlin's wary approach to further NATO enlargement, its attempts to solve conflicts between Moscow and Warsaw, and its apprehension regarding the deployment of the U.S. missile defenses in Poland and the Czech Republic.

As for relations between Russia and Great Britain, this is a story of vain hopes. In early 2000, former British Prime Minister Tony Blair tried to repeat Margaret Thatcher's performance with Gorbachev by helping Vladimir Putin find his way on the world stage after Putin came to power. It soon became evident, however, that relations between the two leaders were not going well. The British leader could not do the favors for Moscow that the Kremlin wanted, as, for example, handing over to Russia Akhmad Zakaev, one of the Chechen separatist leaders, or the fugitive oligarch Boris Berezovsky, the worst of Putin's personal enemies. The Russian authorities could not understand that the British government was unable to give orders to its judiciary. Great Britain failed to find a role as the mediator between Russia and the West.

In the later stages of Blair's premiership and Putin's presidency the dispute over the murder of the former Russian FSB officer Alexander Litvinenko in November 2006 has fueled mounting tensions between London and Moscow. Blair's successor, Gordon Brown, in reacting negatively to plans by Russian energy companies to enter the British market, had caused suspicion in Moscow that he would not be an easy partner for Russia even before he took power. He has confirmed the fears by taking a tough stance on the Litvinenko case and considering curbing cooperation with Russia in education, social affairs, trade, and antiterrorism in response. In July 2007 the dispute escalated with the reciprocal expulsion of diplomats from both countries. Yet both sides have been trying to limit the fallout from the standoff. In any case, London and Moscow have no option but to wait for a change of leadership in Russia before a new page can be opened in their relations.

Paris has been pursuing a fairly flexible policy toward Russia. During Jacques Chirac's presidency, the policy of cajoling Russia fit both the French president's notion of a multipolar world and France's traditional policy of snubbing the United States by flirting with the states causing Washington problems. There was evidence that Chirac even aspired to establish relations with the Kremlin as warm as those that Putin and Schröder enjoyed. As the French political elite was stunned by the Kremlin's sudden decision to cut Western companies, including French Total, from plans to develop the Shtokman gas field,[10] Chirac awarded Putin the Grand Cross Order of the Légion d'honneur. The

French heard about it only in reports from the Russian news agencies. Quite apart from Chirac's personal ambitions, there are solid grounds for favorable relations between Paris and Moscow, including the desire of Russian business to expand into France and the aspiration of French business to invest in Russia. It is, of course, still unclear which agenda toward Russia the new incumbent of the Elysée Palace, Nicolas Sarkozy, will pursue, and what priority Russia will be given in the new French foreign policy. During his election campaign, Sarkozy broke most dramatically with Chirac's support of Russia on human rights, indicating that the rhetoric from the Elysée Palace could have a sharper edge.[11] However, the successful deal with Total allows us to conclude that Moscow has started to build bridges with the new French leader in order to mitigate the cold relations with Brussels and growing tensions with London. Thus, Sarkozy might choose a more moderate line with Russia, understanding the need to have productive cooperation with the key energy supplier of Europe and, who knows, he could like Thatcher, Blair, and some other leaders before him attempt to forge a special relationship with Moscow.

Extremely positive relations underpinned by economic interests have developed between Moscow and Rome. They have not been shaken by the change of Italian prime minister from Silvio Berlusconi, a constant personal advocate of Russia and Putin, to Romano Prodi, with whom the Kremlin had developed good relations during his presidency of the European Commission. Prodi has demonstrated a wish to help the Kremlin with its image problem, which worsened markedly in 2006. "I take note of the new Russia and will do all I can to try to help it win through," Prodi promised Putin at their meeting in January 2007. The expansion of Russian businesses into Italy and the desire of Italian companies to grow their share of the Russian market testify to a lively dialogue between Russia and Italy. Agreements reached by Putin during his visit to Italy in March 2007 on asset swaps between Eni and Russian state companies (Eni decided to buy $4 billion in shares of Russian energy corporations) and Italian participation in the privatization of UES Russia have reconfirmed the Kremlin's ability to promote bilateral relations with Western partners. The majority of other old European states recognize Russia's increasing importance, beyond terms of energy security, and are trying to maintain positive diplomatic relations with the Kremlin, which means not asking awkward questions about the failings of Russian democracy.

If Russia has succeeded in establishing pragmatic relations with "old Europe," it still faces considerable problems with "new Europe." Moscow is highly allergic to Poland, which raises the Kremlin's ire by trying to act as the missionary of democracy in such former Soviet territories as Ukraine and Belarus and reminding Russia about dark chapters in their past relations. The Russian elite cannot control its displeasure with Poland, as is periodically evident when, as if to order, there is a further flare-up of anti-Polish feelings in Russia. If the Kremlin disliked President Alexander Kwasniewski, the coming to power of the Kaczynski brothers has forced Russia to deal with real Polish nationalists. This does not favor any warming of relations between Moscow and Warsaw. Moscow expresses its displeasure with Polish policies both directly, by boycotting certain Polish goods, and indirectly, by attempting to exclude Poland from future energy routes. One might conclude that Russo–Polish relations are a litmus test of Moscow's ability to find a constructive niche in the world arena and to grapple with the legacy of the past, which continues to influence its behavior and is a strong irritant in its relations with former members of the "world socialist system." Positive and benevolent relations with Poland would signal that a new Russia had successfully found a new identity that was not threatening to its neighbors.

The EU and Russia will have to think about building a framework for future relations. In December 2007 the Partnership and Cooperation Agreement (PCA), which forms the legal basis of bilateral relations, will come to an end. Both sides have agreed to draft a new treaty. Meanwhile, the old PCA will be extended automatically unless one side or the other decides to cancel it. So far, there is no consensus even within the EU on what the new treaty should entail. This issue is a subject of debate in Russia as well. Some European analysts, like Katinka Barysch, think that the EU should take its time, putting off substantive negotiations until EU–Russian relations have improved and focusing on making existing agreements work, in particular "the four spaces" and the energy dialogue.[12] There are grounds for such a gradualist approach. If the "road maps" are implemented, they could give a new boost to the relationship. Besides, today, when relations between the two sides have deteriorated, new negotiations could turn, as many observers have anticipated (including in Russia) into an emotional debate and mutual recriminations. Such a debate would bring differences over values and energy into the open, which may detract from the solution of more pragmatic and urgent issues, such as the new visa regime. Besides, a treaty has to be ratified by every EU member, a complicated process.

Once Russia reaches agreements with some of its main partners on its entry into the WTO, its membership will anchor Russia in the international trading system, with no need for a special agreement with the European Union. Thus, for the time being, Russia and the EU will likely muddle through until a new leader in Russia forms a new agenda for its relationship with a united Europe. At the start of the new political cycle in Russia, when the next ruling team is formed, by summer 2008, a much more ambitious dialogue between the EU and Russia will be needed to reenergize mutual interest. Russia and the EU will have to devise a comprehensive and sustainable legal framework to work in, simply because they have so many interlinked interests. The moment inevitably comes when not only European parliamentary bodies but Brussels executives as well will have to restart the dialogue with Russia on norms and principles that cannot be forever postponed—a dialogue that will determine their cooperation on common interests.

We should probably not expect new Russian initiatives from Brussels in the immediate future, since the European Union is preoccupied with matters of European integration. Yet even despite its passive stance on Russia, Europe remains a factor of considerable importance in influencing Russia because of the very existence of the European integration project, the drawing into Europe of the former Soviet satellites, because of the presence of influential European public opinion on what is taking place in Eurasia, and because European integration, a European democracy, and economy are examples for Russia. Many shared economic and security interests and a largely shared culture are capable, if not of bringing them closer together, then at least of mitigating the consequences of misunderstanding and tension in relations that may yet occur, now and in the future. Some analysts strongly believe that Russia and Europe can find a model that will combine Russia's thirst for a great-power role and mainstream European policy, "where the name of the game is integration ... and in this way Russia will continue to be in Europe, but not of Europe. It will be a player, but it will be a player of a different kind."[13] For this to happen, Russia has to change its matrix.

Finally, a word about how Russians feel about Europe. Despite the vacillations in Moscow's policy toward the European Union, most Russians are favorably inclined toward Europe itself. About 70 percent of Russian respondents have a positive attitude toward the European Union, against 20 percent whose attitude is negative. Given the general worsening of relations between Russia and the West, and the United States in particular, the continuing positive feelings of Russians toward Europe keep relations from cooling too much.

Chapter 18

RUSSIA AND THE UNITED STATES: IN SEARCH OF A NEW PARADIGM

Russo-American relations can hardly be understood without taking into account the Russian ruling class's divided attitude toward the United States. It sees Americans as the only nation in the world whose spirit and outlook remotely resemble those of Russians and as the only nation that deserves its attention. The Russian elite is impressed by America's messianism, will to power, and its longing for world preponderance. It perhaps unconsciously imitates the American way of life and the way the United States behaves in the international arena, especially its tough politics and readiness to demonstrate military muscle. It simultaneously loathes Americans for the same reason, purely because Russia cannot afford to behave like America, let alone compete with American might. It lacks the resources to have a global mission of its own and, more importantly, it lacks the ideas needed for such a mission. The Russian political class constantly compares Russia with the United States, and it hates making this comparison and the fact that the comparison is rarely in its favor. Unable to control its emotions, the Russian elite not infrequently lashes out at America, even if that harms its own interests. Russian analyst Andrei Piontkovsky noted that the Russian elite's view of the United States is the "revolt of privileged and well-off people suffering deeply from an inferiority complex, and this complex is not only a Russian, but a global phenomenon."[1]

These ambivalent feelings also underlie the Russian political class's mood swings in its dealings with the United States, which, if they do not shock Americans—unfamiliar as they are with the idea of the subconscious playing such a role in state policy—at least leave them puzzled. The fact that after the fall of the USSR, the United States was and remains the only hegemon still standing evokes even more negative feelings because of the Russian elite's inability to cope with its nostalgia for past Soviet might. In addition, Russia is not used to living in a unipolar world (though it would apparently feel disoriented in a multipolar world). The Russian elite reacts badly to American boastings about American might, virtue, and American claims hailing the United States as a benevolent hegemon or "indispensable nation." The elite has evidently forgotten that during the Soviet period it did not hesitate to define the role of the USSR in analogous terms, annoying some and infuriating others. The point is, however, that the Russian political establishment constantly demonstrates its indignation at American arrogance not because it finds such behavior sickening, as it sickens Europeans, who cannot abide the "benign hegemon" syndrome. The Russian elite is irritated because it cannot afford to behave that way itself. Any advance in American interests, even should such interests coincide with the interests of Russia, dismays the Russian political class. "We don't need a sheriff," Russian politicians say. What they mean is that Russia itself would like to be the sheriff. Even while criticizing Americans, Kremlin functionaries mimic them step by step: the United States has a war on terrorism, so Russia has its own war on terrorism; the United States threatens preventive strikes against countries it dislikes, Moscow declares it may do the same; Washington finds an "axis of evil," and the Kremlin comes up with its own "enemy axis." If anyone criticizes Moscow for its aggressive policies toward other states, the Kremlin propagandists promptly reply, "If the Americans can do that, why can we not do the same?" Russia's politicians just adore maximalism and see consensus and compromise as signs of weakness, almost as American neoconservatives do. Ironically, the Kremlin's shift toward its own conservatism at the end of Putin's term has been justified and legitimized as a response to conservative U.S. unilateralism. The morbid focus of attention on America and the attempt to see the world entirely as reflected through Russia's relations with the United States show up both the limitless pretensions of the Russian elite and its diffidence, its neuroses, and its attempt to disguise them as self-confidence. The one thing that wounds the elite more than anything is that Washington no longer pays much attention to its old sparring partner. That is what the Kremlin really cannot forgive America for. The United States' ignoring of Russia not only humiliates the Russian elite but also reduces opportunities to use its relations with the United States for domestic purposes to strengthen the statist thrust of the regime. Recently Kremlin spin doctors have succeeded in using Russia's humiliation at being ignored by America for mobilization purposes to beef up anti-American feelings.

Russian views of U.S.–Russian relations continue to vary, but the direction in which the perceptions of a major part of the Russian political establishment have evolved has become unmistakable: a significant number of those who formerly believed that robust U.S.–Russian relations would help to promote Russia's domestic transformation and integration into Euro–Atlantic structures have started to express their skepticism about the feasibility of this scenario. Even Russian liberal commentators cannot suppress their frustration, questioning not only the possibility of the U.S.–Russian partnership but also the positive role of these ties in Russia's modernization. The majority of Russian politicians and observers today view the United States with open suspicion, accusing it of using Russia for its own pragmatic ends.

On the American side, those perceptions and moods could hardly provoke anything other than frustration. From the very moment of the Soviet Union's collapse, the United States has been wrestling with the dilemma of "how to balance traditional realpolitik concerns against a liberal-international outlook. Should Washington focus primarily on Russia's foreign and security policy or should it become more actively involved in shaping Russia's postcommunist political and economic transformation?"[2] President George H. W. Bush chose realpolitik in trying to contain the consequences of the nuclear superpower collapse. As noted earlier, the Clinton administration initiated a very different strategy, one of supporting Russia's transformation and integration into the Western community. Clinton devoted great energy and a huge amount of time to U.S. relations with Russia, pursuing the ambitious goal of making Yeltsin's Russia a Western partner and ally, trying to help it dismantle its nuclear weapons and promote a free-market economy and a civil society in Russia.

Clinton's security policy was successful. It helped to fill the vacuum of force left by the collapse of the USSR and diminished the threat of proliferation. The Clinton–Yeltsin partnership stopped the race for strategic nuclear supremacy and, as Zbigniew Brzezinski put it, "codified America's de facto promise to Russia that the U.S. would not exploit its advantage in wealth and technical know-how to obtain decisive strategic superiority."[3] However, in the eyes of Russians this pledge did not survive even Clinton's presidency.

There was also the question of economic reform. Returning back to those days, Strobe Talbott, former U.S. deputy secretary of state, admitted on May 24, 2007, "I think, we can only be self-critical; that is, those of us in the Clinton administration looking back to some extent ... could have used a lot more major up-front support from the outside world. We and Russian reformers should have paid a lot more attention to the structural side of what was necessary in economic reform and ensuring that there would be real rule of law."[4] In terms of building a liberal democracy, Clinton and his team had to watch Yeltsin's neo-patrimonial backlash with anguish.

Regrettably, the Russian prediction and judgment of Clinton's tenure is generally based not on its mission to keep "the political miracle of our era" going, but on the basis of the U.S. strategy in the Kosovo conflict, NATO enlargement, and its support of the unpopular Yeltsin regime. These factors became instrumental in deepening Russia's distrust of Americans. NATO enlargement continues to be the most serious irritant to all Russian political forces. Even liberals perceive NATO enlargement as a reflection of the U.S. conclusion that Russia cannot be transformed, Russia's neighbors should be taken under the umbrella of NATO, and a new *cordon sanitaire* is needed between Russia and the West. In any case, the Clinton administration left the scene amid growing mutual disappointment between Washington and Moscow. Analyzing U.S.– Russian relations in 2001, Thomas Graham wrote: "Indeed, the relationship had reached its lowest point since the breakup of the Soviet Union, and perhaps even earlier."[5] In several years it would become clear that the end of the Clinton era was not the lowest ebb in U.S.–Russian relations, when Moscow and Washington seemed to be on a collision course.

When Putin came to power, he was not in a hurry to build a rapport with Clinton. His intentions were clear. He waited for Clinton's successor to be elected. A new era in U.S.–Russian relations was approaching. Bill Clinton's formula of partnership with Russia in support of its transformation was rejected under George W. Bush, who expressed no interest in Russia or any intention of getting involved in Russian affairs. The new U.S. president embarked on a classic realist approach, trying to engage Russia in the U.S. security agenda and letting Russians solve their problems themselves. After reacting with optimism to Bush's realpolitik, which for the Kremlin meant that the United States would not preach democracy to Russia and would not meddle in its domestic affairs, Moscow was soon dismayed by Washington's downgrading of the relationship.

What motivated the Bush stance toward Russia? From the Russian perspective it seemed that the new U.S. president either did not believe in Russia's reforms or thought that what mattered for America was first of all a stable Russia, acquiescing to the United States. Washington ceased to regard Russia as a foreign policy priority. It was no longer a rival or major influence in world affairs, and the Bush administration evidently did not anticipate any unpleasant surprises from Russia. Along with this loss of interest in Russia, the American establishment lost interest in conceptualizing the processes that were occurring in Russia and Eurasia.

The Putin and Bush relationship began with a scandal when, in the spring of 2001, the Americans exposed Robert Hanssen, who had been working for Moscow for fifteen years. Fifty Russian diplomats suspected of espionage were expelled from the United States. In retaliation, Russia expelled fifty American diplomats, and both sides called it a day. At the Ljubljana U.S.–Russia summit that followed shortly afterward, in June 2001, Bush and Putin unexpectedly found a common language. It was after that meeting that Bush uttered his famous line, "I looked the man in the eye. I found him to be very straightforward and trustworthy, and we had a very good dialogue. I was able to get a sense of his soul." Actually, as it soon became apparent, it was not a matter of Bush's ability to read men's souls, but a decision taken by the American administration to embrace a policy of engagement with Russia. Yet as James Goldgeier and Michael McFaul noted, if Clinton saw his policy of engagement with Moscow as a means of helping Russia to reform, Bush considered it a means of resolving American security issues.[6] Washington wanted to ditch ABM arrangements without time-consuming discussions with the Russians, which Bush accomplished brilliantly by trading on his personal rapport with the Kremlin. To all appearances, Bush rarely raised the question of freedom and democracy in Russia in his discussions with Putin during this period (if he raised them at all). He had no wish to be distracted while resolving questions that were more important to him. Putin was pleased with his meetings with Bush, and we may deduce that they did not discuss anything that could have upset the Russian leader. Bush's realism delighted Moscow, and Putin promptly made his relations with Bush Russia's foreign policy priority, apparently hoping the Americans would upgrade the relationship as well and begin to view Russia as a serious partner.

The chain of unexpected and dramatic events that followed shortly afterward caused the Kremlin to react in a quite extraordinary manner. Putin's response to the tragedy of 9/11 was unambiguous: he unhesitatingly offered help to America. By his telephone call to Bush immediately after the terrorist acts, Putin not only behaved like a pro-Western leader but seemed at the time to have changed the substance of Russia's relations with the United States. Today, motivations behind Putin's pro-American U-turn are more apparent and it can largely be explained by the fact that the terrorist attack on the United States appeared to confirm to Putin that he had been right in warning the world about the threat of international terrorism. It also confirmed his explanations regarding the war in Chechnya, for which the West had condemned him. "I warned you!" This was the message Putin was giving the world and America with his behavior and his rhetoric.

Indeed, the Russian president might have been more cautious in his policy toward the United States, particularly as his advisers were categorically against extending assistance to the United States and the political class continued to be hostile to its former rival. The Russian leader took what was for many Russians an unexpected stance. After 9/11 Putin spent six hours trying to persuade his team that Russia should help the Americans. Though he did not get any support from them, he decided to go ahead with his decision. Upon leaving that meeting, Vladimir Putin made a televised address in which he announced Russia's readiness "to make a contribution to the war on terrorism." Russia really did help America, providing intelligence information about Afghanistan, allowing the United States to use its air space and create bases in Central Asia, and making available Russia's contacts with the Northern Alliance, which opposed the Taliban. Moscow also increased Russian assistance to the Northern Alliance, which fought largely with Russian weapons and, as many Russian observers suspected, with the help of Russian military instructors. In November 2001, Putin flew to a summit in Washington at precisely the moment that Kabul fell and the Taliban was defeated. The Russian leader radiated optimism as he declared, "If anyone thinks that Russia could again become an enemy of the United States, I do not think they understand what has happened in the world and what has happened in Russia." This appeared to be a historic breakthrough in the relations between the former rivals.

At that moment observers in both capitals began to ponder whether Russia and America might work better as a team than either one had with Europe, given that Russia's relationship with the EU was greatly strained. "Russia could assume a more important role as a global U.S. partner. What appears to be evolving are new transatlantic partnerships, unimaginable before the collapse of communism," this author wrote with Angela Stent in the winter of 2002.[7] Equally optimistic was Robert Legvold, who pointed out in August 2002:

> Since the events of September, [the] relationship between the U.S. and Russia has changed more fundamentally, above all because of the revolution in Russian foreign policy. Although incomplete ... the change runs deeper than is often recognized.... The Russian leadership had to make a crucial strategic choice. It was to throw Russia's lot in with the U.S., which also meant Putin was reconciling himself to what could only be called a junior partnership with the U.S. given the asymmetry of power between the two countries.

However, Legvold felt that there were caveats to the new U.S.–Russian realignment, warning, "Common interests there are. Common values remain to be demonstrated."[8] The author and Angela Stent also hedged bets, warning that "the new U.S.–Russian relationship has not been consistently smooth

going," and the transition to a productive partnership demanded that Russia embody Euro-Atlantic values and that the United
States adopt a policy of long-term engagement with Russia
based on the premise that "Russia should be a part of Western
civilization."[9]

Soon it became clear that the Bush–Putin axis in 2001–2002
was built on another premise, one that might be called "a Faust-
ian pact." The United States was silent about Russia's democratic deficits, the war in Chechnya, and growing pressure on
independent media. In return Putin acquiesced to American
policy, particularly the U.S. presence in Central Asia, which had
previously elicited loud Russian protests. For quite some time
the United States treated Putin's growing authoritarianism
leniently. One had the impression that Washington ascribed it
to either the need to push through difficult reforms or did not
care much about Russia's vector, thinking that Russia needed an
"iron hand" to rule it. The main explanation was that Washington needed Russian assistance and partnership in its war on terrorism and nothing else could distract Bush from his major
goal. In any case, the Kremlin's further crackdown on political
freedom and pluralism did not prevent a positive rapport
between the two leaders, to the great frustration of Russian
democrats.

Although the Russian political class continued to fume over
the selfishness of the United States and its lack of respect for
Russia, the Russian president long remained imperturbable,
avoiding gestures that might irritate the Americans. Strobe Talbott, observing Putin's behavior after the unilateral withdrawal
of the United States from the ABM treaty in 2002, expected him
to demand compensation from Washington, as Yeltsin had
always done in such situations. Instead, Putin reacted calmly to
Bush's wrecking of the entire network of agreements on which
the policy of nuclear nonproliferation had been based. He
remarked, "We consider the U.S. decision to be a mistake,"
while emphasizing that it "presents no threat to the national
security of the Russian Federation."[10] Putin wanted to maintain

a constructive relationship (as he understood it) with the United States. He understood the asymmetry of the might and potential of the two countries and had no wish to become embroiled in a fight with Washington. At the same time he could not be happy with Washington's decision. That was the moment when the seeds of future Moscow resentment toward Washington were planted.

Putin was right in his assessment of Bush's desire to eliminate binding agreements and dismantle the arms control structure. As further developments would show, this policy has undermined the nuclear nonproliferation process. Yet the optimistic vector in the U.S.–Russian relationship was preserved. In May 2002, the United States and Russia approved a Joint Declaration on New Strategic Relations that promised, "We are achieving a new strategic relationship. The era in which the United States and Russia saw each other as an enemy or strategic threat has ended. We are partners." In the declaration both sides acknowledged the presence of shared interests in safeguarding stability in Central Asia and the South Caucasus. The declaration laid the foundation for a new stage in the partnership: joint efforts to ensure stability in the post-Soviet territories. That Moscow agreed to an American presence in its own backyard could have been interpreted as a sign of a watershed in the mood of the Russian leadership. Moreover, the declaration provided for cooperation in creating and developing a joint strategic missile defense system. This, however, was the pinnacle of Russo–American relations, after which the mood soon began to falter.

In Washington the change of direction did not immediately register, and Moscow's refusal to support its military operation in Iraq came as an unpleasant surprise. The White House quickly overcame its disappointment and directed its wrath at Chirac and Schröder. This differentiated approach to the participants of the "coalition of the unwilling" was reflected in the axiom "Punish France, ignore Germany, and forgive Russia," which was attributed to Condoleezza Rice. Soon, however, other signs began to indicate that the relationship was far from cloudless.

Looking back, we can imagine that when he entered the Kremlin Putin had several options to choose from with respect to Russia's relations with the United States. The first was to be militant in his public pronouncements but in reality to follow in America's wake as Yeltsin had, agreeing to the role of junior partner. The second option was to oppose American interests, particularly in the former Soviet space. The third was for Russia to distance itself from the United States in areas where Russia had insufficient resources to collaborate with the United States on equal terms, and to continue a dialogue in areas where Moscow could be a full partner. After September 11, 2001, President Putin hoped (as Yeltsin had before him), that an opportunity had arisen for a more ambitious model of relations with America: an equal partnership of Russia and the United States.

How did Putin envisage such a partnership? He never gave details, but his rhetoric and his actions suggest that the Kremlin may have surmised that the United States would not intervene in Russia's internal affairs and would accept that Moscow had a right to do as it pleased within the territory of the former USSR and to expand its role in world affairs. Possibly Putin hoped that the appearance of a common threat from terrorism might make that partnership a priority for both countries. He may have even dreamed about a Russo–American world condominium. It soon became evident, however, that any such hopes were without foundation.

The United States not only had its own understanding of the struggle against terrorism, but had no intention of making Russia its key partner or even an equal partner. It took Russia for granted, overlooked those issues that divided them, and put U.S. interests first, without paying attention to Moscow, in just the same way as it paid scant attention to its Atlantic allies. Washington pursued security interests, trying to avoid any involvement in Russian domestic problems. This political realism regarding the expectations of Washington policy makers did not save U.S.–Russian relations. The Russo–American partnership so much talked about in the early years of Putin's rule—

the joint struggle against international terrorism, the partnership in the nonproliferation of weapons of mass destruction, and the dialogue over energy security—all this business of a "triad" ground to a halt. It became apparent that the partners had entirely different ideas about what the triad constituted and how it entailed the vital interests of each partner.

Chapter 19

WHAT WENT WRONG?

During Putin's second term, the Russian elite began returning to the idea of Russia's superpower role, which demanded an assertive and tough foreign policy. Even loyal Putinists started grumbling about his compromises, "softness," and constant retreats in dealing with the Americans. The Russian elite produced a long list of grudges against the United States: the war in Iraq, retention of the long-obsolete Jackson-Vanik amendment on freedom to emigrate, unilateral repudiation of the ABM treaty, the expansion of NATO, reluctance to strongly support Russia's application to join the World Trade Organization, failure to reciprocate when Russia withdrew its military bases in Vietnam and Cuba, attempts to expand its presence in post-Soviet territories, and an unwillingness to leave Central Asia at the end of the Afghan operation. Moscow felt that Washington should make corresponding concessions each time Russia retreated, even if the retreat resulted from weakness or was entirely in Russia's interests, demonstrating a return to a zero-sum mentality. Thus, when the United States routed the Taliban in Afghanistan, which Moscow had regarded as the main threat to its security in the south, it protected Russia's interests. The Kremlin nevertheless felt the Americans should make a reciprocal gesture and agree to dismantle the U.S. bases in Central Asia. Usually, however, the Americans complained that when pressed about what they really wanted as reciprocity, the Russians remained vague. It was apparent that Moscow was unhappy about nearly everything. Yet most of all, it was unhappy about the things it knew could not be changed in its relationship with the United States. The Kremlin's constant litanies have become its masochistic way of reviving the old phobias, which have been reinforced by American maximalism and its ignoring Russia's grudges.

At some point, Vladimir Putin rejected his previously cautious stance and threw a wrench into the relationship, unleashing a tide of hostile rhetoric. Normally restrained, he began making openly critical remarks about Washington. In December 2004 he stunned an audience when he compared the United States to the colonialists of old: a "strict uncle in a pith helmet instructing others how to live their lives." Soon he declared U.S. concerns on the situation in Chechnya to be "aimed at rocking the Russian Federation." It was a sign that the Kremlin no longer felt constrained by the declaration of a partnership; it had decided to be open in its annoyance with Bush's policies. By 2006 the Russian leader ceased to edit himself when attacking the United States and compared it to "a comrade wolf that knows whom to eat"—"he eats and listens to no one." The reasons for the Kremlin's unhappiness with the United States were evident. Moscow did not get the benefits from the partnership it had expected. On the contrary, it started to suspect Washington of meddling in its domestic affairs and of supporting the "orange virus" in the former Soviet space. Ironically, these suspicions emerged at a time when the U.S. administration was doing everything it could to maintain a neutral stance— demonstrating how edgy and neurotic the Russian political class had become. That the Russian president and Russia's political class began openly and increasingly to encourage anti-American sentiment in society is sufficient testimony to a shift in the Kremlin's position. The ruling team ceased to see the United States as a reliable partner, viewing it instead as a threat. Putin himself was evidently disillusioned with Washington and no longer trusted the United States or its leader and did not try to conceal his new feelings. The change of rhetoric meant that Moscow opted for a revisionist course in its relations with the United States. The shift toward anti-Western mobilizational tactics in domestic policy was reflected in Russia's relations with the United States.

President Bush continued to refrain from criticizing his friend Vladimir. Only once did the U.S. administration gently chide the Kremlin. In an article published in *Izvestia* on January 26, 2004, Colin Powell wrote:

> Certain developments in Russian politics and foreign policy in recent months have given us pause. Russia's democratic system seems not yet to have found the essential balance among the executive, legislative and judicial branches of government. Political power is not yet fully tethered to law. Key aspects of civil society—free media and political party development, for example—have not yet sustained an independent presence.

The general impression was that Washington intentionally closed its eyes to violations of democracy in Russia. American policy makers either failed to understand the foreign-policy implications of the Kremlin's authoritarian shift, underestimated it, wanted to avoid making things worse by lecturing to Putin, or did not have means to influence the Kremlin, which seems to be the most plausible explanation. In the end they seemed to have been taken aback by the Kremlin's growing assertiveness on the international scene and the anti-American thrust of its rhetoric. Gradually, Washington started to view the developments in Russia with increasing alarm: the Yukos affair and Khodorkovsky's arrest in 2003 were seen as the Kremlin's striking a blow against the institution of private property. In addition there was growing state control over the media; the centralization of power; Moscow's meddling in Ukrainian affairs; attempts to push the United States out of Central Asia; support of authoritarian regimes like that of Lukashenko; and finally the passing of a law on nongovernmental organizations in 2006. Yet already by that time, the United States did not have much leverage over Russian developments.

Soon events in the Middle East and failures in the Iraq war forced the Bush administration to shift toward a democracy-promotion ideology and to declare democracy as a means of guaranteeing American security. In this connection, Leon Aron wrote: "The post–9/11 activist U.S. foreign policy, which perceives the promotion of liberty and democracy as the key strategic means of ensuring America's security, cannot but be increasingly at odds with the Kremlin's post-imperial 'restoration.'"[1] Moreover, the democracy promotion agenda was incompatible with the realist course the United States was pursuing toward Russia. In practice, however, the U.S. shift to democracy promotion rhetoric did not much change its cautious approach to Russian domestic developments.[2]

Yet, starting in 2005, Washington could no longer conceal its growing irritation with Moscow's foreign policy and produced a list of its own complaints about Moscow. Not only was there the refusal to support the U.S. operation in Iraq, but also reluctance to endorse American plans for Iran. Moscow supported regimes like Iran, Libya, Syria, and Venezuela, which the United States considered hostile, and was selling them arms. There was dialogue between Moscow and Hamas, the sale of arms to China, sanctions against the newly independent states, and finally, the curtailing of democracy within Russia. Still, Washington continued to make efforts not to overplay idealism and democracy promotion with Russia, trying not to irritate Putin.

What were the reasons it proved more difficult than anticipated to make a reality of the strategic partnership Putin and Bush had proclaimed, and why did the relationship go so sour in the end? "Americans can't tolerate us because we became strong," would be the explanation of Russian pundits and politicians, and this was accepted by many Western observers. If one follows this logic, the relationship between the United States and Germany, a country that became a powerful regional power, should deteriorate as well, yet the two states continue to be close allies. The key reason behind the decline in U.S.-Russian relations in 2006–2007 definitely lies beyond any "weak–strong" dichotomy and beyond the foreign-policy realm. Both states organize power and society quite differently and the existence of common geopolitical interests did not counterbalance the structural and normative incompatibilities between the Russian and U.S. systems, as many experts on both sides hoped. Then why do the relations between Washington and communist China continue to normalize and even appear friendly, a devil's advocate would ask? The U.S.-Chinese constructive dialogue proves that political will, the existence of strategic goals that include understanding of the repercussions of every policy action, and a broad economic agenda might mitigate systemic incompatibilities, at least partially and temporarily. Russo–American relations have been lacking that cushion.

Henry Kissinger, deliberating on the estrangement between the United States and Russia, wrote, "The estrangement falls into two categories: on the American side, disenchantment with domestic trends in Russia, disappointment with Russia's foot-dragging on the nuclear issue in Iran, and reservations about the abrupt way Russia has dealt with the newly independent former parts of the Russian empire. On the Russian side, there is a sense that America takes Russia for granted, demands consideration of its difficulties but is unwilling to respect those of Russia, starts crises without adequate consultation and intervenes unacceptably in the domestic affairs of Russia." Explaining the difficulty in resolving mutual complaints, Kissinger points out that the United States identifies "normalcy and peace with the spread of its political values and institutions," whereas Russia has been seeking it "through a security belt in contiguous territory." He admits that "many Americans criticize Putin for reverting to an autocratic system."[3] In this way, the architect of realpolitik acknowledges the normative limitations of U.S.-Russian relations.

Precisely these limitations affected Bush's foreign-policy real-ism in dealing with Russia. Admittedly, Bush's realism has worked in Kazakhstan, Pakistan, and Saudi Arabia. It does not work in relations with Russia for two interrelated reasons. First, Russia has returned to a system that, for its survival, requires an enemy, reviving the "historical experience" Henry Kissinger mentions; it needs to reproduce the militarist mentality and cannot function in a unipolar world that inevitably brings it on a collision course with the United States. Second, the United States, with its longing for hegemony, cannot be relaxed about the emergence of a state based on different normative values that seeks to recreate its area of global influence. This being the situation, mutual disenchantment has been inevitable.

Other factors have added to the central tension. Moscow became increasingly restive over the resource asymmetry between the two countries, deciding on energy resources to counterbalance the might of the United States. Perceptions also matter. The impression is that Bush and Putin meant two entirely different things by "partnership." Bush apparently saw it as a way of realizing America's security agenda and, seem-ingly, of containing Russian expansionism. Putin saw it as a way of raising Russia's profile and as a guarantee of Russia's global role. U.S. attempts to establish a presence in the territories of the former USSR were interpreted by Moscow as an unfriendly act. Washington saw Russia's exploitation of its energy resources and economic expansion as violating the principles of global energy security and a demonstration of imperialism. Moscow saw America's meek attempts to lecture Russia on democracy as constraining Russia's sovereignty. Finally, the White House, with its "ignore-and-take-for-granted" Russia policy, underestimated the stakes in U.S.–Russian relations. As Andrew Kuchins wrote, "Russia's importance for U.S. interests is underestimated in Washington, especially given our concerns about the prolifera-tion of WMD, radical Islamic-inspired terrorism, and energy security. What other country can potentially promote or thwart our interests on all three of these first-order priorities to the extent that Russia can?"[4] That Washington disregarded Russia as a serious international actor has been a painful experience for the Russian political class. It wasted no time skillfully using the Iraq conundrum to reassert its regional and global presence and trying to undermine U.S. hegemony wherever possible. In so doing, it enjoyed the tacit approval of China and some European states. As the presidencies of Bush and Putin drew to a close, it was clear that, after a period of hope for a constructive partnership (albeit, understood differently) in 2001–2003, neither side continued to harbor illusions about the new reality of their mutual relations.

Some analysts, considering what has obstructed a strategic partnership between Russia and the United States, put an emphasis on other factors. They point to the lack of permanent bodies to guarantee that the political declarations and intentions of the respective governments would be implemented. During the 1990s the Gore–Chernomyrdin commission, by following the technical details of the U.S.–Russian cooperation, acted as a cushion to soften the political winds. When Russia stopped being a priority for the United States, however, such institutions became obsolete. Another reason behind the deterioration of the relationship in the minds of many Russian pundits is the U.S. withdrawal from the arms control dialogue. As developments in 2007 would show, there are undoubtedly issues on the arms control table that need to be resolved. Yet here we are dealing with a paradox: the Russian political elite misses the arms control dialogue with the U.S. because it had served as a confirmation of Russia's superpower status, which means in fact that the Russian political class continues to see the United States as a foe, while at the same wanting to be a key U.S. partner. This contradictory dual identity might puzzle any American counterpart.

Understandably, Washington grew tired of constantly massaging Russian pride, helping to cure Russian complexes, and pretending to deal with an equal. However, the understanding by the U.S. foreign-policy establishment of how dramatic the process is of Russia's shift to a different paradigm within the lifetime of one political generation could have helped to mitigate, at least partially, mutual unhappiness about the relationship. It could hardly prevent the unhappiness and mutual resentment altogether. Finally, there are no common economic interests underpinning U.S.–Russian relations such as exist between Russia and Europe. The United States accounts for only 2.6 percent of Russia's exports, occupying eleventh place, and 4.6 percent of Russia's imports, which places it fifth. Exports to Russia are less than 1 percent of all American exports. According to Russian sources, trade volume between the United States and Russia reached $15.3 billion in 2006. Around $7.7 billion out of $55 billion in foreign direct investment came from the United States. One has to admit, however, that active economic ties between Russia and the EU did not preclude a cooling of relations between them (although the economic factor continues to be operative in the U.S.–Chinese relationship).

Looking back over the past decade, one cannot but note that if Bill Clinton's policy of warmly embracing Russia ended in the mutual disenchantment of Washington and Moscow, then Bush's realpolitik is ending in even worse shape, with a relationship crisis that is not always acknowledged in either capital. At first, it seemed that the personal rapport between Putin and Bush would help to neutralize possible tensions between the two countries. Indeed this occurred on more than one occasion. A moment came, however, when the personal chemistry of which the two leaders were so proud could no longer stem the buildup of mistrust between the two capitals. It has made the situation worse, since there are no other mechanisms that could support the loose fabric of the relationship. Besides, neither leader appears to truly understand the nature of their relationship or the intentions of the other. Bush may have thought his friendly relations with Putin would keep the Russian president within a framework that Washington could understand. Putin believed his friendship with Bush would ensure that the United States would not encroach on territories that Russia considers within its sphere of influence and that the United States would close its eyes to "distinctive features of Russian democracy." In his view, he had made concessions to the Americans on many occasions. He was evidently expecting reciprocal gestures and was disappointed when nothing was forthcoming. "What have we received in return for our concessions to America? They could not even repeal the Jackson-Vanik amendment," one Kremlin official exclaimed. He was right. For Russians, the Jackson-Vanik amendment is a humiliating leftover of the past that reminds them that the Cold War is not over.

Political substance apart, one might wonder how Putin and Bush have retained friendly personal relations for so long (or were they pretending all along?). Not only had they different political agendas, they have completely different political personalities. Bush, with his stubborn consistency and ideological approach, is the antithesis of the chameleon-like Putin, with his ambivalence and flip-flopping. In the end, they have proved that relations based on personal rapport (for which both sides criticized the Clinton–Yeltsin partnership) cannot be sustained unless they are based on a more solid foundation.

The U.S. side, however, has tried, even in 2006, to argue that "the trend has been positive," downplaying the growing rift, whereas the Russian side has been openly critical of the relationship. "I do still think that we have a relationship with Russia that is beneficial to both sides and that is workable on many issues," said Condoleezza Rice on May 1, 2006, still trying to stop the further nosedive of the U.S.–Russian relationship. Inevitably, the question arises of setting standards for judging the success or failure of the relationship. Can it be viewed as successful if serious frictions are avoided between the states and both sides succeed in managing tension, or if their relations are preserved in a stagnant form? How can it be evaluated if cooperation is developed only in a few selected areas? Based on minimal criteria, one can view the U.S.–Russian relationship during the Bush–Putin period positively. Conflicts have been prevented on issues that Washington and Moscow view differently. One can then view relations between Washington and Moscow during the Clinton–Yeltsin years as a stunning success since both sides tried to work within the partnership paradigm. The irony is that a lack of substance in the U.S.–Russian relationship, especially during the Bush–Putin period, has helped to avoid more serious friction. However, judged by maximalist criteria, this relationship fits the crisis formula.

One of the triggers that increased mistrust between Moscow and Washington was the Ukrainian Orange Revolution in 2004, which Moscow continues to this day to believe was instigated by the United States. Another was the realization that the United States did not intend to remove its presence from the CIS, which Putin saw as treacherous. The ex–KGB lieutenant colonel, accustomed to thinking in defensive clichés, decided Russia was being encircled. The last blow to what remained of the Kremlin's trust in the United States was suspicion that the White House saw democracy as a means of subverting the Russian state. It is difficult to judge how far the Russian elite and the president himself believe this. It is not inconceivable that at least some occupants of the Kremlin deliberately invent American bugaboos in order to make the U.S. threat seem more credible. It is also possible that they really do believe that the United States is seeking to weaken Russia. Even moderate Russian politicians now voice suspicion of Washington, asking why Washington is surrounding Russia with a NATO fence and missile defense, warning that it will inevitably provoke a defensive Moscow reaction. In any case, if the Bush–Putin meeting in Ljubljana in June 2001 was a turning point in their personal trust, their summit in Bratislava, Slovakia, in February 2005, when the leaders publicly confronted each other, publicly demonstrated a virtual end of their rapport.

U.S. assistance to Ukraine and Georgia and its readiness to discuss their NATO membership, and Washington's mild criticism of Russian domestic policy have only deepened resentment in the Kremlin. When U.S. vice president Dick Cheney, in Vilnius in May 2006, accused Moscow of using oil and gas as "tools of intimidation and blackmail" and of having "unfairly and improperly restricted the rights of the people," his comments brought a storm of indignation in Moscow. Even Russian liberals viewed it as evidence of a double standard to lecture Russia on democracy yet embrace the authoritarian leaders of Central Asia. Still, this was not the lowest ebb of the relationship.

Meanwhile, Washington stopped pretending. In the spring of 2006, a prominent American thinktank, the Council on Foreign Relations, published a report on relations between the United States and Russia, prepared by a task force headed by Senator Jack Kemp and former vice presidential candidate John Edwards. "U.S.–Russian relations are clearly headed in the wrong direction. Contention is crowding out consensus. The very idea of 'strategic partnership' no longer seems realistic," wrote the authors of the task force, calling for an alternation of "selective cooperation" and "selective opposition" or even "containment" of Russia.[5] Moscow struck back with a report of its own, prepared in the Kremlin, in which the United States was accused not only of trying "wherever possible to encroach on Russia's interests," but also "of continuing to work surreptitiously toward a Russian version of the Orange Revolution."[6] From now on, nothing could prevent the cold shower from getting colder.

When in the spring of 2006, Senator John McCain and Representative Thomas Lantos demanded that Russia be expelled from the G8, they were expressing an opinion widely held in Congress. Even liberally inclined members of the American establishment, like Strobe Talbott, called for a review of U.S. policy toward Russia, saying that the term *partnership* was outdated when talking of Russia, preferring *engagement*. Senator Richard Lugar, who is generally benevolent to Russia and who has made a great contribution to the U.S.–Russian partnership, strongly criticized Russia alongside Venezuela and Iran for having used its energy policy as a form of blackmail.[7]

Bush, however, recognized that despite all the problems, he could not allow the tension to escalate. Washington's problems were piling up, including Iran, and it wanted to restrain Putin's assertiveness. Nevertheless, any shift by Bush to harsher policies with regard to Russia may be seen as an admission that his policy of partnership with Putin had been a failure. Despite many calls to boycott the St. Petersburg G8 summit in the summer of 2006, Bush went to Russia. In the fall of 2006, Russia and the United States reached a bilateral agreement on Russia's WTO membership. These measures mollified Putin, who looked happy and relaxed at the signing of the Russo–American protocol, which opened the way for Russia to join the WTO. At that moment, one might conclude that although Putin had used anti-Americanism in his domestic policy, he was not ready to allow relations with America to deteriorate further. Soon it would become obvious that the logic of losing trust has its own dynamics.

On February 10, 2007, Vladimir Putin gave a speech in Munich that some perceived as the start of a new Cold War between Russia and the United States. Addressing German chancellor Merkel, U.S. defense secretary Robert Gates, Senator McCain, and other Western leaders present in the audience, Putin lashed out against what he called the unipolar world and again delivered a well-known laundry list of Moscow's grievances against Washington. The United States "has overstepped its national borders in every sphere," exhibiting "ever greater disdain for the fundamental principles of international law," Putin said.[8] Little in Putin's speech was new. The president and other Russian leaders had expressed the same grievances many times before. Instead, the audience was caught off-guard by the emotion and energy of Putin's speech, which suggested that he had come to Munich with the express purpose of getting a few things off his chest.

The audience was also taken aback by Putin's intentional rejection of political correctness. It was no secret that Russia's relationship with the West, and particularly with the United States, was far from perfect. In public, however, Western leaders followed the rules of the game and tried to couch their disagreements with Moscow and displeasure with Putin in diplomatic language. Putin cut to the chase and said what he thought of the United States, thereby exposing the full extent of the problems in Russian–U.S. relations. As he did not offer a solution to the problems, however, Putin's candor only made the situation worse by confirming the widespread opinion in the West that improved relations with Russia are highly unlikely during his tenure. Even Putin's supporters in Russia were perplexed by his speech. "This was a chance for Putin to set out a coherent vision of Russian foreign policy for the remainder of his time in office. Regrettably, this opportunity was squandered," analysts close to the Kremlin complained.[9]

What prompted the Russian leader to deliver such a shock to the West, and to the United States, above all? Some Russian observers have suggested that Secretary Gates had aroused Putin's ire when, in remarks to the U.S. Congress at the beginning of February, he grouped Russia with such so-called rogue states as Iran and North Korea. This is far from true. Others maintain that Putin was responding to the U.S. plan to install elements of a missile defense system in Poland and the Czech Republic, although the announcement hardly came as a surprise, since Washington and Moscow had been discussing the issue for nearly a year.

Putin's outburst in Munich was to be expected. It was sparked by several factors, starting with the president's attempt to blame Washington for the collapse of the policy of partnership between Russia and the West. Perhaps he was beginning to consider his foreign-policy legacy and did not want to be remembered as the president who had "lost the West." Putin's speech was also intended to beef up his image in Russia as a strong leader, particularly among the elite, in response to its growing concern over identifying candidates to succeed him in 2008. The president wanted to show both the world and the Russian population that Russia could speak from a position of strength on the world stage. He may have hoped to exploit the anti-

American mood in Europe as well as differences of opinion between the United States and its European allies.

Putin's Munich speech reconfirmed how the Russian president and the Russian elite view their partnership with the United States. They see it as a way to mutual concessions and reciprocity, as a zero-sum game. Moscow perceives Washington's lack of willingness to respond to Russian sensitivities as its intention to weaken Russia and to marginalize it in the international arena. The Russian elite has no doubts that Washington is using "slogans of democratization" to "get access to Russia's natural resources."[10] A whiff of Cold War in the air has become apparent. Yet, as though to prove wrong those doomsayers who predict deep crisis and even imminent confrontation in relations, Putin in Munich pushed the pendulum in the opposite direction. He praised President Bush as his personal friend and invited the U.S. defense secretary to visit Russia, demonstrating the art of handling the "partner-opponent" in Russia's foreign policy. Americans, stunned by Putin's speech, nevertheless played down the seriousness of the rift, undertaking to smooth growing tensions and launching an aggressive diplomatic dialogue with Moscow to assuage the feelings of the Kremlin.

Chapter 20

BUMPS IN THE ROAD

Bush's efforts to woo Russia could not change the vector. Both leaders were moving to the end of their tenures, and neither had the time nor the energy to reverse the dominant trend. The spiral of mutual frustration could hardly have been prevented, taking into account the Kremlin's need to use the United States as a foreign bogeyman for domestic purposes. Russia's strong-arm rhetoric might have been softened by U.S. "preventive" efforts to embrace Russia, for instance, by including Russia in developing the joint missile defense program (an idea Moscow had first raised in 2002). The Bush administration, bogged down in Iraq and overstretched in the global arena, did not pay much attention to Moscow's complaints. "We've done enough coddling of Moscow!" some American observers would say. "Russia is acting like a bully and needs a tough response, not embracing," others would reiterate. From the Russian side, General Yuri Balujevsky, chief of the Russian General Staff, was pretty unequivocal, retorting, "Russia's cooperation with the West on the basis of forming common strategic interests has not helped its military security."[1] Both sides were pushing the ball in the same direction, though in a different way.

The U.S. side for quite a while has been expressing concerns about the state of democratic development in Russia and the

246

derailment of democratic reforms, though mostly through private channels. Recently, the concerns have assumed a more public profile. One example: the comments of U.S. Deputy Assistant Secretary David Kramer on May 31, 2007, in Baltimore, which made a real splash and were perceived as a reflection of what the U.S. administration really thinks about Putin's Russia. Kramer did not mince his words, describing a rather bleak picture of Russia's domestic situation: "Suppression of genuine opposition, abridgement of the right to protest, constriction of civil society, and the decline of media freedom are all serious setbacks. They are inconsistent with Russia's professed commitment to building and preserving the foundations of a democratic state.... The backsliding is multifaceted." Washington was taking the more publicly critical position on Russian domestic developments that it had previously avoided.

In April 2007, the State Department published its report, "Supporting Human Rights and Democracy," with a negative assessment of the state of democracy in Russia. Russian parliamentarians responded by approving a resolution that expressed concern over what they called growing and unprecedented attempts by the United States "to interfere in Russia's internal affairs" and even its "provoking extremist sentiments." When he signed into law legislation supporting a Ukrainian and Georgian bid to join NATO, Bush added to simmering tensions. In his state-of-the-nation address on April 25, 2007, Putin launched a stinging attack on the United States. "The flow of money from abroad used for direct interference in our affairs is growing. Not everyone likes the stable, gradual rise of our country. There are some who are using democratic ideology to interfere in our internal affairs," said Putin sternly. Those "some" Putin had in mind, of course, included the United States.[2] Finally, in his speech on May 9, Victory Day, the Russian president said: "The number of threats is not decreasing. They are only transforming and changing their guise. As during the Third Reich era, these new threats show the same degree of contempt for human life and the same claims to world exclusiveness and diktat." The U.S. embassy in Moscow received assurances from the Russian Foreign Ministry that President Putin had no intention of likening the U.S. administration's policy to that of the Third Reich, but few observers doubted the opposite. One might get the impression that the relationship between the two countries had returned to the pre-Gorbachev period.

During the first term of Putin's presidency, Washington put Russia on the back burner, which explained the lack of U.S. interest in this part of the world and its lack of effort in building a more comprehensive strategy regarding it. Today even if the American establishment understands the significance of Washington's relationship with Moscow, the timing is bad for a fresh breakthrough or even for a smoothing of the relationship. In any case, the arsenal of U.S. instruments for dealing with Russia appears limited, and the U.S. administration has had difficulty in managing the partner–opponent formula of the relationship pursued by Russia. Having no other solutions, the West and the United States have begun desperate efforts to preserve the status quo in their relations with Russia, preventing further deterioration. The Kremlin has succeeded rather skillfully in using both American acquiescence to Russia and American attempts to deter Russia's resurgence game. Russian politicians and government officials like Sergei Lavrov could now afford a condescending tone toward Washington, offering (not without irony) to "help the United States to make 'a soft landing' in a multipolar reality."[3]

By the end of the Putin and Bush terms, one could get confused by the contradictory nature of the relationship between the two countries. The United States and Russia have continued their cooperation on counterterrorism, which appears intensive. The U.S.–Russia Counterterrorism Working Group has been meeting to discuss law enforcement, weapons of mass destruction, terrorist financing, counternarcotics, man-portable anti-aircraft missiles (MANPADS), and transportation security. Nuclear cooperation and nonproliferation cooperation are all in the positive category. In summer 2007, a so-called 123 Agreement to promote civilian nuclear energy cooperation was ready to be signed. Under the START Treaty and the Treaty of Moscow, 7,000 nuclear warheads have been deactivated, and 600 ICBMs and 600 SLBs destroyed. Both countries have renewed (until 2013) the Cooperative Threat Reduction (CTR) program launched to facilitate the dismantling of weapons of mass destruction. At their July 2006 summit in St. Petersburg, Bush and Putin announced the Global Initiative to Combat Nuclear Terrorism, with the goal of preventing nuclear materials from falling into terrorist hands. Russia and the United States continue to work on the Peaceful Use of Nuclear Energy Agreement, which includes enhancing nuclear-fuel-cycle security and the fuel-center initiative. They also continue to work on defense technology cooperation and have begun consultation on post–START (Strategic Arms Reduction Treaty) arrangements (the START Treaty expires in 2009). Both countries have worked closely, despite their many disagreements, over North Korea and Iran (Russia voted in favor of the UN Security Council resolutions on North Korea and Iran), and in the framework of the NATO–Russia Council.

Business relations between the U.S. and Russia have also demonstrated a positive trend. Many American companies that vowed they would never go back to Russia after the 1998 financial meltdown have been back in a Russian market that has been increasingly lucrative in recent years. According to official U.S. sources, American investment in Russia shot up by 50 percent in 2005. Top U.S. companies including Alcoa, Coca-Cola, GM, Procter and Gamble, and Boeing, which in 2006 signed an $18 billion deal to buy Russian titanium, have increased their stake in Russia. In spring 2007, Boeing initiated a contract valued at as much as $2 billion with the Russian airline for the purchase of at least fifteen long-range jets.[4]

Thus, relations between the United States and Russia are complicated and multidimensional. Initiatives in the security area and progress in business relations are apparent but they have not been followed by the extension of constructive cooperation to other levels of partnership, where disagreements continue to prevail. Most importantly, they have not brought mutual trust and have failed to mitigate points of contention that have become more prominent. Among these are Russia's policy toward its neighbors and internal Russian trends.

In the final stages of the Bush and Putin tenures, the two sides have been at loggerheads over three contentious issues that simultaneously reflect the substance and limits of the U.S.-Russian relationship: *Iran, missile defense deployment in Poland and the Czech Republic,* and *Kosovo.*

The continuing Iranian saga demonstrates Russia's concern over American influence. George Perkovich was right when he wrote, "If North Korean or Iranian nuclear weapon capabilities complicate the freedom of [the] U.S. power projection, Russia and China may not see this as entirely bad." Some political circles in Moscow have behaved as though a nuclear Iran would be less dangerous than an American attack on Iran or increased American leverage in the region. We should not, however, oversimplify. Not all Kremlin initiatives have been motivated by a desire to flex muscles or block America and the West, or from a sheer desire to weaken it. Even the pro-Western minority in Russia has been concerned over the straightforwardness of American diplomacy, fearing that the Iraq scenario might be repeated in Iran (a concern shared by China and France). Moscow does not want another Iraq on its borders. At the same time, Moscow has become more apprehensive about Iranian recklessness. Though reluctantly, Moscow supported the United States and its allies in the Security Council twice (in December 2006 and March 2007), approving sanctions against Iran. In the spring of 2007 the Kremlin let it be known that it would not allow Tehran to use tensions between Moscow and Washington to play Russia against the United States.

By March 2007, Russian plans to involve Tehran in negotiations and persuade the Iranians to clarify all International Atomic Energy Agency (IAEA) concerns failed. Iran refused to stop its most sensitive nuclear activity, proving that Moscow had no impact on its policy and could not use Iran as a bargaining chip in trade-offs with the United States. The Russian elite and its leader have understood that Iran's continuing defiance has narrowed Russia's options and been a blow to its reputation. By offering to share the Russian radar facility in Azerbaijan with the United States, Putin proved that he recognized the Iranian threat.

In analyzing the cooling of the relationship between Moscow and Tehran, Dmitri Trenin concluded that the key explanation was not security concerns but business. Russia, with its "national champion" Rosatom, which dealt with the atomic industry, was serious about pursuing its interests globally, including in the United States. That meant significantly greater dividends than Moscow could get in Iran. Economic interests were pushing Russia closer to the West on the Iranian nuclear issue.[5] Whatever the motivation was, it has been a welcome sign, one that proved Moscow and Washington could narrow the field of their disagreements, at least in this area. However, it is too early to tell how sustainable this coming together will be when the Kremlin's attitude toward the United States is dictated by domestic circumstances. There is no evidence that Iran is ready to reverse its nuclear course, and it is difficult to predict how Russia would react to possible further punitive measures against Iran.

In the spring of 2007, U.S. plans to deploy elements of missile defense in Poland and the Czech Republic became another point of contention in the Russo–American relationship. In fact, it was an example of how to create a problem from nothing. The rationale behind U.S. intentions is dubious. Either Washington had not thought about the Russian and European reaction, did not care about it, or misjudged how much its missile defense plan would rile the Kremlin. The Russian outcry could have been prevented if Washington had agreed to involve Moscow in the building of the joint U.S.–NATO–Russia missile system, as the Russians had been suggesting for several years. In any case, considering deteriorating relations with Russia, the deployment of the U.S. missile system should have been postponed until after the changing of the guard at the Kremlin, which has always made the Russian elite nervous and even paranoid. For Moscow's part, its elite hardly perceived ten American interceptors or a radar as an immediate threat to Russian nuclear security. The key reason for the Kremlin's outcry was Moscow's lack of trust in the intentions of the United States. The Kremlin feared that the deployment was part of a plan to "encircle" Russia, to be followed by other actions. As Russian expert Sergei Rogov said, "Bush is not going to stop at that, so more elements of the ABM system may be deployed later," which was precisely what worries Russian politicians. Lavrov raised concerns that missile silos for interceptors could be converted to other uses, including housing intercontinental ballistic missiles.[6]

Russian fears and distrust of American intentions in this context have some basis. It is generally believed in Russia that Washington has broken its promises to Moscow on several occasions, including its reported promise not to expand NATO, which had been enlarged twice. Many people in Moscow remember Clinton's earlier pledge not to rush ahead with NATO, given just before its enlargement. American missile plans fueled opposition in Europe, including Germany, mainly because of Russia's strong reaction. According to German foreign affairs minister Frank-Walter Steinmeier:

> A project of this kind of strategic importance brings up a range of serious issues that should be carefully looked at within the framework of NATO. We have to avoid a situation where the security of a few is achieved at the cost of new mistrust or even insecurity. It is in Germany's and Europe's interest to prevent this.

The Bush administration hardly expected the chain reaction of criticism that followed. If Washington had been handling the issue clumsily, the Kremlin's reaction was out of proportion. It almost seemed as if the Kremlin team had been waiting for such a pretext to prove that America was in fact pursuing policies hostile to Russia. Immediately after Putin denounced plans for missile-defense deployment, his commander of strategic forces, General Nikolai Solovtsov, warned that Russian missiles would target Poland and the Czech Republic if they accepted the U.S. missile system, and that Russia would withdraw from the Intermediate-Range Nuclear Forces (INF) Treaty. Rose Gottemoeller warned,

> This is a conundrum: on the one hand President Putin declares himself the champion of international law and urges all countries to return to the negotiating table. On the other hand, his chief military leaders declare themselves dissatisfied with an important arms control treaty and declare Russia's right to unilaterally withdraw from it.[7]

As it happens, Bush never wanted binding agreements with the Russians on nuclear weapons, giving Moscow an argument to follow suit, and trigger the collapse of the whole arms control framework. It would not be Russia that had initiated the process.

Moscow, by threatening to withdraw from the INF treaty, was playing against its security interests. It would have allowed the United States to threaten to withdraw as well and to build a new generation of intermediate-range missiles, which would mean that the arms race would start again, a race Russia could hardly win. Do Russian politicians understand the Catch-22 they are building for themselves? Some of them do, but even they have been caught in the anti-American tide. It seems that the Kremlin has been intentionally pushing the issue to the edge to see what happens. Perhaps the Americans would back off and make a concession on the issue of interceptors or on some other issue. If not, the whole problem could be forgotten.[8] The story may help to understand the Kremlin's psychology— ready to escalate tensions to the verge of recklessness in an attempt to push its agenda, or it may just demonstrate its ability to provoke suspense and shake up the world without any agenda.

Moscow's outcry had two practical results: first, Europe was unhappy with the United States, finding itself again hostage to relations between Washington and Moscow; second, Russian hawks in the power structure had a pretext to ask for increased defense expenditures.[9]

Meanwhile, the Kremlin has continued its "politics of threat." In May, in his final address to the Federal Assembly on the state of the nation, Vladimir Putin announced Russia's moratorium on implementing the CFE treaty (Conventional Forces in Europe Treaty). The Kremlin's argument seemed irresistible: in 2001 the United States had unilaterally withdrawn from the ABM treaty, explaining that Russia and the U.S. were no longer enemies. "Fine, if we are no longer enemies, then why this fuss about the CFE?" seemed to be the retort. It was difficult to disagree with that. The return to bickering over Cold War relics reflected not only the degree of worsening of the U.S.–Russian relationship, but also a lack of coherent strategies in Washington and Moscow for responding to post–Cold War challenges.

Another point of contention on the U.S.–Russian agenda was Kosovo. Moscow disagreed with the plan proposed by UN special envoy Martti Ahtisaari to grant Kosovo limited sovereignty under international supervision, and insisted that the plan had to be agreeable to Belgrade. Richard Holbrooke, who struck the Dayton deal to end the Bosnian war, immediately jumped in, warning that "European security and stability, and Russia's relationship with the West, were on the line." This message was interpreted by Moscow as being a threat to Russia: "Don't get in the way!" when the Kosovo issue is discussed at the Security Council. Holbrooke's warning only strengthened Russian readiness to say "Nyet!"—returning to the Soviet practice of responding negatively to American initiatives—and to threaten to veto any plan for Kosovo's independence. It is true that Moscow, having no constructive solution to regional conflicts either within or outside the former Soviet space, prefers to postpone the settlement "until better times," which leaves Russia with bargaining chips and the possibility of linking those conflicts with other international issues and anticipated trade-offs. The Russian daily *Kommersant* had a tough comment for the Russian tack in the continuing Kosovo crisis. "Moscow is simply trying to postpone a decision on Kosovo, hoping to use it in its effort to regain its role as an influential actor in the Balkan game," it said.[10]

The feeling is that the Russian position on Kosovo has been more contradictory than that and it does not boil down to simple cynicism. Indeed, having only recently ended (at least formally) its war with Chechnya, Russia views Kosovo's independence with deep apprehension. Despite Moscow's threats to exploit the Kosovo "precedent" by recognizing post-Soviet secessionist territories, the Russian political elite is wary of such a perspective and wants to avoid such a precedent, as do other European countries having separatist forces (Spain being an example).

Irrespective of hidden motives in its delaying tactics and a desire to increase its leverage, Moscow has been right in reiterating that the Serbs are not prepared to accept calmly the loss of a province that means so much to their national identity. At the same time, Russia has allowed Belgrade to use itself as it was used by Milosevic. Again, Moscow could find itself in the same position of losing leverage with Serbia and ending up provoking bitter feelings toward Russia in the Western capitals.

There are few good solutions to the Kosovo endgame. In March 2007, Mark Medish suggested a framework for a negotiated deal that offered a chance for a breakthrough in the Kosovo quandary: essentially "land for peace," plus European integration. The elements of the deal included recognition of Kosovo's sovereignty, followed by a fast membership track for Serbia into the European Union, and a referendum for the northern Serb enclave in Kosovo on association with Serbia. Some variant of this framework, if accepted by the parties, could lead to a durable settlement. We may know soon whether the United States, Europe, and the other parties are ready for such a breakthrough. If the chance to negotiate a comprehensive framework to settle Kosovo's status is lost, the major reason might not be the "Russia factor"—indeed Moscow seems to have kept open the door for last-minute diplomacy—but principally the insistence of the United States on imposed outcomes and the hesitancy of Europe to propose credible alternatives and to offer Serbia a place in a united Europe. Depending on how events develop, Kosovo could remain for some time a political variable in Russia's relationship with the United States, not least because of its ramifications for other "frozen conflicts" such as Transnistria, Abkhazia, South Ossetia, and Nagorno-Karabakh.

These issues have seriously clouded U.S.–Russian relations at the end of Bush's and Putin's presidencies. If not those issues, then other problems might have emerged, such as Georgia's attempt to join NATO, which would have triggered a deterioration in a relationship that has been lacking trust. The Russian president continued to play hardball, forcing the world to freeze in consternation. At a press conference on the eve of the G8 summit in Heiligendamm, Germany, on June 1, 2007, Putin again lashed out at U.S. plans for antiballistic missiles in Europe, noting that "for the first time in history ... elements of U.S. nuclear potential are appearing in Europe," adding, "We absolve ourselves of responsibility for our retaliatory steps." He warned that the American shield would turn Europe into a "powder keg," accusing the United States of an "almost uncontainable hyperuse of force."[11] The day before that press conference, the Russian government announced that it had successfully tested a new intercontinental ballistic missile (ICBM) with multiple warheads that could penetrate any U.S. antimissile shield. Several days later, however, during the G8 summit, Putin unexpectedly proposed a solution. He suggested to Washington the joint use of the Gabala (Azerbaijan) radar station.

It was a brilliant tactical move. The Russian leader proved to the Russian audience that he could be both a tough defender of Russia's interests and a peacemaker. By raising tensions and calming things down, Putin demonstrated to the world that the Kremlin still had an impact on high world politics. In some European states, the Russian president was seen as a problem solver rather than a troublemaker. For the United States, Putin put Bush in a seemingly lose-lose situation. Should Bush refuse Putin's offer, he would prove that the American missile system was directed against Russia; should he accept Putin's offer, he would demonstrate that Russia can dictate terms to the West. By offering Americans the Russian radar station, the Kremlin recognized the Iranian threat and agreed to build an anti-Iranian nuclear shield. Not only in Russian public opinion, but in European public opinion as well, Putin looked like a leader who offered a basis for discussion and joint effort that Washington should have thought about a long time ago. The Russian president appeared to be an excellent tactician who skillfully used the mistakes of the other side. However, tactical victories do not guarantee successful strategy.

Chapter 21

THE BUSH–PUTIN LEGACY

On July 1, 2007, President Bush invited Vladimir Putin to his family's summer home in Kennebunkport, Maine, to sort things out. The result of the "lobster summit" perfectly fit the current model of the U.S.–Russian relationship. As the *Economist* put it, "The two men agreed politely to disagree a lot and co-operate a bit."[1] Putin moved closer to Bush on Iran. Both presidents agreed to start extensive cooperation on civil-nuclear power and to continue dialogue on a new framework for strategic nuclear reductions to replace the START 1 Treaty. The Russian leader continued his "surprise offensive," suggesting to Bush new and unexpected ideas on missile defense cooperation, "We believe that the number of parties to this consultation (on missile defense-LS) could be expanded through the European countries.... We propose establishing an information exchange center in Moscow.... A similar center could be established in one of [the] European capitals.... We are prepared to modernize the Gabala radar. And if that is not enough, we would be prepared to build a new radar." In return Putin expected Bush to abandon the idea of deployment of the missile defense elements in Poland and the Czech Republic.

Vladimir Putin gave his shrewd take on the meeting: "Well, basically, we may state that the deck has been dealt, and we are here to play. And I would very much hope that we are playing the same game." Bush was even more reassuring, giving a positive assessment of their meeting, "We had a very long, strategic dialogue that I found to be important, necessary and productive."[2]

Putin was still enjoying a friendly lunch at Bush's vacation home when one of his tentative successors, Sergei Ivanov, warned that Russia would be ready to move its missiles closer to Europe if Washington pushed ahead with its missile defense plans. Several weeks later, the Kremlin introduced a moratorium on the CFE treaty, continuing its macho posturing. Putin and Bush were definitely not playing "the same game," as Putin had hoped in Kennebunkport. This was anticipated. Putin could not backtrack; he had to look strong in the eyes of the Russian elite. Besides, there were all the signs that he believed he had a chance to restructure international relations and Russia's role at a time when the United States was losing the initiative.

The spat around the U.S. missile initiative and Moscow's world-shaking retaliation said a lot about the state of U.S.-Russian relations, the nature of leadership in both countries, their ability to make strategic decisions, and their capacity to foresee the consequences of those decisions. It was hardly a prudent decision for Washington to move ahead with a missile defense shield at Russia's frontiers, especially when the Russian elite is preparing to solve the presidential succession issue. The decision to proceed provided additional ammunition for the Russian elite to consolidate the nation by returning to a militarist mentality. Besides, after several years of growing mistrust, it was difficult for Washington to persuade the Russian audience that the American shield was neither directed against Russia, nor could it be used against Russia in the future. The Kremlin's behavior at that time was driven by domestic imperatives and principally by the logic of the self-perpetuation of power, which trumped all other considerations. To control this process and guarantee continuity of power, Vladimir Putin has to demonstrate that he remains the only political factor and a formidable force. An especially tough stance in relations with the United States is one of the most effective ways for the Kremlin to prove that. This time it did not stop at using situational toughness with the West. It went further, making an effort to secure a more prominent role for Russia, which (it hoped) would inevitably lead to the gradual dismantling of the unipolar world, or would at least undermine unipolarity. Putin apparently hopes that other world players, including some in Europe, might help him at least to shake the tree. In any case, in the spring and summer of 2007, tensions and squabbles between Washington and Moscow have been viewed in Russia as a test of U.S. dominance and its ability to defend it. There has been a lot of bluff as well as elements of "let us try and see what happens" in this new Kremlin course. So far, the Kremlin has observed redlines it was not ready to cross. It has backed down each time its game threatened to damage relations with the United States beyond repair.

In fact, both Bush and Putin have demonstrated that they are not ready to let tensions escalate into a serious conflict. The Russian leader has invented a formula: when criticizing America he sings the praises of his "friend George." It could become a regular practice for the Russian president to emphasize the "friendly status" of the relationship with the United States, which would work either disarmingly or perplexingly on his American counterpart. All this reflects a new style of Russian diplomacy toward the United States, invented by Vladimir Putin, that can be defined as: "We are friends with you folks, and that means we have the right to tell you what we think about you." The Russian leader, having become skilled in juggling incompatibilities in Russian domestic politics, has proved he can do the same in foreign policy.

President Bush in his turn has continued to woo president Putin, suggesting carrots, including offers of cooperation on the missile defense program. Secretary of State Condoleezza Rice has been intentionally mild in her comments when discussing Russia. In April 2007, during a heated debate with the Russians, she admitted that there were "tensions" and expressed concern over a state that "suppresses dissent." She nevertheless concluded, "We have a pretty good strategic relationship with Russia." (In May 2007 Rice allowed herself to be more candid, saying, "On many things we have done very well, but the fact is that on some others it's been a difficult period.")[3] On June 1, 2007, Bush himself called the Washington–Moscow relationship "complex"—a term previously used chiefly to describe U.S. relations with China.

It is generally understood that the U.S. administration has decided to prevent further backsliding in its relationship with Russia in the interest of solving key U.S. issues. Washington has offered a new formula for dealing with Russia, one that Assistant Secretary of State for European and Eurasian Affairs Daniel Fried has commented on: "Although ours may not be a strategic partnership, it includes partnership on many strategic issues."[4]

Continuing to pursue realpolitik, Washington has been trying to find more subtle tools to demonstrate its concern over Russia's vector by, as David Kramer put it, "pushing back when we must, privately when possible but publicly when necessary, in defense of our values."[5] This approach could be an example of the "transformational diplomacy" advocated by Condoleezza Rice that intends to find a synthesis of idealism and realism.[6] Still, with the Bush term coming to an end, Washington needs simply to preserve the status quo, having no time left to devise a new strategy. As for Putin, continuing his anti-American rhetoric, he has been shy of any action. So far his bark has been worse than his bite. Both sides have moved toward a new stage in their relations that has become a combination of more realistic expectations of each other mixed with mutual disenchantment and prejudice.

There has been a powerful force driving both the U.S. and Russian presidents to pivot: the ticking of the clock. A lack of new ideas, a legacy of setbacks and frustration, and, more importantly, the lack of an effective framework to deal with complicated international issues and the uncertainty of Russia's future explain why the two leaders were stymied in efforts to change the atmosphere. By the end of Bush's presidency, Washington found itself at a dead end, without opportunities to take action regarding Russia that had any chance of improving mutual understanding. A partnership with a state that structured itself on alien terms has been impossible. Confrontation would be destructive for both the United States and for global security. Washington could not afford to isolate and marginalize Russia, as it needs Moscow's support to resolve a whole series of issues affecting U.S. interests. Besides, isolation would merely make Russia more unpredictable. Attempts to pressure the Kremlin would be futile since no Russian leader will take anyone's advice; the Russian public would see doing so as a sign of weakness. On the other hand, indulging the Russian regime encourages statist policies in Moscow and its desire to continue its assertiveness.

As for the Kremlin, its foreign policy has acquired a momentum that would be difficult to alter. Moscow continues to use the United States as an enemy, demonizing it and viewing U.S. hegemony as a constraint against Russia's revival. Thus, the field for constructive dialogue with Washington has narrowed. Even if Moscow and Washington were to agree on a policy toward Iran and North Korea, possibly reaching agreement on other issues and flash points, a return of relations to their previous levels of optimism would hardly occur.

The outgoing leaders have no time left to reorder priorities or come up with new initiatives. Bush has to concentrate on Iraq, which is central to American politics. Russia has already become a side issue in U.S. politics. As for Putin, he too is likely preparing for his exit from the Kremlin. The moment has come for crisis management, conflict prevention, and damage control. Both countries are awaiting the appearance of new governing teams unburdened by what happened in the past. Until then, the most the outgoing teams can do is to keep the dialogue going and avoid generating new tensions. The cyclical and up-and-down character of the U.S.–Russian relationship reconfirms the conclusion that it has deep roots. In some areas the American and Russian vectors are irreconcilable, at least at this historic juncture, which undermines agreements on common interests. Many expected the opposite outcome, with common interests softening structural incompatibilities. That has not happened. Summing up the evolution of U.S.–Russian relations after the collapse of the Soviet Union, one could argue that in the area of security both states have managed relations well in eliminating the threat of a nuclear confrontation despite Moscow's constant concern that Russia is being encircled. In reality, no one in the Kremlin believes a U.S. attack on Russia is feasible, and hardly any Americans believe that Russia might become a serious adversary. In terms of America's impact on Russia's transformation, the conclusion seems unexpected: the Russian political elite has succeeded in using U.S. realpolitik, and even the very existence of the United States, to strengthen the centralized state and perpetuate its authoritarian regime. One could argue, however, that without American attempts to help Russia's transformation, the result might have been worse.

Pondering the evolution of relations between the two countries in the last years of the Bush–Putin tenures, Robert Legvold predicted "either the status quo plus or the status quo minus," explaining that, in the first case, "the uneasy balance between cooperation and discord will continue," and in the second case that the relationship could "descend to another level."[7] There are domestic and foreign policy drivers in both countries that work in favor of the continuing stagnation of U.S.–Russian relations, which include the shifting balance between cooperation and disagreement. For the time being, there are factors that push both sides to "keep company" with one another, but such socializing comes of necessity. To be sure, the section of the Russian establishment that sees its survival as depending on close relations with the West would try to avoid further distancing itself from the West, which is a crucial prerequisite of Russia's cooperation with the United States. The question remains, however: will both sides contain the logic of distrust and its ramifications?

With presidential elections approaching in both countries, during which the "Russia card" and the "America card" could be played (though hardly actively in the United States), it seems unlikely that relations will seriously improve or that any improvement would be sustainable. During the previous election campaign, the Republicans made a point of attacking Clinton and the Democrats for having "lost" Russia. This time a similar maneuver may be expected from the Democrats. In Russia, anti-Americanism has become a criterion of patriotism for the Russian elite, which parades it vigorously at election time. The Democrats' victory in the U.S. mid-term elections in fall 2006 deepened Moscow's sense of foreboding because of its stubborn belief that relations are traditionally less relaxed with the Democrats than with the Republicans. Russian politicians were evidently overlooking the fact that U.S.–Russian relations were conducted very much along Cold War lines during Reagan's terms in office, and they were a good deal warmer during Clinton's presidency.

The new arrivals in the Kremlin and the White House will inherit a difficult legacy. They will have to redefine the relative importance that Russia and the United States have for each other and decide what the best political and conceptual framework is for their relationship.[8] Having sized each other up, Moscow and Washington will have to deal again with the back-burner "cooperation package" of the war on terror and energy security, now complicated by the politicizing of the issue (not without Russia's involvement). They will need to restart the dialogue on nuclear disarmament.[9] The long-standing agenda, known only too well in both capitals, includes such positive, however marginal, achievements as cooperation in the conquest of space and the peaceful use of nuclear energy, which will help to keep the U.S.–Russian relationship afloat. If the new leaders decide to reenergize their dialogue, they will have to ponder new challenges and think about the compatibility of their interests in addressing them, which means going beyond the well-known list. One would expect small steps to be more feasible than grandiose projects. Thus, Sergei Lavrov's initiative, addressed to NATO, on cooperating in fighting drug trafficking from Afghanistan is a step that could revive cooperation between Russia and NATO in the struggle against the Taliban. There is growing understanding in Russian political circles that the anti-American orientation of the new Afghan opposition will sooner or later acquire an anti-Russian flavor. More large-scale ideas have been on the table for a long time, including building a joint U.S.–NATO–Russia missile defense system. Breakthrough initiatives—like cooperation between Russia, Europe, China, and the United States in Central Asia and between Europe, Russia, and the United States in the Caucasus, not only in achieving common security goals in those regions but in enhancing their modernization—and joint efforts in rebuilding the Russian Far East and Siberia, do not seem plausible today.[10] The success of any project ideas for a future Russo–American relationship will depend, finally, not on the personal chemistry of their leaders but on how both states deal with systemic incompatibilities.

Experience shows that if Russia and the United States continue to move within the current paradigms, it would be overly optimistic to expect that the new leaders in Washington and Moscow will succeed in building a stable and productive relationship solely on the basis of the common interests of their countries. The divergence between their civilizational standards will inevitably produce different interpretations of those interests Moscow and Washington are assumed to share. Take international terrorism, for example. Moscow and Washington have yet to agree on a definition of a terrorist organization. The United States classifies Hamas and Hizballah as terrorist organizations, while Moscow does not. This means that the mere quantity of issues discussed will not lead to functioning Russo–American cooperation. Without a shared normative outlook and political will to find points of consensus, one cannot exclude that their dialogue may instead serve to deepen existing mutual prejudice.

How can consensus be reached if each side looks differently at the world and its role in the world? One has to be aware that the United States continues to strengthen its hegemony, viewing it as the guarantee of its national interests, which is incompatible with the existence of any other state's longing to be a geopolitical pillar, especially when that state promotes different values. Russia, on the contrary, is again trying to secure its comeback as a global power, which for the Russian elite is key to Russia's existence. It perceives the United States as a constraint, which means that so far Russia and the United States have competing strategic agendas.

At this time, seeking points of mutual engagement, quite apart from its results ("dialogue for dialogue's sake"), might be a way to prevent Russia and the United States from drifting further apart while they wait for more substantial grounds for their partnership to appear. We have, however, to avoid excessive hope that the new initiatives of the new leaders, their personal relations, and an active dialogue will build an opportunity "to start anew," that this time will be successful. Deliberating on how to restore U.S. relations with Russia, former adviser to President Bush, Thomas Graham, has defined the principle of reciprocity. The American approach should be "to respect Russia's choice and preferences," "recognize Russia as an integral part of European civilization," and "demonstrate understanding of the problems Russia is facing." The American side should expect Russia to "refrain from interpreting our appeal to common values as a cynical ploy," to be "aware of the difficulties the U.S. is facing," and to "recognize that they themselves are responsible for the state of affairs in Russia."[11]

The key precondition for productive cooperation or selective partnership between Russia and the United States is a strengthening of U.S. multilateralism and its active engagement of Russia, as well as the transition of Russia to democratic standards. If those conditions are absent, a repetition of the vicious circle that we have been watching will be inevitable, with new hopes becoming mere delayed disappointments.

Might we expect U.S.–Russian cooperation to promote Russia's integration with the West and help Russia's modernization? Its results could be contradictory. As noted, so far this cooperation has helped Russia to preserve the status quo. The existence of the United States has been used by the Kremlin to consolidate its current system of rule. Yet history sometimes allows for unpredictable and seemingly unrealistic things to happen, such as Gorbachev's foreign-policy breakthrough, which helped the Soviet Union's liberalization. Theoretically, a new foreign-policy pattern that could be reflected in a real, not imitation, partnership between the United States and Russia might facilitate a new round of democratization in Russia. This could be successful not only should Russia suddenly gets its own de Gaulle or Churchill in the Kremlin as well as a change of mood toward democratization within the political class, but also if the United States makes Russia's integration into the West its mission. Today the suggestion sounds too idealistic, but the future may offer new chances to make it possible.

It would be naïve to hope that, should Russia restructure itself on a democratic basis, relations between Russia and the United States would be perfect and the tensions between their interests much less destructive if shorn of Russia's normative hostility. One can anticipate that U.S. hegemony will continue to be a key irritant, even for a democratic Russia, simply because of its history, tradition, and mentality. There are grounds for optimism as well. First, the Russian elite, despite its anti-American feelings, tries to be integrated into the West on the corporate and personal level; second, there are no deep roots of anti-Americanism within the Russian population; third, the United States and Russia will definitely be allies in the event of geopolitical and civilizational conflicts; fourth, American and Russian societies have so far been the only societies with messianic aspirations ready to pursue goals that are not directly linked to their pragmatic economic interests. This fact can make them future partners in pursuing a global agenda.

For now, the suspicion the elites of both countries feel toward each other inevitably affects the attitudes of the wider public. In 2006, 43 to 47 percent of Russians had positive feelings toward the United States, whereas in the 1990s that figure reached 68 percent. An analogous trend is seen in the United States. In 1997, 20 percent more Americans viewed Russia more positively than negatively, while in 2006 the proportion was 53 percent favorable and 40 percent unfavorable. Happily, the cooling of relations between "official" Moscow and Washington has not led to a marked rise in hostility between individual Russians and Americans. On the whole, Americans continue to have a benign attitude toward Russia, with 71 percent of those surveyed hoping that Russia will become a democracy in ten years' time. Russians have a more favorable perception of the United States than many Europeans do. In 2006, 43 percent of Russians were positively inclined toward the United States, as against 39 percent of the French, 37 percent of Germans, and 23 percent of Spaniards. There is, however, an indisputable trend for the perception of the United States among the Russian public to worsen. In early 2007, the number of Russians favoring closer ties with the United States was 13 percent, against 31 percent who favored closer ties with countries that oppose American influence. In spring 2007, during the escalation of anti-American propaganda, 43 percent of the Russian respondents believed that the United States constituted a threat to other countries because of its longing for economic domination. Thirty-three percent blamed it for its attempt to "spread American-style democracy."[12] The anti-American propaganda gushing from Russian television sets continues to have an effect.

One can only hope that the common sense of ordinary people will not allow relations to deteriorate to the point of a real freeze. We need to recognize, however, that a new cycle of mutual suspicion is inevitable as long as the two countries have different outlooks and base their lives on different principles.

Chapter 22

UNSTABLE STABILITY, OR
ON SHOOTING YOURSELF
IN THE FOOT

The world has given up discussing Russia's reforms and is now more interested in how stable Russia is and whether it is going to let off fireworks while the rest of the world tries to get on with its business. There are no visible signs to suggest that the system that Russian presidents Boris Yeltsin and Vladimir Putin have set up will be undermined in the near future. On the contrary, all the evidence suggests that society is stable and under control. Let us not forget, however, that this is Russia, a country that constantly surprises observers with sudden U-turns. What seems solid today may turn into tectonic lava tomorrow, threatening to submerge not only Russia but to spill out beyond its borders.

Let us enumerate the factors that ensure order in Russia. The price of oil is crucial to Russian stability. Oil revenues flow into the Stabilization Fund, which is the regime's safety net. If there is social tension, the authorities can dip into this pocket and calm things down by handing out money to the malcontents. Economic revival continues, which keeps the part of society with consumer appetites happy. People have not yet fully recovered from their weariness after the upheaval of the Yeltsin era, and its memory is one of the crucial factors of stability in post-Yeltsin Russia; even when dissatisfied, people have no burning desire to take to the streets and demand policy changes. They are disillusioned with the opposition, both of the left and the right. They are in no hurry to support it and are content to wait for new faces to appear. Remnants of the old opposition from the Yeltsin times have lost their combativeness but continue to occupy niches of protest, merely hindering the appearance of a more dynamic and, for the Kremlin, a more dangerous opposition. The Kremlin is also adept at stealing the opposition's more appealing slogans. It has succeeded in bringing on board celebrities capable of influencing public opinion, and these are now working for the Kremlin, hoping for various favors in return. The directors of major theaters are hoping for new theater buildings; the directors of leading hospitals are hoping for new equipment; performers hope to perform at top venues; politicians want money and the Kremlin's support for their election campaigns and a promise that they will be reelected; political advisers hope for permanent employment at high salaries. In short, the political and intellectual classes have signed on.

Particularly noteworthy is the loss of the intelligentsia's old spirit of dissent. Present-day society lacks that ferment of dissatisfaction that the intelligentsia and dissidents provided in Soviet times. The regime is in fact not too repressive (yet!), allowing those in opposition to survive, if only after driving them into a ghetto and restricting their access to the public. The oppositionists socialize with one another through clubs, the coteries of the few remaining small opposition parties, and finally on the Internet. That there are such safety valves creates the impression of some level of freedom. The Kremlin and its spin doctors are to be congratulated on the ingenious way they have clogged the political arena with clones formed and financed by the Kremlin: parties, mushrooming youth movements, a public chamber, and a state council. These fronts create the illusion that there is an active political life and reduce opportunities for the emergence of vibrant social and political movements.

The Kremlin is constantly ready to react to shifts in the public mood. If the populace is upset by the regime's social welfare policies, the Kremlin initiates "national projects" to improve social welfare. If people are tired of corruption, the Kremlin reacts instantly by arresting a dozen corrupt officials, many of whom are subsequently quietly released. When people are irritated by the privileges granted to the authorities and bureaucratic apparatus, the latter quickly decide to remove the flashing lights from their cars that give them priority in traffic. This tactic of reacting rapidly to discontent works. The regime, of course, is also reaping the benefit of a reaction that always appears after revolutionary upheavals: the period of stabilization as the population gradually recovers from the agitation of a period of radical change.

Of course, for slumbering Russia, the institution of leadership is immensely important. When everything is vague and fragile, when there is no sense of progress, and when faith in the future has evaporated, society sees its salvation in its leader. People see the corruption of the regime but place the leader above officialdom, exempt him from criticism, and, even though they are aware of the extent of his culpability, have no desire to part with their remaining illusions about the only political institution with power resources—the presidency. Russia's attitude to Vladimir Putin is, however, gradually beginning to change. If initially he was supported because people hoped he would revive Russia, he is now a president of hopelessness, supported because the populace can see no alternative.

It is amazing just how self-contradictory the attitudes of post-Soviet citizens can sometimes be. In early 2007, 32 percent said they were satisfied with the country's progress, while 65 percent of respondents said they were dissatisfied. Only 12 percent believed the economic situation in the country would get better, and 14 percent thought it would get worse. Sixty-nine percent expected no change for the better. Only 25 percent of those surveyed believed the government could improve the situation, and 16 percent had no faith that the government would do anything. Despite this, an overwhelming majority of people, 77 percent of those surveyed, approved of the president's actions (against 22 percent who did not), even though they knew very well that his is the only real authority in the country and it is the president who controls the government they view as pathetic.[1] Russians continue to see the president as being above politics, his regime, and his system, and they seek in this way to retain at least some belief in order, since rejecting a leader in a country that has no other institutions threatens chaos.

People in Russia no longer take any interest in politics because they do not see how it can help them to improve their lives. A gap has opened up between people's personal interests and the tools of politics. Only 26 to 34 percent of Russians under age forty follow political events; among those aged fifty years and above, the number rises to 46 percent. This is the departing generation, knocked out of action by the failed revolution of the 1990s. The political apathy of Russians surprises observers who, when they compare Russia and China, conclude that the Chinese are far more acutely aware of injustice and more actively express their dissatisfaction with the authorities (to judge from the 87,000 protest demonstrations and strikes in China in 2005).[2] Among Russians, only 3 percent of those surveyed in 2006 said they would take to the streets to protest against actions by the authorities. The majority prefer to express their discontent by whining, as they did under the Soviet regime. Local protests, which are a constant feature in Russia, attract no mass support or even sympathy from the rest of society. It really appears that the bulk of the population, following all the accumulated stress and endless misfortune they have experienced, have given up looking for a way out, lost the will to fight back, and have resigned themselves to their misfortunes.

This appearance of apathy and indifference may, however, be deceptive. Slowly but surely systemic factors are emerging that will gradually undermine this docility. There are three such long-term factors, engendered not by adventitious circumstances but by the way society is organized. The first is the fundamentally illogical nature of democratically legitimized authoritarianism. The regime's determination to retain power obliges it to fix election results, which weakens legitimacy, and a regime that has lost legitimacy can be repudiated at any moment. The second factor is the regime's determination to maintain the status quo while simultaneously redistributing resources. This pits one elite group against another and destabilizes the political situation. The third factor is the inevitable appearance of discontent when power is excessively centralized. If popular discontent cannot be expressed in parliament and the mass media, it will sooner or later spill out into the streets. In addition to these systemic factors, others can appear: conflicts between the centralization of power and the greater independence the regions need for their survival; between the regime's attempts to manage business and the needs of the market; and between state expansion and its attempts to control society and the population's aspirations to run its own affairs.

Russia is truly providing ever more evidence for the view that a system constructed on the principle of "transmission belts" of power—top-down governance—can work only if a flawless mechanism of subordination is in place. The latter is maintained primarily through fear, secondly through violence, and thirdly through a mobilizing ideology, which in the case of Russia used to be communism. If any one of these modules is missing, the pyramid of power starts to be shaky. What do we have in Russia? The security ministries are corrupt and cannot protect the authorities effectively. In some factions of the population the old fear of authority is embedded in the population's genes. It has been reawakened, forcing people to return to the Soviet type of passivity and of paying lip service to official policy. In other segments of the urban population, especially among the younger generation, fear of the Kremlin evaporated during Yeltsin's time. These people can hardly be consolidated on the basis of a mobilizing ideology. Moreover, in a centralized system, the breakdown of any one of its branches causes the breakdown of the entire system since all its elements exist in a pyramid of subordination. The lack of independent institutions to resolve conflicts between interest groups means that the conflicts destabilize the system from within. When conflict is hidden, the political process becomes more unpredictable, and a centralized system is impotent in the face of unpredictability.

The population is also being freed from direct dependence on the state. Forty-five percent of Russians say they are already independent of the state. A considerable portion of these people withdraw into private life. Quite often they are dissatisfied with the way the authorities operate but do not protest because they are able to survive without them. Russia's status quo is built on the reciprocity principle: the authorities allow society to choose its own way of survival on condition that it will not meddle in politics, and it anticipates that the people will tolerate the authorities' means of survival. However, the moment the regime impinges on the interests of the people, they will seek to unite and may challenge the Kremlin. In Russia, groups of malcontents have begun to organize spontaneously, such as motorists, investors cheated of their money, mothers of soldiers, and environmentalists. This is civil society in the making, with millions already drawn into it. It is soon going to create problems for a state that does not recognize the rule of law and continues to harass people. There is also the fact that all of Russia's political institutions are dependent on the president's approval rating, a fall in which would jeopardize the entire system.

We should not overlook *the law of unintended consequences*. On more than one occasion, the regime has produced effects quite the opposite of what it expected. The attempted monetarization of welfare benefits in kind in 2004, intended to reduce the state's spending on social welfare, came to an abrupt end when the authorities took fright at widespread popular protest and threw millions of extra dollars into pacifying it. The Kremlin's meddling in the 2004 Ukrainian presidential election in support of a pro-Russian Viktor Yanukovich eventually benefited the pro-Western Viktor Yushchenko. The 2005 gas conflict with Kiev was intended to strengthen Gazprom's position as a supplier of hydrocarbons but only obliged Europe to look elsewhere for its energy supplies. The Kremlin's astonishing capacity for shooting itself in the foot is evident in the regime's determination to shield Iran from sanctions, which leaves it pandering to extremist regimes near Russia's borders. There is no guarantee that the law of unintended consequences will not apply again when the Kremlin, attempting to consolidate its position, finally saws away the bough on which it is sitting.

A measure of the regime's anxiety about the possible reactions of a society that it understands less and less is the extent to which the ruling team is preoccupied with mimicry, creating pro-Kremlin parties, docile movements, and associations that will either divert public activism into a safe channel or at least disorient the population. Rebellious youths have only to start setting up their own movement along the lines of the protest movements in Ukraine and Serbia when another movement of the same name (set up by the Kremlin) springs up instantly and takes to the streets. The resulting confusion makes it more difficult to organize real protests.

Confirmation of the authorities' fears and anxieties is also to be seen in its attempts to remove even the remotest chance of an initiative unsanctioned by the Kremlin during the election campaign. Accordingly, throughout 2005 and 2006, the Duma, at the behest of the Kremlin, was frantically passing amendments to electoral legislation to ensure that the "party of power"—as the pro-Kremlin's party of the moment, United Russia, is dubbed—was victorious. The Kremlin either bans all forms of protest or intimidates protesters while simultaneously seeking to discredit them in the eyes of the public. Protest actions by the now-banned National Bolshevik Party, brutally suppressed by the authorities in 2005–2006, were the first sign that a possible era of street protests is to be expected in Russia, where opportunities for the legal expression of dissatisfaction are denied. Yet the suppression of extremist protest did not help. Soon, new protest formats emerged, among them the most hated in the Kremlin: the Other Russia opposition movement formed in

2006 by former prime minister Mikhail Kasianov, former world chess champion Garry Kasparov, the leader of the National Bolsheviks, and writer Eduard Limonov, known for his radical views.[3] The first attempt of the Other Russia to organize a dissenters' march through the streets of Moscow took place in December 2006 under banners demanding the defense of freedom. The authorities banned the march, although they had previously allowed demonstrations by the communists and the nationalists. The Other Russia was given permission to gather only in the square. Two thousand people calling on the regime to observe the constitution were surrounded by eight thousand militiamen, soldiers, and riot police with dogs and the latest technology for dispersing demonstrations. Overhead, militia helicopters circled, and the movement's supporters were arrested on all manner of pretexts even before they reached the square.

The opposition, however, did not get scared and took to the streets regularly. The dissenters' marches in March–April 2007 in St. Petersburg, Moscow, and Nizhni Novgorod ended with ugly scenes of dissenters being roughed up, people's skulls being broken, and harassment and beating of the press. The authorities prepared thoroughly for an "intimidation operation," summoning reinforcements of riot police from all over Russia, hoping that provincial security forces would not be soft on the protesters. The world was shocked by the brutality of the law-enforcement organs. Even the press representative of the presidential administration had to admit that the reaction of the law-enforcement agencies to the dissenters' marches "was exaggerated." Some observers thought that the authorities were driven by fear and behaved foolishly, damaging their own reputation. The motivations behind their intimidation tactic, however, are likely more complicated. There was no reason to suppose that at this time the Kremlin feared losing power, having as it did such an amazing presidential approval rating. Several thousand protesters in the streets (even with five thousand protesters in St. Petersburg) hardly presented an immediate threat to the government. Nevertheless, it was the growing insecurity of the Kremlin clans, unsure of their future and with a continuing paranoia because of the example of the 2004 Ukrainian "Orange Revolution," that prompted them to use preemptive measures to frighten potential dissidents and the opposition. They wanted to make it clear that they were ready to use force without hesitation to nip protests in the bud. Harassing dissenters also sent a message from Kremlin hardliners, not only to a potential opposition, but also to competing clans within the Kremlin. The message boiled down to the following: "Don't get in our way!" In this manner, the Kremlin brought an end to the Gorbachev and Yeltsin epochs of tolerance for political struggle.

The authorities do not conceal their suspicion that the dissent is the result of foreign meddling, that the Other Russia movement and its members are Western stooges, and that all the dissenters' marches have been part of a covert operation to destabilize Russian society. It is difficult to tell whether Putin and his team really believe this or whether they need to invent a pretext to move to a harsher regime. Finally, there is widespread speculation that the use of violence on the streets of major Russian cities has one further and possibly primary explanation, an attempt by hard-liners to ruin Putin's reputation, especially in the West, and to force him to stay. We can only speculate as to how grounded these suspicions are. "The Kremlin now has its external and internal enemies," wrote the Russian daily *Novaya gazeta*. "It is armed and ready for the upcoming elections, or to revise the constitution."[4]

The dissenter marches in the spring of 2007 and the state's brutality against street protesters might become the watershed that ends a period of soft authoritarianism and opens a new period, one that could mean sliding toward harsher authoritarian rule. If this were true, to what extent is Putin personally responsible for that slide? It is hard to believe that the decision to crack down on the Other Russia movement and the street protests could have been taken without his knowledge, which leads to the conclusion that the president may have been the one to cross the line first. If the crackdown happened without his knowledge, then it means that he has begun to lose influence, a conclusion that is less plausible. Perhaps the president has behaved in his usual way: informed about a problem, he mused, letting his subordinates guess what it was that he really wanted. One tough decision that he acquiesced to silently meant the beginning of a tough policy, with all levels in the chain of command trying to be "more catholic than the pope." This is typical of Russian government's top-down decision making. One word from Putin: "Stop!" is enough to stop the harassment of the Russian opposition. In May 2007 the president remained silent, and his silence gave the state carte blanche to clean house. It had to, simply because in the view of Kremlin strategists any tolerance of the opposition will bring more people to the streets next time, which may turn Moscow into Kiev and Red Square into Maidan Square. This would mean the end of the Russian system, which can function only by keeping the lid on the kettle. Sooner or later, however, this kettle will blow up.

Independent Russian observers (and there are still quite a few of them) writing on Internet sites predict that the actions of the authorities sooner or later will provoke the young to take to the streets. They will do this to demonstrate their disagreement with the Kremlin's desire to keep them under control, herding them into government-sponsored organizations. Russian journalist Andrei Kolesnikov wrote, "There are signs that the mood of dissent is starting to spread in society and increasing numbers of young people are beginning to sympathize with the protest rallies simply because they do not want to allow the authorities to impinge on their rights to have their own views."[5] The All-Russia public opinion research center has registered that in 2007 more than one quarter of the population has been willing to take part in rallies and demonstrations (in 2006, 17 percent were prepared to do so). According to the Levada Center, the protest constituency in Russia in 2007 amounted to 20 percent of the population. An editorial in the pro-Kremlin journal *Expert* expressed real concern: "Million of protesters in London against Blair's Iraq policy would not bring [the] British state to collapse, but an opposition rally of 100,000 in Russia could abolish the system."[6]

The more busily the Kremlin's spin doctors try to mold a domesticated "civil society," shutting off every escape valve for protest, the more likely it becomes that a section of real society will decide to move outside the tightly controlled political arena. A structured opposition integrated into the system is a precondition for a stable state and society. Forcing the opposition out of politics is always damaging to the system. No less than 61 percent of Russians want a genuine opposition, only 25 percent disagreeing. Some 47 percent do not believe they have such an opposition, as against 30 percent who do.[7] The Russian people are waiting for effective opponents of the regime to appear, and demand always stimulates supply.

New techniques of organizing street protest will undoubtedly be seen, paralleling what has occurred in a great variety of countries from Serbia to China. Protest can suddenly flare up, organized, for example, through text messaging. Internet communication is a tried-and-tested means of bringing protesters out into the streets, as witnessed in Ukraine and Belarus. To call a meeting of several thousand people who do not know one another, you do not need political parties, access to television, or a leader. You need only to put out an appeal on the Internet that strikes a chord with your audience, and you will have a flash mob event. How will the Kremlin's cumbersome machinery for preventing organized protest cope with such an elusive, spontaneous element that can spring up at any time anywhere? The authorities would have to shut down the Internet, which is hardly possible. If they tried to do that, the Kremlin would soon learn the elementary truth that the strength of public protest is directly proportional to the extent to which a society is hermetically sealed. The collapse of the Soviet Union showed how closed systems come to an end. Has this lesson been lost on the post-Soviet Russian authorities?

Chapter 23

WHAT MIGHT DETONATE
AN EXPLOSION?

An alarming element in present-day Russia is the development in the North Caucasus of clannish regimes of a totalitarian nature supported by federal bayonets and subsidies. Moscow has become hostage to peripheral dictators like Ramzan Kadyrov in Chechnya and to other sultanistic regimes it created in an attempt to stabilize the situation in the region. Now those dictators and their clans are blackmailing the Kremlin, demanding ever more money and power. In the process, they are passing all responsibility for the situation in their republics on to Moscow. North Caucasian sultanism strengthens anti-Russian and Islamic sentiment in the region and creates a basis for terrorism, not only in Chechnya but also in other North Caucasus republics. In 2005 an attempt at armed revolt with Islamic slogans took place in Nalchik, the capital of the Kabardino–Balkarian Republic. The revolt was directed against law-enforcement agencies guilty of atrocities and was crushed with exceptional brutality. This uprising was a warning that the population, and primarily young people, might take up arms against corrupt local regimes or, indeed, against Moscow, which supports corrupted local authorities. A chain reaction of protest could easily explode throughout the region.

The Kremlin finds itself facing a deadlock in the North Caucasus. The attempt to impose presidential rule from Moscow is likely to provoke a new Caucasian war in which both the local elites and those who oppose them—who until now have been tearing at each other's throats—will unite against Russia. To leave things as they are is tantamount to turning the region into a zone that is bristling with weapons, parasitic on Russia, heading in the direction of Islamic fundamentalism, and increasingly threatens the stability and integrity of Russia itself. Already, detachments of paramilitaries from the North Caucasus are extending their activities outside their own republics. Units from the Chechen security forces, which comprise mainly ex-rebel fighters, are turning up fully armed in the central regions of Russia and are helping to resolve business disputes. The soldiers of the Chechen Vostok Battalion, headed by clan leader Sulim Yamadaev, intervened in St. Petersburg. He had been hired by one of the competing sides in a commercial conflict. Kadyrov paramilitaries, led by his security ministers, went to Moscow and murdered his opponent in a busy Moscow street while Russian law-enforcement agencies turned a blind eye. Who is to say that one of the contending factions within the Kremlin will not hire the Chechen units to decide the power struggle in Moscow? Armed to the teeth, turbulent, and increasingly fundamentalist, and counting among their populations a growing number of uneducated and unemployed young people, the North Caucasus could destabilize the whole of Russia. This is a real concern of the Russian population: 44 percent of Russians do not believe the war in Chechnya is over; about 65 percent think that the situation in the whole North Caucasus is unstable; 10 percent think it is explosive; and only 16 percent believe that it is calm. This is the legacy that Yeltsin and Putin have left the next Russian president.[1]

There is a danger also from situational factors that today work in favor of stability but tomorrow may have the opposite effect. The Russian authorities have virtually no contingency plans for the possibility of a fall in the price of oil, smugly assuming that the energy appetites of China and India, together with the war in Iraq, will keep it at a high level. Other tools of the regime for ensuring stability are the popular movements created by the Kremlin. Who is to say that such youth movements as *Nashi* (Ours), *Mestnye* (Locals), and the *Molodaya Gvardiya* (Young Guard) will not go the same way as the nationalistic *Rodina* (Motherland) Party? After being likewise set up by the Kremlin, *Rodina* became a loose cannon because of the ambitions of its nationalistic leader, Dmitri Rogozin. The Kremlin had to remove the Motherland Party from the Moscow elections and expel some of its overly ambitious politicians.

It might be more difficult to keep even the pro-Kremlin youth movements on a leash. The gangs of young Putin supporters created by the Kremlin in the wake of the Ukrainian Orange Revolution started by harassing opposition politicians Garry Kasparov and Mikhail Kasianov and then went after foreign diplomats, attacking the British and Estonian ambassadors. The young are playing the game with evident enthusiasm, becoming more aggressive each time. They have already understood their strength and are eager to do "big projects." The moment may come when the young wolves will feel they are being manipulated and will want to become an independent force. And someone might emerge who will lead this destructive blind force that can be turned into a dangerous political weapon. The Russian authorities may never have read the story of Frankenstein and seem unaware of how experiments creating monsters may end.

Finally, let us consider the paradoxes of the president's approval rating, which for now is working in favor of stability. In 2006, of the 76 percent of the population who said they supported President Putin, only 17 percent considered him a successful leader. The rest believed he was unable to cope with the tasks he should be dealing with, with the exception of foreign policy. The paradox of support for a leader who is considered unsuccessful only serves to confirm the hopelessness that is rife in Russia: the people support a leader whose possibilities and potential they consider limited because there is no one else. Yet

Vladimir Putin has to leave the political scene and his approval rating cannot be transferred to his successor. This fact might have a serious destabilizing effect.

The growth of nationalistic sentiment and xenophobia in Russia is even more alarming. Xenophobia has always been endemic in Russia, but it was never allowed public expression. It hid behind imperial ideology. Now ethnic nationalism is often fanned by factions within the ruling elite. In its search for external or internal enemies, the elite focuses on immigrants, the West, liberals, or those of the newly independent states who do not want to come under Russia's wing. When the representatives of the establishment talk about banning particular ethnic groups from certain professions and introducing quotas for immigration, it further incites the xenophobes. The anti-Georgian campaign unleashed by the regime during one of its periodic confrontations with Tbilisi in the fall of 2006 shows that ethnicity can become a driver of both Russian foreign and domestic policy.

The forces of law and order do not react to increasingly frequent racially motivated assaults on Tadjiks, Chechens, Armenians, and others of non-Slavic origin by skinheads. The lack of reaction shows that the authorities do not know what to do about the ethnic aggression that is spreading through the land. Its underlying causes continue to accumulate. The general atmosphere of the fight against terrorism provokes suspicion of non-Russians. The growing corruption and arbitrariness of the government authorities engender a sense of powerlessness. Social and regional stratification arouses envy among the dispossessed, of the better-off strata of the population or of national groups, which stick out among the majority Slavic faces. A desire to find an object for retaliation is the result. Nationalism and xenophobia are the simplest and most primitive defense reactions of people when survival is difficult. Channeling aggression toward "aliens" (immigrants, non-Slavs) is advantageous to the regime and the bureaucracy. Today some 56 percent of Russians support the slogan "Russia for the

Russians." Polls demonstrate that the size of the nationalist vote in Russia has grown over the past ten years from 25 to 40 percent. In 2007, 30 percent of Russians were conscious of interethnic tension, while 64 percent did not feel it, and 6 percent were "don't knows." In Moscow, however, the number of those conscious of it is much higher (58 percent) versus 40 percent who are not aware of it, and 2 percent who "don't know."[2]

Regular pogroms and racist killings in several Russian cities (St. Petersburg, Voronezh, and Moscow) began in 2003. Since 2005 they have occurred almost monthly. According to data from independent centers, 450 people were attacked and injured in racist attacks in 2005, and 500 in 2006. The rising wave of racism is disturbing. Even the Kremlin is beginning to worry and is easing off, moderating the dose of its nationalistic messages. If, however, some Kremlin factions begin to assert that their "Russian project" "does not mean victimizing other nationalities," others continue to call for the defense of the rights of the "indigenous population" and stir up hatred for "aliens." A public that is fearful and unsure of its future becomes susceptible to simplistic ideas, of which "Russia for the Russians" is the most readily understood. In the process, the struggle against fascism and extremism has been devalued by the regime itself, since it continually applies these epithets to the opposition. The upshot is that Russia is approaching a transfer of power in an atmosphere in which the ruling group has unleashed national–populist moods, trying to maintain an archaic mentality and suspicion of the outside world, which, for some social groups, might be far more attractive than communist, social-democratic, or liberal alternatives.

In this context certain developments may be important. The growth of Russian nationalism may undermine imperialist moods that have lingered in the popular consciousness. The evolution of some Russian politicians who had previously proclaimed imperial slogans (Vladimir Zhirinovsky and Dmitri Rogozin, for instance) and who have now exchanged their expansionist rhetoric for isolationism should be confirmation enough of this evolution. Russian analyst Emil Pain, however, alerts us to a new phenomenon, which he defines as a "revival of the imperial syndrome." This syndrome means imperial sentiments blended with nationalism. This explosive mix may become a key obstacle to the democratization and modernization of Russia.[3]

In the fall of 2006, a succession of assassinations took place in Moscow at a level that shows that Russia is still far from achieving anything resembling normality. They were the murders of the first deputy chair of the Central Bank, Andrei Kozlov, who was well known as a consistent champion of an ethical financial system, and of one of the most outstanding journalists of the opposition and a champion of human rights, Anna Politkovskaya. As if a signal had been given that it was once again all right to murder competitors and opponents, one killing followed another—of bankers, people in business, top officials, and mayoral candidates. Russians returned to the 1990s, when contract killings were the most effective way of resolving problems. Unexpectedly, society discovered that the assassins had never gone away. They are again in demand. Under Yeltsin, yearly 19 people were killed for every 100,000 of the population, while under Putin the figure is now 22. In the United States, 5 people for every 100,000 are killed, while in Europe there are 1 or 2 murders for every 100,000. Russia has the third highest rate in the world for the murder of journalists, after Iraq and Algeria. During Putin's presidency 13 contract-style killings of journalists have occurred, and this despite the fact that Russia boasts no fewer than 550 law enforcement officers for every 100,000 of the population, as against 300 in Europe.

Russia's relapse into resolving problems with small arms tells us some unwelcome truths about Putin's legacy. The president has not fulfilled the task he set himself upon assuming office—to restore order and ensure the personal safety of the population. That the state is not based on the rule of law has resulted in a society that lives according to the law of the jungle. The rise to power of members of the security ministries and their lack of accountability at least partially explains why violence has become a political tool. It is less important whether the president himself initiated this change or whether it is the fault of his entourage or the logic of the neo-patrimonial regime. What really matters is that a shift has occurred in Russia toward more violence and the use of brutal force in political and everyday life.

It is an unrewarding task to speculate about how stable a closed social system can be that works in its own interests. Let us imagine an unexpected combination of untoward events: the radical reform of the outdated and still subsidized housing, an increase in fuel bills, transport snarl-ups in major cities, a rise in the rate of inflation, unrest among students who are to be drafted into the army, a technical failure like the 2005 power shortages in Moscow; a series of ethnic riots; and terrorist acts and the usual inability of law-enforcement organs to effectively respond to them. These events might well stir up the most stoical and inert of societies. But in Russia, any surfacing of discontent is cause for concern, not only for the regime but also for civil society. Social tension in the absence of powerful liberal democratic forces, in a country where liberal democracy itself is automatically associated with a worsening of living conditions and where there is a lack of a consolidated group of pragmatists who understand the need to reform Russia, will play into the hands of populist nationalism. If a lurch to the right were to happen, we would have to agree with those occupants of the Kremlin who mutter darkly that today's regime is the acme of civilization compared with what might replace it. The whole problem, of course, is that today's authorities have provided the basis for a populist national tide, and the longer the present system continues, the stronger that tide may become.

Increasingly, there are signs that the ruling elite, outwardly so confident, has been less and less certain of its future. "We are downright scared," one of the stars in the Kremlin firmament admitted. This is only too evident from the furious setting up of tame organizations, the support for servile politicians, the exclusion from public view of independent individuals, the petty-minded control of elections, and the isolation of society from Western influence. An indication of the ruling class's anxiety about its future in Russia is the extraordinary burgeoning of the Russian population of London and other Western capitals, the continuing draining from Russia of billions of dollars' worth of what is now known as "capital export," and the reluctance of Russian business to invest in Russia. The same mood of uncertainty manifests itself among ordinary people as consumer frenzy. People are not saving. They are spending today because they have no faith in tomorrow.

Society, noting the agitation of a regime that tries simultaneously to intimidate it and to be liked by it, sees that the authorities lack self-confidence. It also sees that this lack in itself can invite tests of its durability. Thus, one has to be prepared for any unexpected turn of events in Russia, not least something the regime may itself instigate as it tries to forestall adverse circumstances.

Chapter 24

RUSSIA: GOING NOWHERE FAST

A fter the fall of communism, Russia faced a challenge that no state in the world had faced before. Not only did it have to give up its global mission to be the pole of an alternative civilization, spheres of influence, and its territorially integrated (contiguous) empire, it also had to radically alter the principles on which the state and society were organized. Russia had to renounce a project it had been attempting to implement for centuries, one it seemed at times to be doing entirely successfully. That these challenges had to be faced simultaneously and that they were interrelated, contradictory, and multidimensional, made it exceptionally difficult to respond to them. Russia nevertheless seems to have rejected the instruments of mass repression, territorial expansionism, the regulatory role of the bureaucracy, and the sanctity of personalized power. It has tried to adopt the fundamental values of the West: the rule of law, the primacy of the rights and freedoms of the individual vis-à-vis the state, and the right to private property. These values were set down in a constitution that, for the first time in Russian history, acknowledged and declared: "The basic rights and freedoms of the individual are inalienable and belong to each person from birth." Previously, rights and freedoms in Russia were something that only the higher authorities could bestow.

The Russian political class, however, proved incapable of introducing Western values in practice. The Russian elite, taken unawares by the collapse of the USSR, never considered leaving the Soviet period behind completely and creating a law-governed state. It limited itself to devising new ways of realizing its group interests. It can no longer be doubted that, at the present stage of Russia's historical development, liberal democracy has suffered a defeat.

The hybrid produced through the efforts of presidents Boris Nikolayevich and Vladimir Vladimirovich tells us that Russia has failed to take on board liberal principles and Westernize, but neither does it want to return to the classic Russian system (even if it did, perhaps it is too late because the clock has been broken beyond repair). Power in Russia remains personalized, but it is no longer rooted in the public mind as something inevitable and God given. In effect, the Soviet model of the bureaucratic state has been revived, only now without the communist ideology and its former repressive mechanisms. Society has emerged from a patriarchal culture but has not yet fully evolved into a new culture, and random fragments of the old and new cultures coexist in its consciousness. In trying to imitate the rule of law, pluralism, and freedom while hanging on to top-down governance, Russia is immobile and now finds itself either becalmed or marooned, in the doldrums of history, unable to move forward or backward, stuck between civilizations and historical epochs. Its future direction is unclear. At home, there is a desire to disguise the emphasis on authoritarianism as democracy. Abroad, Russia lays claim to a partnership with the West and membership of Western organizations, all the while openly opposing it. On the one hand, Russia regards itself as part of Europe and European culture, which it really is. On the other hand, Russia's politics and the organization of its power and society remain alien to Europe and the West generally. The attempt to combine incompatible elements is masked by exercises in mimicry that are presented as pragmatism. In reality, they point to the inability of both the ruling class and Russian society to leave the past behind (or a lack of energy for this), although they also have no wish to remain in the past indefinitely.

Russia is made up of contradictions, and the disparity between appearance and reality in the country is likely to confound observers who prefer precise calculations. It may sound absurd to many Russians at least, but it might well be more difficult for Russia to transform itself according to the norms of European civilization than it would, for instance, for China and some Southeast Asian countries. Deliberating on the liberal–democratic transformation of Southeast Asia, Francis Fukuyama wrote that "traditional political Confucianism ... could be jettisoned relatively easily and replaced with a variety of political-institutional forms without causing the society to lose its essential coherence." In his view, Asian democracy could be built "not around individual rights, but around [a] deeply engrained moral code that is the basis for strong social structures and community life."[1] In contemporary Russia because of the lack of a "deeply engrained moral code" and other mechanisms that could guarantee social coherence, the task of building a new political system might prove to be a harder and less predictable exercise. The Russian state and society are still organized around principles that are not compatible with liberal democracy.

Here I have in mind not only the primacy of the state. After all, all societies were built on this principle, some of them only recently, at the end of the twentieth century. They managed not just to abandon this principle, but also to find ways to combine the legacies of their historical, cultural, and religious traditions with the liberal-democratic rules of self-organization. In the Russian case, the primacy of the state has always been linked, not just to its superpower status, but also to the existence of real or imagined threats, both internal and external, which in turn required the militarization of people's everyday lives and the subjugation of the very foundations of society to militarist goals. In short, Russia developed a unique model for the survival and reproduction of power in a state of permanent war. This situation was maintained even in peacetime, which was always a temporary state in a Russia that was constantly either preparing for war against an external enemy or pursuing enemies at home. As Russian political scientist Igor Klyamkin explained, "Russia has always developed by annihilating the boundary between war and peace, and its system simply could not and still cannot exist in a peaceful environment."[2] The militarist model has been intended to legitimize the supercentralized state in the eyes of the people. In its militarization and its view of the world around it as hostile, Russia differs from other countries that have consolidated on the basis of the primacy of the state before transforming themselves and placing the interests of society and the individual above those of the state.

Putin's presidency has demonstrated, perhaps unwittingly, both the possibilities and the limits of using elements of militarist thinking to preserve the traditional state. On Putin's watch the Kremlin has returned to the tactic of seeking out "enemies" in both Russia and abroad in order to justify the centralization of power. Among the enemies "appointed" by the Kremlin, we find Belarus, Georgia, Ukraine, the West, nongovernmental organizations, liberals, and oligarchs. To date this tactic has worked well, but it has its limits. At some point the witch hunt could lead to a battle between clans within the elite, as happened under Stalin. Such a battle would begin to undermine the stability of the state and the security of the elite. This model also hampers the dialogue between the Russian elite and the West as well as the elite's ability to use the West to ensure its own survival. The Kremlin evidently recognizes the limits of the militarist paradigm. It is trying not to cross the line beyond which Russia would remove itself from the community of developed nations, marginalizing itself, something the political class tries to escape. This fact proves how far Russia has extricated itself from the past, even in trying to perpetuate some of it.

Vladimir Putin has been exceptionally lucky in his leadership. The sky-high price of oil and surging world demand for hydrocarbons have allowed the president to conduct a new experiment using the traditional Russian paradigm. He has tried to remove militarization as the foundation of the Russian state, leaving only some of its fragments and stereotypes, and to replace it with the energy superpower model. The elite views energy resources as a key instrument of both "hard" and "soft" power as well as a guarantee of Russia's global status and the centralized state. The substitution of energy for militarism has been successful, but because of the nature of energy resources and Russia's increasing integration in global economic interdependencies, this new means for preserving the primacy of the state has a limited potential. As Russia's energy resources approach exhaustion, continued reliance on them could ultimately undermine the old Russian system, generating rot and degradation. It remains unclear how and when this might occur, whether it would eventually bring down the centralized state, and what would replace it.

Westernization and democratization of Russia may lead to the very result nationalists and anti-Westernizers have predicted: not just the undermining of the old state, but its evolution toward a looser federation or confederation, or even the fragmentation of Russia. Yet the attempt to prop up an archaic state by using such artificial political prostheses as energy resources and hunting for "enemies" will make the final act even more dramatic. It remains to be seen when the elite will recognize that in its current form Russian civilization has spent itself and how this elite might try to reform Russia before it becomes impossible to preserve it within its current borders and in its current form.

Meanwhile, it seems that Russia is still firmly held in the embrace of its political tradition. Does this mean it will forever be the hostage of its history, geography, culture, and form of governance, imposed on Muscovy centuries ago by the Golden Horde of the Mongols? Is there no suggestion from history that the Russian nation might be capable of adopting freedom? Even Richard Pipes, who usually inclines toward pessimism where

Russia is concerned, acknowledges that there have been exceptions to Russia's totalitarian tendencies in its history. He sees the
Novgorod Republic as such an exception, which during its rise
in the fourteenth and fifteenth centuries "encompassed most
of Northern Russia, granted its citizens rights which equaled
and in some respects even surpassed those enjoyed by contemporary Western Europeans."[3] There were other times of progress
when Russia began to introduce civil rights and freedoms.
Among these were the Assemblies of the Land of the sixteenth
and seventeenth centuries; the reign of Peter the Third with his
edict guaranteeing the freedoms of the gentry and the demilita-
rization of the state; the decrees of Catherine the Great, who
borrowed ideas from the European Enlightenment and tried to
adapt them to Russia; Alexander II's local government, legal and
military reforms, and his manifesto on the emancipation of the
serfs; the October Manifesto of 1905; the convening of a State
Duma; and the reforms of Piotr Stolypin. Russia's history has
not been an unmitigated tale of autocracy. Russia constantly
borrowed Western principles of governance and adapted them
to its needs. However, these reforms did not weaken autocracy
but gave it a new lease on life.

The failure of the liberal-democratic project in recent years is
seen as confirmation that Russia is incapable of living in freedom not only by supporters of Russia's great-power status but
also by some Western observers. The failure is grist for the mill
of those who see Russian development in terms of cyclical theory, from liberalization to restoration and back again, or in the
context of continuity theory, as the constant replication of a traditional matrix. Both these theories reflect a fatalistic view of
Russia as doomed to be an autocracy and facing nothing but
ruin if it ceases to be. This narrative might seem to confirm that
conclusion, but matters are much more complicated. Russian
history is neither a mechanical shifting between reform and
counterreform (one step forward, one step back); neither is it
circular, though it often appears to be. In reality, each successive
reform moves Russia a little further forward, driving society

toward greater openness. Successive restorations do not take the country back to its starting point, but leave a little more freedom. The Putin restoration does not take Russia automatically back to the Soviet Union. It is a backsliding that nevertheless leaves society to its own devices. The regime appears to be telling the population, "Do as you please, only do not try to seize power." Leaving society alone, giving it the right to seek its own salvation (but not the right to interfere in politics or claim ultimate control over property) is an advance in terms of social autonomy compared with the communist period, when the regime aimed to keep society entirely straitlaced.

Russia is gradually coming out of its shell, opening up to the world in a way that cannot be restrained for long. Not even Russian traditionalists want to live in a hermetically sealed country like North Korea. After each warming of the climate in Russia there is a reversion to personalized power and state lawlessness, but each time, the regime loses some of its earlier might and is obliged to retrench and limit its power and ambitions, and try to look civilized.

The time is coming when the political regime will no longer be able to function in an authoritarian way. It will be unable to provide what society requires of it: stability and a higher standard of living, not to Soviet but to Western levels. We may find that the current period is the last gasp of an authoritarianism whose return was possible only because of the pain of the Yeltsin reforms, its chaotic way and its failure, and the high price of oil. Together these may have artificially prolonged the life of a system that is already expiring and historically doomed. Thus, Russia passes through its cycles and circles, but each time it does so at a different level and in a new historical context. The attempts to understand Russia's developments by addressing its tradition, mentality, and culture tend to be instructive but insufficient to explain new aspects of Russian life or to provide any real clue as to what its next stage may be.

If liberal trends were cut short in the early twentieth century because society was not yet ready for freedom, the defeat of

Russia's liberal project in the early twenty-first century is more explicable in terms of the Russian elite's not being ready for freedom or political competition. We should not overstate the maturity of ordinary Russians or their ability to follow the rule of law; they are still politically inactive and seem incapable of coming together to force the regime to take their interests into account. The Russian public has no experience of civil associations, no experience of life in a country where the powers of the state are separated between the executive, legislature, and judiciary. The people of Russia are, however, increasingly ready to move toward European standards and norms. They already feel themselves to be Europeans. They increasingly long to be rid of a corrupt state that burdens them and to enjoy the personal well-being that people in the West enjoy. Because development has become globalized, and because Russia is now a reasonably economically developed country with a population reasonably educated and informed about the rest of the world, there is no call for it to repeat all those stages that Great Britain passed through on the path to liberal democracy since the era of Magna Carta. The further problem remains, however, of how to enable the people to recognize the link between their economic aspirations and freedom, between security, stability, and reform.

The Russian elite is trying desperately to keep society in a state of drowsy oblivion, both by playing on its subconscious, reactivating old myths, and by not allowing the demons of the past to die. It is the Russian elite that is incapable of performing in a context of political pluralism, which is the principal force keeping Russia in its current deadlock. The Russian ruling class can, indeed, be called elite only in a purely conventional sense. It is a mishmash of sundry groups (like Putin's St. Petersburg brigade) raised to the highest positions in the land through the workings of mere chance. Most of them lack more than managerial talent. They also lack (and this is more serious) the ability or desire to take into account the national interest. The main aims of the ruling class propelled into power as a result of the collapse of the USSR are not difficult to guess: they aim to line their pockets, to control whatever property they have managed to get their hands on, to prevent the emergence of new faces inside their ranks (that is, people who might redistribute their property or undermine their positions), and to keep the public ignorant of where their real interests lie.

Unlike the Soviet elite, the new Russian political class has emergency landing sites in the West to which it can parachute with its families at the drop of a hat. The comprador elite cleverly disguises its commercial mediation in the sell-off of Russian resources using nationalist rhetoric. Having this Western escape hatch has two consequences: it may prevent the ruling class from attempting to cling to power by violent means, and it also bolsters its cynicism, general lack of commitment, and inability to understand and promote the national interests of the country.

The elite imposes its will on society not by force, as it used to, but by imitating, and thereby discrediting, freedom. "You live in a democratic state," the elite informs the public. "You have courts, a parliament, a multiparty system. What else do you want?" When, however, Russia's citizens see that all the institutions of the state are corrupt and that democracy appears to mean that the bureaucracy can do whatever it pleases, they are likely to question the need for democracy. When, under the guise of liberalism, technocrats who lack any sensitivity to social costs impose deregulatory decisions on them, the people wonder what the use of liberalism is and why they need it. To this day, the Yeltsin period, which the population remembers as a time of a widening gap between rich and poor and a dramatic fall in the general standard of living while the democratic band played on, evokes revulsion on the part of the public against democratic values. Those traditionally called liberals in the government caused anger and disgust by their ostentation and blatant disregard of the predicament of ordinary people, and this now automatically spills over to a rejection of those who still attempt to raise the banner of liberalism. Mikhail Khodor-

kovsky, while in jail with time to think over Russian developments, has rightly observed that the defeat of liberalism
occurred also because people "could not stand the sight of liberals in thousand-dollar jackets" at a time when deprived families had nothing to clothe their children with. Still, not all
liberals of the 1990s understood that truth.

Will not Russia's citizens at some point demand real freedom from their elite in the way the Ukrainians did, whose mentality and culture are close to that of Russians? And why are
Ukrainians more willing to embrace competition in politics and
the rule of law than Russians are? The answer can only be that
the Ukrainian public does not lay claim to great-power status
and that the great majority of Ukrainians are prepared to join
the West, at some cost to their sovereignty. A substantial part of
Russian society would also at some point be willing to jettison
the myth of superpower status in return for prosperity and well-
being. It is just not ready do so for the time being. Russians
continue to follow the elite, and the elite fears that repudiating
great-power status would pull the rug out from under it. The
elite would have to renounce its acts of global derring-do and
create a normal country, although governing a normal country
is something the political class today is clearly incapable of
doing. In a free country, the present elite would certainly be
thrown out. Maintaining a claim to great-power status is still
one of the chief obstacles to Russia's emancipation. The political class continues to foster popular phobias and complexes,
insisting that Russia is fated to glory and a special destiny. It
busily tries to prevent the populace from thinking in less exalted
categories and seeking a decent and dignified life for themselves.

That individuals who think of themselves as liberal democrats choose to be employed by an illiberal regime works to the
advantage of bureaucratic authoritarianism. The failure of the
Yeltsin generation of liberal democrats to form a united opposition to the regime, their ignoring (with the honorable exception of the Yabloko Party) of issues of equality and justice, also
hinders Russia's transformation. In the Baltic states, Moldova,

and Ukraine, moving closer to the West was seen as a reaffirm-
ing of national identity, and the nationalism of these states facilitated an embracing of liberal democracy. In Russia, on the
contrary, nationalism rejects the West and its ideologies. Since
the collapse of the Soviet state in the 1990s, many people,
including quite a few liberals, believe that Russia can survive
only as a centralized state and a superpower. They are convinced
that repudiating these principles will precipitate a new collapse,
but now it will be the collapse of the Russian Federation.
Russia's future trajectory largely depends on whether the liberals and democrats succeed in persuading the people that,
although they oppose personalized power and great-power
ambitions, they have no wish to see Russia implode but are
merely striving to create a law-governed state that would act as
a center of attraction for its neighbors. As long as the liberals
and democrats are considered antinational and antipatriotic,
they have no prospect of becoming the leading force in Russian
politics.

Meanwhile, strengthening authoritarian trends in Russian
political life have put Russian liberals and democrats in a
painful dilemma, one seemingly without a solution: either to
preserve the role of the systemic opposition and take part in
public politics, including elections, or to shift to the role of radical, anti-systemic, and anti-regime opposition, without the
hope of a role in public political life. The role of the systemic
opposition includes the endorsement of the key principles of
the current system, the rejection of any claim to real power, and
a readiness to collaborate with the authorities. Those who
choose the second option will have to face the inevitable threat
of being pushed outside the political arena and of becoming the
object of state harassment. Previous political ambivalence in
Russia that included elements of pluralism and political struggle has gradually been replaced with the state monopoly, which
means submission by all actors to the Kremlin's rules of the
game. All political forces have to make a choice that will affect
their future activity and make them either partners—and

elements of the regime—or opponents, with consequences that are already known.

During the first term of Putin's presidency, opposition to the regime still had, though in a form more limited than before, the opportunity to act within the system, that is, to be present in the parliament and to have some access to the national television channels and media. Now, only a tamed opposition, that is, the forces and political actors who are allowed to disagree with one another over trivia but who do not risk criticizing the regime, are allowed to remain. Ironically, the Communist Party has preserved its oppositional role, which proves that the ruling elite does not find communists to be a threat, and the Kremlin and the communists have found a modus vivendi. The situation with the communists can be defined as an anti-systemic factor working in the interests of the system—not the only paradox in the Russian reality. As in Yeltsin's time, the Kremlin needs the communists in the role of bogeymen, in order to look constructive. Communists are from time to time invited to the national television channels and even have permission to organize their rallies, consolidating the left electorate and preventing it from moving to more radical opposition. Meantime, liberals have been marginalized and are denied avenues of self-expression. The Kremlin's reaction to liberal opposition has been much more severe compared with the Kremlin's attitude to the Communist Party, which demonstrates that liberal democracy is the alternative that seriously worries the Kremlin.

At the end of 2006 and through 2007, fragmentation within the liberal-democratic movement continued without much assistance from the Kremlin. Some liberals and democrats (for instance the leaders of the Republican Party, Vladimir Ryzhkov and Vladimir Lysenko, who were denied registration) supported the Other Russia movement that had become a version, albeit weak, of the People's Front. The "old parties," the Union of Right Forces (SPS) and Yabloko, have decided to follow their own paths. This could have been expected in the case of SPS, which has been moving in the Kremlin orbit. The leader of

Yabloko, Grigory Yavlinsky, has distanced his party from the Other Russia movement in an attempt to preserve the role of a moderate and constructive opposition to the regime. It is a daunting task in a situation where political pluralism has been wiped away. Soon the Other Russia movement began to split, proving how difficult, if not impossible, it is for the opposition to unite when stagnation and passivity prevail in a society apprehensive of new turmoil. Russian democrats continue their effort to challenge the regime and its succession project by preparing to take part in the Duma elections and even presidential elections. By August 2007 Grigory Yavlinsky, Mikhail Kasianov, Viktor Gerashchenko (former head of the Russian Central Bank), and former Soviet dissident Vladimir Bukovsky announced that they would run for the presidency on the opposition platform. So far the opposition has failed to consolidate around one presidential candidate, which makes the whole opposition campaign a futile effort.

The Kremlin's crackdown on political pluralism and its tightening of the screws have narrowed the breathing space of the democrats. Moderates may still find opportunities for legal activity by distancing themselves from the radical opposition, which has been the Kremlin's chief target for harassment. However, moderates' participation in a rubber-stamp legislature cannot change the nature of the regime, and will turn into more decorative ornaments. Down the road, the moderate opposition may find itself without its electorate, which has begun to radicalize. Yabloko members in St. Petersburg already take part in Other Russia rallies—a painful Catch-22 situation for democratic opposition parties of the Yabloko type. To continue the political struggle by legitimate means in a continually shrinking legal space could end with their marginalization or worse: turning into an element of the system they have been fighting against. Adopting a more radical stance would force them to take to the streets, leaving them without the legal means to present their views. The parliamentary elections in December 2007 will demonstrate whether the regime can leave a niche for moderate liberal opposition. This is an experiment that will also show how Russia could be democratized in the future. Will it be done through legal activities of the opposition in public institutions and its participation in elections, or through street protests if the authorities totally eradicate dissent from the political stage? To date, the system has moved in the latter direction, which leaves no scope for an independent moderate opposition.

Chapter 25

CAN THE WEST HELP THE RUSSIAN LIBERAL PROJECT?

What part the West has played or may yet play in the fate of Russia's liberal project is highly contentious. Assessments in both Russia and the West include confidence that the West's role in Russia's development has been overestimated, that it was not significant before and is negligible now. An opposite assessment is that the establishment of the current political regime in Russia would never have been possible without support and legitimization by the West. Ivan Krastev has been pretty tough on the Western impact, saying,

> Managed democracy in Russia was justified as the best way to prevent a communist restoration. For this reason, it appealed not only to some Russian liberals but also to Western governments.... The establishment of managed democracy in Russia would never have been possible without the endorsement of the West.[1]

Within Russia, the criticism of Western democracies and their policies toward Russia is increasing in all political factions, even among liberals. Liberals consider, with frustration, that the Western community has no interest in Russian reforms and suspect the West has struck a deal with the Kremlin in order to pursue its security and energy interests. Representatives of statist, nationalist, and even moderate factions believe the West is constantly meddling, trying to subvert the independence of the Russian state and weaken it, viewing Russia as a potential competitor or enemy. Ultimately, at the beginning of the twenty-first century, different political forces in Russia, from the liberals and Westernizers to the populists and nationalists, have come together in disappointment, criticism, and even condemnation of the West. How much impact does the West really have in Russia, and how important is it to Russia's liberal transformation, if at all?

At the end of Vladimir Putin's presidency, the West has considerably less scope for influencing Russia's development than it had in the 1990s. Now marginal at best, the West needs to appreciate its limitations and be aware that its efforts may be counterproductive should it fail to understand Russian reality, what is possible in Russia today and what is not. There are a number of reasons why the "Western factor" has become less significant in Russia.

In its policy toward Russia, the West has always been torn between its desire for constructive relations with the Kremlin in order to achieve its economic and security goals, which require it to refrain from preaching to the Russian leadership, and attempts to influence Russia's democratic reorientation. To date, it has failed to strike a balance between those two goals, as reflected in the permanent zigzagging of its Russia policy. The problem of energy security obliges consumer countries (meaning primarily Western democracies) to humor to the supplier countries, most of which are far from democratic regimes. The West's desire to keep Russia as one of its dependable and responsible suppliers of hydrocarbons obliges Western governments, especially in Europe, to close their eyes to the "special features" of Russian democracy. Security and energy concerns, as well as fears of Russia's destabilization should it again begin to democratize, constrain Western attempts to defend its values in relations with Russia and to remind the Kremlin of the standards Russia has subscribed to.

The domestic challenges faced by the Western democracies—immigration, problems relating to the coexistence of different cultures, the tension between economic efficiency and social welfare, and the stumbling of the European integration project—force the West to concentrate on its own problems. This focus leaves it less time and energy to assist the transformation of other states. It is particularly difficult to assist in the democratization of hybrid regimes, like Russia's, that have learned to construct façades and desperately resist efforts to influence their development from the outside. Here the West's efforts may even result in supporting hybrid regimes in their mimicry. These regimes have become skilled not only in defending themselves from "foreign interference in internal affairs" but in using the West in the interests of their stability and in their game of pretending and imitating.

In Russia, frightened by the "color revolutions," the authorities are trying by all the means at their disposal to block the Western factor. The Kremlin's propagandists are adept at discrediting the West's intentions toward Russia. Russian politicians, not least among them President Putin, have become highly accomplished at deflecting Western criticism with verbal gymnastics. Whenever Russia is criticized for corruption, lawlessness, the killing of journalists, brutality in Chechnya, or civil rights violations, the politicians find corresponding examples in Western practices, reminding us of the Enron saga, the corruption of Spanish mayors, the harassment of ethnic Russians living in Latvia and Estonia, the misdeeds of American soldiers in Iraq, the Guantánamo base and the Abu Ghraib prison, and failed efforts by the Bush administration to promote democracy in the Middle East. "In any case, *mafia* is not a Russian word," Putin once noted in response to criticism of Russia by the leaders of the European Parliament. The result of anti-Western and anti-American propaganda is that Russians form the impression that the West has no moral ground for telling them how they should behave or how to construct a successful society. The Kremlin has become successful in provoking suspicion toward Western intentions and, sometimes, the behavior of Western politicians helps the Kremlin's efforts. The key Russian politicians reiterate: "The West does not like us. It constantly criticizes us because we are now strong and independent and will not allow it to order us around. We have to be on guard because their advice will return Russia back to a Yeltsin-type chaos." These arguments strike a chord with the Russian population.

The elite does its best, not without success, to inculcate the idea that Western assistance in building democracy and the work of Western nongovernmental organizations (NGOs) within Russia is aimed at subverting the state. The impression is that the Kremlin insiders sincerely believe this. The United States is the recipient of most of the accusations, and President Putin himself here takes the lead in blasting America. One may conclude that the Russian political regime has found fairly effective ways of deterring Western influence by first using imitation techniques and anti-Western propaganda. Next, it finds Western weaknesses and points to double standards in Western behavior, which often leaves the West at a loss as to how to respond. Third, it harasses Russian nongovernmental organizations and movements that receive Western assistance and pursue a liberal agenda. (In today's Russia, discrediting liberal democracy means discrediting the West, and vice versa.)

Now that the Kremlin has successfully nullified political pluralism and the opposition, its major priority is the insulation of its citizenry from Western influence. Russian and foreign NGOs have become the inevitable victims of the new campaign. In January 2006 President Putin signed a bill into law imposing tough control on local and foreign NGOs functioning in the country. Major efforts are directed against Western organizations and those Russian NGOs that accept foreign funds. The ruling class tries to close off Russian society not only from the promotion of Western democracy but also from any Western assistance.

In the 1990s Russia was eager to learn the principles of democracy and readily embraced various forms of Western assistance in solving its social, educational, environmental, and health care problems. Today, even Russian liberals feel uncomfortable about Western influence and the concept of "democracy promotion." One has to admit that the inept way it has been implemented, primarily by its key architect, the United States, has helped the Russian authorities build their anti-Western and anti-American campaign. Thomas Carothers comments in this regard, "Democracy promotion has come to be seen as a code word for 'regime change.'" Carothers is also right in saying that "the damage that the Bush administration has done to the global image of the United States as "a symbol of democracy and human rights by repeatedly violating the rule of law at home and abroad has weakened the legitimacy of the democracy-promotion cause."[2] Anyway, Western activity will be counterproductive if it is rhetorical, self-serving, and hypocritical. In Russia's case, the authorities have succeeded in making independent civil and political forces, and in particular the recipients of Western assistance, Western stooges in the eyes of the population.

A simplistic understanding of democracy assistance, its clumsy promotion by Western donors, and the Kremlin's suspicion that this assistance is a disguise for other purposes results not only in the ineffectiveness of the effort itself, it also endangers the liberal community targeted by this assistance. A recent example is the State Department's report "Supporting Human Rights and Democracy: The U.S. Record 2006," which includes a long list of U.S. government activity in funding NGOs, promoting the rule of law, advocacy training for prosecutors and defense lawyers, and (among other things) promoting "free and fair elections." The United States "continued to provide programming and technical support to Russian watchdog organizations [and] nonpartisan training for political parties," says the report.[3] While the Russian regime is engaged in a search for the enemy, this statement is the kiss of death for NGOs and liberal parties since any such assistance puts its recipients in a vulnerable position. Moreover, any foreign assistance to political parties is forbidden by a new Russian electoral law.

Recent developments in Russia and the nature of its relations with the West have demonstrated that the previous model for the Western–Russian partnership, based on the premise of Russia's transformation and integration into the West, has proved to be premature. A new formula is needed for the relationship that would include a more subtle Western approach to Russian transformation. Building this new formula forces both sides to deliberate on some crucial questions. Does the West still want Russia to be part of its civilization? Does Russia want to pursue that goal? Or are both sides moving toward an entirely different model of the relationship, one that will exclude Western influence on Russia's development and in which the West will agree to be excluded?

The search for a new balance of values and interests in the relations between Russia and the West continues. The new leaders coming to power in Russia, major European countries, and the United States will have to deal with the new Russian challenge. The leaders that presided over the period of the Soviet Union's collapse, including Mikhail Gorbachev, Helmut Kohl, François Mitterrand, Ronald Reagan, George H. W. Bush, and Margaret Thatcher, and the next political generation that came to the fore when Russia and the new states were dealing with the painful issues of their state building (I have in mind Boris Yeltsin and Bill Clinton) succeeded in coping with the security agenda. They also left hope for Russia's integration into the Western world. The generation of leaders that is leaving today, or has recently left the political scene—Tony Blair, George W. Bush, Jacques Chirac, Vladimir Putin, and Gerhard Schröder— have undermined the hope that Russia will be brought into the Western orbit. There have been serious objective reasons for their failure to integrate Russia into the West, having to do first of all with the complexities of Russia's transformation. Yet those leaders all bear a share of responsibility for Russia's and the West's moving apart.

Is the West ready for a new project of engaging Russia, this time more cautiously and with advance planning? The debate in the West between the two schools of thought, realist and idealist, on whether to help Russia with its transformation or pursue instead only geopolitical interests in the relationship, has intensified. Western realists have persuasive motives for withdrawing their active support for Russia's transformation. Indeed, the political climate in Russia constrains Western efforts to influence Russian reforms and disallows ambitious assistance to foster democracy. Why try to help if Russia has decided to follow its own "special path"? Why try to preach democracy to a society that gives its authoritarian leader massive support? Besides, any hint of promoting democracy might hamper the realization of Western strategic interests with Russia. Let the Russians sort out their problems before the West begins a new attempt to support their reforms, realists say. In a discussion on Russia, organized by *American Interest*, Hugh Ragsdale and Paul Stepan argued,

> What are the U.S. interests in Russia? They are simple and unmistakable and two in particular are critical: cooperation on nuclear proliferation and the monitoring and suppression of terrorism.... When the U.S. government is not attacking Russian political practice, it is eagerly soliciting its assistance in issues beyond the easy reach of U.S. strength.... Russians are going to do government [in] their own way. It is beyond America's capacity to do much about it, except to poison their regard for the U.S. and its interests in the attempt.[3]

Russian pragmatists among analysts and politicians frustrated with the chill in relations are trying to find ways to reengage Russia and the West, unequivocally supporting the approach of "no more democracy preaching" and a shift to an interest-based policy.

The problem is that to date the realism that dominated the policies of key Western powers toward Russia did not help the West and Russia to realize mutually acceptable common interests and did not prevent their relationship from deteriorating. The proponents of the new version of realism fail to notice the causality between, on the one hand, the way Russia is organized and, on the other, the way it reacts to the West. The divergences between Russia and the West would not vanish if the West were to stop expressing concerns over Russia's normative trajectory. They may become even more pronounced. Recent experience has proved that the dichotomy between standards and interests is artificial since interests in the end are rooted in values. That is why there is no guarantee that the Kremlin would be ready to be a predictable partner of the West and even cooperate with the West when it views the West as an alien civilization built on different standards. All this means is that the West must take a keener interest in Russia's transformation, not for philanthropic reasons but for the sake of its strategic interests and its own well-being. Russian pragmatists who preach a need to return to realpolitik and advise the West to accept Russia as it is in fact not only reject Russia's liberal trajectory, but by doing so, they undermine any chance of building a solid basis for the relationship. Moreover, sooner or later they will be forced to become engaged in anti-Western rhetoric simply because one cannot be friendly with the West while supporting "Russia as it is."

I support Joseph S. Nye, who argues:

> If the West were to turn its back on Russia, isolation would reinforce the xenophobic and statist tendencies present in Russian political culture and make the liberal course more difficult. A better approach would be to look to the long run, use the soft power of attraction, expand exchanges and contacts with Russia's new generation, support its participation in the WTO and other market institutions, and address deficiencies with specific criticism rather than general harangues or isolation.[4]

The realists, however, are right to express their concerns as to what should be the new engagement formula and how to implement it. The devil is always in the details.

Indeed, the West continues to influence Russia by its very existence. Russia formulates its own policies by reacting to the West, arguing with it, and rejecting or copying it. To a considerable extent it is thanks to the influence of the West (primarily Europe) that Russia has numerous nongovernmental organizations; an ombudsman for human rights; trial by jury; and community service as an alternative to army service. Russians appeal to the European Court of Human Rights in Strasbourg when they cannot obtain justice in Russia. In 2005, Russians lodged a record 8,500 complaints against the Russian state, or 20.8 percent of all the complaints filed.

The question is, should the West quietly wait for Russia to be ready for its new democratic revolution? Such tactics would mean preserving the status quo, as some Western politicians and pundits exasperated with revisionist Russia would suggest. Or should it be an active strategy that will look ahead with the goal of integrating Russia in the future through a gradual transformation, which could be more protracted than many of us believed in the 1990s? The West at the moment has no answer to these questions. Meantime, the recent emergence of a resurgent and angry Russia is a warning for the West that an unreformed Russia cannot be friendly toward the West.

Western leaders and proponents of a wait-and-see tactic for Russia have to understand that the lack of a common Western strategy for Russia and support of the status quo in Russia will inevitably end with Russia becoming more alienated from the Euro-Atlantic community. Given all the constraints, the West can create an environment conducive to Russian reforms. Three imperatives, it seems, are crucial here: *understanding, strategy,* and *engagement.* Russians interested in moving toward the West expect it to understand the contradictory nature of Russia's evolution, as well as its obstacles and potential. Without understanding of Russian dilemmas and choices, the West will continue to be wrongfooted by this restive country, something that has happened more than once in the past decade. Moreover, the West will continue to be stunned by Russian developments. As George Soros has candidly admitted, "Russia seems to be emerging as a new kind of player on the international scene.... Although I follow developments in Russia fairly closely, I have been taken unawares. In this respect I am no different from the rest of the world."[5]

Russians hoping for Russia's transformation would expect the West to furnish a coherent and subtle strategy for dealing with the Kremlin leadership, the political class, and society. How the concept of reengaging with Russia, with the goal of its future integration, is defined—as selective engagement, pragmatic engagement, cooperation, or dialogue—does not matter. More important is that it should assure the Russian population, now disenchanted with the West, that the West has high stakes in and a serious commitment to its relations with Russia. In addition, the West should assure Russians that it is interested in Russia's successful reforms and its joining the Western community. Engagement with Russia should include cooperation with it in those areas where their interests overlap: in counterproliferation, combating international terrorism, energy security, and climate change. Further, true engagement presupposes that the two sides will learn to avoid the zero-sum game that allows the Russian elite to feel confident, and the Western establishment (or some circles) to see this zero-sum game as an adequate response to Russia's newly acquired cockiness.

The West has tools for influencing Russian perceptions and attitudes that it is not using, or using rarely or badly. Russia is a member of such Western clubs as NATO, the G8, the Council of Europe, and the Parliamentary Assembly. Russian leaders—Gorbachev, Yeltsin, and Putin—have signed a series of documents committing Russia to strengthening the rule of law, civil society, respect for human rights, freedom-of-the-press guarantees, and the independence of the judiciary. Today the West has the opportunity to remind Moscow about the obligations it undertook when joining those clubs and signing those documents. On those occasions when Western leaders have had to remind the Kremlin of its obligations, their insistence has yielded results. Under pressure from its G8 partners (primarily the United States), Russian authorities jettisoned a harsher version of the law on nongovernmental organizations.

Only too frequently, however, Western leaders try not to upset the Kremlin by raising contentious matters in private talks with Russian leaders. There has hardly been any attempt by Western leaders to make furtherance of the economic interests of the Russian elite in the West conditional on a commitment by the Kremlin to follow the Universal Declaration of Human Rights, the Helsinki Final Act, or the principles of the Council of Europe. The West often takes the easiest black-and-white approach, either trying to put pressure on the Kremlin or becoming excessively amiable toward it (with the second approach predominating). Both approaches indirectly contribute to strengthening Russian authoritarianism, which has learned to exploit the West and its actions in the interests of self-preservation.

If the Western community wishes to show greater initiative in encouraging Russia's liberal project, it will have to rethink one or two customary approaches to promoting democracy. One would be an attempt to assist in the formation of independent institutions (parties, trade unions, and a parliament), the organization of elections, or the formation of youth movements like those that were prime movers in the revolutions in Georgia, Serbia, and Ukraine. The Moscow establishment has succeeded in erecting insurmountable barriers to such Western activity in Russia, which is regarded as interference in its internal affairs, while the acceptance of such aid by Russians is regarded as anti-state activity. For the same reason, Western observers will find it far more difficult, if not impossible, to monitor Russian elections effectively in the future. In terms of "bridge building," the West's first priority today should be to prevent Russian society from being cut off from the outside world and to counter any further growth of anti-Westernism.

Several key tools in this context may be useful: *openness, information, support of NGOs, business, social projects,* and *success stories.* In terms of openness, the West needs to move beyond a state-to-state dialogue that both Russian and Western elites pursue, often without much profit. Instead it needs to facilitate contacts between Russian society and Western society. Thus far, the Western leaders (apparently tired of the Russian puzzle) have lost interest in bringing together stakeholders in both Russia and the West interested in cultivating the relationship. Particularly important are student and professional exchanges and the easing of the visa regime between Russia and Western countries. Undoubtedly, the opposite is currently happening. Western broadcasting in Russia needs to be expanded; instead, it has been reduced. Efforts to assist Russian civil society need to continue but new forms of this assistance should be discussed that will not make NGOs aliens in Russian society. Allowing Russian business to enter Western markets, and minimizing the barriers to those Russian exports that are competitive in the global market, would be an important instrument of engagement and keeping Russia more open.

Social projects in Russia that would help to improve the West's image in the eyes of the Russian population might be an effective way of implementing a new engagement policy (I have in mind assistance in fighting lethal diseases, solving ecological problems, and cooperation in educational projects). It is also important to help create an example of successful transformation that would help Russians to discard their belief that they are genuinely unsuited to democracy and convince Russian society that it can be reformed (just as Poland's transformation and integration into Europe has persuaded Ukrainians that they can follow suit). The success stories of Ukraine and Belarus, two nations culturally and historically close to Russia, could provide a high-profile argument in favor of freedom and democracy for ordinary Russians.

Finally, the West should at all costs avoid isolating Russia, even if Moscow does everything it can to marginalize itself. It is a test for the Western community to provide engagement with Russian society without support of its bureaucratic–authoritarian regime.

Admittedly, we have to recognize that the logic of the Russian system may bring an increasing closing off of society from the outside world, which will reduce all opportunities for outside influence. Even so, the West may still be able to aid the Russian liberal project indirectly by practicing what it preaches. If the West renounces its dual standards, observes its own ideals, provides for the welfare of the Western community, and demonstrates to Russian society a genuine interest in its successful revival, it will enhance the attractiveness of the liberal alternative for Russia.

Chapter 26

HOW TO STOP
SUICIDAL STATECRAFT

The world's need for energy supplies, the force of inertia, the efforts of the Russian elite to discredit democracy, the passivity of society, and the lack of a strong liberal opposition—all serve to prolong Russia's drifting in the doldrums of history. Sooner or later, however, it will be impossible for Russia to ignore the question of how long it can continue to exist simultaneously in the past and the future, to move backward and forward at the same time, imitating development and reforms while trying to preserve the status quo. An important factor continues to make it especially difficult to escape from this impasse. That factor is war and its repercussions. I will return to the war in Chechnya: Yeltsin's war accelerated the demise of Russia's reforms. Putin's war in Chechnya not only squeezed him into the presidency but also continues to legitimize his personalized power. Moreover, this was a new kind of war—against the internal and external enemy—which has implications for Russia's development that at the moment are difficult to grasp. In the wake of the 2004 tragedy in Beslan, Putin defined the situation with a single word: "war." He thereby provided himself with the justification for further moves to centralize power. Officially, the war in Chechnya was declared over. Yet it remains unclear whether it has really ended, or whether it might restart, this time in other Northern Caucasus republics, or what its consequences will be for Russia, its understanding of its mission, its nature, and its territorial integrity. In any case, the war's impact on Russian domestic politics may facilitate the establishment of a new authoritarian regime after Putin is gone.

Two Chechen wars resulted in the degeneration of the troops who have fought in Chechnya, a consolidation of corruption of authorities and institutions involved in the North Caucasus, an outburst of Russian nationalism and Islamic radicalism; and, finally, they have become one of the reasons behind the failure of Russian reforms. Not a single state has ever succeeded in pursuing reforms while fighting a civil war. That is what the two Chechen wars have brought Russia—simultaneously facilitating the centralization of power and conjuring up conflicts the regime cannot resolve. For Russia to emerge from the past, a line needs to be drawn through its militaristic paradigm of development and attempts to use war for the regime's purposes. This will also require a reevaluation of the wars Yeltsin and Putin waged in the North Caucasus and a search for a way to overcome their effects on the minds of Russians.

The war in Vietnam had a tremendous impact on an entire generation of Americans, who eventually coped with the trauma by reflecting it in art. Francis Ford Coppola's *Apocalypse Now* was one of the means by which America found closure. In Russia the war in Chechnya continues to influence domestic developments and the mentality of the Russian people. Society tries not to think about it, represses it, tries to forget it, and deludes itself that the problem of Chechnya does not affect it and never affected it. The country refuses to face up to the surreptitious and destructive influence those two wars continually have on the way people feel, think, and behave, not only in the Northern Caucasus or neighboring Russian regions, but in the whole of Russia. Until society is prepared to reassess the war in the Caucasus, the war cannot end, either in people's minds or in reality. Meanwhile, hundreds of thousands of people— soldiers and civilians— have been subjected to the savagery of two Chechen campaigns that became civil wars, coloring life in Russia with their tragedy. The ongoing Chechen syndrome is reflected in the fact that the public cannot decide whether Russian servicemen should be put on trial for murdering Chechen civilians. Time and time again, the Russian courts acquit war criminals whom society sees as heroes, further consolidating the cult of lawlessness and brutality in the country. Putting off the need to find closure for the wars in Chechnya by rethinking their consequences and solving the problems of the Northern Caucasus leaves Russia unable to put an end to its militaristic paradigm, to recognize the value of human life, or to face its responsibility for the tragedies suffered by other peoples because of the actions of the Russian state. Without this, it will be impossible for Russia to move forward to *a post-post-Soviet future.*

The future of the present Russian experiment of adapting democratic means to suit the needs of authoritarianism is obvious—it has none. Describing policy during the presidency of George W. Bush, Zbigniew Brzezinski uses the expression "suicidal statecraft," coined by Arnold Toynbee to define the process whereby a state following a militarist course undermines itself:[1] "For America, suicidal statecraft will end with a change of leadership and a change of policy. In the case of Russia, suicidal statecraft and its repudiation will be an unpredictable process that may convulse not only Russia, but the post-Soviet territories."

Does this mean that Russia, stuck at a fork in the road, will be unable to emerge from its stagnation of many long years, or that it is doomed to some catastrophic scenario? Current trends give no grounds for optimism. The ruling class and Russian society itself are drifting downstream with no thought of where the drift will take them. Mutually incompatible trends within the system and society itself, combined with a historical weariness after failed revolutions and numerous weaknesses disguised by demonstrations of strength (which are often imitations of strength or strength that soon turns into a weakness), make it difficult to generate the energy needed to change things. The elite has not forgotten the Gorbachev period, which it sees as proof that if you weaken control over society, events will spiral out of control and it may have to face the collapse of the Russian Federation. One can hardly expect a liberal-democratic upsurge in the context of stagnation and mass disenchantment with reforms. Such an upsurge can only be triggered by a crisis or by the imminent threat of one. Sometimes, looking at the state of the country, it seems that a crisis would be preferable to hopeless, terminal decay. There is no guarantee, however, that a crisis in Russia will usher in a golden age of freedom. The elite may deal with a crisis by merely changing rhetoric, policies, or personalities in the Kremlin, while the old system continues unchanged, as happened in 1991, 1993, 1998, and 2000. It may be that before Russia has another opportunity to turn to liberal democracy, it will have to free itself not only of illusions about the beneficence of mild authoritarianism but also from the temptation to try to resolve its problems with a nationalistic, totalitarian regime. Russian nationalists dreaming about a real "iron hand" have good reason to support Putin's regime today. They hope it will facilitate their coming to power. Totalitarianism in Russia cannot be sustained in the long term first of all because the elite is afraid to use repression on a mass scale. But it may attempt to turn to totalitarian mechanisms to defend its position in a moment of crisis. Everything depends on when the next crisis, which will demonstrate the unviability of the system, occurs, what sort of condition Russia is in at the time, and the state of mind of its political class and its society.

It remains unclear what effect the remaining elements of Russia's hybrid nature will have on its future development. The democratization of similar regimes in Mexico, Serbia, and Ukraine has shown that hybrids, because they afford some level of freedom, can raise the population's aspirations for a real democracy. So far, however, Russia has been out of luck; its underdeveloped democratic institutions have produced disaffection and only encouraged the population to seek to survive under the strong, personalized regime.

Even with these anxieties, complexes, and constraints, the desire to see Russia reborn as a liberal state is still alive. A significant section of the population recognizes that there is an impasse and ponders what needs to be done to move forward along liberal lines. In Russia there are far more people who want to live in freedom than one might suppose. It is true that when Russians are asked about their priorities, they reply that the most important ones are security, stability, and their standard of living. In 2006 75 percent regarded these as most important, while only 13 percent mentioned democracy. However, only 12 percent of these respondents agreed that the interests of the state are more important than those of the individual. Fifteen percent considered that the rights of individuals can be sacrificed to those of the state; 44 percent believed that people should fight for their rights; and 21 percent said that the interests of the individual are more important than those of the state. This was a breakthrough in the thinking of a people who for centuries have been brought up to revere the state and their leader.

Yet, we have to acknowledge a growing split in people's thinking in recent years. People support the idea of a "special path" for Russia while wanting to see it move closer to the West. They dislike the state but also want it to help them; they demand the expulsion from Russia of its "non-native" population but want other states to become part of Russia. They want order and freedom, and democracy and strong leadership, but cannot find a proper balance. Politics and its major elements and tools (such as political parties, parliament, the judiciary, the media, and opposition) have been intentionally and completely discredited. In the eyes of the population, this leaves the presidency as the only viable political institution. Putin and Putin's epoch have returned Russia to the key elements of the old matrix, and his successor will have to deal with that legacy.

In spring 2007, 64 percent of Russian respondents said that they trusted the president; 42 percent trusted the church; 31, the army; 27, the media; 24, the security services; 19, the government, 17, the judiciary, 16, prosecutors, 13, parliament, and 7, political parties. This is a devastating verdict of society on current Russian politics and a reflection of its deep dissatisfaction with existing political institutions. This does not mean that the same people do not want these institutions to be active and effective—after the brutal dispersal of the dissenters' marches, around 60 percent of respondents said that they believe that the opposition has the right to express its views. Thus, at the end of Putin's political cycle, we note increased social disenchantment with politics, fear of change, and a longing for the status quo and stability. At the same time, in the bleak picture the polls paint of the popular mood, one can see glimmers of hope. Amid a statist and nationalist outburst, according to the pro-Kremlin VTsIOM survey center, 47 percent of respondents said that Russia should not fight for superpower status (34 percent said it should). Asked what will guarantee the well-being of Russia, only 29 percent mentioned presidential "verticality," that is, top-down governance; 43 percent chose the "strengthening of civil rights" (12 percent chose neither, and 18 percent held no view).[2] According to another poll done by the Levada Center, in July 2007 85 percent of respondents approved of Vladimir Putin's performance as president (14 percent disapproved). At the same time, 41 percent were satisfied with the situation and 56 percent of respondents were dissatisfied.[3] That means that those who approve of the activity of personalized power disapprove of the reality this power has created.

The regime is deliberately trying to keep the minds of the public in a schizophrenic state, obstructing the formation of a civil culture and legal mentality. If the demand for a "special path" and an "iron hand" strengthens in Russia, it will not be because of the inability of Russians to live in a democratic and free society, but because they have been deliberately disoriented and trapped by fears, phobias, and insecurity intentionally provoked by the ruling elite. They have blindly followed a corrupt and immoral Russian political establishment that has offered them a false semblance of a solution.

For now, however, Russia's main problem is that the potential instigators of a new democratization are divided. What needs to happen for them to gain sufficient strength to come together to oppose the existing rot? A grassroots protest? Economic collapse? A technological disaster? Given that the forces of liberal democracy are weak, a great deal depends on how the pragmatists within the ruling elite behave, whether they recognize that retaining a lawless state is not only ruinous for the country but also provides them with no safeguards for their own future. Who specifically are likely to be the prime movers of a new transformation: representatives of business, the pragmatists within the federal authorities, a new generation of liberals, regional elites, the media community, or the younger generation of educated people? This remains unclear. It seems likely that a spearhead battalion will be formed from members of all these groups, and so far there is no way to predict who exactly will become its driving force.

There are signs that a new environment is gradually forming within Russian society and that conditions are ripening for a renewed impulse toward systemic change. The simple fact that society has become urbanized has forced a break with archaic political stereotypes. Business has succeeded in surviving and creating fairly efficient conditions for production. Its dynamism has come up against the constraints of a corrupted state not subject to the rule of law. The population would like to live the way Europeans do.

Finally, the younger generation is able to escape from the pressures of the state into its own world of Internet associations and is developing its own subculture. Millions of young people participate in blog sites and post their diaries on the Internet. In 2006, 1.2 million Russians subscribed to *LiveJournal*, created by Brad Fitzpatrick, and Soup, a Russian Internet company, is expected to have 4.1 million Russian subscribers by 2008. This phenomenon is growing exponentially and is producing a social group that the regime cannot control. These young people are not interested in democracy today, but they may start taking an interest if their personal freedoms are threatened. They may then demand freedom for society in general. For the potential initiators of a social breakthrough to make their appearance, to become aware of the need to organize, and to see that what is needed is not merely a change of political personalities but a reform of the regime, Russia needs a radical change in public opinion. There has to be a recognition that society's problems can be addressed only by adopting new standards. This is how the Ukrainians in 2004 came to fundamentally reform their government. As events there showed, that is when people begin to adapt and get used to new values and principles, a process that may provoke disappointments. But those already are a different type of disappointment.

Chapter 27

PARADOXES AND HOPES

Russia's evolution since 1991 has sometimes seemed chaotic and devoid of logic, but there are patterns, often paradoxical, where positive developments have occurred as a consequence of negative developments, and vice versa, when one barrier has been successfully eliminated and simultaneously another one has been strengthened or produced. The results of actions often can be contrary to those intended. Complexity, ambiguity and the contradictory nature of the Russian landscape result not only from the *multidimensionality* of its transformational process, which is historically unprecedented, but also from the fact that Russia is stuck, pretending and believing that it is moving. This creates appearances that are deceptive, reality that is confusing, and tensions that cannot be resolved without producing another set of tensions. Let us add to that personal factors—arrogance, incompetence, ignorance, the self-aggrandizing habits and vested interests of the ruling elite, coupled with passivity and apathy of a people totally worn out by the 1990s, dreaming of an unchangeable status quo and afraid of more turmoil.

I will single out several "transition traps," but the list of multiple barriers—structural and situational—Russia has encountered on the path to democracy and civil society, and of ironic twists of history and reality that produced unexpected outcomes, could be extended.

- *Success Can Be Detrimental.* The stalling of democratic reforms is, to some extent, a result of the economic success and mild authoritarianism of the regime. This makes part of society believe it can be moderately prosperous and successful without liberal democracy.

- *The Uncertainty of Certainty.* The Russian political elite has cracked down on political pluralism and competition in its search for certainty. The result is that the certainties are now less fixed. Neither Putin nor Russia can know what will happen after 2008. And Putin's successor will hardly know how to deal with Putin's legacy, which is a more important unknown than the name of the successor.

- *The Instability of Stability.* The more the elite strengthens stability by using an obsolete model of the overcentralized state, the more it undermines it. Removing opportunities for expressing criticism within the framework of official institutions forces the opposition into the streets, turning criticism into destructive protest and rendering stability brittle.

- *The Impotence of Omnipotence.* This paradox, formulated by Guillermo O'Donnell in reference to Latin American countries, operates in Russia too. The concentration of all the powers of the state in a single pair of hands inevitably weakens the leader and makes him a hostage of his entourage, even if he succeeds in creating the impression of a strongman.

- *Digging One's Own Grave.* By eliminating competition and political pluralism, and by preventing discussion of systemic alternatives, the ruling class creates a situation where positive change will be needed to forcefully remove the current ruling elite from power.

- *The Dilemma of the Captive Mind.* This dilemma was formulated by Polish sociologist Piotr Sztompka and deals with the specific personality syndrome of "homo sovieticus." The components of this syndrome include: passivity, avoidance of responsibility, conformism and opportunism, helplessness, "parasitic innovativeness," primitive egalitarianism, and passionless envy. Meanwhile, the market and democracy require the opposite: activity and innovation, responsibility, etc. The Russian system perpetuates the "homo sovieticus" syndrome.

This is not an exhaustive list, and new Catch-22s are constantly arising. Perhaps the greatest challenge for transforming Russia will be the need for its leadership to start the new reforms, of which the most radical will be dividing state power among independent institutions. Will a new leader be prepared to embark on political self-castration and hand over some of his powers to other institutions? This is Russia's metaproblem for which no solution was found under Yeltsin and Putin.

A number of laws govern the Russian postcommunist system. The most fundamental is the *law of failure.* When a liberal opposition is not ready to take power, society may have to pursue a false avenue before recognizing that it leads to a dead end. Only after hitting a wall does it start looking for another way out of its predicament. A leader has to fail spectacularly to demonstrate that the trajectory taken was wrong. Gorbachev's failure to reform the USSR showed that it could not be reformed. Yeltsin's attempt to create a functioning capitalism with the aid of technocrats and oligarchs demonstrated the limits of that form of capitalism. Putin's destiny may be to confirm that Russia cannot be modernized from above, in which case his success as an authoritarian modernizer will only delay Russia's finding the road to genuine democracy and an effective market economy. So if by his own limited lights Putin succeeds, he fails; and if he fails, he succeeds. One could expect that Putin's failure to pursue modernization should demonstrate to Russia that successful czarism is a twenty-first century oxymoron and should bring the liberal transformation of Russia forward. So far there are no signs that it is going to happen. At the moment, in the people's eyes and in the eyes of the West, Vladimir Putin is not a failure. He has succeeded in skillfully replacing the modernization agenda with a search for stability. The price of oil has helped him to do the trick. Yet, the future will inevitably help to clarify matters and we will see the difference between failure and success.

I have already mentioned the *law of unintended consequences* and how it works in Russia. In the case of succession, this law means that the regime, trying to ensure self-perpetuation, creates a situation where the successor has to consolidate his power by repudiating his predecessor and his legacy.

Russia has to conceptualize the problems that arise as it climbs out of the past and embarks on its journey toward the kind of open society Karl Popper wrote about. The Russian public has yet to decide how much freedom and pluralism it is ready for, as nationalistic complexes remain inflamed and populist moods are on the rise. How can a lawless state be restructured without plunging Russia back into chaos? This dilemma reflects the eternal quandary of Russian reformers, which has often caused them to stop halfway or to turn back.

In the future, there would seem to be *three* ways for Russia to go: the present stagnation may continue; there may be a systemic crisis; or there may be a breakthrough to liberal democracy. For now, Russia continues to stagnate. Some optimists believe this scenario will push Russia toward liberal reforms. Stagnation, however, cannot lead to reform, it never did. It is more likely that it will end either in a crisis and an attempt to resolve it through repressive authoritarianism, or it will end with decay without a chance for Russia to get on its feet. Several years ago I thought that an avalanche-like collapse, unexpected ruin, disintegration—all these frightening and theatrical options are not for Russia. Today I am more pessimistic, watching how Russia is squandering the chance created by the oil bonanza to modernize itself. Failure to do this in the next ten to fifteen years would mean that we have to consider the threat of a state collapse and Russia's disintegration. If this were to happen, the world will likely be appalled by the catastrophe and its global repercussions. Even if the worst could be avoided, stagnation is not much better—that would mean the slow spreading of rot, which might not always be visible but in the end would lead to the disintegration of the people's will, of the Russian spirit of adventure and of political and intellectual courage, and it would mean muddling through for decades. This is the price of stabilizing the current Russian reality and the price of squandering the opportunity.

What matters most for Russian society and the elite is to put an end to the stagnation and to find the means of bringing about the liberal transformation of Russia, in its present geographical configuration, before its relapse into old habits becomes irreversible and it reaches the point of no return. Each additional year that stagnation continues, however, reduces the probability of a liberal-democratic modernization. The opportunity is still there, but for how much longer will the window remain open—five, seven, ten years?

If Russia should try once more to realize its liberal project, it will face new issues. Russia is unlikely to be able to transform its enormous territory without the cooperation and assistance of the Western democracies, primarily in developing Siberia and the Far East, and perhaps also in modernizing the North Caucasus. Russia will need to abandon its stubborn aspiration to self-sufficiency and its pathological sensitivity over its sovereignty, when it is in any case increasingly dependent on the consumers of Russian natural resources. Inviting foreigners to resolve managerial and economic tasks is nothing new for Russia, but for the Western democracies to be willing to be included in a new Russian project, they will have to be persuaded that Russia is really embarking on the creation of a law-governed state. Moreover, Western cooperation is unlikely to be unconditionally acceptable to Russia. The West will need to bear in mind just how difficult completing joint initiatives on the territory of Eurasia may prove, and how painful it will be for the Russian elite to maintain its position while Russia is becoming integrated into the Western world. If Western politicians indulge in displays of petty egoism or fail to recognize the magnitude of the challenge, they may send Russia back in the direction of a restoration. There is no need for Russia to become a full member of such organizations as NATO, the EU, and other Western forums in order to become part of the community of liberal democracies. Tailor-made forms of association and partnership may ease Russia's integration into European civilization.

The West should not expect a liberal Russia to prove an easy and agreeable partner, or to manifest much gratitude. Shared values do not necessarily lead to shared national interests or to full unanimity on how the world should be ordered and governed. This fact has been amply demonstrated by the frictions between Europe and the United States during the two terms of the Bush administration, with an idiosyncratic perspective of the world perpetually articulated by France. It is not impossible, indeed it is probable, that post-post-Soviet Russia will experience tension and disagreements with its Western partners. Neither is there any doubt that in times of trial Russia will stand with the West, if only because Russian society is concerned about the same things that threaten the West. These are primarily extremist radical Islam and nuclear proliferation, but also include the consequences of China's transformation into another superpower. Yet, there may come a time when we see democratic Russia allied with the West not on the basis of a war against common dangers, but on the basis of shared values.

Russia continues to drift, but the moment will surely come when the inability of bureaucratic authoritarianism to modernize the country and its failure to continue imitating stability and progress will become clear to Russians. Will the Russian political class have the courage to change the rules it plays by and move toward a state governed in accordance with the rule of law before it loses ground? Will it instead seek its salvation in an aggressive autocracy, and will the populace go along with that? This will be a test of whether Russia is capable of recognizing that it cannot build a successful state until it abandons its old system. Will it find the strength for a renaissance as a liberal democracy and finally bring another chapter of its dramatic history to a close? Soon we will know the answer to this question. If Russia finds the courage to start anew, this historic endeavor will affect the entire global order. God grant that this time Russia's attempt to break through to the future will be a success.

POLITICAL CHRONOLOGY

1989

March 26: Yeltsin is elected deputy of the Congress of People's Deputies of the Soviet Union, the new Soviet legislature.

July 29–30: The Interregional Group of Deputies, the first Russian democratic opposition in the Soviet parliament, is formed.

1990

May 16: Opening session of the newly elected Russian parliament, the Congress of the People's Deputies of the Russian Socialist Federal Republic (RSFR).

May 28: Boris Yeltsin is elected chair of the Supreme Soviet of the Congress of the People's Deputies.

June 8: Russian parliament votes for the precedence of Russian laws over Soviet laws.

June 12: Russian parliament declares Russia's independence. Yeltsin and members of his team leave the Communist Party.

August 1: Russian Parliament adopts a law on the media that liquidates censorship.

August 31: Russian parliament endorses the law on Russia's control over the natural resources on its territory.

December 12: The United States approves a $1 billion food credit for the USSR.

1991

January 12: Soviet troops attack the television center of Vilnius, Lithuania (fourteen civilians are killed).

February 9: Referendum on independence in Lithuania.

March 31: Referendum on independence in Georgia.

April 23: In Novo-Ogarevo, the representatives of the nine Soviet republics approve a new union treaty on the creation of the Union of Sovereign States suggested by Mikhail Gorbachev.

July 1: Dissolution of the Warsaw Pact and the formal end of the Cold War.

July 10: Yeltsin is sworn in as the first president of Russia.

July 7: A new $1.5 billion food credit is approved by the United States for the USSR.

June 12: Yeltsin is elected president of the Russian Federation.

July 31: Gorbachev and Bush sign the START 1 treaty.

August 19–21: Soviet nomenclatura coup to try to save the USSR.

August 24: Gorbachev resigns from his post as General Secretary of the Communist Party of the Soviet Union (CPSU).

August 29: Russian parliament dissolves the CPSU.

September 2–5, October 28: Fifth Congress of the People's Deputies of Russia gives Yeltsin power to rule by decree and to implement economic reform.

September 6: Mikhail Gorbachev recognizes the independence of the Baltic states.

September 11: James Baker arrives in Moscow to learn who is in charge, Gorbachev or Yeltsin.

September–October: Collapse of negotiations in Novo-Ogarevo between Gorbachev and the leaders of the Soviet republics on the creation of the Union of Sovereign States.

October 28: Congress of People's Deputies of Russia endorses Russia's path to sovereignty and dismantles Soviet ministries.

November 6: The creation of the new Russian government of liberal technocrats with Yegor Gaidar as deputy premier and economic and finance minister. The government is officially headed by Yeltsin, but informally First Vice Premier Gennadi Burbulis is in charge.

November 25: Gorbachev fails to persuade the leaders of the republics to sign a new union treaty, which could be the basis of the Union of Sovereign States.

December 1: Referendum in Ukraine on independence.

December 8: Agreement in Belovezha Puscha between Yeltsin, Ukrainian president Leonid Kravchuk, and Belarusian leader Stanislav Shushkevich results in the dissolution of the Soviet Union.

December 21: Meeting in Alma-Ata of the leaders of the Soviet Republics legitimizing the dissolution of the USSR and creating the NIS (Newly Independent States).

December 25: The last television address of Gorbachev, who leaves the Kremlin, signaling the end of the Soviet era. "Society has achieved freedom ... did not learn to use it," says Gorbachev in his final address to the nation.

1992

January 29: The start of "shock therapy"; prices are liberalized and skyrocket by a factor of ten to twelve.

January–February: Yeltsin's entourage fragments. Right-wing and left-wing opposition to Yeltsin is formed. First opposition rallies in Moscow.

January: Vice President Alexander Rutskoi starts to fight against Yeltsin. Parliament disapproves of Yeltsin and his government.

February 1: Yeltsin's first trip to the United States and his meeting with George H. W. Bush.

March 21: Tatarstan declares its independence from Russia. The threat of Russia's fragmentation.

April 6: VI Congress of People's Deputies and the emergence of parliamentary opposition to Yeltsin's course, headed by speaker Ruslan Khasbulatov. Democrats also begin to attack Yeltsin, who prefers authoritarian governance.

May: Restructuring of the Gaidar–Burbulis government. The pragmatists, including Viktor Chernomyrdin, join the government.

Summer: General Alexander Lebed, commander of the 14th Army in the Transnister republic, enters politics and becomes a vocal critic of the Kremlin.

December 1: VII Congress of the People's Deputies confronts the president and forces the resignation of Gaidar.

December 14: Chernomyrdin becomes the new prime minister. The liberal–technocratic period in Russian politics is over.

1993

January 2–3: At a summit in Moscow, Bush and Yeltsin sign the START 2 treaty.

March 12: VIII Congress of People's Deputies opens, and the confrontation between the president and the opposition escalates. Yeltsin loses initiative.

March 25: Yeltsin addresses the nation and declares a state of emergency. The opposition threatens him with impeachment.

March 26: IX Congress of the People's Deputies finds a compromise between Yeltsin and the opposition. The congress adopts a decision to organize a referendum to show whom society supports: the president or parliament.

April 3–4: At a summit in Vancouver, Canada, the U.S. announces a $1.6 billion assistance package for Russia.

April 25: President Yeltsin wins in the referendum on trust, albeit by a minimal margin.

May–June: The Constitutional Assembly representing various forces discusses a new Russian constitution.

July 9: G7 countries in Tokyo announce a $28.4 billion assistance package for the former Soviet Union.

September 21: Yeltsin issues Decree N1 400, which disbands parliament and introduces presidential rule. Parliament, headed by Yeltsin's opponents Vice President Alexander Rutskoi and Speaker Ruslan Khasbulatov, disobeys.

October 3–4: Open confrontation between the president and the opposition. Yeltsin uses tanks to dismantle parliament. The events end in bloodshed. The leaders of the opposition are put in jail.

September 13: Yegor Gaidar again joins the government as minister of the economy and first deputy premier.

December 12: Elections to new parliament—the State Duma—and referendum on the new constitution, which introduces a superpresidential republic.

1994

January 16: Gaidar leaves the government in protest over the ending of reforms.

Spring: Anti-NATO campaign in Moscow and clouds over U.S.–Russian relations.

April 28: Signing of the Treaty of Public Consent. The Kremlin tries to guarantee stability in Russia.

April 20: Creation of the Collective Security Treaty Organization (CSTO), which includes Russia, Kazakhstan, Tadjikistan, Kyrgyzstan, Uzbekistan, Georgia, and Belarus. The treaty is an attempt to form a new post-Soviet military alliance under the leadership of Russia. In 1999 Azerbaijan, Georgia, and Uzbekistan refuse to extend their membership in the organization, although later Tashkent reconsiders its decision and rejoins.

Spring: Yeltsin's bodyguard, Alexander Korzhakov, gains leverage in the Kremlin circle, and clans begin to rule Russia.

August 29: Russian troops leave the Baltic states, which acquire full sovereignty.

September 8: Russian troops leave Poland, and the last foreign troops leave Berlin.

October 11, "Black Tuesday": The collapse of the ruble sends the Russian economy into crisis.

November 26: Russian troops disguised as Chechen opposition forces attack Chechnya and are defeated by those loyal to Chechen President Johar Dudayev's forces.

November 29: Meeting of the Russian Security Council, which decides to use the army against Chechen separatists.

December 1: Russian troops enter Chechnya, and the first Chechen war starts.

December 31: Federal troops attack Grozny and are defeated by separatists.

1995

January: Russian troops shell Chechen cities with rockets and bombs. The war with the separatists becomes bloody. Society demands peace.

February 8: Five hundred thousand miners from 228 Russian mines go on strike, demanding a salary increase. Yeltsin's regime loses support in society.

Spring: Yeltsin becomes physically unfit and loses the ability to perform the functions of his office. His approval rating plunges to 4 percent.

May 9–10: Clinton in Moscow persuades Yeltsin to start NATO–Russia talks and to join the Partnership for Peace Programme.

June 2: The Paris Club agrees to reschedule Russia's $9.5 billion debt.

June 8: Yeltsin negotiates with Ukrainian president Leonid Kuchma on the issues in contention between Russian and Ukraine.

June 14–19: Chechen terrorists headed by Shamil Basayev attack Budenovsk, killing hundreds of civilians. Prime Minister Viktor Chernomyrdin accepts the demands of the separatists.

June 23: Peace negotiations begin between Moscow and Chechen separatists with the participation of OSCE representatives in Grozny.

July 29–30: The agreement on a peaceful settlement of the situation in the Republic of Chechnya is signed. It deals with military questions, including the return of federal troops to Russia. The settlement of political and economic issues is postponed. The agreement is soon violated by both sides.

August: Bosnian Serbs shell Sarajevo, NATO launches air strikes, and the relationship between Russia and the West sours.

September 10: Yeltsin supports the idea of a union with Belarus.

December 17: Parliamentary election in Russia.

1996

January 9: Yevgeny Primakov replaces Andrei Kozyrev as foreign minister. A new wave of terrorist acts. Chechen terrorists attack the provincial city of Kizliar.

February 1–6: Russian oligarchs organized by Boris Berezovsky meet at the World Economic Forum in Davos and decide to help Yeltsin with his reelection campaign.

April 19–21: Clinton informs Yeltsin of the timetable of NATO enlargement.

April 21: Chechen president Johar Dudayev is killed, allegedly by a Russian rocket.

Spring: Yeltsin begins his presidential campaign. He strikes a deal with the oligarchs: "auctions for shares."

June 11, 28, and July 11, 28: Terrorist acts in the Moscow metro and in buses; terrorist acts in the Northern Caucasus.

June–16, July 3: Two rounds of presidential elections. Yeltsin is sick but steals the elections in the second round. The Kremlin makes a trade-off with General Alexander Lebed, who helps Yeltsin win and gets the position of secretary of the Security Council.

August 17: Russian military gets the order to stop its actions in Chechnya.

August 30–31: General Lebed signs a peace treaty with Aslan Maskhadov, the new leader of the Chechen separatists in Khasavyurt. The general becomes the most popular politician in Russia and starts threatening Yeltsin's power.

October 15: General Lebed is fired.

November 5: Yeltsin undergoes heart surgery but returns to political life.

December 3: Nationwide strike against wage arrears. Of 189 coal mines, 154 stop work.

1997

February–March: Yeltsin opposes membership of the former Soviet Republics in NATO.

March 27: Boris Nemtsov, the governor of Nizhni Novgorod, joins the government as deputy premier and together with Anatoly Chubais attempts to restart social and economic reforms.

April 28: The president signs a decree spelling out the basic principles of the structural reforms of the "natural" monopolies.

May 12: Yeltsin and Maskhadov sign a treaty on peace and mutual relations between Russia and Chechnya. The first Chechen war is officially over.

May 22: Yeltsin and Belarusian president Lukashenko sign a charter on union between Russia and Belarus.

May 27: At a summit with NATO leaders in Paris, Yeltsin signs the NATO–Russia Founding Act.

July 21: Yeltsin signs a law listing seven mineral deposits that may be developed by outside partners in accordance with the law on production sharing that was adopted in 1995. Yeltsin signs a law on privatization that prohibits further shares-for-loans schemes.

Summer: Wars between technocrats and oligarchs and among oligarchs for power and property. Svyazinvest auction rigged by the oligarchs. Liberal technocrats headed by Anatoly Chubais lose influence.

September 17: Russia joins the Paris Club.

September–October: The rise of Boris Berezovsky and his gang. Berezovsky against Chubais; confrontation of clans.

Fall: Political establishment looks for Yeltsin's successor. Parliament confronts Yeltsin and his government. The collapse of the technocrats. Premier Chernomyrdin accumulates influence and threatens the position of Yeltsin's "political family."

1998

January 22: Chernomyrdin promises to cut off the flow of Russian technology to Iran.

March 9–12: Chernomyrdin's visit to the U.S., where he is presented as a future Russian leader.

March 23: Yeltsin fires Chernomyrdin and appoints Sergei Kiriyenko, one of his younger ministers, as the new premier.

May 16–17: At a summit in Birmingham, Russia officially becomes a member of the G8.

May 4: Yeltsin signs a decree that facilitates Russian citizens' obtaining of foreign passports.

Summer: Financial crisis in Russia. The International Monetary Fund and the World Bank, under pressure from Clinton, give Russia credits to stabilize its financial situation.

August 17: Financial collapse and default. The decision to default is taken by a group of technocrats and is questioned as partisan. Oligarchs succeed in saving their money.

August 24: Yeltsin fires the government and its premier, Kiriyenko.

September 11: Yeltsin appoints Yevgeny Primakov as the new premier. Primakov, supported by the State Duma, forms a left-wing cabinet.

Fall: Various elite groups prepare for a change of power in the Kremlin. Moscow Mayor Yuri Luzhkov and Primakov demonstrate their intention to fight for power.

October: Kosovo crisis escalates, and Russia's relations with the West and the United States again begin to deteriorate.

November 14: Democratic politician Galina Starovoitova is killed.

December 16: The first Iraq war starts. Moscow disapproves of the American military campaign.

1999

January: Relations between Primakov and Yeltsin's "political family" go sour. New confrontation between parliament and the president.

Spring: The political situation in Russia becomes tense: a war of all against all. The Kremlin loses control over events. The war of compromats starts in earnest. Public Prosecutor Yuri Skuratov supports charges against Yeltsin's family. The Duma and the Council of Federation prepare to impeach the president.

March 17: A newcomer from St. Petersburg, Vladimir Putin, is appointed as the new secretary of the Security Council.

March 18: NATO forces bomb Belgrade. Relations between Russia and the West continue to worsen.

March 19: The first NATO enlargement after the end of the Cold War. The Czech Republic, Hungary, and Poland are invited to begin accession talks at the Alliance's Madrid summit in 1997, and on March 12, 1999, they become the first former members of the Warsaw Pact to join NATO.

March 23: Flying to Washington on a visit, Primakov makes a U-turn and returns to Moscow to protest U.S. actions in Serbia.

March 24: NATO air strikes against Serbia begin.

May 12: Yeltsin fires Primakov as a potential rival and prevents his own impeachment.

May 19: Appointment of the new premier, Sergei Stepashin. From now on any prime minister is considered a potential Yeltsin successor.

June 16: The United States and Russia agree to the terms of Russia's participation in the NATO-led Kosovo peacekeeping forces.

August 7: Invasion of Chechen terrorists headed by one of the leaders of the separatists, Shamil Basayev, of Northern Caucasus republic Dagestan.

August 16: Parliament confirms the appointment of Vladimir Putin as the new premier.

September 9 and 13: Apartment houses bombed in Moscow. Hundreds are killed.

September 16: Apartment houses bombed in Volgodonsk. Russians feeling threatened seek security.

September 30: Russian troops enter Chechnya and the second Chechen war starts.

September–October: The emergence of new Kremlin parties, Unity and Fatherland, which represent warring factions of the elite, the Yeltsin group and the Primakov–Luzhkov clan.

November 14: Yeltsin publicly embraces Putin and confirms that he is the "only choice for Russia."

November 18: Clinton at the OSCE summit in Istanbul criticizes Russian actions in Chechnya. Yeltsin agrees to allow OSCE monitors to enter Northern Caucasus.

December 17: New Russian parliamentary elections.

December 14: Yeltsin informs Putin of his resignation and appoints Putin his successor.

December 31: Taped broadcast of the final Yeltsin message to the nation. Yeltsin leaves his post, creating an opportunity for preterm presidential elections.

2000

January 10: Russia adopts its new Concept of National Security, which changes its rhetoric regarding the relationship with the West. The term "partnership" is replaced with the term "cooperation."

January 25: Summit of the states, members of the Union of Independent States; discussion of regional security strategy and military cooperation. Trend toward the emergence of a new military alliance.

January–February: Putin begins reenergizing relations with the West. He calls George Robertson, secretary general of NATO; restores cooperation with NATO, broken during the Kosovo conflict; and invites Tony Blair to St. Petersburg. Putin hints at Russia's possible interest in joining NATO.

February 1: On Russia's initiative, a multilateral meeting on the Middle East conflict begins in Moscow. Russia resumes interest in global issues.

March 26: New presidential elections. Putin is elected president of Russia.

May 7: Inauguration of the new president.

May 13: Putin undertakes political reform, creating superregions (okrugs) governed by his representatives. It is the basis for his new top-down mechanism of governance.

August 12: The submarine *Kursk* sinks, triggering the first crisis of Putin's leadership. Putin's approval rating plummets.

June 13: Oligarch Vladimir Gusinsky is arrested, evidencing a new policy toward the oligarchy and independent media corporations controlled by business.

July 21–23: G8 summit in Okinawa, Japan, a coming-out party for Putin.

October: Putin starts his anti-oligarchic campaign to squeeze the oligarchs from power.

October 30: EU–Russia summit in Paris.

November: Introduction of the new state symbols and return to the Soviet anthem; crackdown on independent media.

2001

February 18: Spy scandal in Washington involving highly placed FBI agent Robert Hanssen breaks.

March 21: New security ministers are appointed. Sergei Ivanov is appointed defense minister. Boris Gryzlov, leader of the "Unity" party, replaces Vladimir Rushailo as Interior minister.

Spring: Putin continues cleansing the political scene of oligarchy. Construction of a "managed democracy."

April 3: The end of the most powerful independent television channel, NTV. The Kremlin attacks what is left of Gusinsky's media empire, newspaper *Segodnia,* and the magazine *Itogi.*

April 3: The president in his address to the Federal Assembly promises to fight corruption.

April 12: Creation of the "party of power," United Russia, based on "Unity" and "Fatherland." Putin endorses the new party.

May 30: The new ruling team takes over Gazprom. Alexei Miller is appointed its chair, replacing Rem Vyachirev.

May 1: Bush delivers a speech at the National Defense University and declares that "today Russia is not our enemy." He calls for moving beyond the 1972 anti-ballistic missile (ABM) agreements.

May 17: EU–Russia summit in Moscow

June 15: Creation of the Shanghai Cooperation Organization, which includes China, Russia, Kazakhstan, Kyrgyzstan, Tadjikistan, and Uzbekistan.

June 16: U.S.–Russian summit in Ljubljana. Personal bond formed between Putin and George W. Bush.

July–August: Putin cultivates a multivector diplomacy, beginning a dialogue with Beijing and hosting North Korean Kim Jong Il in the Kremlin.

September 11: Immediately after the terrorist attack on America, Putin calls Bush and offers help.

Fall: Russia cooperates with the United States in preparation for the Afghan war.

November 13: Putin arrives in Washington for a summit meeting. At that moment Kabul falls.

November 14–15: Bush and Putin meet in Crawford, Texas.

November 16: Tony Blair suggests the creation of the Russia–NATO Council and upgrading Russia's role in the relationship with the alliance. New members of NATO and U.S. defense secretary Donald Rumsfeld oppose the initiative.

December 13: The United States withdraws from the ABM treaty.

2002

January: The last independent television channel, owned by Berezovsky, is closed. All television channels are now under control of the state.

Spring: The residents of Voronezh take to the street protesting housing reform.

May 24: U.S.–Russian summit in Moscow. Strategic Offensive Reduction Treaty is signed and a declaration on new strategic relations is endorsed.

Summer: Warm relations between Moscow and the United States. White House praises Moscow and views their relations as "the best in history."

May 28: The NATO–Russia Council is formed and Putin sits together with all NATO leaders.

May 29: The EU–Russia summit in Moscow. Romano Prodi arrives in Moscow and brings a long-awaited present: the EU recognizes Russia's market-economy status. Washington soon does the same, improving Russia's chances of joining the World Trade Organization (WTO).

September 11: Moscow delivers an ultimatum to Tbilisi, warning it about the possibility of strikes at terrorist bases on Georgian territory.

October 23: Terrorist act at the Dubrovka theater in Moscow. Separatists seize eight hundred hostages. The attempt by federal forces to free hostages with the help of an unknown gas leaves 120 dead.

November 11: EU–Russia summit in Brussels. Discussion of the outcomes of the five-year cooperation between Russia and the European Union. The Kaliningrad transit issue is raised as well as Russia's membership of the WTO.

2003

February 23: In Kiev Putin announces that if Iraq disobeys the Security Council it might be worth considering harsh measures against it.

February–March: Russia and the United States differ on how to approach Iraq. The "coalition of the unwilling" is formed with the active role of France.

March 19: The beginning of the second Iraq war.

May 20: Western leaders take part in the festivities of the three hundredth anniversary of St. Petersburg. The U.S. president pointedly ignores his Atlantic allies but is warm to Putin.

May 31: EU–Russia summit in St. Petersburg, which elaborates the idea of four "common spaces" of cooperation between Russia and the EU: economic space; the space of freedom, security, and human rights; the space of external security; and the space of science, education, research, and culture.

October 5: Presidential election in Chechnya. Akhmad Kadyrov, former separatist who has switched sides, is elected the new Chechen leader. Putin starts "Chechenization" of the separatist republic.

October 25: The arrest of Mikhail Khodorkovsky, which signals the end of Russian oligarchic capitalism.

November 6: EU–Russia summit in Rome details their cooperation ("road maps") in the "common spaces."

November 22–23: The Rose Revolution in Georgia and the emergence of the Mikhail Saakashvili regime.

December 7: Parliamentary election and defeat of the liberal parties. The PACE (Parliamentary Assembly of the Council of Europe) delegation issues a conclusion: "The elections were free but unfair." The Kremlin's "United Russia" has the majority of seats.

2004

January 26: U.S. Secretary of State Colin Powell visits Moscow. His visit is preceded by an article in *Izvestia* criticizing Russian domestic policy.

February 9: The EU approves the resolution "Relations with the Russian Federation," which expresses disappointment with its relations with Russia.

February 24: Putin fires premier Mikhail Kasianov.

February–March: Growing tensions in relations between Russia and the EU.

February 22–23: The U.S.–Russia summit in Bratislava, Slovakia. Bush and Putin sign joint declarations on cooperation in the energy area and nuclear field. Bush promises to support Russia's membership accession process in WTO and tries to discuss democracy with Putin.

March 5: Mikhail Fradkov is appointed premier.

March 14: Putin is reelected with a landslide majority for a second term.

March 13: The Tulip Revolution in Kyrgyzstan. Collapse of Askar Akayev's presidency.

March 29: Bulgaria, Estonia, Latvia, Lithuania, Romania, Slovakia, and Slovenia join NATO.

Spring: Introduction of administrative and cabinet reforms.

April 26: Meeting of the defense ministers of the Shanghai group and their decision to begin joint military exercise in the Urals region to "prevent destabilization."

April 27: In Luxembourg, Moscow and the EU sign a compromise that facilitates solving a cargo transit block between Russia's mainland and its enclave, Kaliningrad.

May 1: New expansion of the EU.

May 9: The president of Chechnya, Akhmad Kadyrov, is assassinated.

Summer: A new chill in U.S.–Russian relations. The United States is bogged down in Iraq.

May 21: The EU–Russia summit in Moscow. Discussion of the "road maps" (for the four common spaces), the Kaliningrad transit issue, and the rights of Russian-speaking minorities in the Baltic states.

Summer: The last blow to Yukos and the trial of Khodorkovsky and Lebedev. The government sells Yuganskneftegaz, the leading company of the Yukos conglomerate.

Summer: Deterioration of the relations between Russia and Georgia; tensions on the border between Georgia and South Ossetia.

September 1: Terrorists attack Beslan school with more than 1,000 children and adults. More than 300 children die during the rescue operation.

September 26: Putin introduces new political initiatives proposing the scrapping of the elections of governors and switching to a proportional system for the Duma elections. The Beslan massacre is used as a pretext to launch a new strengthening of the presidential "pyramid of power."

November 25: EU–Russia summit in The Hague. Discussion of the "road maps" continues.

2005

January: People take to the streets protesting government reform on the "monetization" of social benefits.

March 8: The leader of the Chechen opposition and former president of Chechnya, former Soviet colonel Aslan Maskhadov, is killed. The ransom for his head is announced as $10 million, which helped to locate Maskhadov.

May 2: Arrest in the U.S. of former atomic energy minister Yevgeni Adamov, accused of the embezzlement of $9 million in American assistance.

May 10: The EU–Russia summit in St. Petersburg; approval of the "road maps" for the four common spaces.

May 25: Blackouts in Moscow, Tula, Kaluga, and Riazan create serious disruption in the life of the region.

Spring: The Kremlin starts to build loyal youth movements (*Nashi*, *Molodaya Gvardiya*, and *Mestnye*).

May 31: Khodorkovsky and his colleague Platon Lebedev are convicted and sentenced to nine years in jail.

July: The U.S. Congress approves $85 million in support of Russian democracy.

August 4: A Russian submarine is rescued by a British crew.

September 16: Gazprom announces the list of its foreign partners in the exploration of the Shtokman gas field. The list includes Chevron, ConocoPhilips, Total, Statoil, and Hydro.

October 13: One hundred fifty separatists attack a government building in Nalchik, the capital of Kabardino-Balkaria.

November 29: Meeting of the foreign ministers of the CSTO, which adopts a decision initiated by Russia to create a peacekeeping force.

November 4: The "Right March" of Russian nationalists in Moscow becomes a demonstration that shows the rising nationalist tide.

November–December: The Orange Revolution in Ukraine and the deterioration of relations between Russia and the Yushchenko team.

December 29–January 1: Gazprom raises the gas price for Ukraine.

2006

January 12: Amendments to NGO (nongovernmental organizations) law are adopted by the Duma limiting the activity of nongovernmental organizations.

January 22: The Public Chamber, a new body formed by the Kremlin to represent Russian civil society, convenes for its first meeting.

May 4: U.S. Vice President Richard Cheney speaks in Vilnius, Lithuania, and criticizes Russian domestic policies and its use of energy resources for political purposes.

May 24–25: EU–Russia summit in Sochi, where an agreement on facilitating the visa regime between both sides and on readmission is approved.

July 10: Shamil Basayev, one of the leaders of Chechen terrorists and an organizer of numerous terrorist acts on Russian territory, is killed.

July 11–12: Conference of the "Other Russia" opposition movement provokes a bitter reaction from the Kremlin.

July 15–17: G8 summit in St. Petersburg hosted by Vladimir Putin.

August 30: Ethnic conflict in the town of Kondopoga in Karelia, where the clashes between the Russian population and the Chechens start, demonstrating the level of xenophobia in Russia.

September 13: Moscow starts a blockade of Georgia and deports its citizens in response to the arrest of its intelligence officers in Tbilisi.

September 13: The first deputy chair of the Central Bank, Andrei Kozlov, is killed, which is the first murder of a representative of the government during Putin's tenure.

September 22–23: Trilateral meeting of Angela Merkel, Jacques Chirac, and Putin in Paris, where they discuss energy policy and other irritants in relations between Russia and Europe.

October 7: Anna Politkovskaya, one of the fiercest Putin critics, is murdered. Putin says that "her murder has brought more problems than her articles."

September 23: At the Russian–German–French summit in France, Putin informs Merkel and Chirac about a plan to redirect the gas flow toward Europe instead of the United States.

October 9: The head of Gazprom, Alexei Miller, announces that Gazprom intends to explore the Shtokman gas field without foreign partners.

October 12: Merkel informs Putin of Germany's decision to create an energy alliance within the European community without "third countries" and asks Putin to ratify the Energy Charter that Russia finds "not corresponding to its interests."

October 20: Informal EU–Russia summit in Lachti, Finland, where Chirac tries to prevent criticism of Russia by other EU members.

October 28: Creation of the second "party of power"—"A Just Russia"—under the leadership of the speaker of the Council of Federation, Sergei Mironov.

November 12: Referendum on independence in pro-Russian South Ossetia and the election of its president, which further deepens the mutual hostility between Russia and Georgia.

November 14: Dmitri Medvedev, a presidential hopeful, is appointed to be in charge of "national projects."

November 23: Alexander Litvinenko, a former Federal Security Bureau (FSB) officer who was granted asylum in the UK and later became a British citizen, dies from being poisoned by polonium-210. A former Russian intelligence officer, Andrei Lugovoi, is suspected of murder.

November 24: EU–Russia summit in Helsinki. Russia refuses to ratify the Energy Charter.

November 27–28: At the 2006 Riga summit, NATO heads of state declare that the Alliance intends to extend further invitations to countries that meet NATO standards to join NATO at the next summit, in 2008.

November 28: Heads of the Newly Independent States, convene a meeting in Minsk that shows that the future direction of the alliance is uncertain.

2007

February 9–10: Munich Conference on Security Policy; Putin speaks and causes shock waves in the West.

February 15: Putin appoints a new defense minister, Anatoly Serdyukov, and moves Sergei Ivanov to the post of first vice premier.

March 11: Elections in the fourteen regions become a rehearsal for the parliamentary elections scheduled for December. Elections bring victory to the key "party of power" — "United Russia."

March 26–27: Official visit to Russia of Chinese president Hu Jintao and the opening of the Year of China in Russia.

March–May: Government crisis in Ukraine. Russia watches warily but does not try to interfere.

April 26: President Putin threatens to suspend unilaterally Russia's compliance with the CFE (Conventional Forces in Europe) Treaty (the 1990 original and the 1999 unratified amendment) unless the treaty accommodates Russia's interests and is ratified by NATO allies.

April 30–May 5: Crisis in Russian relations with Estonia over the replacement of the monument to Soviet soldiers. The EU defends Estonia.

May 17–18: EU–Russia summit in Samara and attempts by both sides to stop further deterioration of the relationship. The sides discuss the ongoing Russian ban on Polish meat imports, the status of Kosovo, and Iran. Progress is made in discussion of visa-free regime between the EU and Russia.

May 29: Russian military announce the first successful test launch of the RS-24, a new ICBM with multiple independent warheads.

June 4: Putin warns that Moscow could take "retaliatory steps" if Washington proceeds with its plans to build a missile defense system for Europe.

June 7: Putin offers the United States to share Russian radar station at Gabala (Azerbaijan).

June 8: G8 summit in Heiligendamm (Germany). President Putin continues to try to persuade Americans to build a common missile defense system, acknowledges the Iranian threat, and argues that Russia "will develop according to the common principles that apply to all civilized countries."

June 11–15: Extraordinary Conference of the State-Parties to the Treaty on Conventional Forces in Europe Vienna initiated by Russia. The Kremlin wants ratification of the 1999 adapted CFE Treaty by NATO countries by an arbitrary deadline (July 1, 2008).

June 12–14: St. Petersburg Economic Forum brings 9,000 participants from 65 countries. Putin proposes to create a Eurasian regional equivalent of WTO. Sergei Ivanov plays the role of successor.

July 1–2: The "Lobster Summit" of Bush and Putin in Maine.

July 7–8: The Other Russia splits. Mikhail Kasianov leaves the movement to form his own party.

July 17: Russia introduces moratorium on its compliance with CFE treaty.

July 20–24: Tit-for tat expulsion of four diplomats between Moscow and London in the continuing spat around the Litvinenko poisoning and Moscow's refusal to extradite the suspect in the poisoning case.

July 25: Vladimir Putin meets with top-ranking officers of Russian power structures and stresses the task of military build-up to "strengthen the fighting capability of the army and navy."

July 25: Russia–NATO Council meets in Brussels. There is discord around the CFE, missile defense, and Kosovo.

August 1: Russian expedition plants a flag in the seabed under the North pole, claiming a sector of the continental shelf the size of western Europe. Dispute over the Arctic begins.

August 3: Russian military announce resuming building aircraft carriers and decision to "restore [its] naval presence in the Mediterranean Sea."

August 8: Russian strategic bombers resume their practice of flying long-haul missions to areas patrolled by NATO and the United States.

August 9: Henry Kissinger publishes an article in the *International Herald Tribune* calling for support for Putin's proposal to link Russia's radar installation to the U.S. and NATO defense system.

August 13-18: Reinforcements are dispatched to Ingushetia and other North Caucasus republics to deal with the resurgence of rebel activity. North Caucasus is area of violence again.

September 12: Mikhail Fradkov government resigns and Putin submits to the State Duma the candidacy of the new prime minister Viktor Zubkov.

Parliamentary and Presidential Election Results

Parliamentary Election Results, 1993

Party	Party Leader	Single-List Seats	Total Mandate Seats	Percentage of Duma Seats	Party-List Vote
Liberal Democratic Party of Russia (LDPR)	Vladimir Zhirinovsky	59	5	64	22.92
Russia's Choice	Yegor Gaidar	40	24	64	15.51
Communist Party (KPRF)	Gennadi Zyuganov	32	10	42	12.40
Women of Russia	Alevtina Fedulova	21	2	23	8.13
Agrarians	Mikhail Lapshin	21	16	37	7.99
Yabloko	Grigori Yavlinsky	20	7	27	7.86
Party of Russian Unity and Accord (PRES)	Sergei Shakhrai	18	4	22	6.73
Democratic Party of Russia	Nikolai Travkin	14	1	15	5.52
Other Parties		0	21	21	?
Independents		0	130	130	?
Total:		**225**	**220**	**445**	

Parliamentary Election Results, 1995

Party	Party Leader	Single-List Seats	Total Mandate Seats	Percentage of Duma Seats	Party-List Vote
Communist Party (KPRF)	Gennadi Zyuganov	99	58	157	22.30
Liberal Democratic Party of Russia (LDPR)	Vladimir Zhirinovsky	50	1	51	11.18
Our Home Is Russia	Viktor Chernomyrdin	45	10	55	10.13
Yabloko	Grigori Yavlinsky	31	14	45	6.89
Other Parties		0	65	65	?
Independents		0	77	77	?
Total:		**225**	**225**	**450**	

Parliamentary Election Results, 1999

Party	Party Leader	Single-List Seats	Total Mandate Seats	Percentage of Duma Seats	Party-List Vote
Communist Party (KPRF)	Gennadi Zyuganov	67	46	113	24.29
Unity	Sergei Shoigu	64	9	73	23.32
Fatherland–All Russia	Yuri Luzhkov, Yevgeny Primakov	37	29	66	13.33
Union of Right Forces	Boris Nemtsov	24	5	29	8.52
Liberal Democratic Party of Russia (LDPR)	Vladimir Zhirinovsky	17	0	17	5.98
Yabloko	Grigori Yavlinsky	16	4	20	5.93
Other Parties		0	16	16	?
Independents		0	107	107	?
Total:		**225**	**216**	**441**	

Parliamentary Election Results, 2003

Party	Party Leader	Single-List Seats	Total Mandate Seats	Percentage of Duma Seats	Party-List Vote
United Russia	Boris Gryzlov	120	100	220	37.57
Communist Party (KPRF)	Gennadi Zyuganov	40	11	51	12.61
Liberal Democratic Party of Russia (LDPR)	Vladimir Zhirinovsky	36	0	36	11.45
Motherland	Sergei Glaziev	29	8	37	9.02
Other Parties		0	32	32	?
Independents		0	71	71	?
Total:		**225**	**222**	**447**	

Presidential Election Results, 1991

Candidate	Percentage of Vote
B. Yeltsin	57.3
N. Ryzhkov	16.85
V. Zhirinovsky	7.81
A. Tuleev	6.81
A. Makashov	3.74
V. Bakatin	3.42

Presidential Election Results, 1996, Round I

Candidate	Percentage of Votes
B. Yeltsin	35.28
G. Zyuganov	32.03
A. Lebed	14.52
G. Yavlinsky	7.34
V. Zhirinovsky	5.7
S. Fedorov	0.92
M. Gorbachev	0.51
M. Shakkum	0.37
Y. Vlasov	0.2
V. Bryntsalov	0.16
A. Tuleev	0

Presidential Election Results, 1996, Round II

Candidate	Percentage of Votes
B. Yeltsin	53.82
G. Zyuganov	40.31

Presidential Election Results, 2000

Candidate	Percentage of Votes
V. Putin	52.94
G. Zyuganov	29.21
G. Yavlinski	5.8
A. Tuleev	2.95
V. Zhirinovsky	2.7
K. Titov	1.47
El. Pamfilova	1.01
S. Govorukhin	0.44
Y. Skuratov	0.43
A. Podberezkin	0.13
U. Dzhabrailov	0.1

Presidential Election Results, 2004

Candidate	Percentage of Votes
V. Putin	71.31
N. Kharitonov	13.69
S. Glaziev	4.1
I. Khakamada	3.84
O. Malyshkin	2.02
S. Mironov	0.75

NOTES

Chapter 1

1. The essence of Yeltsin's character and his political nature was reflected well in his memoirs, *The Struggle for Russia* (New York: Times Book, 1994) and *Midnight Diaries* (New York: Public Affairs, 2001).

2. On Boris Yeltsin's rule, see also Leon Aron, *A Revolutionary Life* (New York: St. Martin's Press, 2000); Michael McFaul, "Yeltsin's Legacy," *Wilson Quarterly*, Spring 2000; Peter Reddaway and Dmitri Glinski, *The Tragedy of Russia's Reform: Market Bolshevism against Democracy* (New York: USIP Press, 2001); Stephen Kotkin, *Armageddon Aborted: The Soviet Collapse, 1970–2000* (New York: Oxford University Press, 2001); *Yeltsinskaya Epocha: Esse Politicheskoi Istorii* (Yeltsin's Epoch: Essays of Political History) (Moscow: Vagrius, 2001); George W. Breslauer, *Gorbachev and Yeltsin as Leaders* (Cambridge, U.K.: Cambridge University Press, 2002); Michael McFaul, *Russia's Unfinished Revolution: Political Change from Gorbachev to Putin* (Cornell: Cornell University Press, 2002); Leonid Mlechin, *Kreml'. Prezidenty Rossii. Strategiya Vlasti—ot Borisa Yeltsina do Vladimira Putina* (The Kremlin. Presidents of Russia: A Strategy of Power—From Boris Yeltsin to Vladimir Putin) (Moscow: Centerpoligraph, 2003); Viktor Sheinis, *Vzliet i Padenije Parlamenta* (The Rise and Collapse of the Parliament) (Moscow: Moscow Carnegie Center and Indem, 2005).

3. On the influence of Russia's historic legacy on current political developments, see Alexander Achiezer, Igor Klyamkin, and Igor Yakovenko, *Rossiyskaya Istoria: Konets ili Novoe Nachalo?* (Russia's History: The End or the New Beginning?) (Moscow: Novoye Izdatel'stvo, 2005).

4. Ralf Dahrendorf, *Reflections on the Revolution in Europe* (London: Chatto and Windus, 1990), p. 79.

5. Adam Przeworski, *Democracy and the Market: Political and Economic Reforms in Eastern Europe and Latin America* (Cambridge, U.K.: Cambridge University Press, 1991), p. 187.

6. Axel Hadenius, ed., *Democracy's Victory and Crisis* (Cambridge, U.K.: Cambridge University Press, 1997), p. 408.

7. Giuseppe Di Palma, *To Craft Democracies: An Essay on Democratic Transitions* (Berkeley: University of California Press, 1990), p. 210.

8. *Vedomosti*, April 24, 2007.

9. Mikhail Krasnov, interview with *Novaya gazeta*, April 24–May 5, 2007; for an analysis of the Yeltsin constitution, see Mikhail Krasnov, *Personalistski Rezhim v Rossii: Opyt Institutsionnogo Analiza* (The Personalized Regime in Russia: The Experience of the Institutional Analysis) (Moscow: Liberal Mission, 2007).

10. Joseph A. Schumpeter, *Capitalism, Socialism, and Democracy* (New York: Harper and Brothers, 1947), p. 290.

11. Strobe Talbott, *The Russia Hand* (New York: Random House, 2002), p. 121.

12. Talbott, *The Russia Hand*, p. 52.

13. Angela Stent, "America and Russia," in *Russia's Engagement with the West: Transformation and Integration in the Twenty-First Century,* ed. Alexander J. Motyl, Blair A. Ruble, and Lilia Shevtsova (Armonk, New York: M. E. Sharpe for *Political Studies Review,* 2004), pp. 264–5.

14. Arnold Horelick and Thomas Graham, *U.S.–Russian Relations at the Turn of the Century* (Washington, D.C.: Carnegie Endowment for international Peace, 2000), p. 19.

Chapter 2

1. *Kommersant-Vlast'*, April 27, 2007.

2. See the discussion on Yeltsin's legacy in *Izvestia*, April 26, 2007.

3. Peter Reddaway and Dmitri Glinski, ibid., p. 631–632.

4. Archie Brown, "The Real Yeltsin Legacy," *The Guardian*, April 27, 2007.

5. Strobe Talbott, *The Russia Hand* (New York: Random House, 2002), p. 10.

6. Leon Aron, "The Yeltsin Legacy," http://www.American.com, April 23, 2007.

7. Stefan Hedlund, "Vladimir the Great, Grand Prince of Muscovy: Resurrecting the Russian Service State," *Europe-Asia Studies*, vol. 58, no. 5 (July 2006): 793.

8. George W. Breslauer, *Evaluating Gorbachev and Yeltsin as Leaders*, in Archie Brown and Lilia Shevtsova, eds., *Gorbachev, Yeltsin, and Putin: Political Leadership in Russia's Transition* (Washington, D.C.: Carnegie Endowment for International Peace, 2001), p. 64.

9. *New York Times*, April 29, 2007.

10. Martin Wolf, "How Russia Slipped on the Road to Yeltsin's New Era," *Financial Times*, April 25, 2007.

Chapter 3

1. Ljudmila Telen, *Pokolenie Putina* (Putin's generation) (Moscow: Vagrius, 2004), p. 14.

2. During the first Chechen war in 1994–1996, an overwhelming part of the society was against the war. In January 1995, 54 percent of those polled were in favor of the withdrawal of Russian troops; 27 percent supported the introduction of troops (19 percent were undecided). During the second Chechen war, which began in 2000, 43 percent supported the introduction of troops into the republic, 43 percent expressed doubts about the purpose of this step, and 11 percent had difficulty answering (VTsIOM polls, January 28, 2000, www.VTsIOM.ru, January 2000).

3. Guillermo O'Donnell, "Tensions in the Bureaucratic-Authoritarian State," in *The New Authoritarianism in Latin America*, ed. D. Collier (Princeton, N.J.: Princeton University Press, 1979), p. 292. The bureaucratic–authoritarian regime that has emerged in Russia resembles Guillermo O'Donnell's delegative democracy, which rests on the premise that "whoever wins elections to the presidency is thereby entitled to govern as he or she sees fit, constrained only by the hard facts of existing power relations and by a constitutionally limited term of office." In contrast to a delegative democracy, the Russian bureaucratic authoritarian regime is based on the appointment of the successor and total control on the part of the high executive over the entire political scene.

4. On the evolution of Putin's rule see, *Ot Piervogo Litsa: Razgovory s Putinym* (From the First Person: A Conversation with Putin) (Moscow: Vagrius 2000); *Putin 1 and Putin 11: Results of the first term and the Prospects for the Second*, ed. Yuri Fiodorov and Bertil Nygren (Oslo: National Defense College, 2004); *Leading Russia: Putin in Perspective*, ed. Alex Pravda (Oxford, U.K.: Oxford University press, 2005); *Gorbachev, Yeltsin, and Putin: Political Leadership in Russia's Transition*, ed. Archie Brown and Lilia Shevtsova (Washington, D.C.: Carnegie Endowment for International Peace, 2001); Peter Baker and Susan B. Glassner, *Kremlin Rising: Vladimir Putin's Russia and the End of Revolution* (New York: Scribner, 2005); Anna Politkovskaya, *Putin's Russia: Life in a Failing Democracy* (London: Owl Books, 2007); Richard Sakwa, *Putin: Russia's Choice* (Routledge, 2003); Andrew Jack, *Inside Putin's Russia: Can There Be Reform Without Democracy?* (Oxford: Oxford University Press, 2007); Puti Rossijskogo Postkommunisma (Paths of Russian Post-Communism), eds. Maria Lipman and Andrei Riabov (Moscow: Izdatelstwo R. Elinina, 2007).

Also see the discussion on Putin's regime and leadership, "The Russian Enigma," *American Interest*, vol. 11, no. 2 (November–December 2006), and "The Russian Enigma," vol. 11, no. 2, (November–December 2006); vol. 11, no. 4 (March–April 2007).

Chapter 4

1. Francis Fukuyama, "The Primacy of Culture," *Journal of Democracy*, January 1995.

2. Larry Diamond, "Thinking about Hybrid Regimes, "*Journal of Democracy*, April 2002.

3. Ivan Krastev, "Democracy's Doubles," *Journal of Democracy*, April 2006.

4. Stephen Kotkin, *Russia under Putin: Democracy or Dictatorship?* (Washington, D.C.: Foreign Policy Research Institute, March 6, 2007), www.fpri.org.

5. Andrew Wilson, *Virtual Politics: Faking Democracy in the Post-Soviet World* (New Haven: Yale University Press, 2005), p. xiii.

6. Guillermo O'Donnell, "Horizontal Accountability in New Democracies," *Journal of Democracy*, vol. 9, no. 3 (July 1998): 115.

7. Roderic Lyne, Strobe Talbott, and Koji Watanabe, *Task Force Report to the Trilateral Commission: Engaging with Russia: The Next Phase* (Trilateral Commission, June 30, 2006).

8. Stephen Sestanovich, "Putin's Invented Opposition," *Journal of Democracy*, vol. 18, no. 2, 2007.

9. Robert Dahl, *Polyarchy: Participation and Opposition* (New Haven: Yale University Press, 1971), pp. 33–5.

10. Research by the World Bank in 2005 indicates that the value of bribes paid to officials by Russian business rose from $5.7 billion in 2002 to $8.7 billion in 2005, that is, by 53 percent. According to the liberal Indem Foundation, the value of bribes paid to bureaucrats by Russian business has increased from $33 billion in 2001 to $316 billion in 2005, or almost half the Russian gross domestic product. Thus, for example, the size of the bribe (or cut) that business is obliged to pay the ministries of education and health is 20 to 30 percent of the value of the contracts, while bribes in military procurement can be as high as 70 percent.

11. Kirill Rogov, "Kapitalizacija Poriadka" (Capitalization of Order), *Novaya gazeta*, April 2–4, 2007.

12. Vladimir Nazarov, "Osobennosti Suverennogo Federalizma" (The Peculiarities of Sovereign Federalism), *Vedomosti*, April 23, 2007.

13. We could extend the list to include the members of his kitchen cabinet, for instance, the obscure Kovalchuk brothers.

14. Guillermo O'Donnell, "Delegative Democracy," *Journal of Democracy*, vol. 5, no. 1 (January 1994).

Chapter 5

1. James MacGregor, *Transforming Leadership: A New Pursuit of Happiness* (London: Atlantic Books, 2003), pp. 22–7.

2. George Breslauer, "Evaluating Gorbachev and Yeltsin as Leaders," in *Gorbachev, Yeltsin, and Putin*, p. 51.

3. Archie Brown, "Introduction," in *Gorbachev, Yeltsin, and Putin: Political Leadership in Russia's Transition*, ed. Archie Brown and Lilia Shevtsova (Washington, D.C.; Carnegie Endowment, 2001), pp. 6–7.

4. Alex Pravda, ed. "Introduction," *Leading Russia: Putin in Perspective: Essays in Honour of Archie Brown* (Oxford: Oxford University Press, 2005) p. 25.

Chapter 6

1. For an analysis of the pragmatist position, see Igor Klyamkin and Tatiana Kutkoviets, *Kremlevskaya Politologia: Kak Nas Uchat Ljubit' Rodinu* (The Kremlin School of Political Science: How They Teach Us to Love the Motherland) (Moscow: Liberal Mission, 2006).

2. Andranik Migranian, "Ot Politicheskogo Chaosa k Poriadku" (From Political Chaos to Order), *Izvestia*, April 17, 2007.

3. Vladislav Surkov, "Osnovnyje Tendentsii i Perspektivy Razvitija Sovremennoi Rossii" (Key Tendencies and Perspectives of Development of Contemporary Russia), www.Polit.ru; Vladislav Surkov, "Suverenitet Vazhnee Democratii" (Sovereignty Is More Important than Democracy), *Nezavisimaya gazeta*, July 13, 2005.

4. For a discussion between pragmatists and idealists, see "Rossijskoje Gosudarstvo: Vchera, Siegodnia, Zavtra" (The Russian State: Yesterday, Today, Tomorrow), www.liberal.mission.ru; Lilia Shevtsova, "Kogo Ochraniajut Nashi Ochraniteli" (Who Is Being Protected by Our Defenders), www.liberal.ru, July 2007.

5. Quoted in *Nezavisimaya gazeta*, December 15, 2006.

6. www.Levada.ru, "Obshchestvo" (Society), 2007.

7. Minxin Pei, "Beijing Drama: China's Governance Crisis and Bush's New Challenge," *Policy Brief* 21 (Washington, D.C.: Carnegie Endowment for International Peace, November 2002).

Chapter 7

1. See www.Levada.ru, "Politika" (Politics), April 2007.

2. Associated Press, June 9, 2007.

Chapter 9

1. On Russian oligarchs see David Hoffman, *The Oligarchs: Wealth and Power in the New Russia* (New York: Public Affairs, 2002); Chrystia Freeland, *Sale of the Century: Russia's Wild Ride from Communism to Capitalism* (New York: Crown, 2000); Paul Khlebnikov, *Godfather of the Kremlin: Boris Berezovsky and the Looting of Russia* (New York: Harcourt Brace, 2000).

2. William Thompson, "Putin and the Oligarchs," in *Leading Russia: Putin in Perspective*, ed. Alex Pravda (Oxford: Oxford University Press, 2005), p. 181.

3. State officials sitting on the boards of state companies earn good allowances. For example, Vladimir Yakunin, the head of the Russian railroad, received $817,000 in 2006 for serving as chairman of the board of directors of Transcreditbank. As the head of the railroad, Yakunin received a salary that amounted to $1 million in 2006. Top managers of Gazprom receive about $1.3 million annually and in addition, some of them, like Alexei Miller, the head of Gazprom, receive around $623,000 for serving on the board of directors of Gazprom. See *Vedomosti*, July 11, 2007.

4. Ibid., p. 52.

Chapter 10

1. Grigory Yavlinsky, *Rossijskije perspektivy: Ekonomicheskii I politicheskii Vzgliad* (Russia's Perspectives: Economic and Political Views) (Moscow: Galea Print, 2006).

Chapter 11

1. www.gks.ru, *Kommersant*, January–June 2007; *Vedomosti*, January–June, 2007

2. Anders Aslund, "Russia's Challenges as Chair of the G-8," Policy Briefs in International Economics, March 2006; www.iie.com.

3. Economic growth in the first half of 2007 amounted to 11.5 percent in China and 9.4 percent in India.

4. *Novyje Izvestia*, March 6, 2007.

5. www.gks.ru; *Kommersant*, December 2006, January–May 2007; *Vedomosti*, January–June 2007; Alexei Kudrin, *Rol' Stabfonda v Makroekonomicheskoi Stabil'nosti* (The Role of the Stabilization Fund in Macroeconomic Stability), www.liberal.ru.

6. "The clouds will start to gather two years from now: imports have been growing at a much faster rate than exports, and in 2009 the positive trade balance will be negated. A year later the budget surplus will evaporate as well. The obvious consequence will be a decline in the ruble's nominal exchange rate," wrote Alexander Kiyatkin, predicting the capital outflow and banking and financial collapse. Alexander Kiyatkin, "Drugaya Rossiya" (A Different Russia), *Smart Money*, N22, June 18, 2007.

7. Yegor Gaidar, *Padenije Imperii: Uroki dlja Sovremennoj Rossii* (The Collapse of the Empire: Lessons for Contemporary Russia), (Moscow: Rosspen, 2006).

8. According to Viktor Pleskachevsky, president of the Professional Association of Registrars, over 75 percent of property in Russia belongs to the state, while only 25 percent is privately owned. According to Julian Cooper, in 2005 the state owned/controlled companies in the top 25 accounted for 36 percent of total sales of the top 400 companies. In 2007 this share amounts to 50 percent or more.

9. According to independent sources, between 1998 and 2004 state-controlled oil companies increased their output by 75 percent, while the increase for privately owned companies was 132 percent. During the five years from 1999 to 2004, the annual increase in oil production was 8.5 percent, while, after the nationalization of Yukos, it fell to 2.7 percent. Even more damning evidence of the state's destructive influence is the fact that between 1999 and 2005 Gazprom increased annual production by 2 percent, while the increase in 2005 fell to 0.8 percent.

10. Alexander Shokhin, *Kommersant*, November 23, 2006.

11. Admittedly, Donald Evans, the former U.S. secretary of commerce, rejected the chairmanship of Rosneft, and Sir Richard Sykes, the former boss of GlaxoSmithKline, turned down an offer to be the nonexecutive chair of Severstal.

12. Vadim Radujev, "Suverenitet i Kapital" (Sovereignty and Capital), *Vedomosti*, April 27, 2007.

Chapter 12

1. Alexei Kudrin, *Rol' Stabfonda v Makroekonomicheskoi Stabil'nosti* (The Role of the Stabilization Fund in Macroeconomic Stability), www.liberal.ru.

2. William Tompson and Rudiger Ahrend, *Economic Surveys: Russian Federation* (Paris: OECD, July 2004), p. 6.

3. Terry Lynn Karl, *The Paradox of Plenty: Oil Booms and Petro-States* (Berkeley: University of California Press, 1997).

4. *Izvestia*, December 31, 2006.

5. *Kommersant*, January 27, 2007.

6. Foreign investors were forced to sell their shares at a discount, and (according to the Russian press) Shell alone lost from $1.5 to $2 billion in the process.

7. Gazprom according to independent media did not have the wherewithal to buy a controlling interest in the Sakhalin-2 project and had to borrow money for the purpose.

8. See Michel Stott, "CEOs Ignore Russia's Murky Politics in Rush to Invest," Johnson Russia List, June 10, 2007.

9. Siemens managers admit that they have spent about $556 million in bribes to the authorities and representatives of special services in Eurasia since the end of the 1990s.

10. Natalya Grib, "Pljus Gazifikacija Vsiej Evropy" (Plus Gasification of Entire Europe), *Kommersant*, June 26, 2007.

11. Guy Chzan and David Gauthier-Villars, "Total Settles for Less," *Wall Street Journal*, July 13, 2007.

12. Vladimir Milov, *The EU–Russia Review*, vol. 1 (May 2006), EU Russia Center, www.eu-russiacenter.org.

Chapter 13

1. www.gks.ru, *Kommersant, Vedomosti*, January–July 2007.

2. Vladimir Popov, Russia Redux? March–April 2007 www.http://newleft review.net.

3. Murray Feshbach, XDR-TB in Russia, www.cdi.or/russia/johnson, January 29, 2007.

4. *Vedomosti*, March–July 2007.

5. Interview with Yevgeni Yasin, *Rossijskaya gazeta*, March 28, 2007.

6. *Novye Izvestia*, August 7, 2007.

7. *Rossijskaya gazeta*, March 30, 2007; *Vedomosti*, March 30, 2007.

8. *Rossijskaya gazeta*, August 4, 2007.

9. www.Levada-center.ru, *Obshchestvo* (Society), 2007.

10. www.VTsIOM.ru, April 2007.

11. www.Levada-center.ru, *Obshchestvo* (Society), May 2007.

12. Ibid.

Chapter 14

1. Deliberating on the influence of the Kosovo crisis on Russia's relations with the West, Celeste Wallander wrote, "Kosovo exemplified how military capable NATO is, and how Russia has little influence in Europe." Celeste A. Wallander, "Russian Foreign Policy in the Wake of the Kosovo Crisis," in *U.S.–Russian Relations*, Aspen Institute Congressional Program (August 6–20, 1999), vol. 14, no. 3.

2. Sergei Medvedev, "Russia at the End of Modernity: Foreign Policy, Security, Identity," in *Russia and the West at the Millennium: Global Imperatives and Domestic Policies*, ed. Sergei Medvedev, Alexander Konovalov, and Sergei Oznobishchev (Garmisch-Partenkirchen: George C. Marshall European Center for Security Studies, 2002), p. 51.

3. Sergei Karaganov, "Farsovaya 'Cholodnaya' Voina" (A Farcical Cold War), *Rossijskaya gazeta*, December 27, 2006.

4. Roderic Lyne, "We Need to Be Patient with Russia," *International Herald Tribune*, July 12, 2006.

5. Roderic Lyne, Strobe Talbott, and Koji Watanabe, *Task Force Report on Engaging with Russia: The Next Phase* (The Trilateral Commission, June 30, 2006) p. 6.

6. Robert Legvold, "Russian Foreign Policy during Periods of Great State Transformation," in *Russia's Foreign Policy in the Twentieth Century and the Shadow of the Past*, ed. Robert Legvold (New York: Columbia University Press, 2007).

Chapter 15

1. Bobo Lo, "Evolution or Regression? Russian Foreign Policy in Putin's Second Term," in *Toward a Post-Putin Russia,* ed. Helge Blakisrud (Oslo: Norwegian Institute of International Affairs, 2006), p. 58.

2. Sergei Lavrov, "Summiruja Rossijskuyu Vnieshnjuyu Politiku" (Summarizing Russian Foreign Policy), *Kommersant,* December 21, 2006.

3. Vladimir Frolov, "Cho Dlya Nas Zapad Poslie Mjunchena?" (What Is the West to Us after Munich?) *Izvestia,* February 28, 2007.

4. Lavrov, "Summiruja Rossijskuyu Vnieshnjuyu Politiku."

5. Sergei Ivanov, "Russia Must Be Strong," *Wall Street Journal,* January 11, 2006.

6. Robert Legvold defined Russia's relations with the West as being based on a desire to be "with, although not necessarily as part of, the West, or without and perhaps against the West." Robert Legvold, U.S.-Russia-Europe: Cooperative Efforts. Aspen Institute, Thirty-Third Conference, August 12–18, 2006, Aspen Institute, Congressional Program, vol. 25, p. 7.

7. Zbigniew Brzezinski, *The Choice: Global Domination or Global Leadership* (New York: Basic Books, 2005).

8. On Russia–China cooperation, see C. Fred Bergsten, Bates Gill, Nicolas Lardy, and Derek Mitchell, *China, The Balance Sheet: What the World Needs to Know Now about the Emerging Superpower* (New York: Center for Strategic and International Studies and Institute for International Economics, 2006), pp. 134–5.

9. In comparison, annual trade between China and the United States in 2006 amounted to $260 billion and with the EU, to $270 billion.

10. Vladislav Inozemtsev, *Le Monde Diplomatique,* Russian edition, April 2007, p. 4.

11. Coit D. Blacker, "Russia and the West," in *The New Russia Foreign Policy,* ed. Michael Mandelbaum (New York: Council of Foreign Relations, 1998), p. 188.

12. Andrew Kramer, "Putin Plays Down IMF and WTO," *New York Times,* June 11, 2007.

13. Isaiah Berlin, *The Soviet Mind: Russian Culture under Communism,* ed. Henry Hardy (Washington, D.C.: Brookings Institution Press, 2005), p. 90.

14. Andrei Grachev, "Putin's Foreign Policy Choices," in *Leading Russia. Putin in Perspective,* ed. Alex Pravda (Oxford, U.K.: Oxford University Press, 2005), p. 273.

Chapter 17

1. Dmitri Trenin, *Integracijai Identichnost: Rossija kak Novyj Zapad* (Integration and Identity: Russia as the New West) (Moscow: Europe, 2006), p. 124.

2. Angela Stent, "Berlin's Russia Challenge," *National Interest*, no. 88 (March–April 2007): 46.

3. Sergei Karaganov, "Realnyje Cojuzy i Pustyje Deklaracii" (Real Treaties and Empty Declarations), *Rossijskaya gazeta*, April 6, 2007.

4. Dov Lynch, "Struggling with an Indispensable Partner," in *What Russia Sees*, ed. Dov Lynch, Chaillot Paper, no. 74 (January 2005).

5. Lynch, "Struggling with an Indispensable Partner."

6. "The old Europe" acquiescence to the Kremlin's policy is viewed with frustration by the Russian liberals. Europeans "recognize Russia as vast storeroom of raw materials ... and an important market for their companies but flatly refused to recognize it as a political subject," wrote Vladislav Inozemtsev, "Putina Ozhidayut na Sledujushchem Summite Voc'merki" (Putin Is Expected at the Next G-8 Summit), *Vedomosti*, June 14, 2007.

7. "The Bear Necessities of Life," *Economist*, November 23, 2006.

8. *RIA Novosti*, May 18, 2007.

9. *Vedomosti*, May 18, 2007.

10. In July 2007 Gazprom returned to negotiations with Total regarding its possible participation in developing the Shtokman field.

11. *Moscow Times*, May 4, 2007.

12. Katinka Barysch, *The EU and Russia: Strategic Partnership or Squabbling Neighbors* (London: Center for European Reform, 2006).

13. Iver B. Neumann, "Russia as a Great Power," in *Russia as a Great Power: Dimensions of Security under Putin*, ed. Jakob Hedelskog, Vilhelm Konnander, Bertyl Nygren, Ingmar Oldberg, and Christer Pursianen (London: Routledge, 2000).

Chapter 18

1. Andrei Piontkovsky, "Vyzovy 21 Vieka i Russkaya Politicheskaya Elita" (Challenges of the Twenty-First Century and the Russian Political Elite), *Mir Peremen*, no. 2 (2006): 36.

2. Angela Stent, "America and Russia," in *Russia's Engagement with the West. Transformation and Integration in the Twenty-First Century*, ed. Alexander J. Motyl, Blair A. Ruble, and Lilia Shevtsova (Armonk, N.Y.: M. E. Sharpe, 2005), p. 263.

3. Zbigniew Brzezinski, *Second Chance: Three Presidents and the Crisis of American Superpower* (New York: Basic Books, 2007), p. 3.

4. Strobe Talbott, interview, March 22, 2007, www.state.gov.

5. Thomas Graham, "U.S.–Russian Relations: Risks and Prospects," Wilton Park Conference, September 21, 2001, www. cdi.org/Russia.

6. James M. Goldgeier and Michael McFaul, *Power and Purpose: American Policy toward Russia after the Cold War* (Washington, D.C.: Brookings Institution Press, 2003).

7. Angela Stent and Lilia Shevtsova, "America, Russia and Europe: A Realignment?" *Survival*, vol. 44, no. 4 (Winter 2002–2003): 122.

8. Robert Legvold, "U.S.–Russian Relations Ten Months after September 11," in *U.S.–Russia Relations: A New Framework*, Twenty-Seventh Conference, August 15–21, 2002, Aspen Institute, Congressional Program, vol. 17, no. 5: 6, 12.

9. Stent and Shevtsova, *America, Russia and Europe*, pp. 128–9.

10. Strobe Talbott, *The Russia Hand* (New York: Random House, 2002), p. 418.

Chapter 19

1. Leon Aron, "Institutions, Restoration, and Revolution," American Enterprise Institute, Spring 2005, www.aei.org.

2. Thomas Carothers wrote, "... The notion that democracy promotion plays a dominant role in Bush policy is a myth.... The administration has followed a firmly realist line toward Russia and China." Thomas Carothers, "The Democracy Crusade Myth," The National Interest online, www.nationinterest.org/, May 6, 2007.

3. Henry Kissinger, "Overcoming Tensions," *Khaleej Times*, April 4, 2007.

4. Andrew Kuchins, "Russian Democracy and Civil Society: Back to the Future," Testimony prepared for the U.S. Commission on Security and Cooperation in Europe, February 8, 2006.

5. Council on Foreign Relations, *Russia's Wrong Direction: What the United States Can Do and Should Do*, John Edwards and Jack Kemp, chairs, Stephen Sestanovich, project director, Independent Task Force Report 57, 2006.

6. *Moskovskije novosti*, September 24–28, 2006.

7. Washington's growing suspicion of Russia has also had practical consequences. In July 2006, the U.S. State Department introduced sanctions against the Russian companies Rosoboronexport and Sukhoy in retaliation for arms sales between Moscow and the governments of Hugo Chávez, Iran, and Syria (sanctions against Sukhoy were later rescinded following further review). Putin responded by reneging on promises to supply the United States with liquefied natural gas (LNG) and to include American companies in the exploration of the Shtokman field.

8. Vladimir Putin, www.lenta.ru, February 13, 2007.

9. Vladimir Frolov, "A Missed Opportunity to Lead the World," *Russia Profile*, February 20, 2007.

10. Sergei Lavrov, *Izvestia*, December 31, 2006.

Chapter 20

1. Associated Press, February 9, 2007.

2. www.Kremlin.org, April 25, 2007.

3. Sergei Lavrov, *Izvestia*, December 31, 2006

4. David Kramer, deputy assistant secretary for European and Eurasian affairs, remarks to the Baltimore Council on Foreign Affairs, Baltimore, Maryland, May 31, 2007, www.state.gov.

5. Dmitri Trenin, *New Times*, April 9, 2007.

6. Some Russian politicians suspected that the U.S. missile deployment was aimed intentionally at provoking a Russian reaction and a nuclear race that Russia could not win while exhausting Russian resources. That criticism from Moscow caught the Bush administration by surprise proves that there were no grounds for accusing the United States of such Machiavellianism.

7. Rose Gottemoeller, "The INF Conundrum," *Nezavisimaya gazeta-dipkurier*, March 5, 2007.

8. Russian society supported a tough response to the United States. In spring 2007 sixty-seven percent of Russians viewed the deployment of U.S. missiles as a threat to Russia; only 9 percent considered the Iranian nuclear program, and 6 percent the North Korean nuclear program, as more serious threats to Russia. This was an unintended consequence of U.S. foreign policy, which helped the Kremlin's domestic agenda. www.Levada-center.ru, May 2007.

9. Before the scandal, the Defense Ministry announced a $189 billion program to rebuild Russian military might, which would include new intercontinental ballistic missiles, submarines, aircraft carriers, and a mysterious "fifth-generation" fighter plane. Now the military could ask for more.

10. *Kommersant*, May 12, 2007.

11. Interfax, June 4, 2007.

Chapter 21

1. "America and Russia," *Economist*, July 7–13, 2007.

2. Remarks by President Bush and President Putin after their meeting, Kennebunkport, Maine, July 2, 2007.

3. Associated Press, May 10, 2007.

4. Daniel Fried, "Russia: In Transition or Intransigent?" Testimony, Commission on Security and Cooperation in Europe (Helsinki Commission), May 24, 2007.

5. David Kramer, deputy assistant secretary for European and Eurasian affairs, remarks to the Baltimore Council on Foreign Affairs, Baltimore, Maryland, May 31, 2007, www.state.gov.

6. Speech by Condoleezza Rice at Georgetown University, Washington, D.C., January 18, 2006, www.state.gov.

7. Robert Legvold, "U.S.–Russia–Europe: Cooperative Efforts," Aspen Institute, Thirty-Third Conference, August 12–18, 2006, Congressional Program, pp. 10-11.

8. For ideas on moving from a limited alliance to a productive partnership between Russia and the United States, see Angela Stent and Lilia Shevtsova, "America, Russia, and Europe: A Realignment?" *Survival*, vol. 44, no. 4 (Winter 2002–2003): 128–33; and Stent, "America and Russia," in *Russia's Engagement with the West. Transformation and Integration in the Twenty-First Century*, ed. Alexander J. Motyl, Blair A. Ruble, and Lilia Shevtsova (Armonk, N.Y.: M. E. Sharpe, 2005), pp. 276–7.

9. In terms of nuclear disarmament, Rose Gottemoeller warned that, until Moscow and Washington observe their own obligations in reducing their nuclear arsenals, it will be difficult to persuade other countries, primarily Iran and North Korea, to comply with the policy of nuclear nonproliferation. Gottemoeller, "The INF Conundrum."

10. Zbigniew Brzezinski wrote, "To retain Siberia, Russia will need help; it cannot do so on its own, given its demographic decline and what is emerging next door in China." *The Choice: Global Domination or Global Leadership* (New York: Basic Books, 2005), p. 103.

11. Thomas Graham, "Dialectika Siily I Slabosti" (The Dialectics of Strength and Weakness), *Vedomosti*, June 29, 2007

12. www.Levada-center.ru, 2006–2007.

Chapter 22

1. www.Levada-center.ru, April–May 2007.

2. Albert Keidel, "China's Social Unrest: The Story behind the Stories," Policy Brief 48 (Washington, D.C.: Carnegie Endowment for International Peace, 2006).

3. In July 2007 the Other Russia movement split when Mikhail Kasianov decided to form his own party.

4. *Novaya gazeta*, April 22–24, 2007.

5. www.Gazeta.ru, April 28, 2007.

6. "'The Others Do Not Belong Here," *Expert*, April 23–May 6, 2007, p. 21.

7. www.Levada-center.ru, April 2007.

Chapter 23

1. In early August 2007, hundreds of Interior Ministry police reinforcements from Russian regions were dispatched to Ingushetia, as the violence in the North Caucasus grew, signaling a resurgence in rebel activity.

2. www.Levada-center.ru, April–June, 2007.

3. Emil Pain, "Empire in Itself. On the Revival of the Imperialist Syndrome," in *After Empire* (Moscow: Liberal Mission Foundation Press, 2007), p. 115.

Chapter 24

1. Francis Fukuyama, "The Primacy of Culture," *Journal of Democracy*, vol. 6, no. 1 (January 1995), p. 12.
2. www.polit.ru, January 2007.
3. Richard Pipes, "Why the Bear Growls," *Wall Street Journal*, Match 1, 2006.

Chapter 25

1. Ivan Krastev, "Democracy's 'Double,'" *Journal of Democracy*, vol. 17, no. 2 (April 2006), p. 59.
2. Thomas Carothers, "The Backlash against Democracy Promotion," *Foreign Affairs*, vol. 85, no. 2 (2006), p. 56.
3. Hugh Ragsdale and Paul Stepan, "Don't Feed the Bear," *American Interest*, vol. 11, no. 4 (March–April 2007), p. 92.
4. Joseph S. Nye, "Russia's Fragile Power," *Korean Times*, February 11, 2007.
5. George Soros, *The Age of Fallibility: Consequences of the War on Terror* (New York: Public Affairs, 2006), p. 195.

Chapter 26

1. Zbigniew Brzezinski, "The Dilemma of the Last Sovereign," *American Interest*, vol. 1, no. 1 (Autumn 2005), p. 30.
2. www.Levada-center.ru, April 2007, May 2007; *Niezavisimaya gazeta*, February 20, 2007; www.Vtsiom.ru, January 2007.
3. Alexei Levinson, "Chto Podderzhivayet Verchi?" (What Supports the Top?), *Vremia novostei*, July 24, 2007.

INDEX

ABOUT THE AUTHOR

Lilia Shevtsova, senior associate of Carnegie Endowment for International Peace, co-chairs the Russian Domestic Politics and Political Institutions Project. She is an associate fellow at the Chatham House, Royal Institute for International Affairs (London). She is a member of the WIIS (Women in International Security) Advisory Board, of the Board of the Institute for Human Sciences at Boston University, the Executive Board of the New Eurasia Foundation, and the Board of the Liberal Mission Foundation; she serves on the editorial boards of *American Interest, Journal of Democracy, Pro et Contra*, and *Demokratizatsiya*. She has been a visiting professor at the University of California at Berkeley and at Cornell University, and a fellow at the Woodrow Wilson International Center for Scholars. She is author of *Putin's Russia* and *Yeltsin's Russia: Myths and Reality*, all published by the Carnegie Endowment.

Arch Tait learned Russian at Latymer Upper School, London; Trinity Hall, Cambridge; and Moscow State University. He has a Ph.D. in Russian literature from Cambridge and began translating in earnest in 1986 after a meeting with Valentina Jacques, then editor of the magazine *Soviet Literature*. From 1993 he was the UK editor of the *Glas New Russian Writing* translation series, whose editor-in-chief was Valentina's successor, Natasha Perova. To date he has translated fourteen books, 30 short stories, and 25 articles by most of the leading Russian writers of today. His most recent translations are Anna Politkovskaya's *A Russian Diary* and Andrei Piontkovsky's *Another Look Into Putin's Soul*.